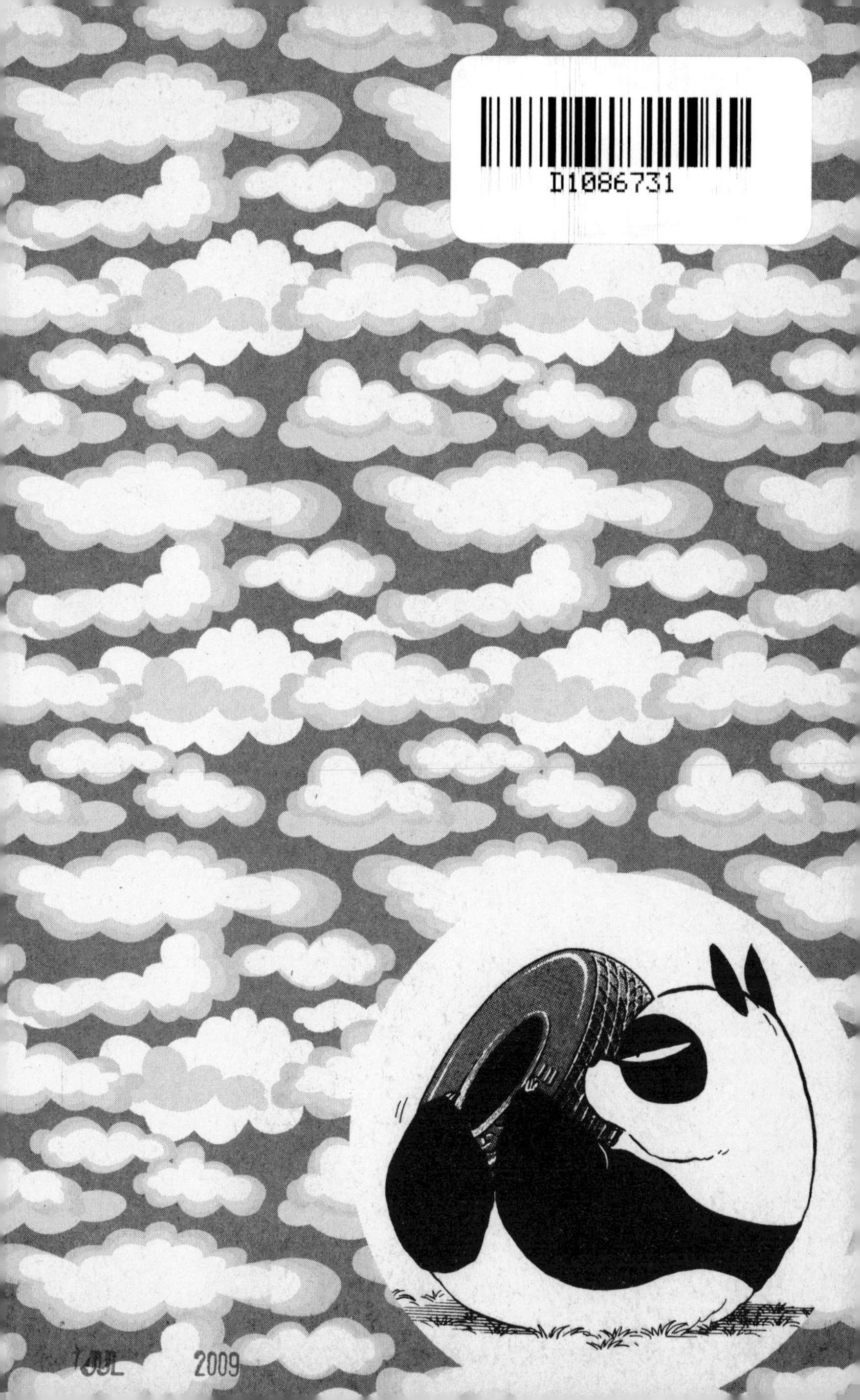

VOL. 18
Action Edition

Story and Art by
RUMIKO TAKAHASHI

English Adaptation/Gerard Jones and Toshifumi Yoshida
Touch-Up Art & Lettering/Wayne Truman
Cover and Interior Design/Yuki Ameda
Editor (1st Edition)/Julie Davis
Editor (Action Edition)/Avery Gotoh
Supervising Editor (Action Edition)/Michelle Pangilinan

Managing Editor/Annette Roman
Director of Production/Noboru Watanabe
Editorial Director/Alvin Lu
Sr. Director of Acquisitions/Rika Inouye
Vice President of Sales & Marketing/Liza Coppola
Executive Vice President/Hyoe Narita
Publisher/Seiji Horibuchi

© 1988 Rumiko Takahashi/Shogakukan, Inc. First published by Shogakukan, Inc. in Japan as "Ranma 1/2." New and adapted artwork and text © 2005 VIZ, LLC. The RANMA 1/2 logo is a trademark of VIZ, LLC. All rights reserved. The stories, characters, and incidents mentioned in this publication are entirely fictional.

No portion of this book may be reproduced or transmitted in any form or by any means without written permission from the copyright holders. For the purposes of publication in English, the artwork in this publication is printed in reverse from the original Japanese version.

Printed in Canada.

Published by VIZ, LLC
P.O. Box 77010
San Francisco, CA 94107

1st Edition Published 2001

Action Edition
10 9 8 7 6 5 4 3 2 1
First Printing, April 2005

www.viz.com

PARENTAL ADVISORY
RANMA 1/2 is rated T+ for Older Teen. This volume contains violence and suggestive situations. Recommended for older teens (16 and up).

store.viz.com

Ranma 1/2

VOL. 18 — Action Edition

MARION COUNTY PUBLIC LIBRARY
321 MONROE STREET
FAIRMONT, WV 26554

STORY & ART BY
RUMIKO TAKAHASHI

STORY THUS FAR

The Tendos are an average, run-of-the-mill Japanese family—on the surface, that is. Soun Tendo is the owner and proprietor of the Tendo Dojo, where "Anything Goes Martial Arts" is practiced. Like the name says, anything goes, and usually does.

When Soun's old friend Genma Saotome comes to visit, Soun's three lovely young daughters—Akane, Nabiki and Kasumi—are told that it's time for one of them to become the fiancée of Genma's teenage son, as per an agreement made between the two fathers years ago. Youngest daughter Akane—who says she hates boys—is quickly nominated for bridal duty by her sisters.

Unfortunately, Ranma and his father have suffered a strange accident. While training in China, both plunged into one of many "cursed" springs at the legendary martial arts training ground of Jusenkyo. These springs transform the unlucky dunkee into whoever—or whatever—drowned there hundreds of years ago.

From then on, a splash of cold water turns Ranma's father into a giant panda, and Ranma becomes a beautiful, busty young woman. Hot water reverses the effect...but only until next time. As it turns out, Ranma and Genma aren't the only ones who have taken the Jusenkyo plunge—and it isn't long before they meet several other members of the Jusenkyo "cursed."

Although their parents are still determined to see Ranma and Akane marry and assume ownership of the training hall, Ranma seems to have a strange talent for accumulating surplus fiancées...and Akane has a few stubbornly determined suitors of her own. Will the two ever work out their differences and get rid of all these "extra" people, or will they just call the whole thing off? What's a half-boy, half-girl (not to mention all-girl, *angry* girl) to do...?

CAST OF CHARACTERS

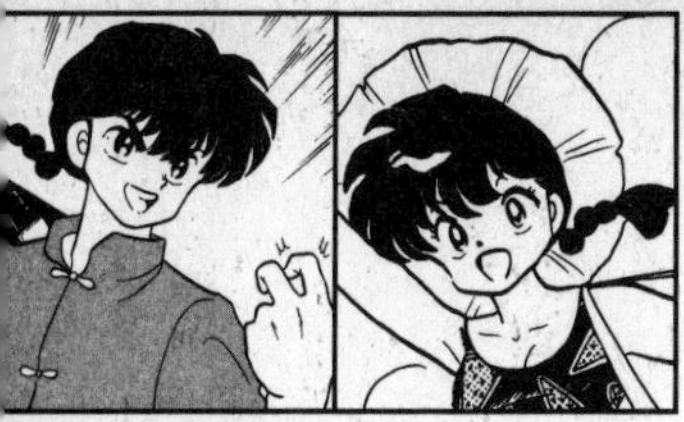

RANMA SAOTOME
Martial artist with far too many fiancées and an ego that won't let him take defeat. Changes into a girl when splashed with cold water.

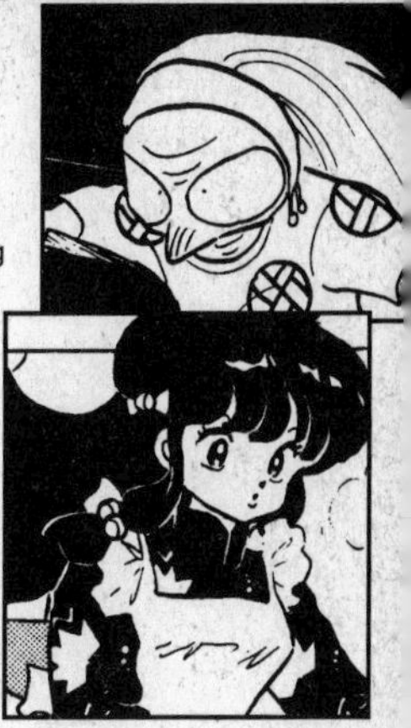

COLOGNE and SHAMPOO
Chinese-Amazon warriors who followed Ranma to Japan because of a tradition mandating that women bested by men marry those men, and women bested by women kill those women. Mm-hmm, really nothing out of the ordinary.

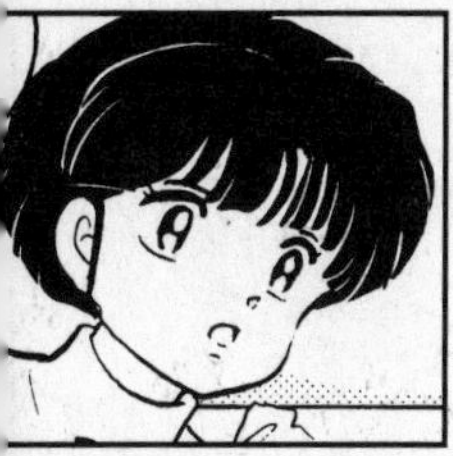

AKANE TENDO
Martial artist, tomboy and Ranma's reluctant fiancée. Has no clue how much Ryoga likes her, or what relation he might have to her pet black pig, P-chan.

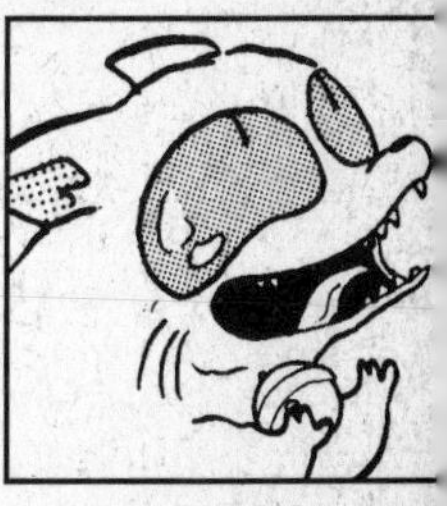

GHOST CAT
A.k.a. "Mao Mo Lin." Otherworldly spirit fixated on making Shampoo his bride.

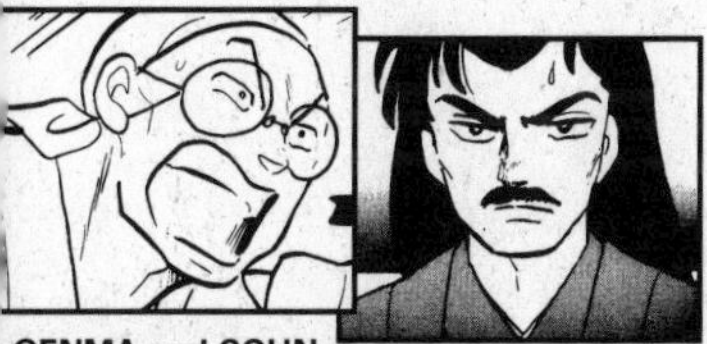

GENMA and SOUN
Buffoonish (to clown a phrase) former disciples of the panty-raiding Happosai. Also fathers to Ranma and Akane, respectively. (Genma turns into a roly-poly panda).

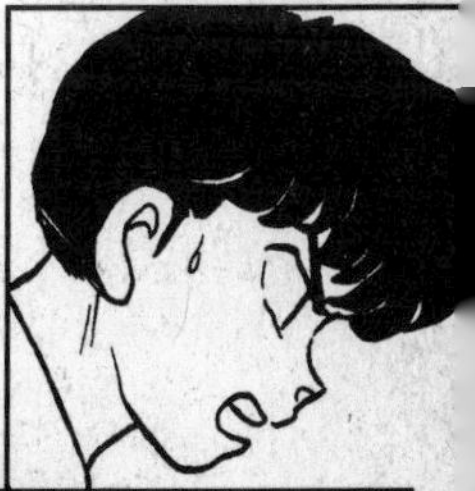

TATEWAKI and KODACHI KUNO
Terrible brother-sister twosome equally determined to win the pig-tailed girl/Ranma-darling as their own.

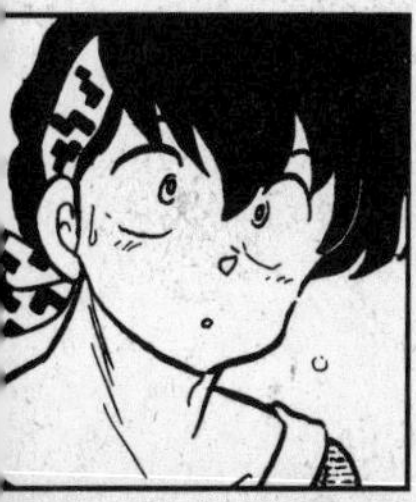

RYOGA
Skilled martial artist with absolutely no sense of direction. Loves Akane a lot, loves turning into her pet black pig "P-chan" (NOT!), and *really* loves beating the snot out of Ranma.

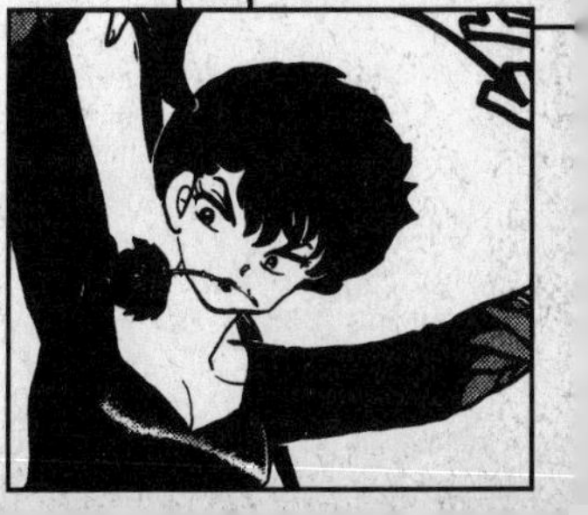

CONTENTS

Part 1
THE LION'S ROAR

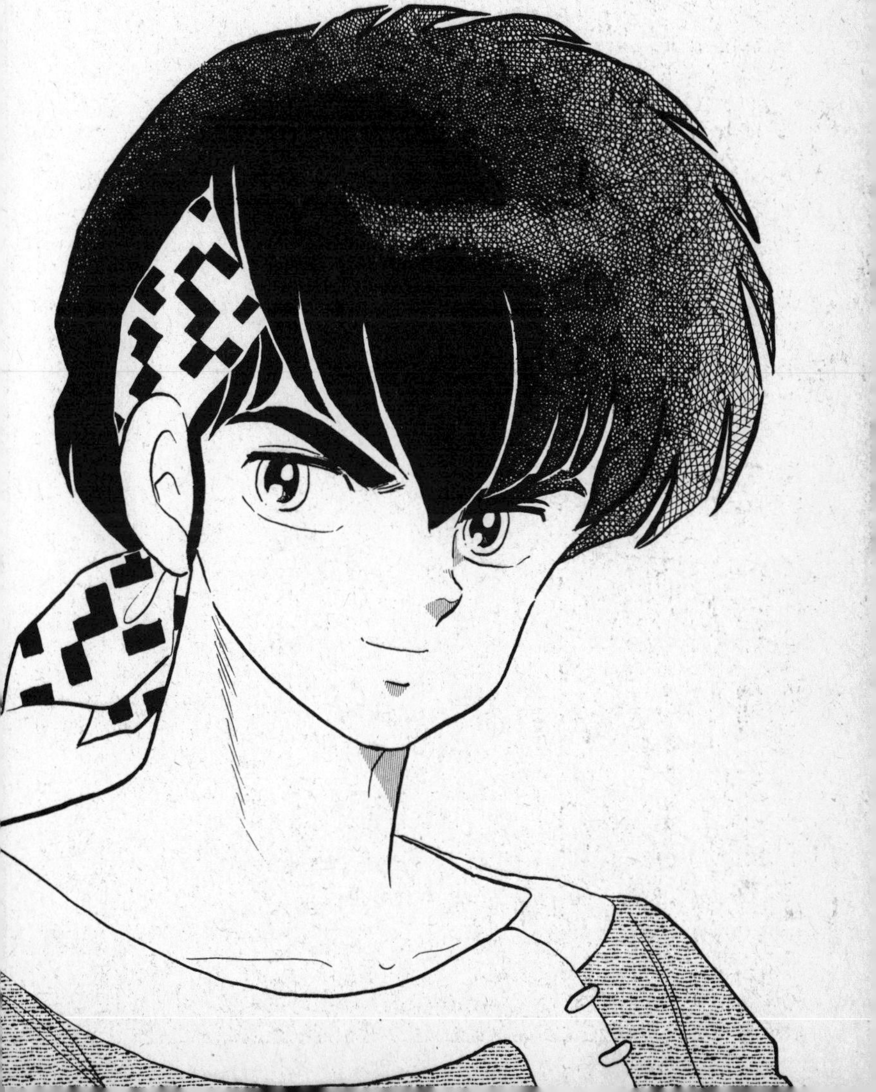

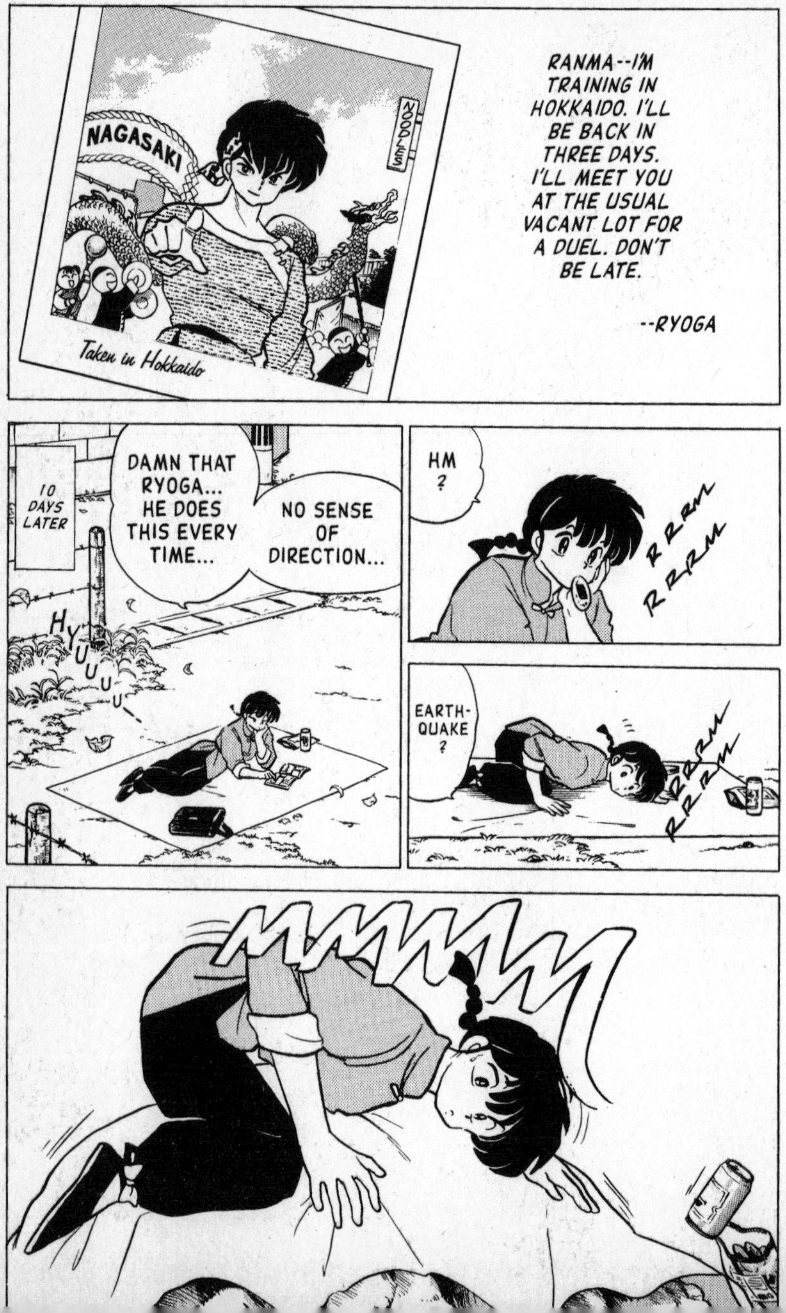
NAGASAKI
NOODLES
Taken in Hokkaido
RANMA--I'M TRAINING IN HOKKAIDO. I'LL BE BACK IN THREE DAYS. I'LL MEET YOU AT THE USUAL VACANT LOT FOR A DUEL. DON'T BE LATE.
--RYOGA
10 DAYS LATER
DAMN THAT RYOGA... HE DOES THIS EVERY TIME...
NO SENSE OF DIRECTION...
HYUUUU
HM ?
RRRM RRRM
EARTH-QUAKE ?
RRRM RRRM

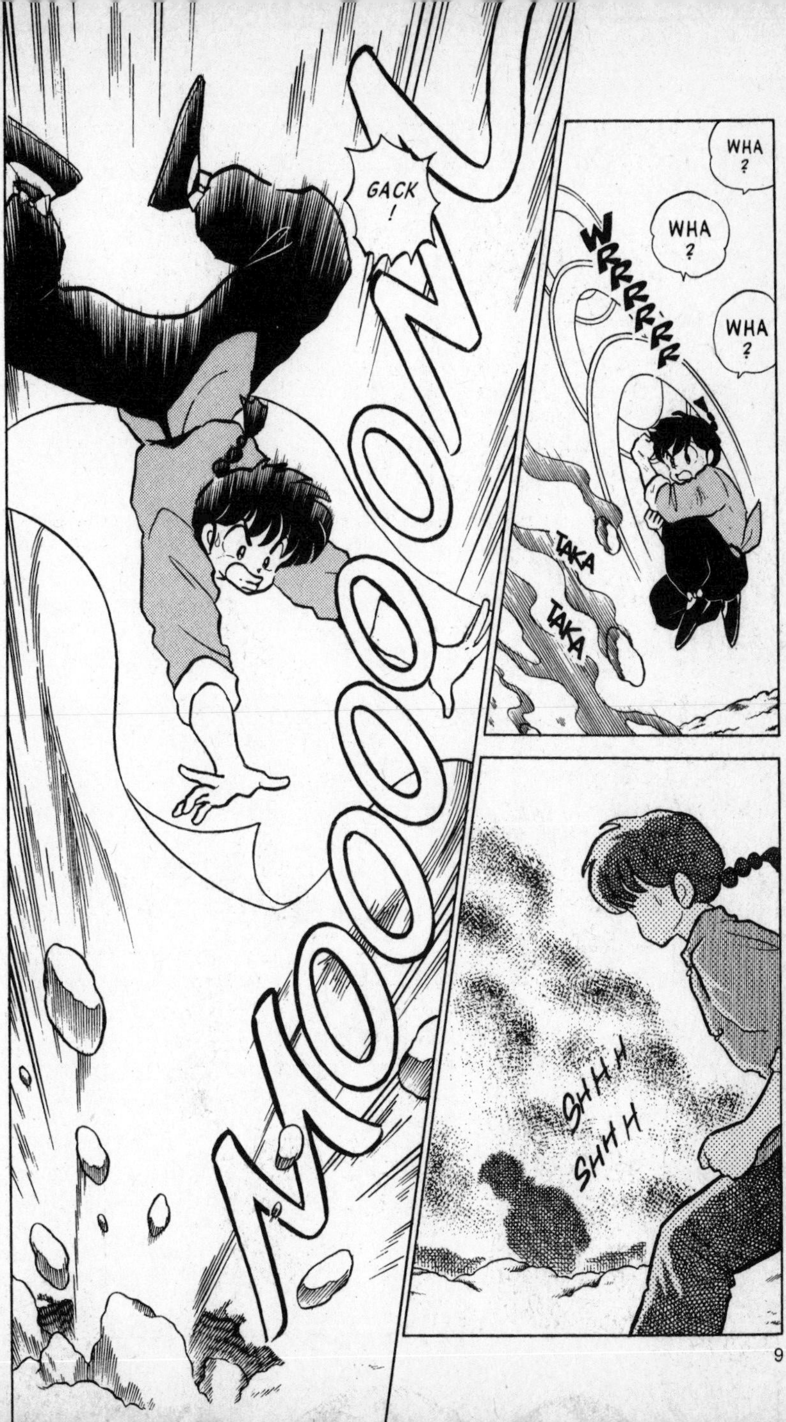
GACK !
MOOOOOON
WHA ?
WHA ?
WHA ?
WRRRRRRRR
TAKA
TAKA
SHHH
SHHH

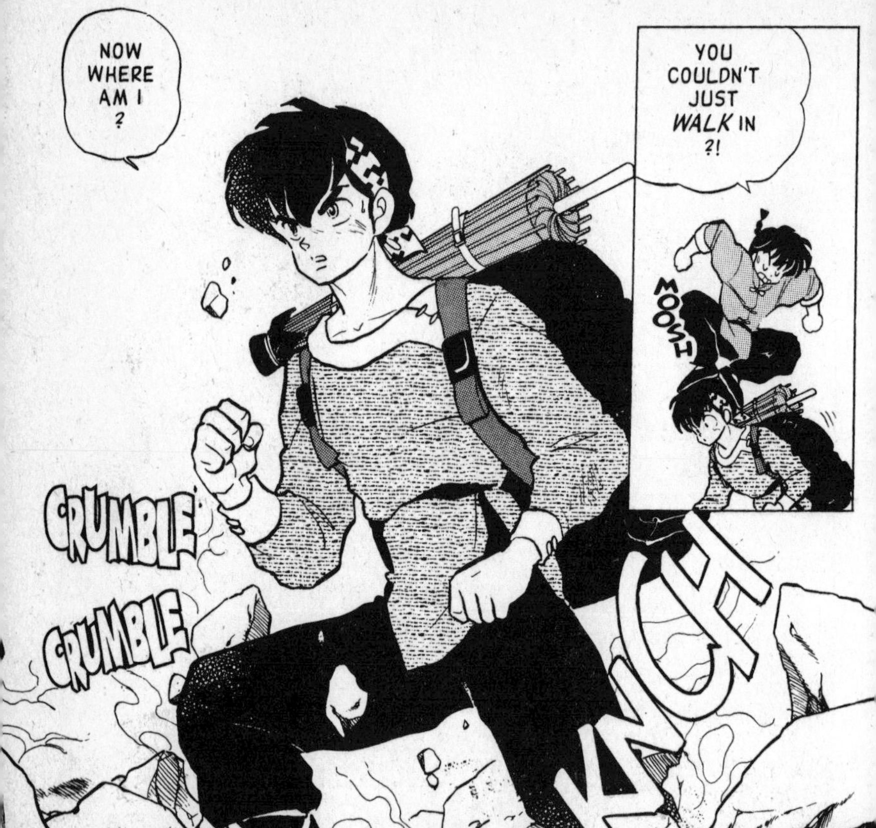
NOW WHERE AM I ?
CRUMBLE
CRUMBLE
KNCH
YOU COULDN'T JUST *WALK* IN ?!
MOOSH

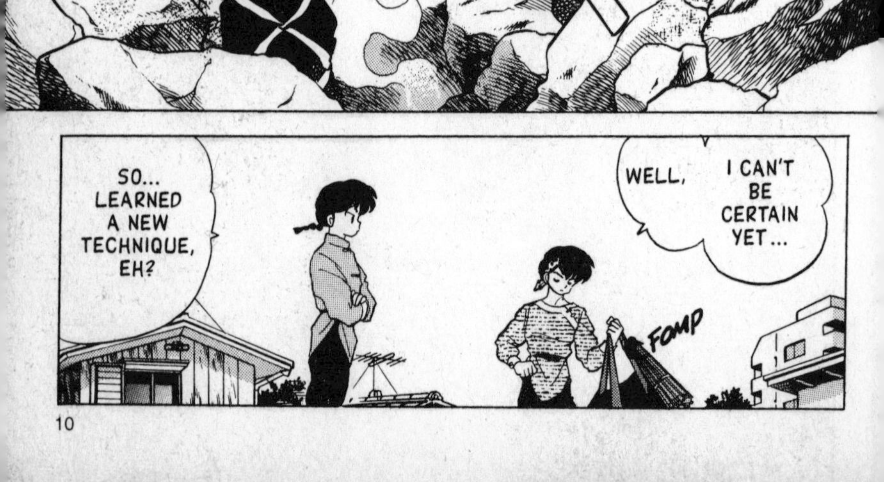
SO... LEARNED A NEW TECHNIQUE, EH?
WELL,
I CAN'T BE CERTAIN YET...
FOMP

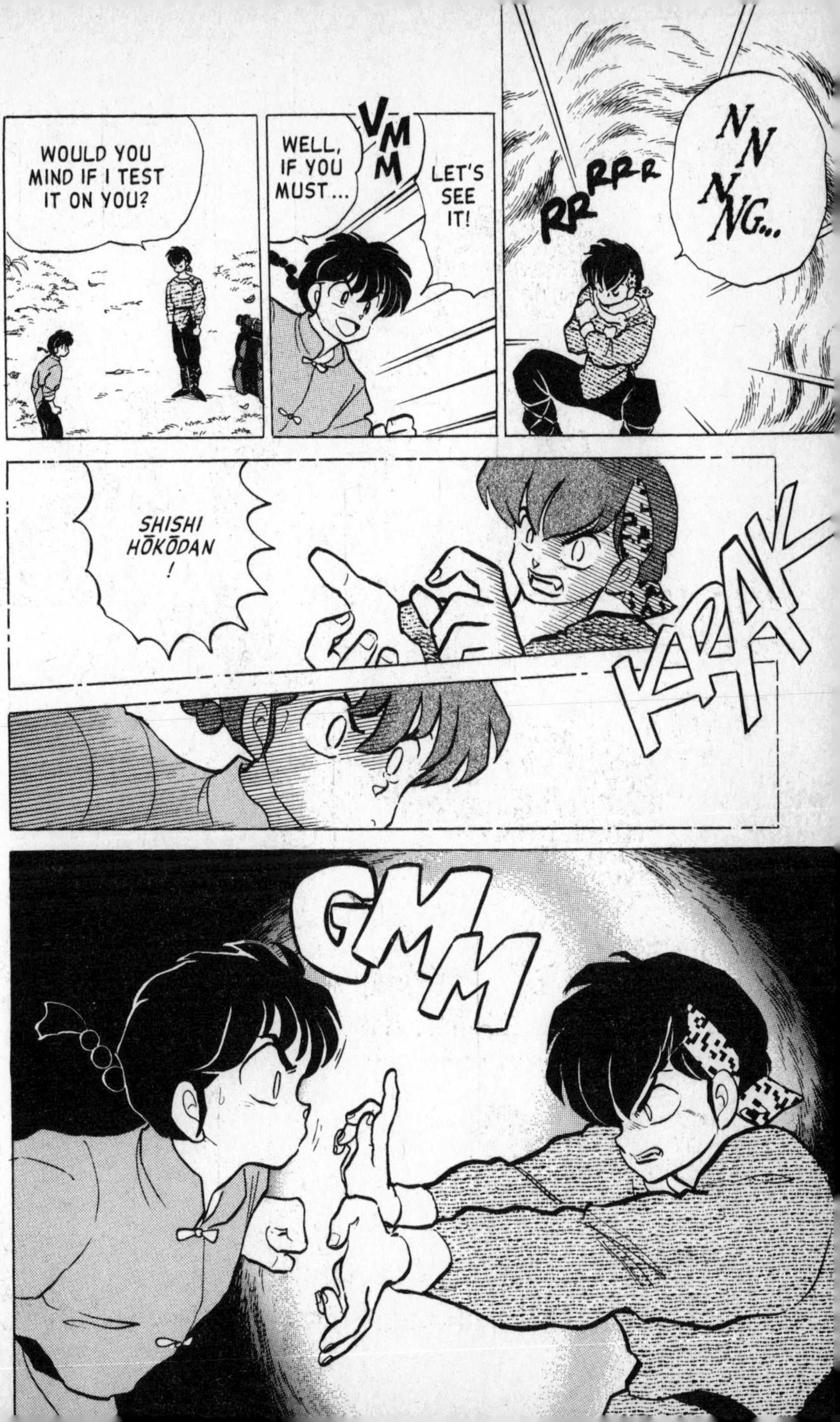
WOULD YOU MIND IF I TEST IT ON YOU?
WELL, IF YOU MUST...
VMM
LET'S SEE IT!
RRRRRR
NNNNG...
SHISHI HŌKŌDAN!
KARAK
GMM

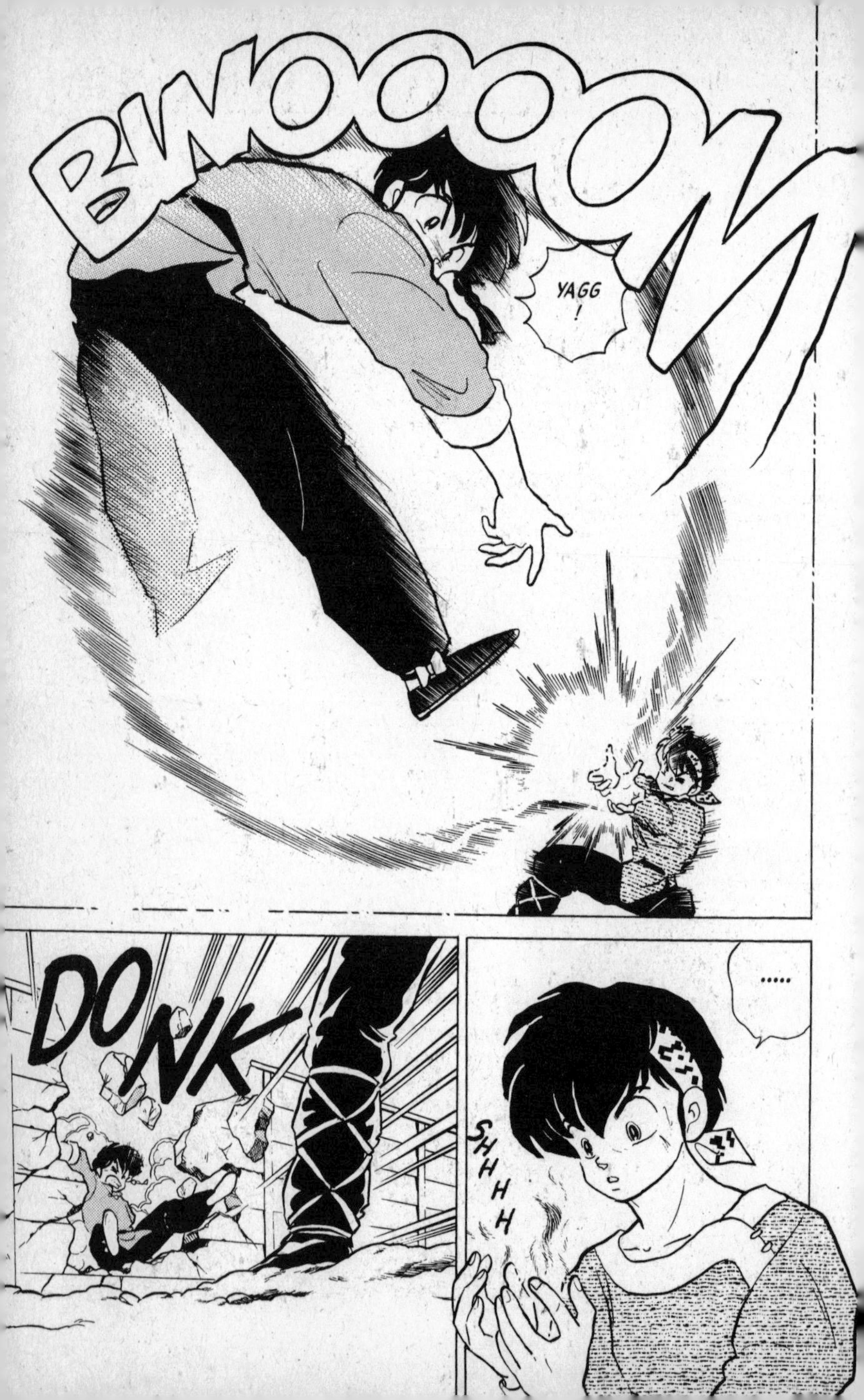
BWOOOOOM
YAGG!
DONK
SHHHH
.....

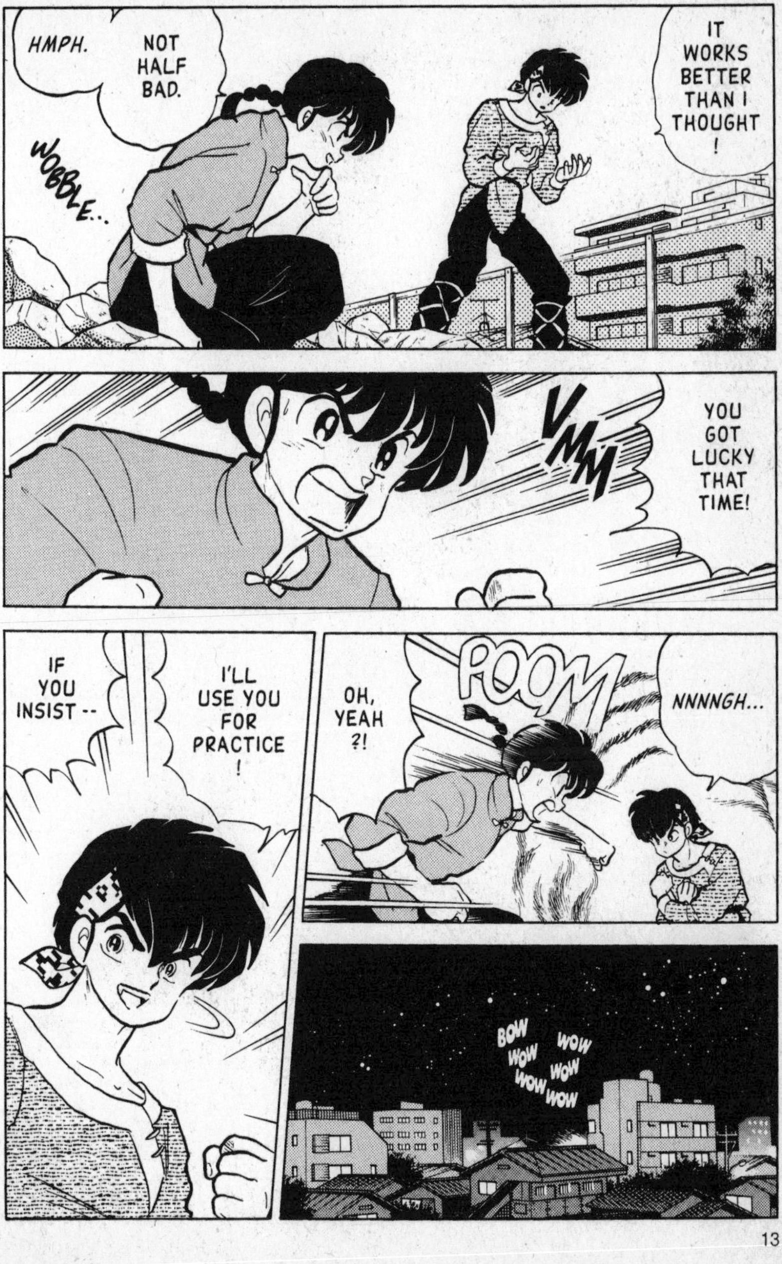
HMPH.
NOT HALF BAD.
WOBBLE...
IT WORKS BETTER THAN I THOUGHT!
VMM
YOU GOT LUCKY THAT TIME!
IF YOU INSIST --
I'LL USE YOU FOR PRACTICE!
OH, YEAH?!
POOM
NNNNGH...
BOW WOW WOW
WOW WOW WOW

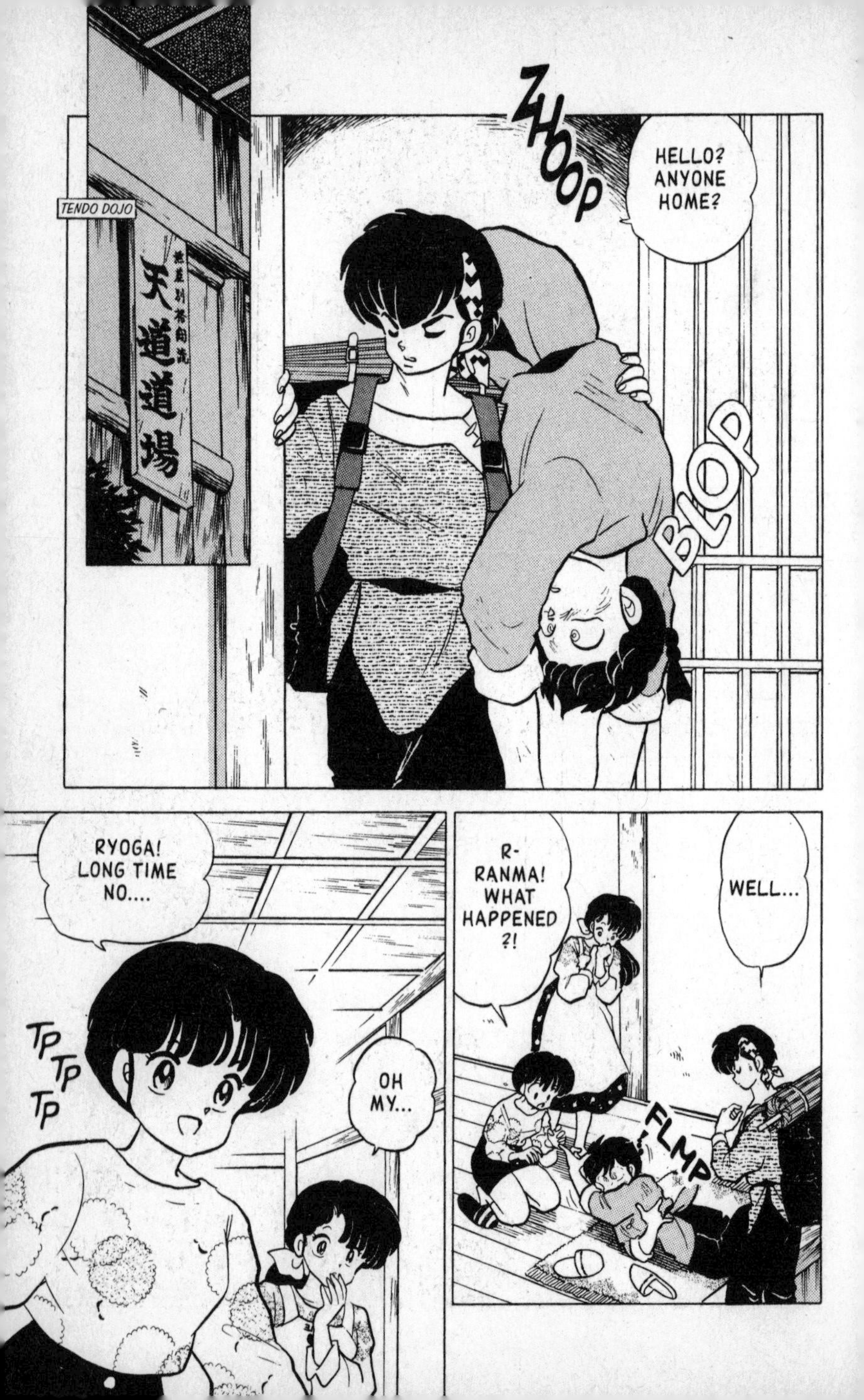
TENDO DOJO
天道道場
ZHOOP
HELLO? ANYONE HOME?
BLOP
RYOGA! LONG TIME NO....
TP TP TP TP
OH MY...
R-RANMA! WHAT HAPPENED ?!
WELL...
FLMP

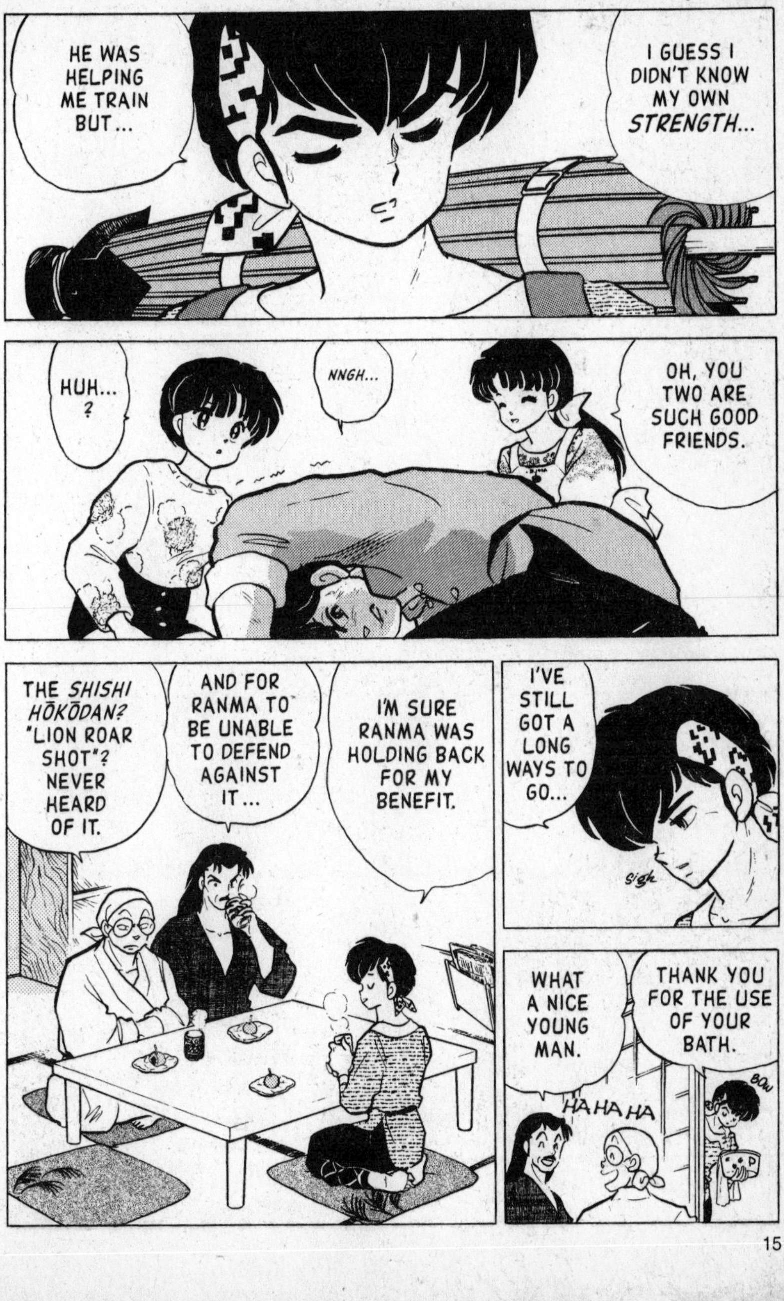
HE WAS HELPING ME TRAIN BUT...
I GUESS I DIDN'T KNOW MY OWN *STRENGTH*...
HUH...?
NNGH...
OH, YOU TWO ARE SUCH GOOD FRIENDS.
THE *SHISHI HŌKŌDAN?* "LION ROAR SHOT"? NEVER HEARD OF IT.
AND FOR RANMA TO BE UNABLE TO DEFEND AGAINST IT...
I'M SURE RANMA WAS HOLDING BACK FOR MY BENEFIT.
I'VE STILL GOT A LONG WAYS TO GO...
sigh
WHAT A NICE YOUNG MAN.
THANK YOU FOR THE USE OF YOUR BATH.
HA HA HA
BOW

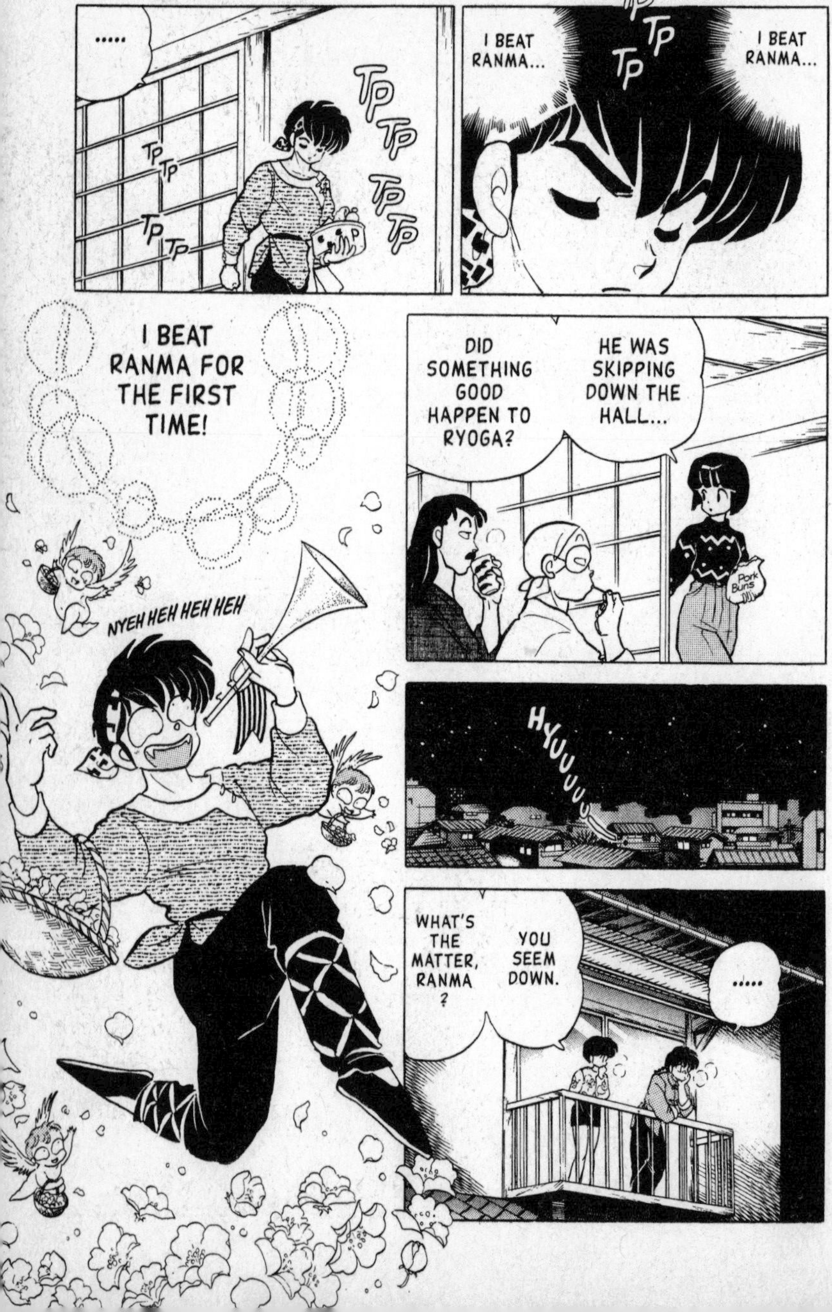

......
TP TP TP TP
TP TP
TP TP
I BEAT RANMA...
TP TP TP
I BEAT RANMA...
I BEAT RANMA FOR THE FIRST TIME!
NYEH HEH HEH HEH
DID SOMETHING GOOD HAPPEN TO RYOGA?
HE WAS SKIPPING DOWN THE HALL...
Pork Buns
HYUUUUU
WHAT'S THE MATTER, RANMA?
YOU SEEM DOWN.
......

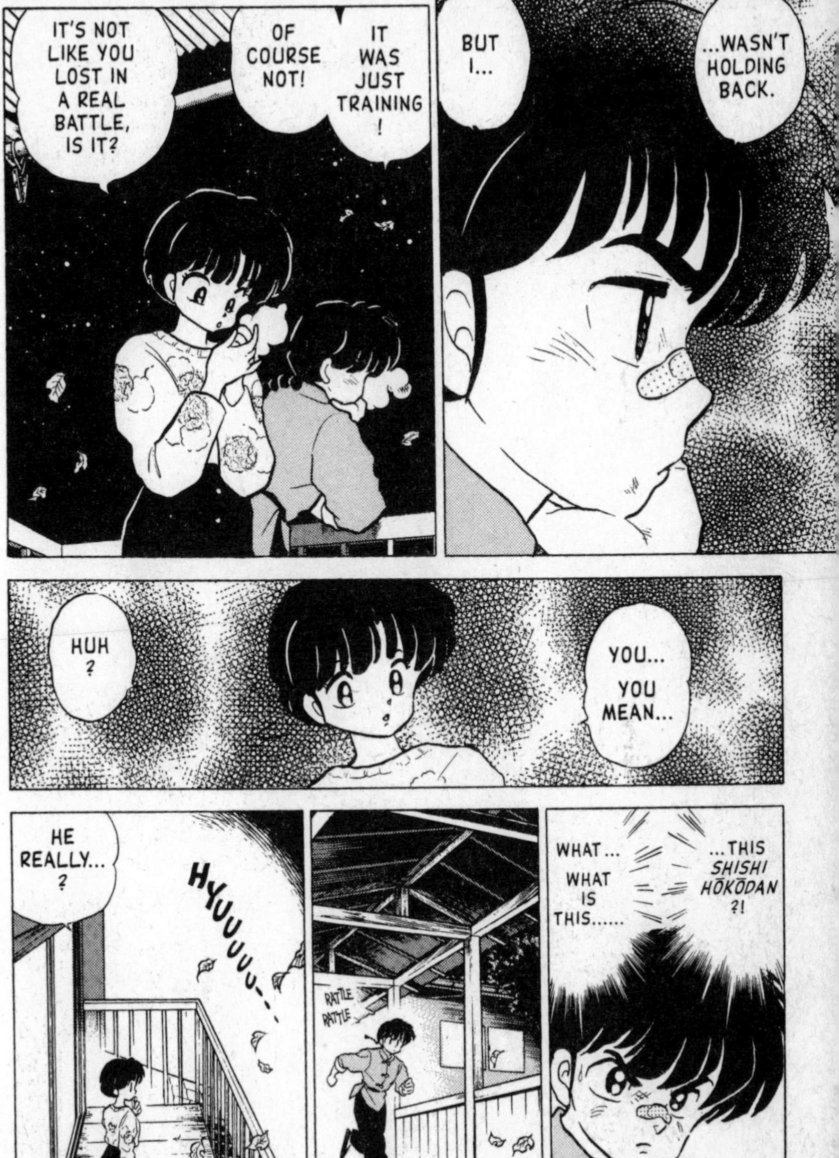
IT'S NOT LIKE YOU LOST IN A REAL BATTLE, IS IT?
OF COURSE NOT!
IT WAS JUST TRAINING!
BUT I...
...WASN'T HOLDING BACK.
HUH?
YOU... YOU MEAN...
HE REALLY...?
HYUUUUU...
RATTLE RATTLE
WHAT... WHAT IS THIS......
...THIS SHISHI HŌKŌDAN?!

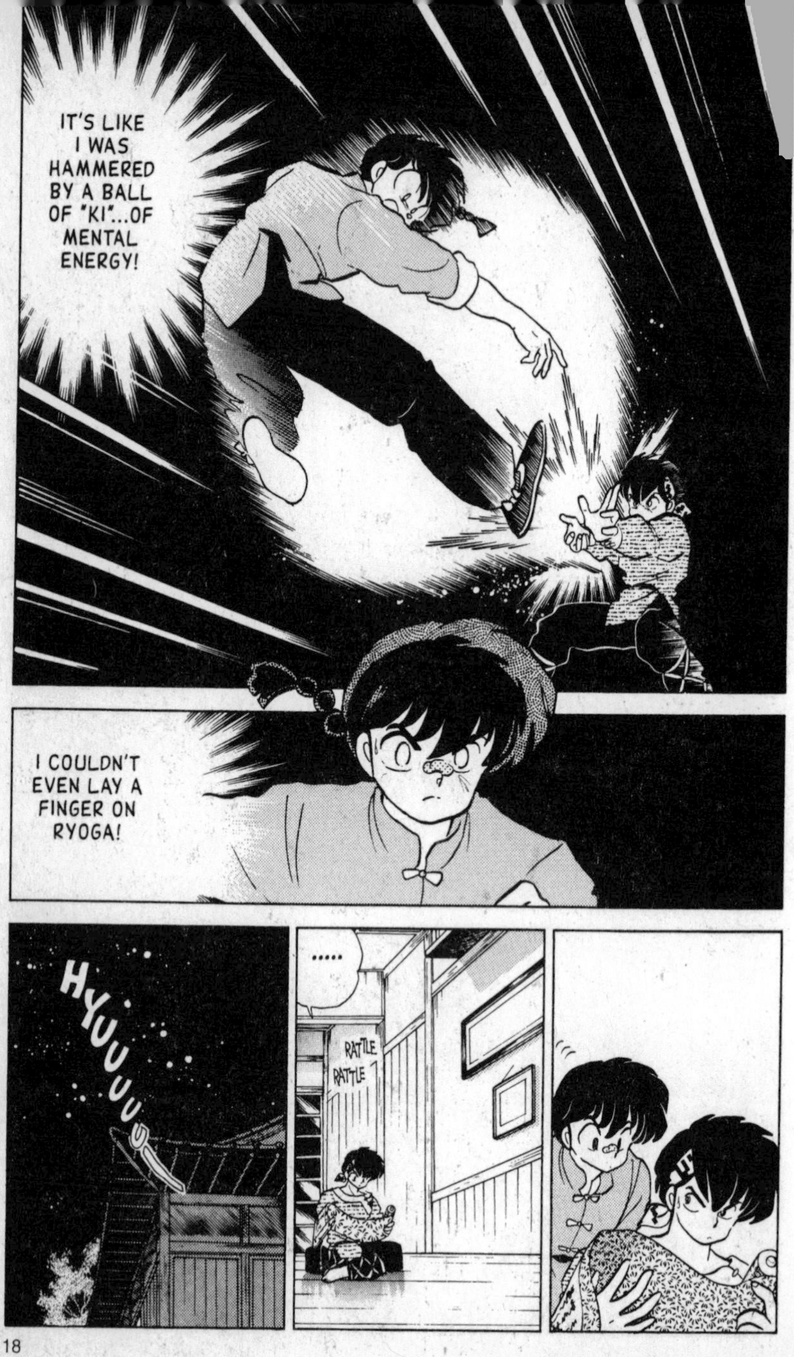
IT'S LIKE I WAS HAMMERED BY A BALL OF "KI"...OF MENTAL ENERGY!
I COULDN'T EVEN LAY A FINGER ON RYOGA!
HYUUUUU
......
RATTLE RATTLE

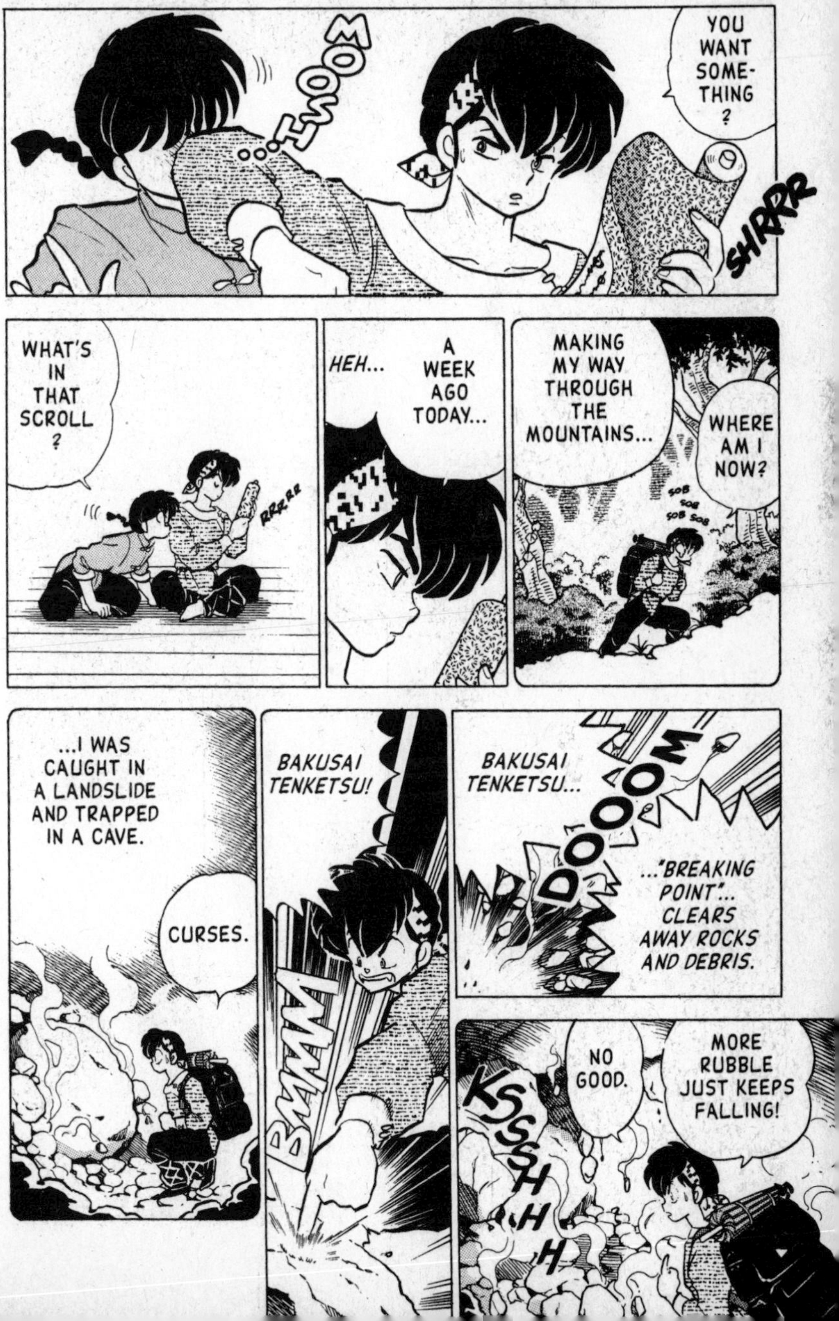
WOOOM...
YOU WANT SOMETHING?
SHRRR
WHAT'S IN THAT SCROLL?
RRRRR
HEH...
A WEEK AGO TODAY...
MAKING MY WAY THROUGH THE MOUNTAINS...
WHERE AM I NOW?
SOB SOB SOB SOB
...I WAS CAUGHT IN A LANDSLIDE AND TRAPPED IN A CAVE.
CURSES.
BAKUSAI TENKETSU!
BMMM
BAKUSAI TENKETSU...
DOOOOOM
..."BREAKING POINT"... CLEARS AWAY ROCKS AND DEBRIS.
NO GOOD.
MORE RUBBLE JUST KEEPS FALLING!
KSSSHHH

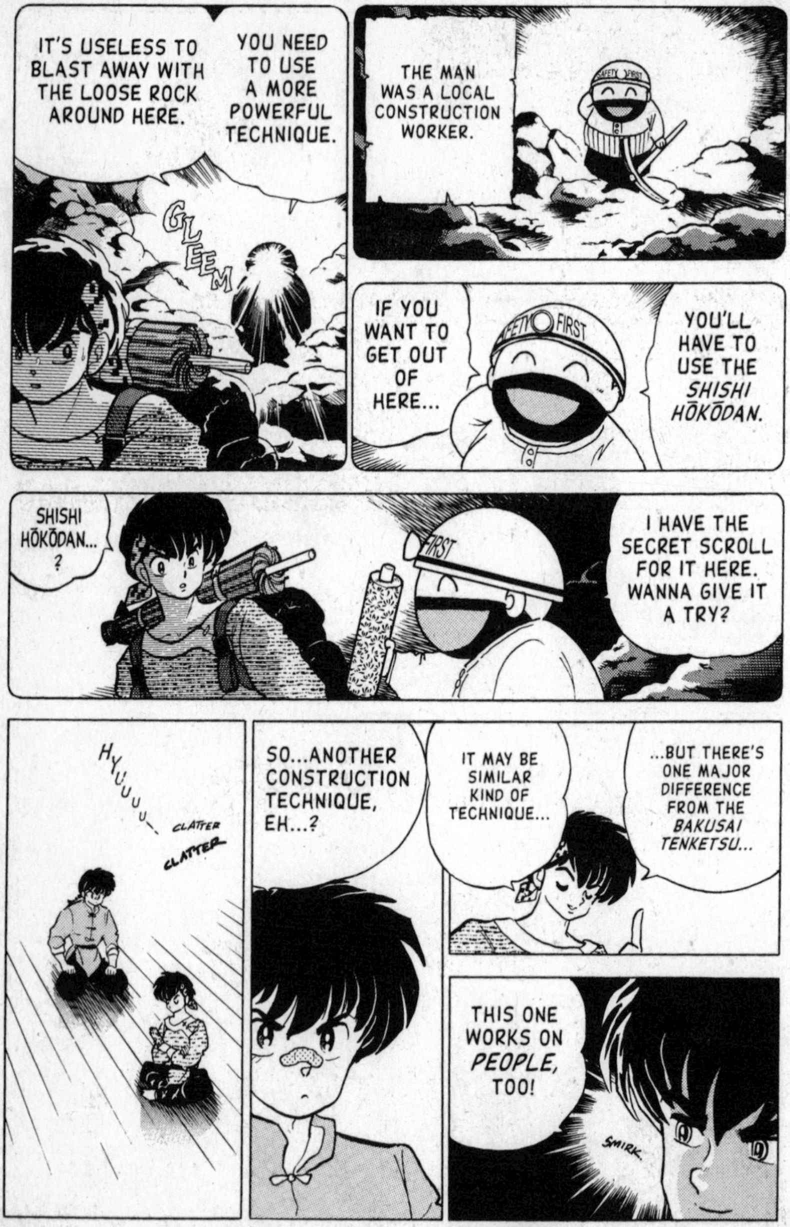
IT'S USELESS TO BLAST AWAY WITH THE LOOSE ROCK AROUND HERE.
YOU NEED TO USE A MORE POWERFUL TECHNIQUE.
GLEEM
THE MAN WAS A LOCAL CONSTRUCTION WORKER.
SAFETY FIRST
IF YOU WANT TO GET OUT OF HERE...
YOU'LL HAVE TO USE THE *SHISHI HŌKŌDAN.*
SHISHI HŌKŌDAN...?
I HAVE THE SECRET SCROLL FOR IT HERE. WANNA GIVE IT A TRY?
HYUUUU-
CLATTER
CLATTER
SO...ANOTHER CONSTRUCTION TECHNIQUE, EH...?
IT MAY BE SIMILAR KIND OF TECHNIQUE...
...BUT THERE'S ONE MAJOR DIFFERENCE FROM THE *BAKUSAI TENKETSU...*
THIS ONE WORKS ON *PEOPLE,* TOO!
SMIRK

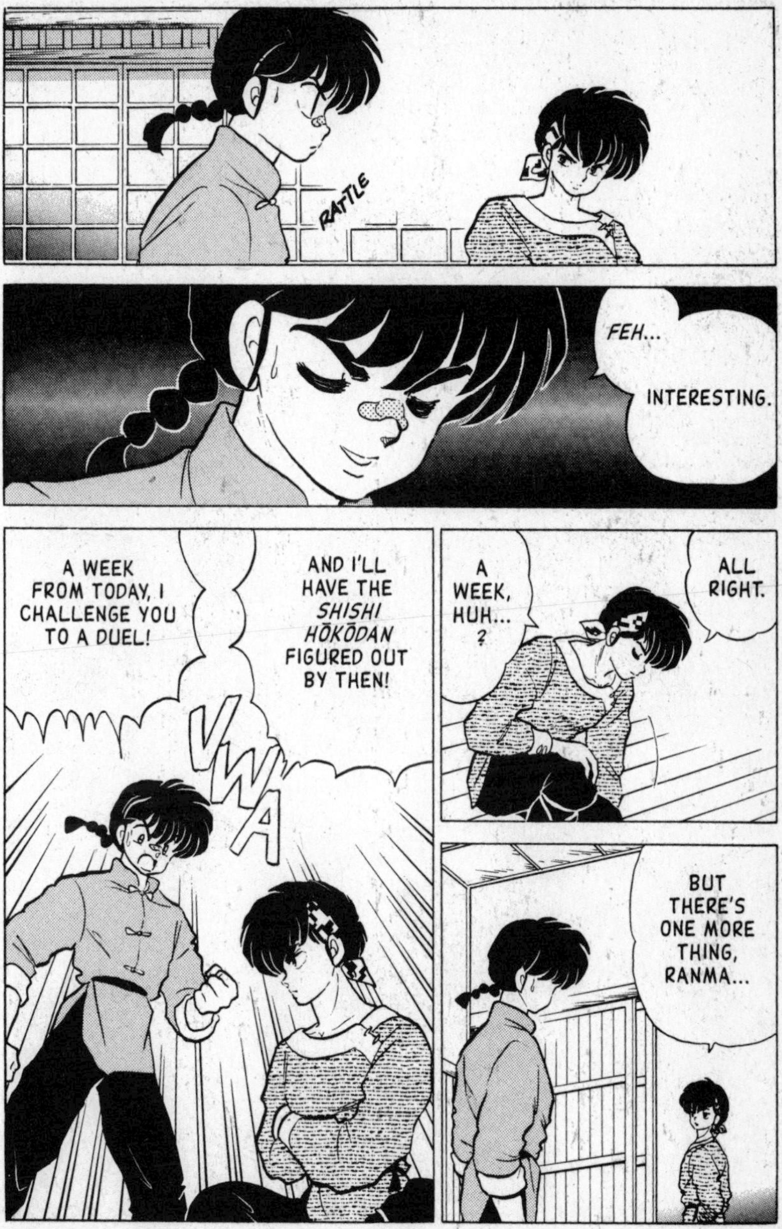
RATTLE
FEH...
INTERESTING.
A WEEK FROM TODAY, I CHALLENGE YOU TO A DUEL!
AND I'LL HAVE THE *SHISHI HŌKŌDAN* FIGURED OUT BY THEN!
VWA
A WEEK, HUH... ?
ALL RIGHT.
BUT THERE'S ONE MORE THING, RANMA...

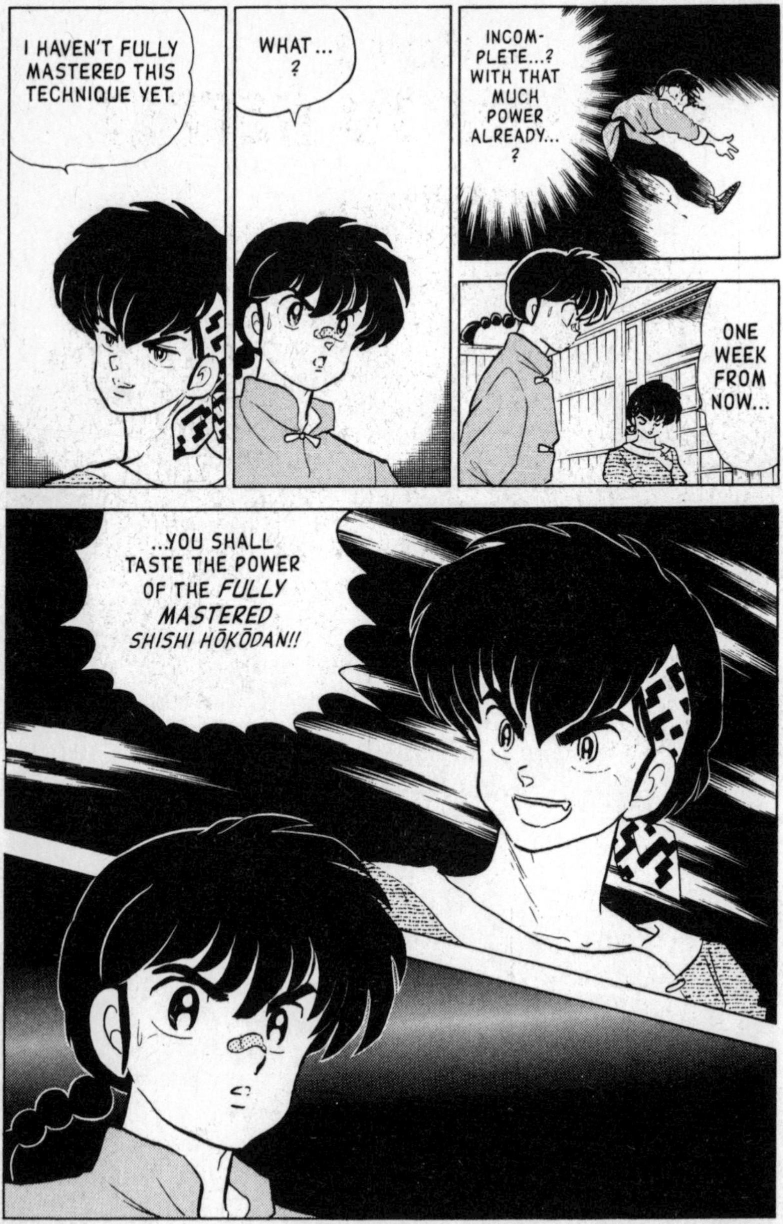
I HAVEN'T FULLY MASTERED THIS TECHNIQUE YET.
WHAT... ?
INCOMPLETE...? WITH THAT MUCH POWER ALREADY... ?
ONE WEEK FROM NOW...
...YOU SHALL TASTE THE POWER OF THE *FULLY MASTERED SHISHI HŌKŌDAN!!*

Part 2
PRELUDE TO DEFEAT

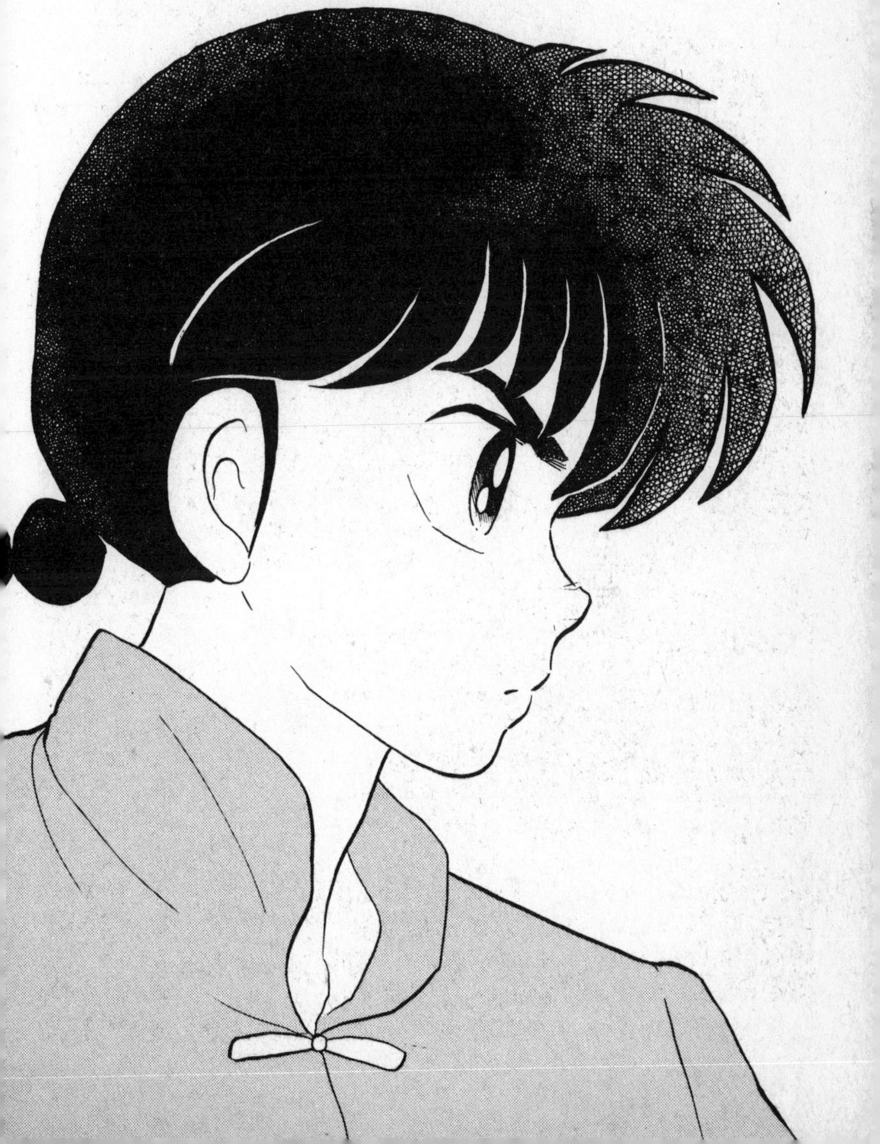

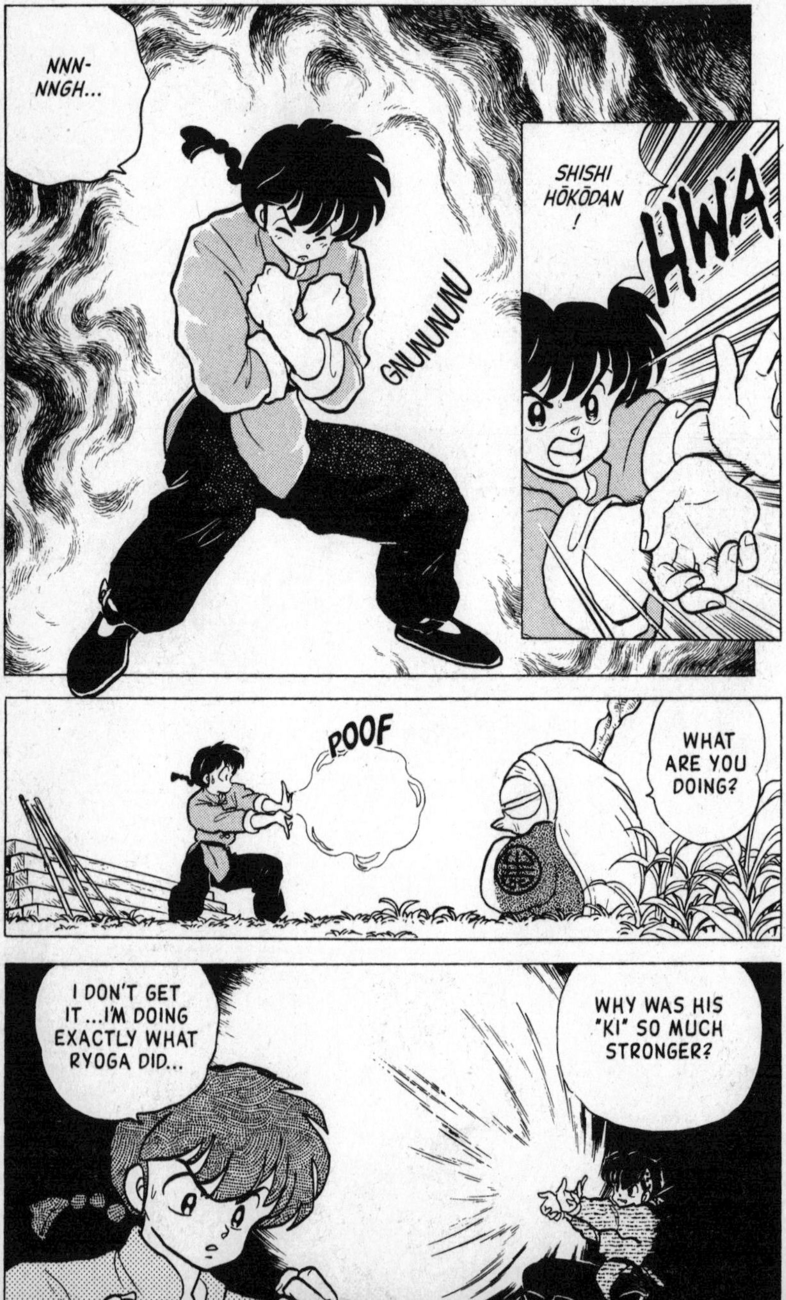
NNN-NNGH...
GNUNUNUNU
SHISHI HŌKŌDAN !
HWA
POOF
WHAT ARE YOU DOING?
I DON'T GET IT...I'M DOING EXACTLY WHAT RYOGA DID...
WHY WAS HIS "KI" SO MUCH STRONGER?

HEY! YOU MUST KNOW THE SECRET BEHIND THE *SHISHI HŌKŌDAN*, RIGHT?!

TELL ME!

YESSS...

I CAN SEE RYOGA MASTERING IT...

BUT YOU, SON-IN-LAW...

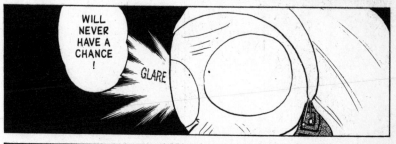

WILL NEVER HAVE A CHANCE!

GLARE

OH, GIMME A--!!

GIVE IT UP!

PNG!

I'LL NEVER... ...HAVE A CHANCE?

A WEEK FROM TODAY, I CHALLENGE YOU TO A DUEL!

FRUIT

MAN...IF I CAN'T FIGURE THIS OUT...

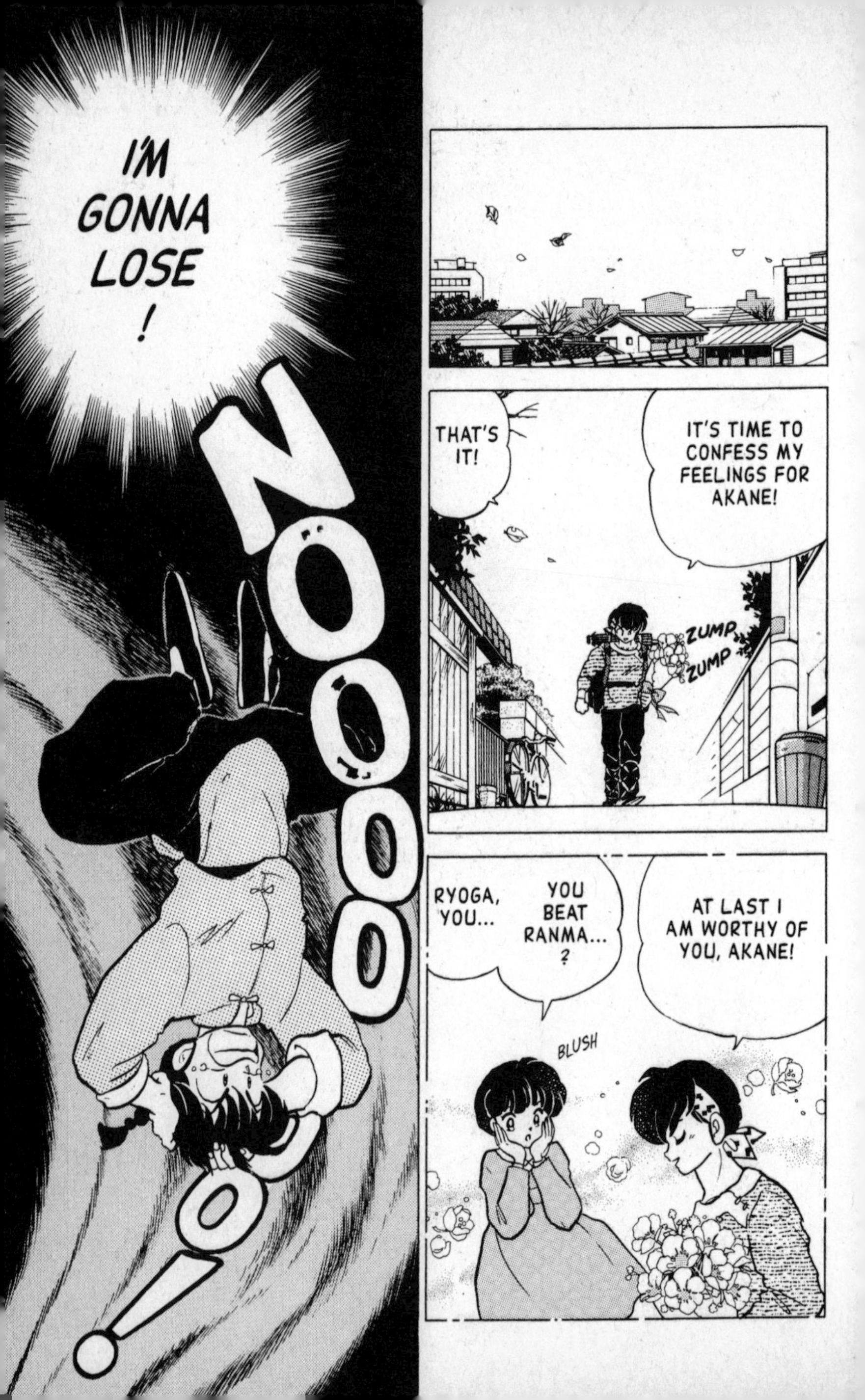
I'M GONNA LOSE!
NOOOOO!
THAT'S IT!
IT'S TIME TO CONFESS MY FEELINGS FOR AKANE!
ZUMP ZUMP
RYOGA, YOU...
YOU BEAT RANMA...?
AT LAST I AM WORTHY OF YOU, AKANE!
BLUSH

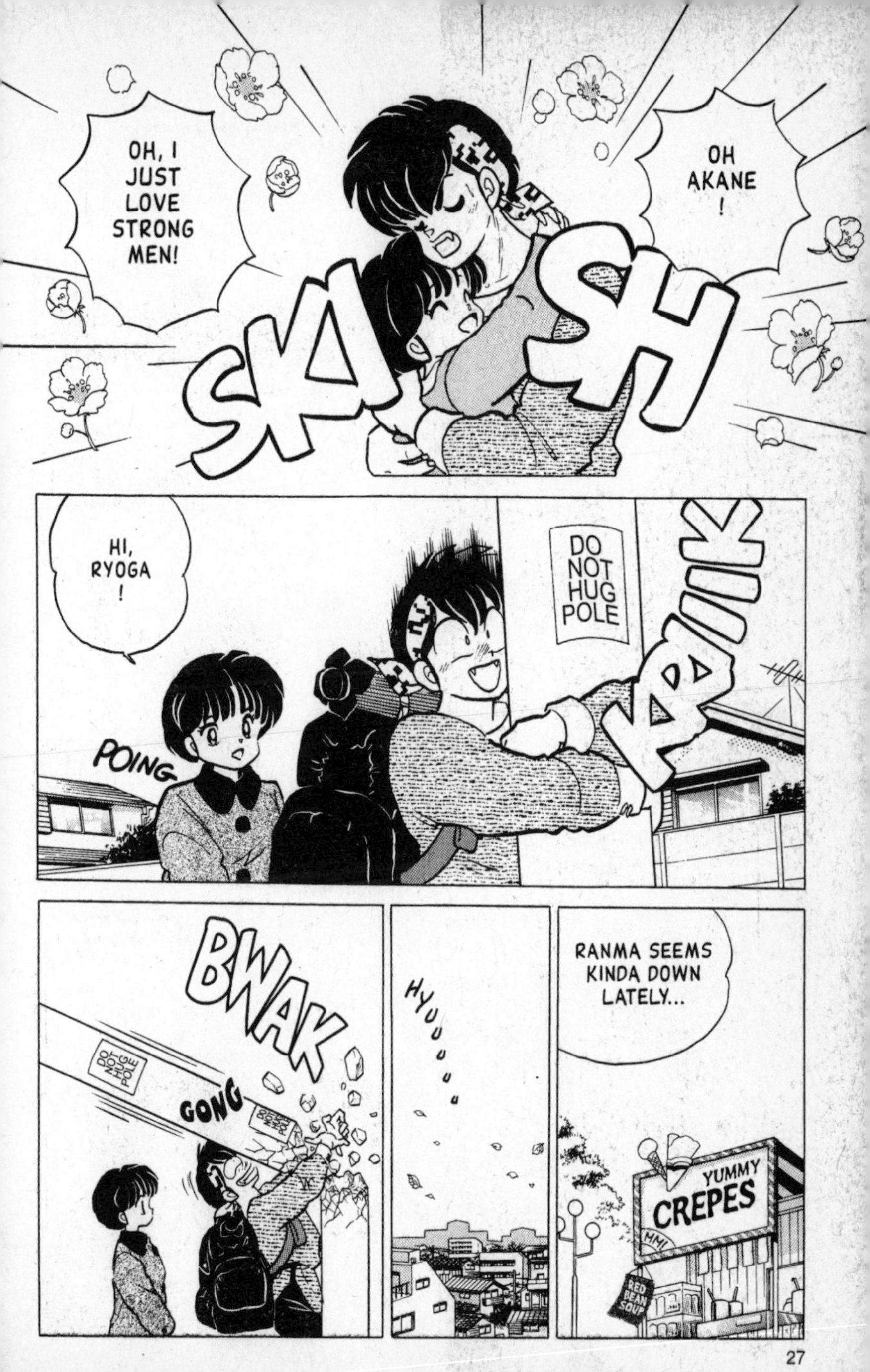
OH, I JUST LOVE STRONG MEN!
OH AKANE !
SKLASH
HI, RYOGA !
DO NOT HUG POLE
KRAK
POING
BWAK
DO NOT HUG POLE
GONG
HYUUUUUU
RANMA SEEMS KINDA DOWN LATELY...
YUMMY CREPES
MM!
RED BEAN SOUP

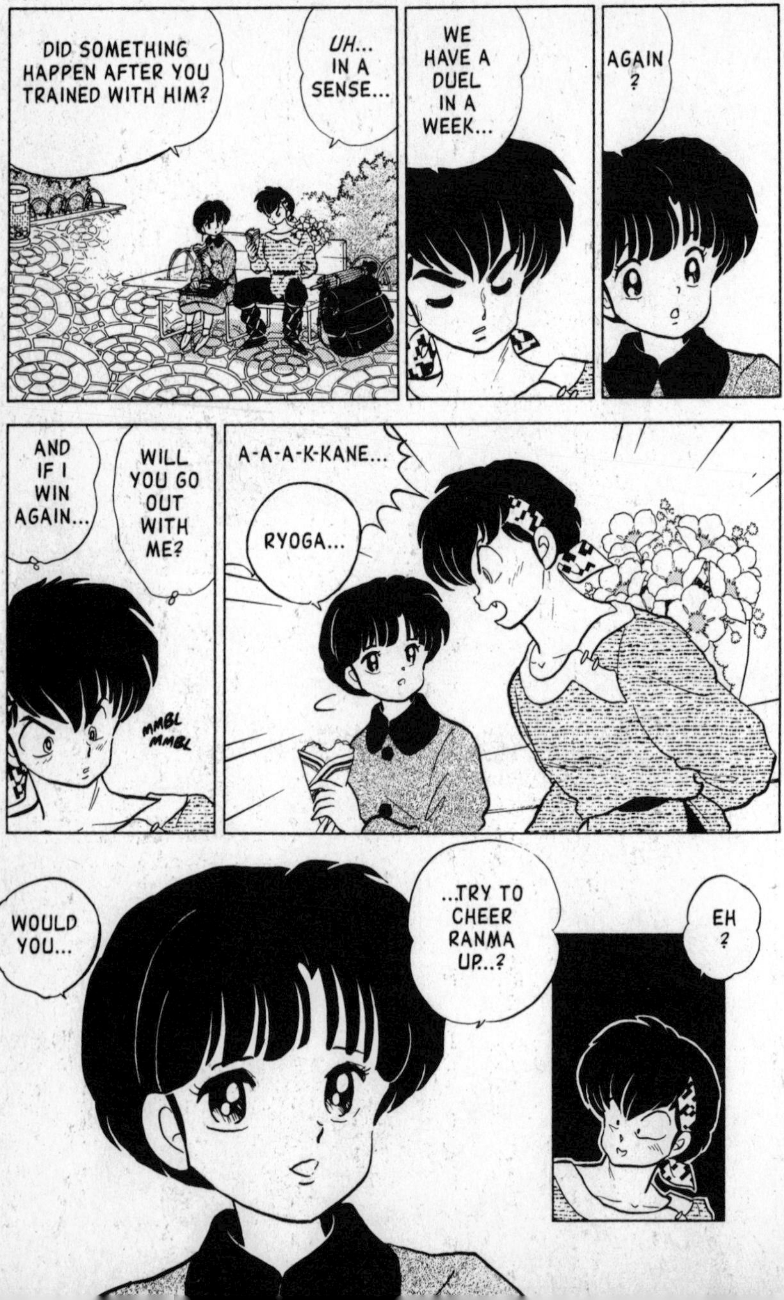
DID SOMETHING HAPPEN AFTER YOU TRAINED WITH HIM?
UH... IN A SENSE...
WE HAVE A DUEL IN A WEEK...
AGAIN?
AND IF I WIN AGAIN...
WILL YOU GO OUT WITH ME?
MMBL MMBL
A-A-A-K-KANE...
RYOGA...
WOULD YOU...
...TRY TO CHEER RANMA UP...?
EH?

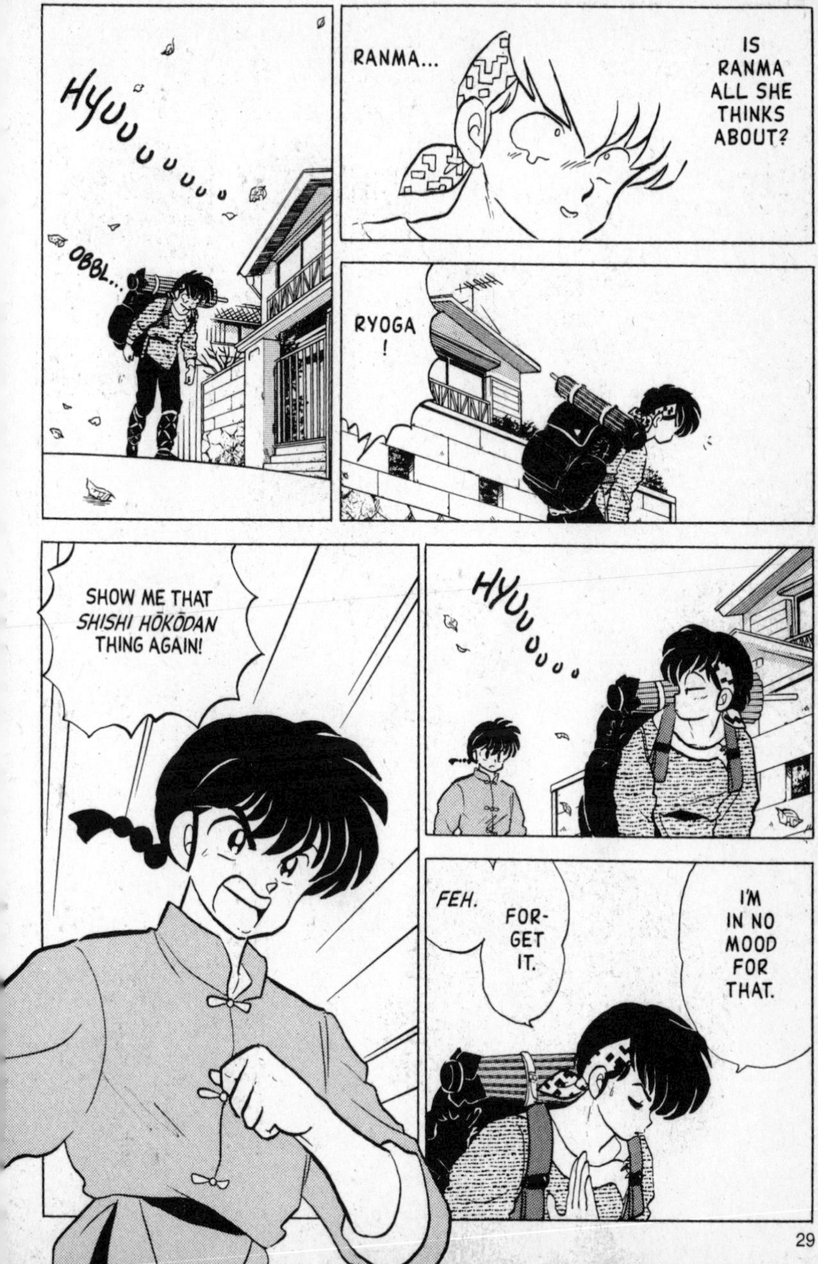
HYUUUUUUUU
OBBL...
RANMA...
IS RANMA ALL SHE THINKS ABOUT?
RYOGA!
SHOW ME THAT *SHISHI HŌKŌDAN* THING AGAIN!
HYUUUUUU
FEH.
FOR-GET IT.
I'M IN NO MOOD FOR THAT.

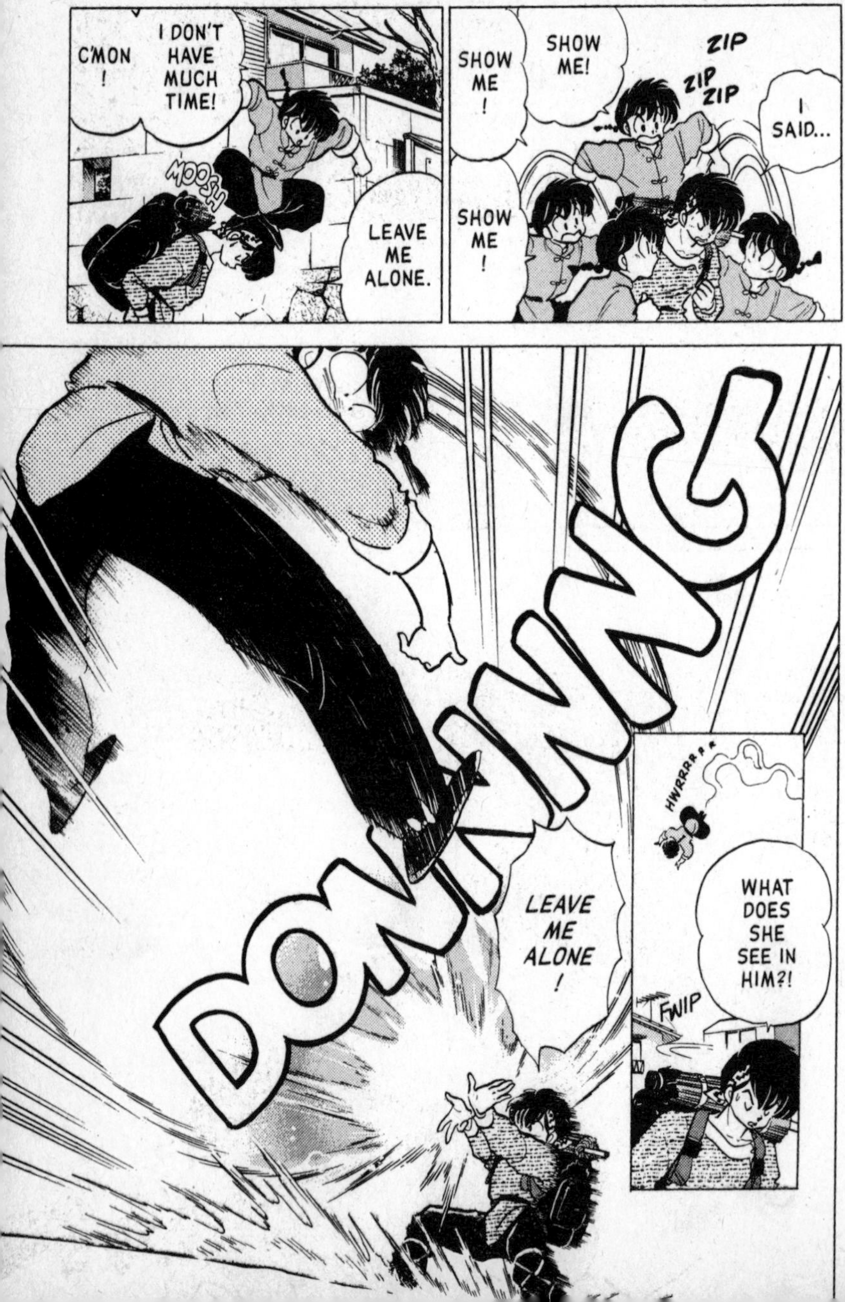
C'MON !
I DON'T HAVE MUCH TIME!
WOOSH
LEAVE ME ALONE.
SHOW ME !
SHOW ME!
ZIP
ZIP ZIP
I SAID...
SHOW ME !
LEAVE ME ALONE !
HWRRRR
WHAT DOES SHE SEE IN HIM?!
FWIP

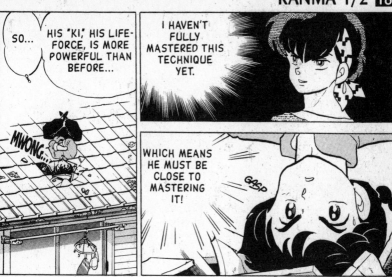

SO... HIS "KI," HIS LIFE-FORCE, IS MORE POWERFUL THAN BEFORE...

I HAVEN'T FULLY MASTERED THIS TECHNIQUE YET.

MWONG...

WHICH MEANS HE MUST BE CLOSE TO MASTERING IT!

GASP

I GOTTA HURRY!

I GOTTA GET A LOOK...

...AT THAT *SHISHI HŌKŌDAN* SCROLL OF HIS!

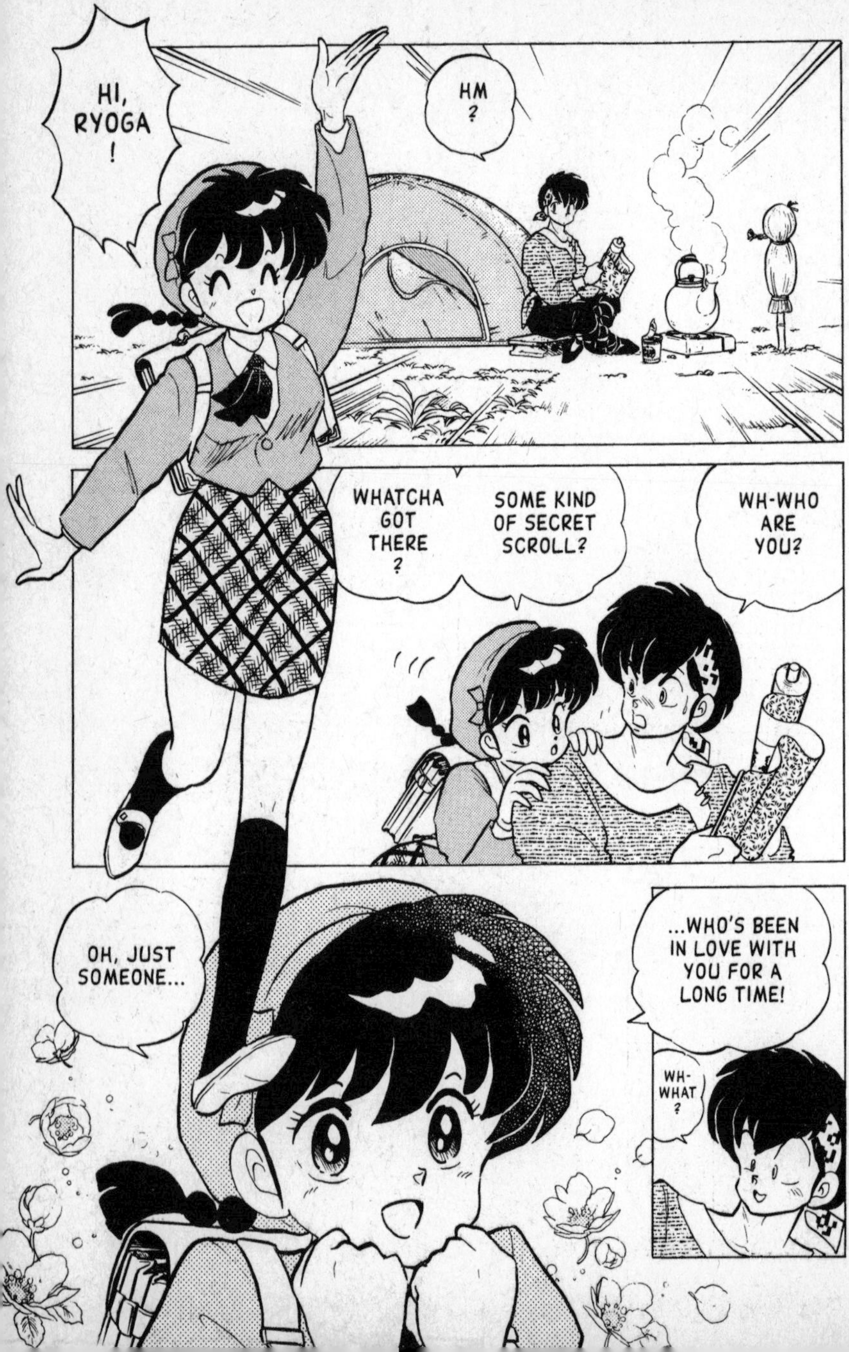
HI, RYOGA!
HM?
WHATCHA GOT THERE?
SOME KIND OF SECRET SCROLL?
WH-WHO ARE YOU?
OH, JUST SOMEONE...
...WHO'S BEEN IN LOVE WITH YOU FOR A LONG TIME!
WH-WHAT?

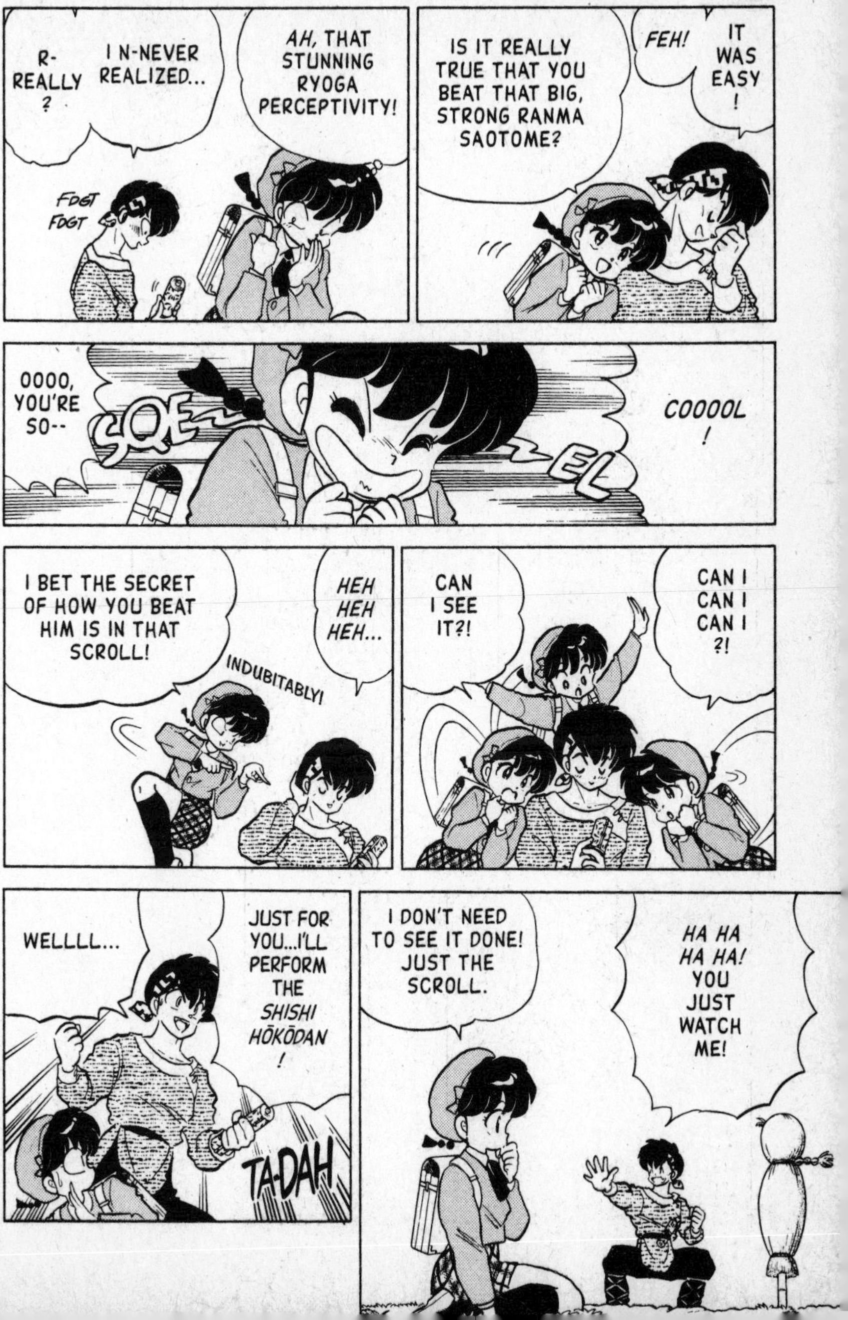
R- REALLY ?
I N-NEVER REALIZED...
AH, THAT STUNNING RYOGA PERCEPTIVITY!
FDGT FDGT
IS IT REALLY TRUE THAT YOU BEAT THAT BIG, STRONG RANMA SAOTOME?
FEH!
IT WAS EASY !
OOOO, YOU'RE SO--
SQE
EL
COOOOL !
I BET THE SECRET OF HOW YOU BEAT HIM IS IN THAT SCROLL!
HEH HEH HEH...
INDUBITABLY!
CAN I SEE IT?!
CAN I CAN I CAN I ?!
WELLLL...
JUST FOR YOU...I'LL PERFORM THE SHISHI HŌKŌDAN !
TA-DAH
I DON'T NEED TO SEE IT DONE! JUST THE SCROLL.
HA HA HA HA! YOU JUST WATCH ME!

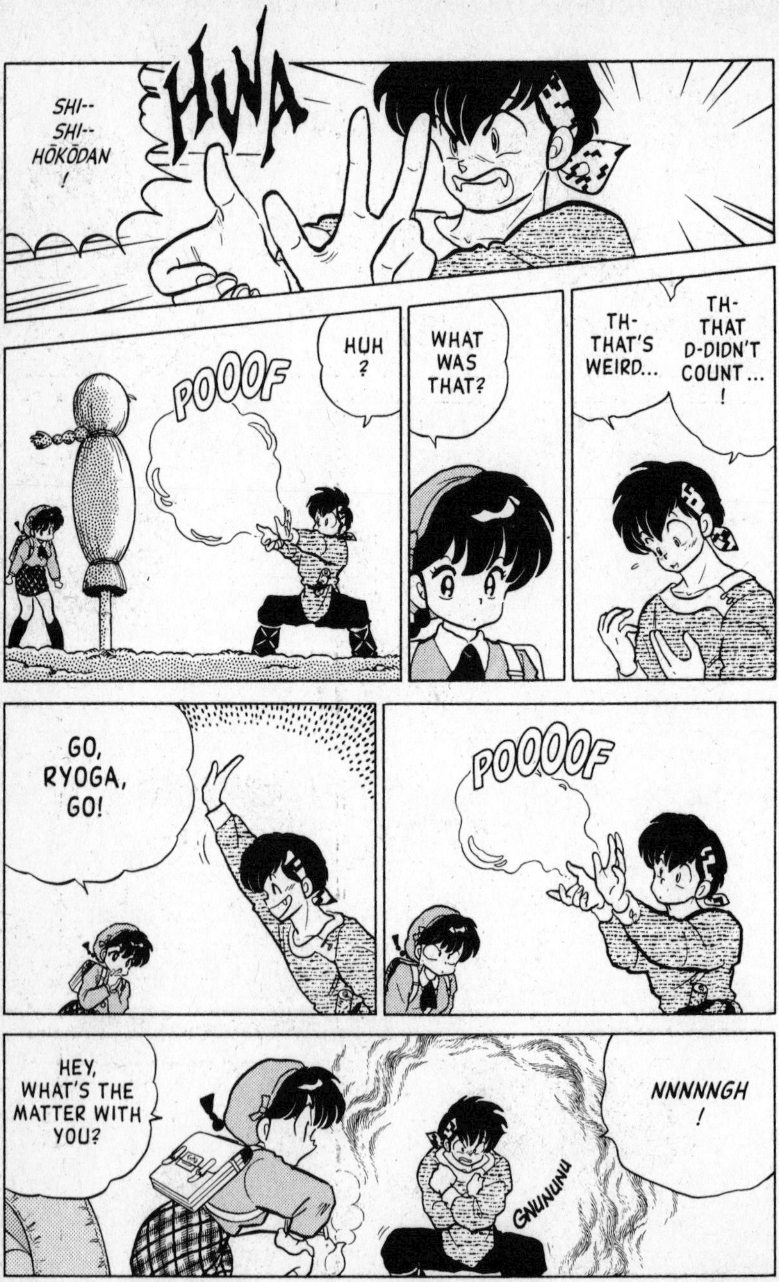
SHI-- SHI-- HŌKŌDAN !
HWA
POOOF
HUH ?
WHAT WAS THAT?
TH- THAT'S WEIRD...
TH- THAT D-DIDN'T COUNT... !
GO, RYOGA, GO!
POOOOF
HEY, WHAT'S THE MATTER WITH YOU?
GNUNUNU
NNNNNGH !

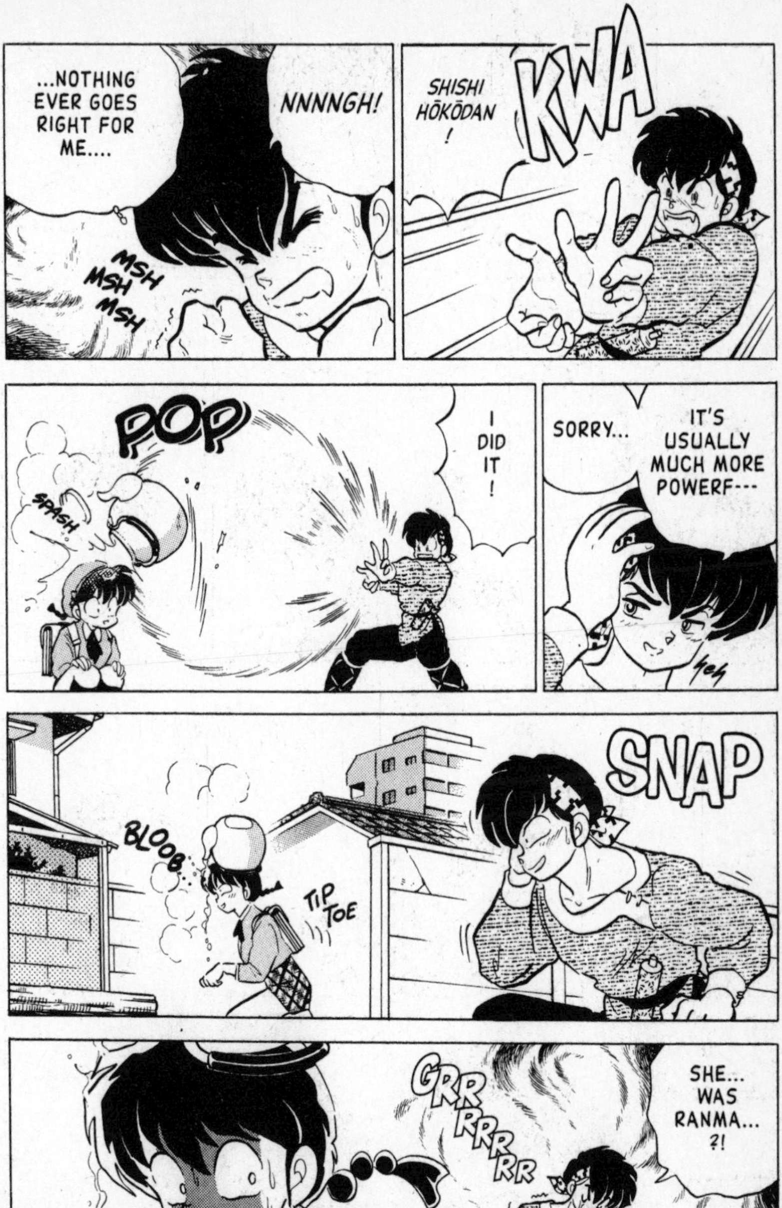
...NOTHING EVER GOES RIGHT FOR ME....
NNNNGH!
MSH MSH MSH
SHISHI HŌKŌDAN !
KWA
POP
SPASH
I DID IT !
SORRY...
IT'S USUALLY MUCH MORE POWERF---
heh
SNAP
BLOOB
TIP TOE
GRRRRRRRR
SHE... WAS RANMA... ?!

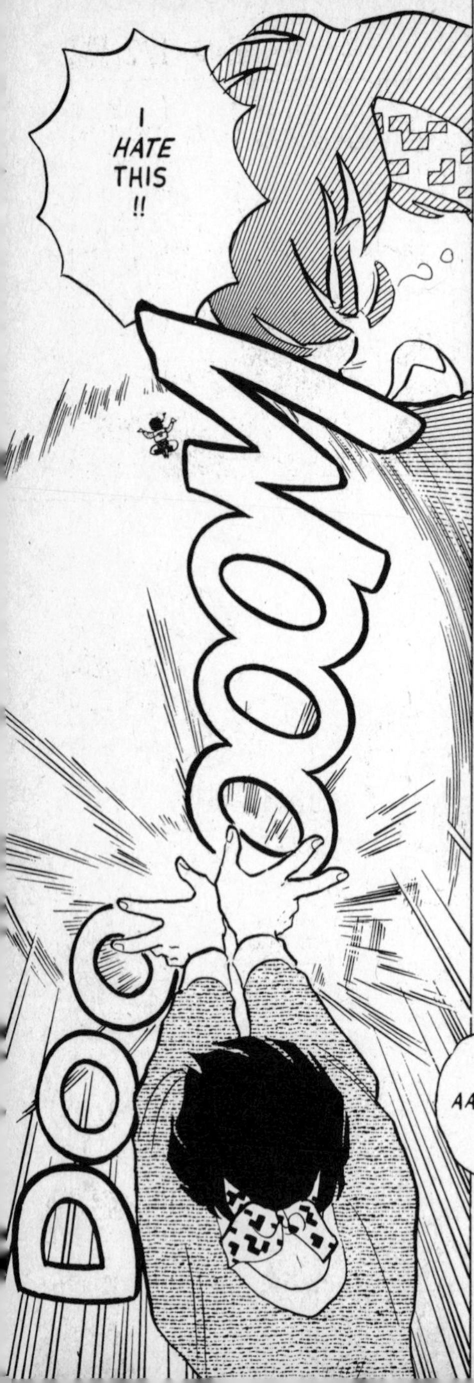
I HATE THIS !!
DOGOOOM
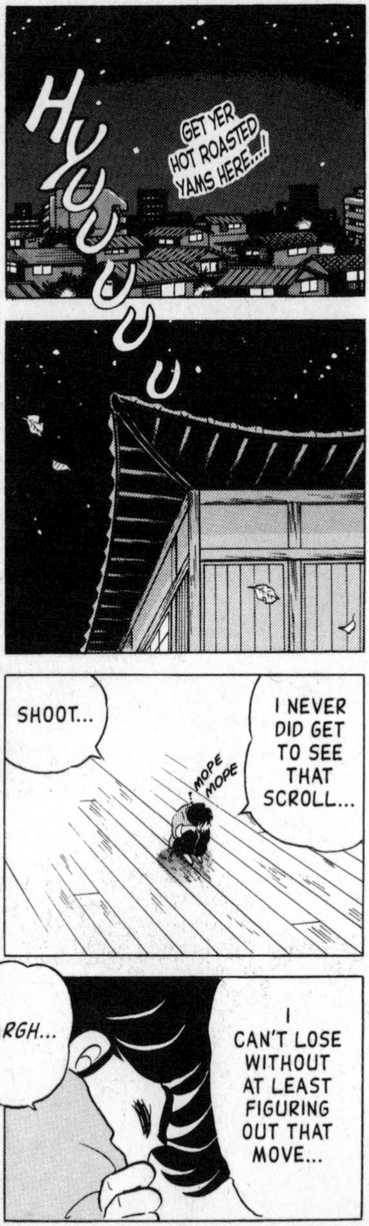
HYUUUUUU
GET YER HOT ROASTED YAMS HERE...!
SHOOT...
I NEVER DID GET TO SEE THAT SCROLL...
MOPE MOPE
AARGH...
I CAN'T LOSE WITHOUT AT LEAST FIGURING OUT THAT MOVE...

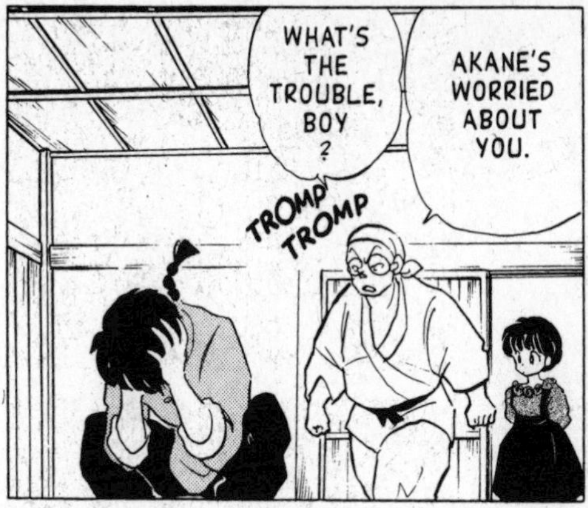
WHAT'S THE TROUBLE, BOY ?
AKANE'S WORRIED ABOUT YOU.
TROMP TROMP

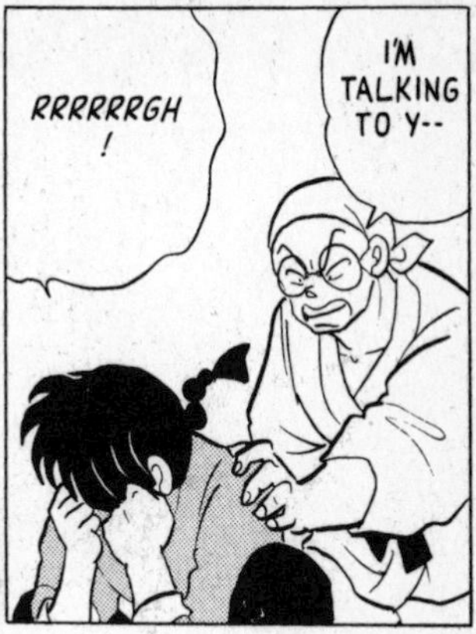
RRRRRRGH !
I'M TALKING TO Y--

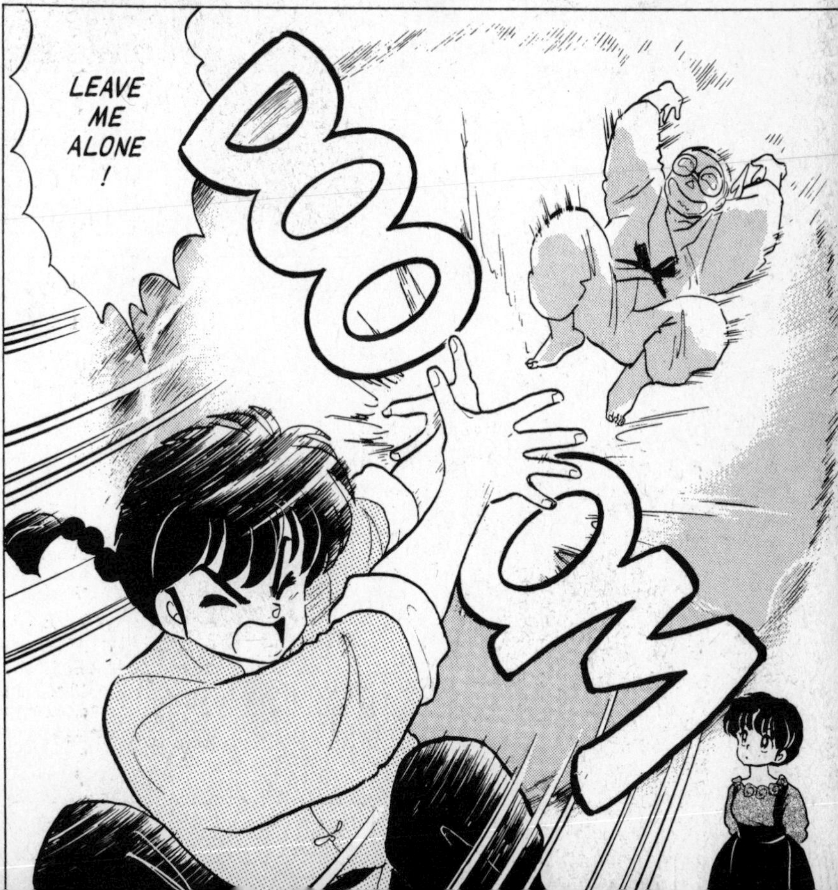
LEAVE ME ALONE !
BOOM

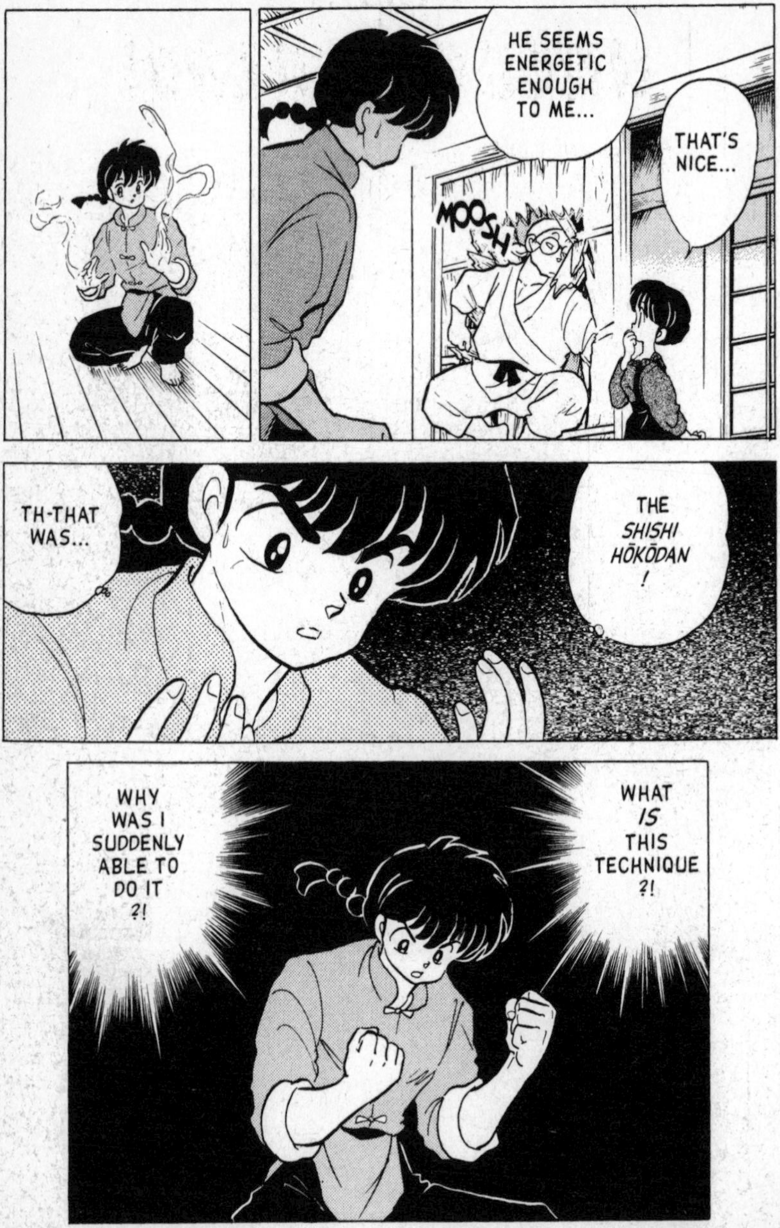
HE SEEMS ENERGETIC ENOUGH TO ME...
MOOSH
THAT'S NICE...
TH-THAT WAS...
THE *SHISHI HŌKŌDAN* !
WHY WAS I SUDDENLY ABLE TO DO IT ?!
WHAT *IS* THIS TECHNIQUE ?!

Part 3
UNLUCKY BLOW

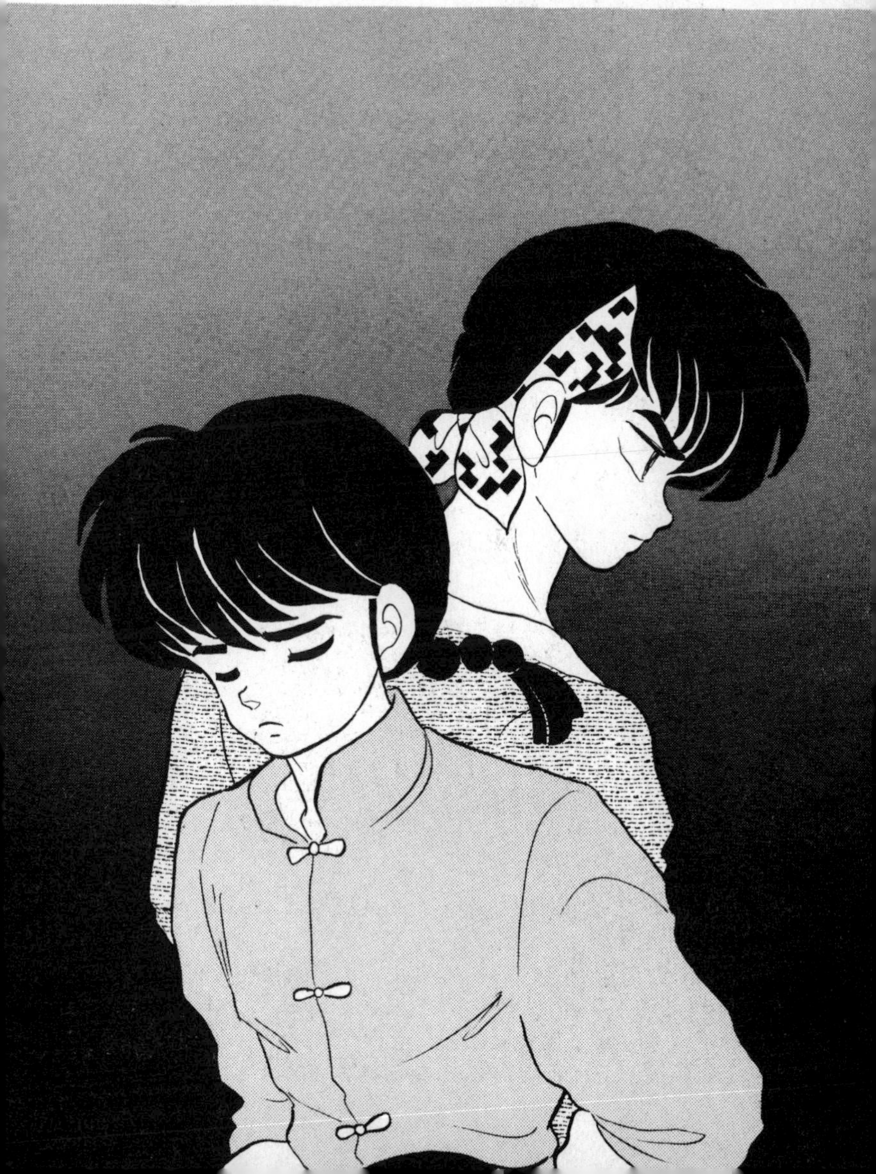

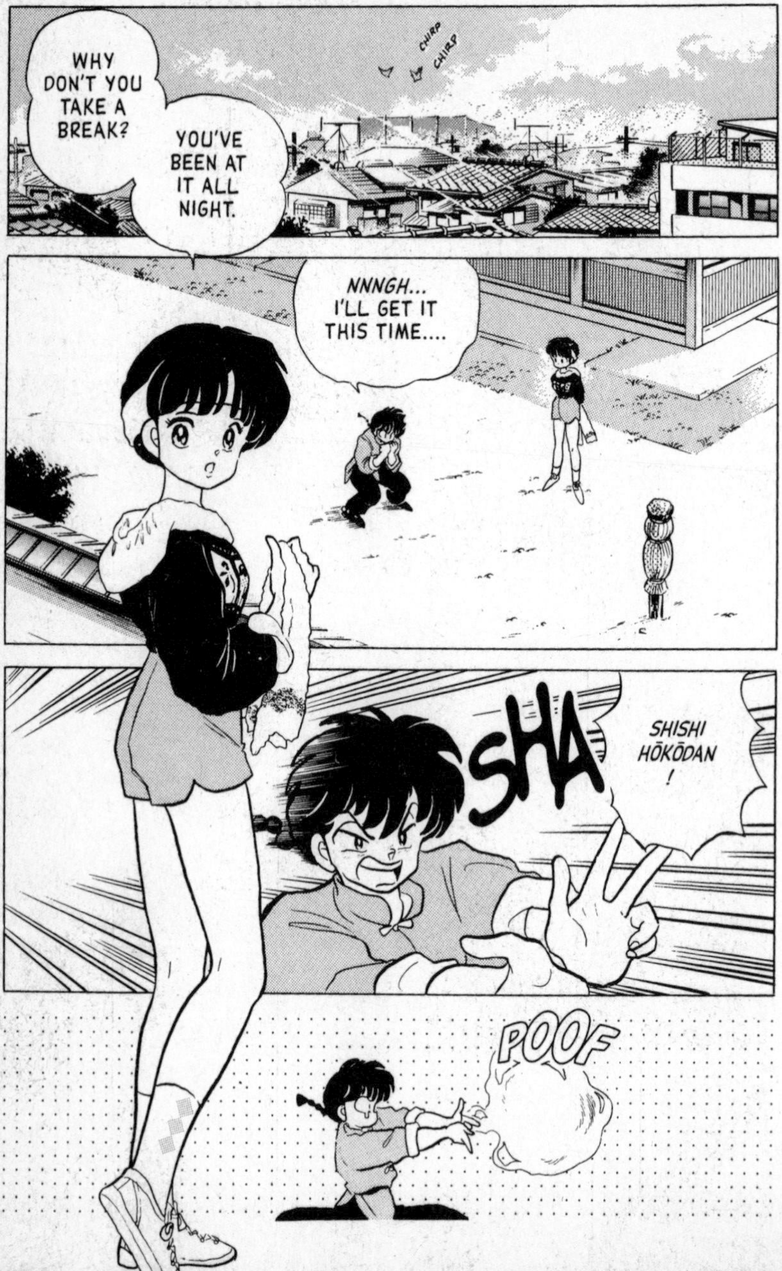
CHIRP
CHIRP
WHY DON'T YOU TAKE A BREAK?
YOU'VE BEEN AT IT ALL NIGHT.
NNNGH... I'LL GET IT THIS TIME....
SHA
SHISHI HŌKŌDAN!
POOF

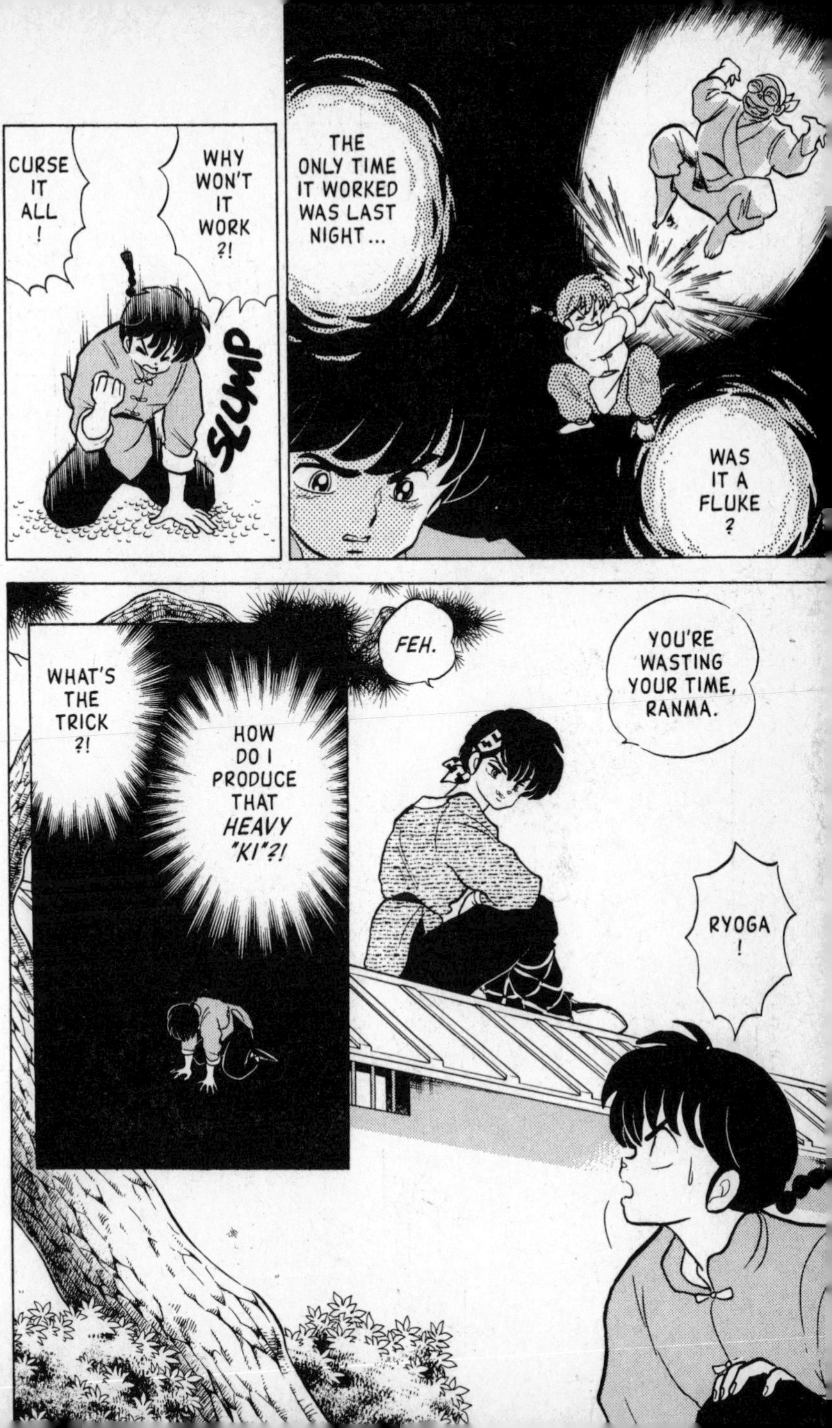
CURSE IT ALL !
WHY WON'T IT WORK ?!
SLUMP
THE ONLY TIME IT WORKED WAS LAST NIGHT...
WAS IT A FLUKE ?
WHAT'S THE TRICK ?!
HOW DO I PRODUCE THAT HEAVY "KI"?!
FEH.
YOU'RE WASTING YOUR TIME, RANMA.
RYOGA !

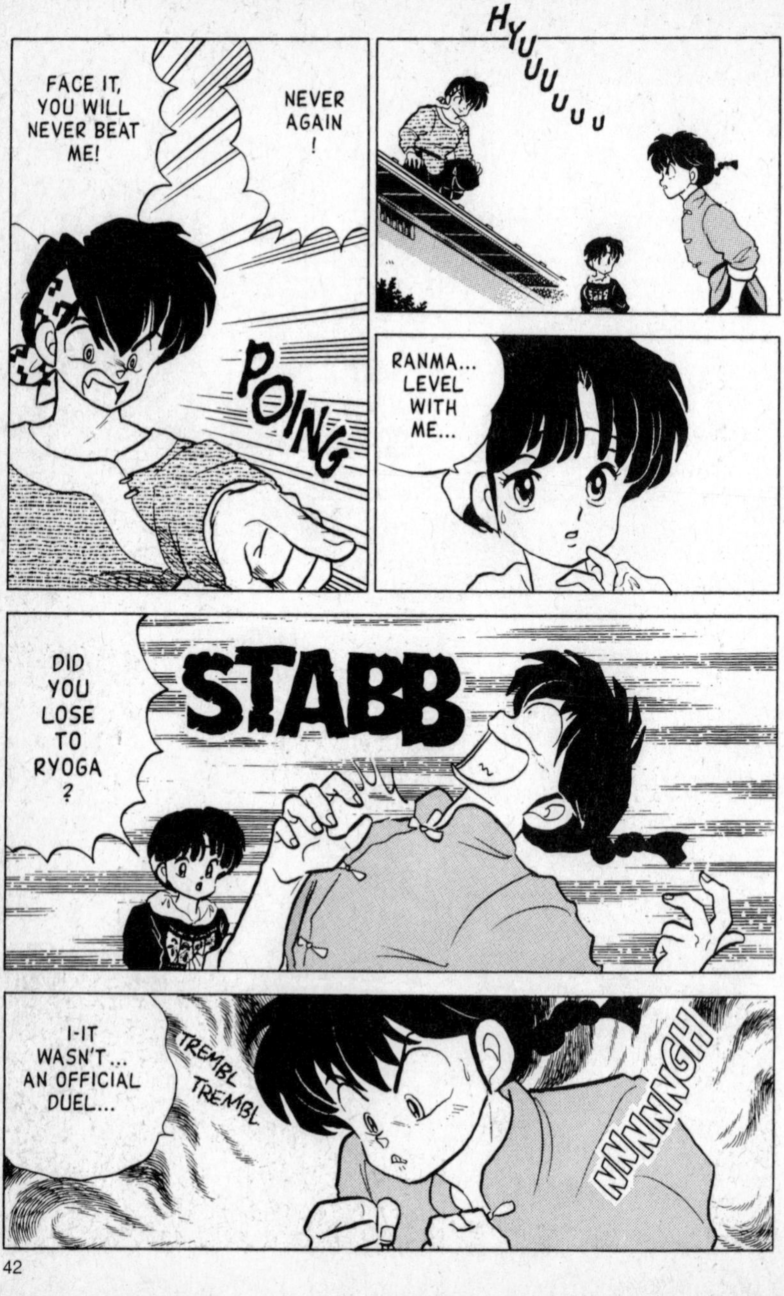
FACE IT, YOU WILL NEVER BEAT ME!
NEVER AGAIN !
POING
HYUUUUUU
RANMA... LEVEL WITH ME...
DID YOU LOSE TO RYOGA ?
STABB
I-IT WASN'T... AN OFFICIAL DUEL...
TREMBL TREMBL
NNNNNGH

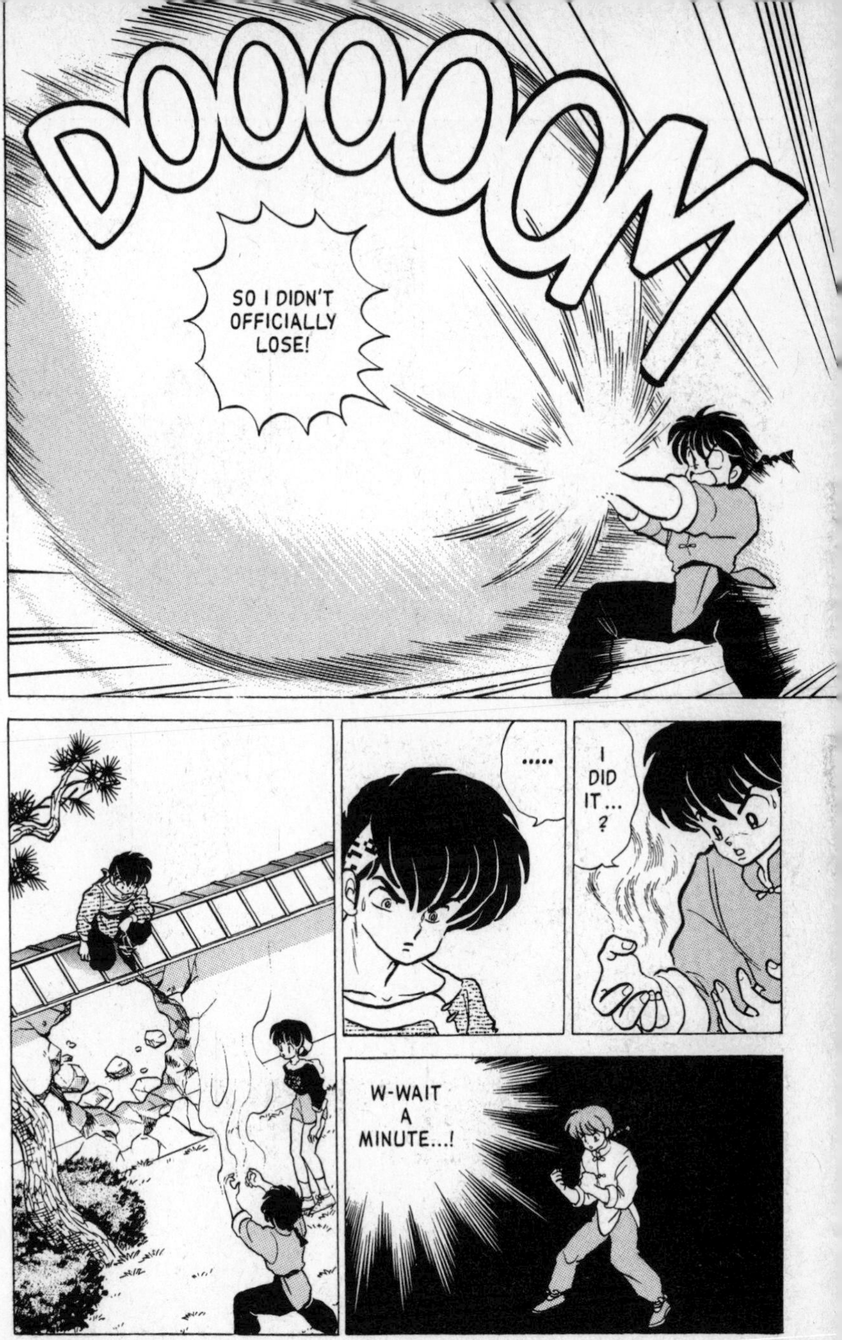
DOOOOOM
SO I DIDN'T OFFICIALLY LOSE!
.....
I DID IT...?
W-WAIT A MINUTE...!

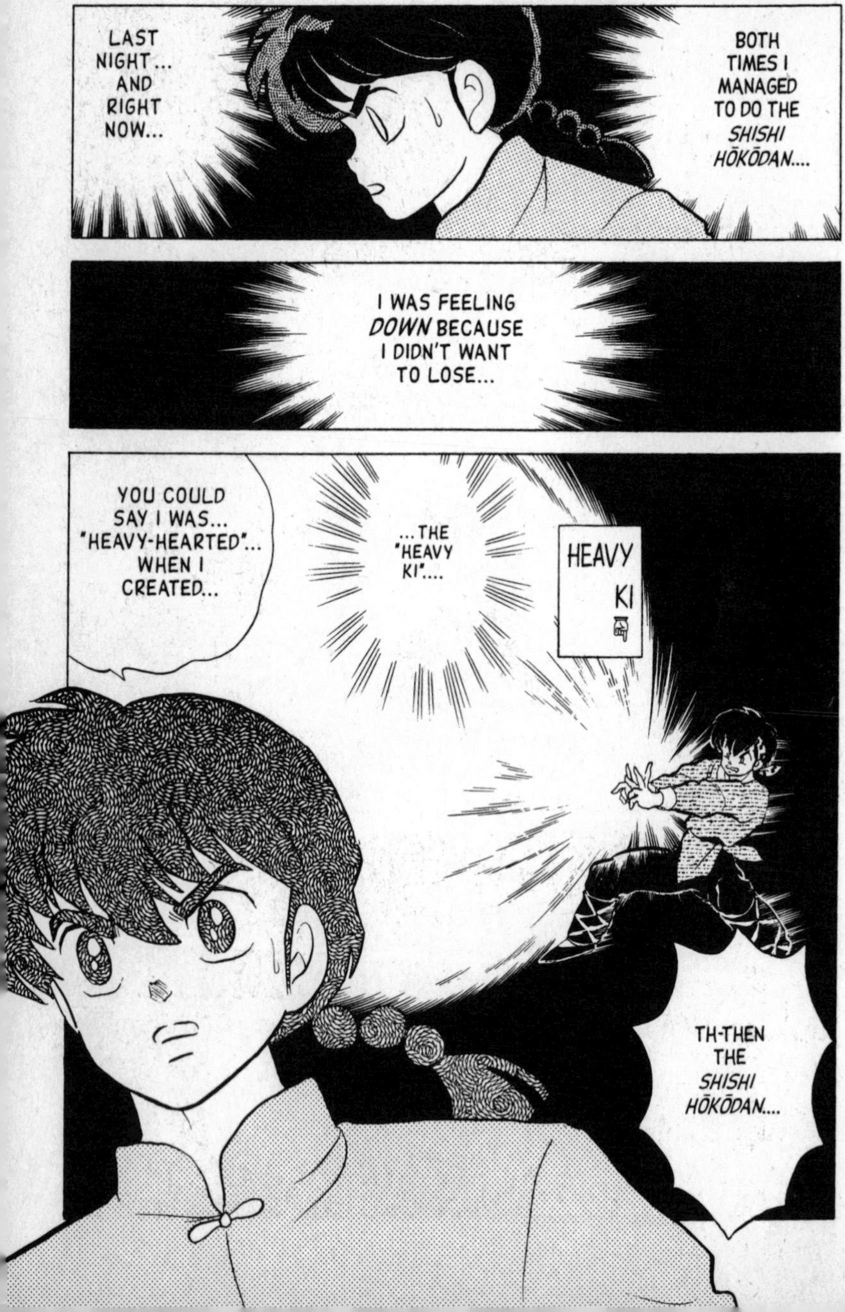
LAST NIGHT... AND RIGHT NOW...
BOTH TIMES I MANAGED TO DO THE *SHISHI HŌKŌDAN*....
I WAS FEELING *DOWN* BECAUSE I DIDN'T WANT TO LOSE...
YOU COULD SAY I WAS... "HEAVY-HEARTED"... WHEN I CREATED...
...THE "HEAVY KI"....
HEAVY KI
TH-THEN THE *SHISHI HŌKŌDAN*....

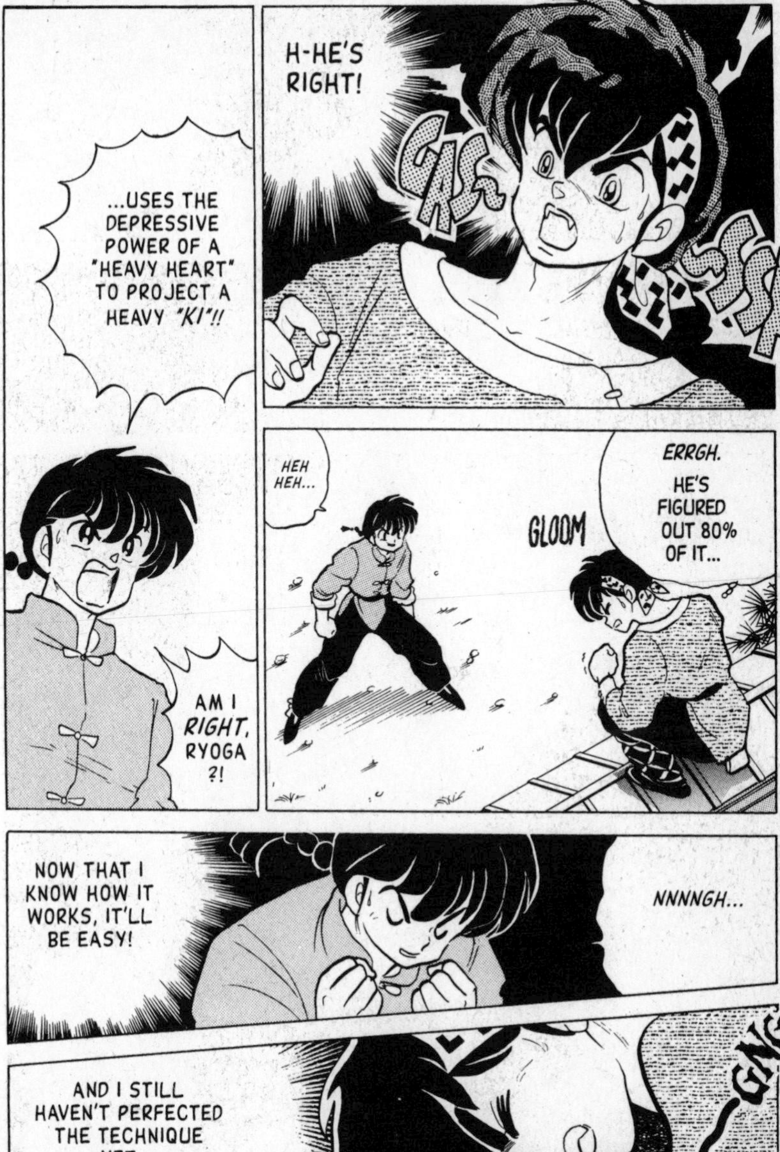
...USES THE DEPRESSIVE POWER OF A "HEAVY HEART" TO PROJECT A HEAVY "KI"!!
AM I RIGHT, RYOGA ?!
H-HE'S RIGHT!
GASP
HEH HEH...
GLOOM
ERRGH.
HE'S FIGURED OUT 80% OF IT...
NOW THAT I KNOW HOW IT WORKS, IT'LL BE EASY!
NNNNGH...
AND I STILL HAVEN'T PERFECTED THE TECHNIQUE YET...
—GNG

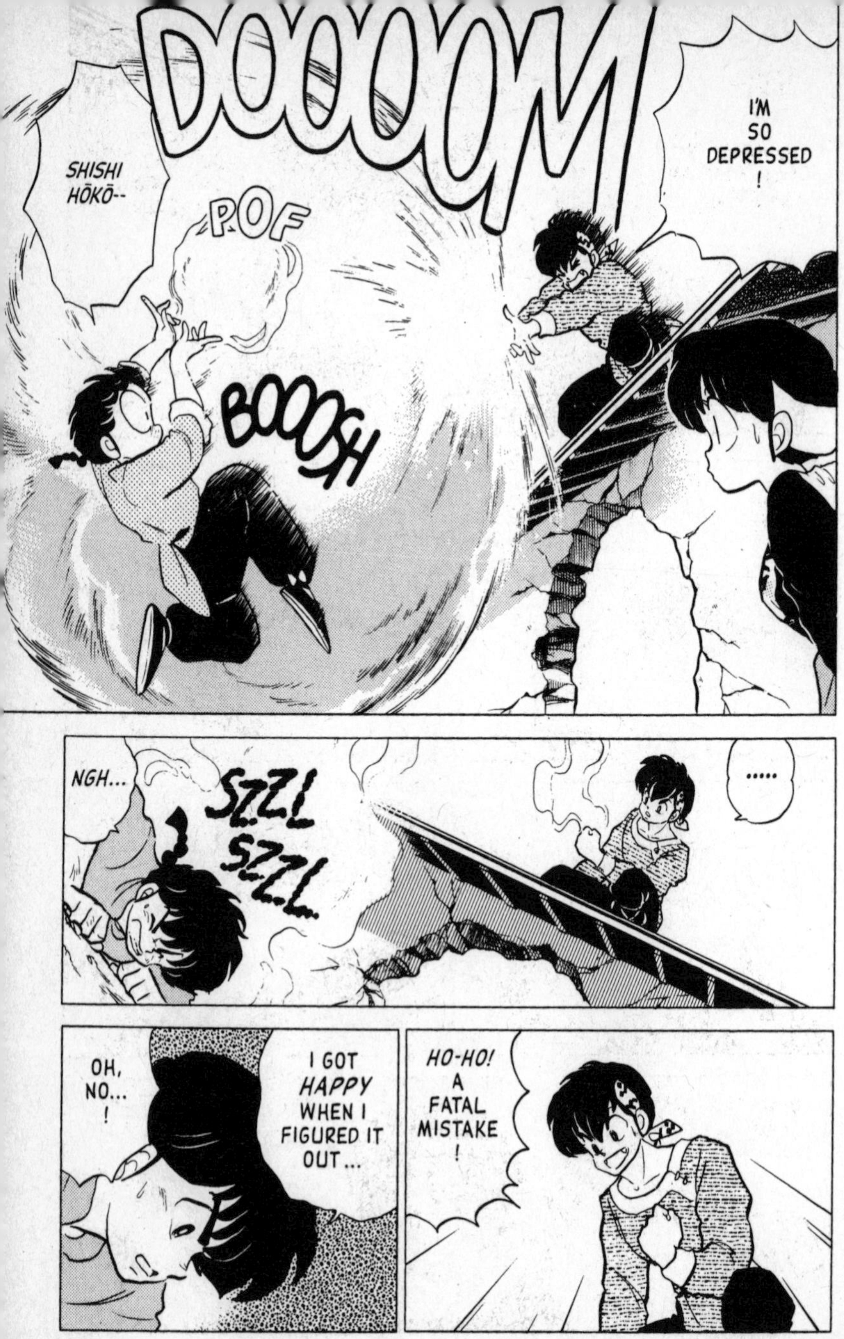
DOOOOM
SHISHI HŌKŌ--
I'M SO DEPRESSED!
POF
BOOOSH
NGH...
SZZL SZZL
.....
OH, NO...!
I GOT *HAPPY* WHEN I FIGURED IT OUT...
HO-HO! A FATAL MISTAKE!

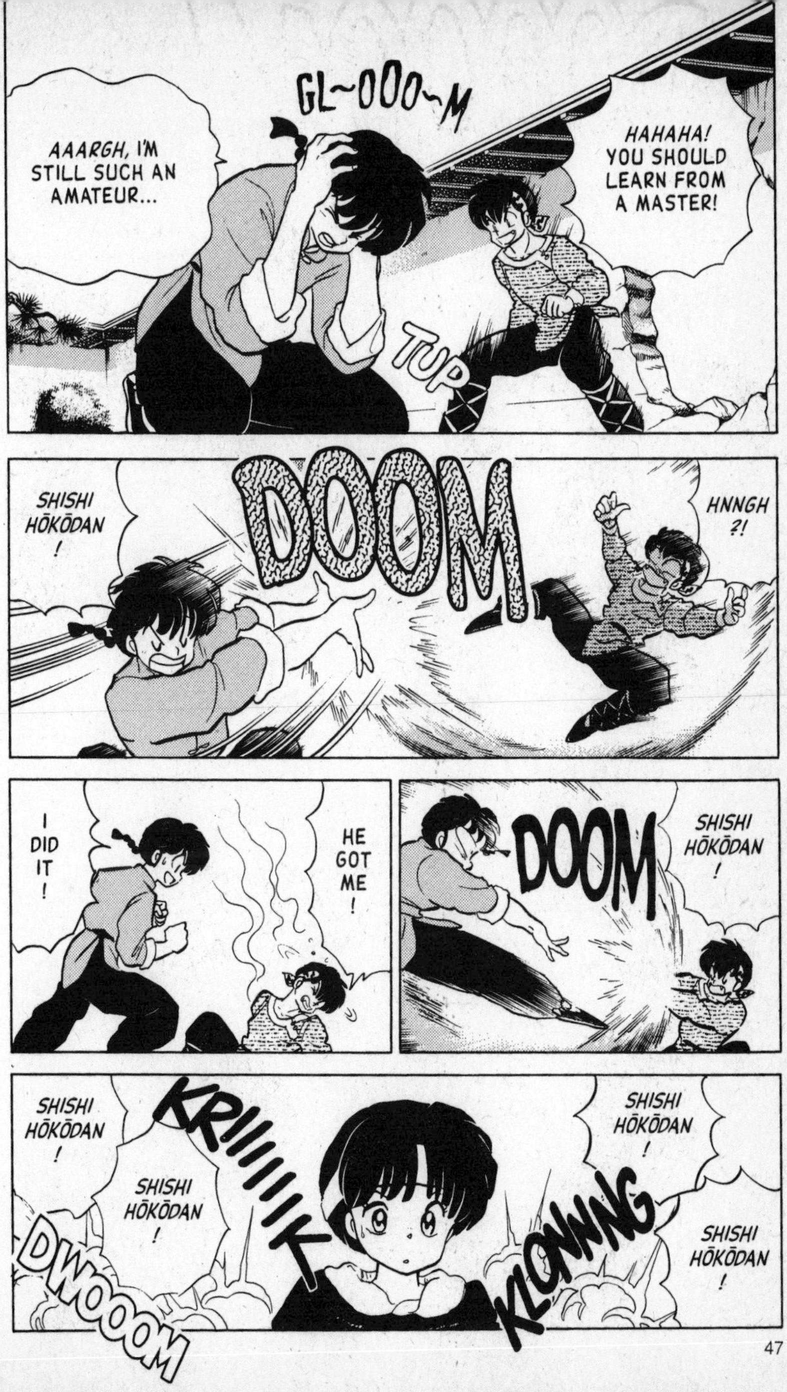
AAARGH, I'M STILL SUCH AN AMATEUR...
GL~OOO~M
HAHAHA! YOU SHOULD LEARN FROM A MASTER!
TUP
SHISHI HŌKŌDAN !
DOOM
HNNGH ?!
I DID IT !
HE GOT ME !
DOOM
SHISHI HŌKŌDAN !
SHISHI HŌKŌDAN !
KRIIIIIIK
SHISHI HŌKŌDAN !
DWOOOM
KLONNNG
SHISHI HŌKŌDAN !
SHISHI HŌKŌDAN !

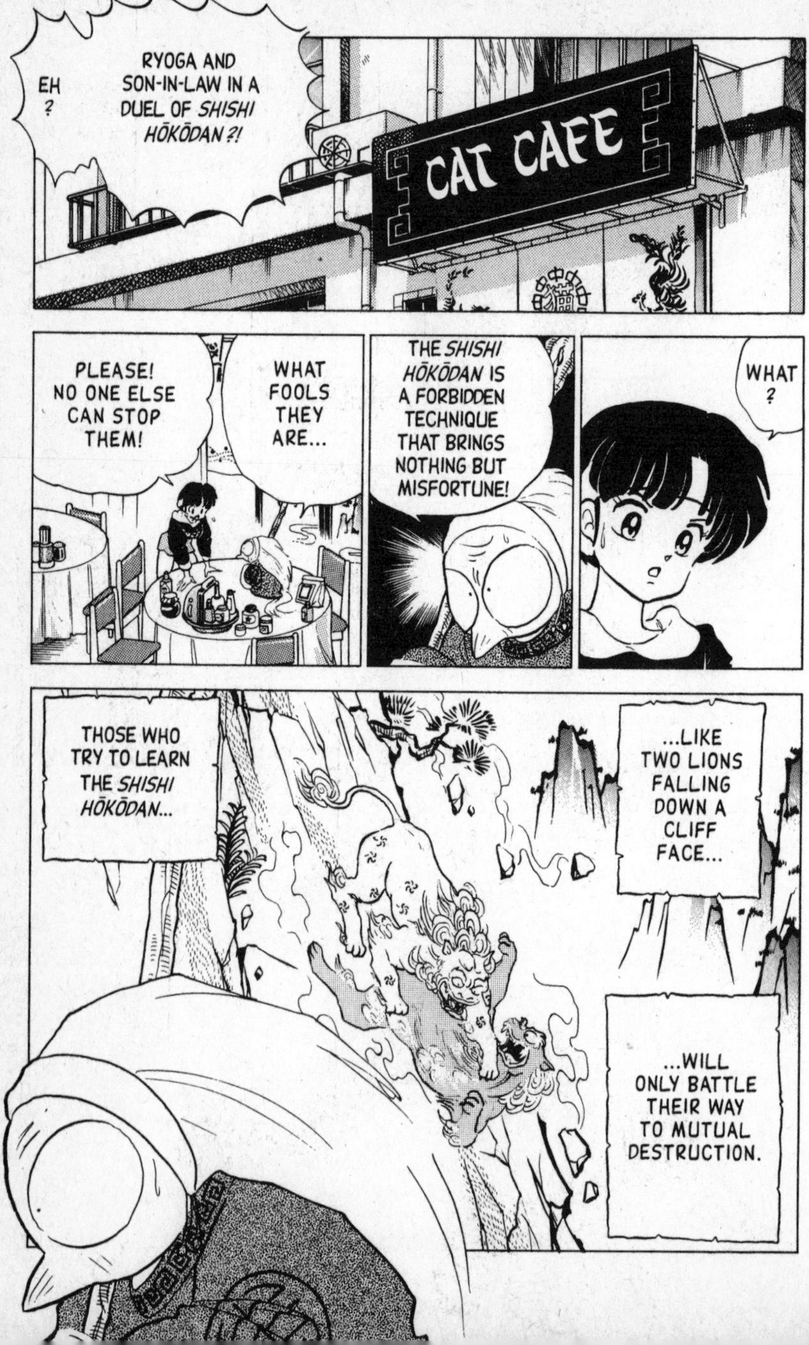
EH ?
RYOGA AND SON-IN-LAW IN A DUEL OF SHISHI HŌKŌDAN ?!
CAT CAFE
PLEASE! NO ONE ELSE CAN STOP THEM!
WHAT FOOLS THEY ARE...
THE SHISHI HŌKŌDAN IS A FORBIDDEN TECHNIQUE THAT BRINGS NOTHING BUT MISFORTUNE!
WHAT ?
THOSE WHO TRY TO LEARN THE SHISHI HŌKŌDAN...
...LIKE TWO LIONS FALLING DOWN A CLIFF FACE...
...WILL ONLY BATTLE THEIR WAY TO MUTUAL DESTRUCTION.

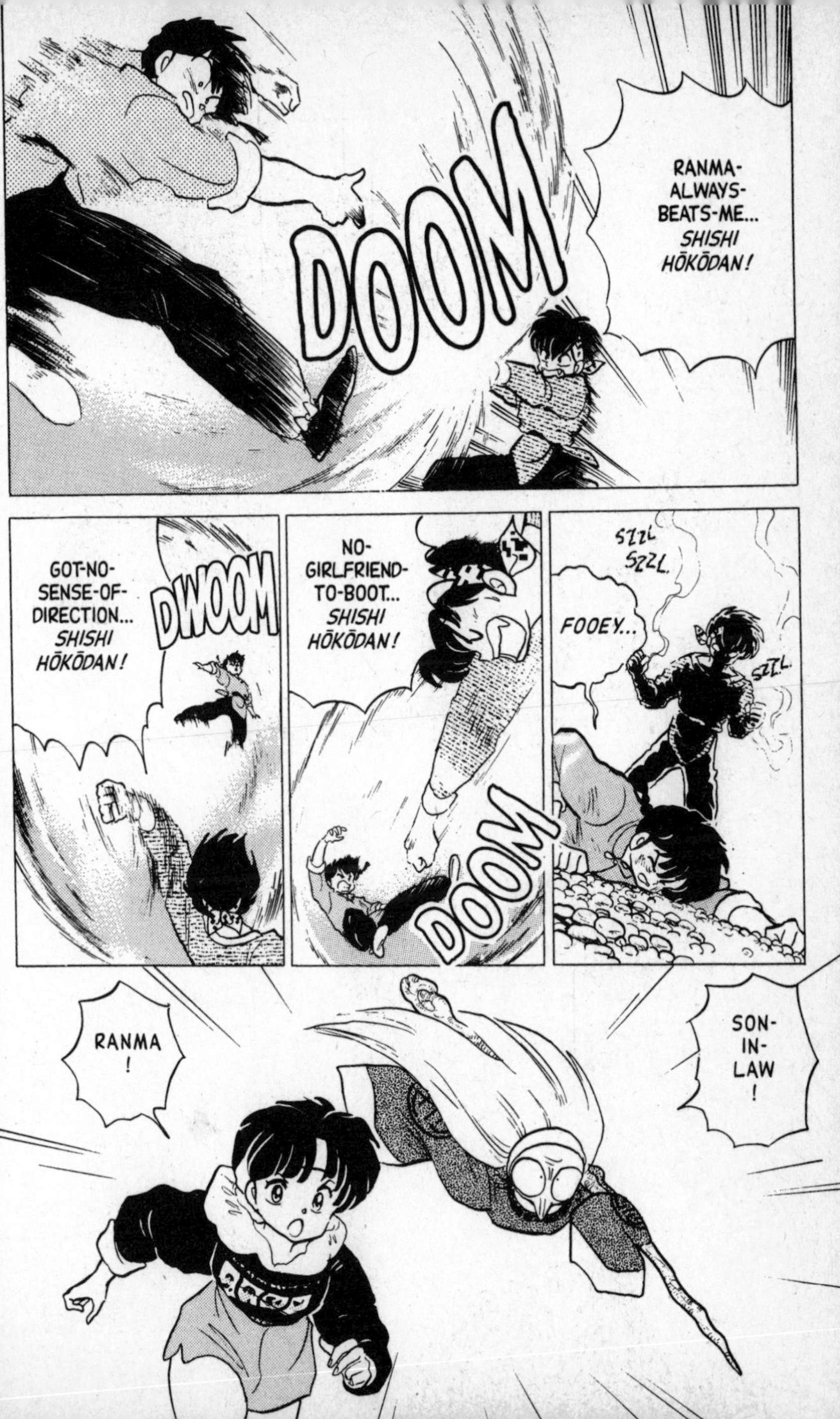
DOOM
RANMA-ALWAYS-BEATS-ME... SHISHI HŌKŌDAN!
GOT-NO-SENSE-OF-DIRECTION... SHISHI HŌKŌDAN!
DWOOM
NO-GIRLFRIEND-TO-BOOT... SHISHI HŌKŌDAN!
DOOM
SZZL SZZL
FOOEY...
SZZL
RANMA!
SON-IN-LAW!

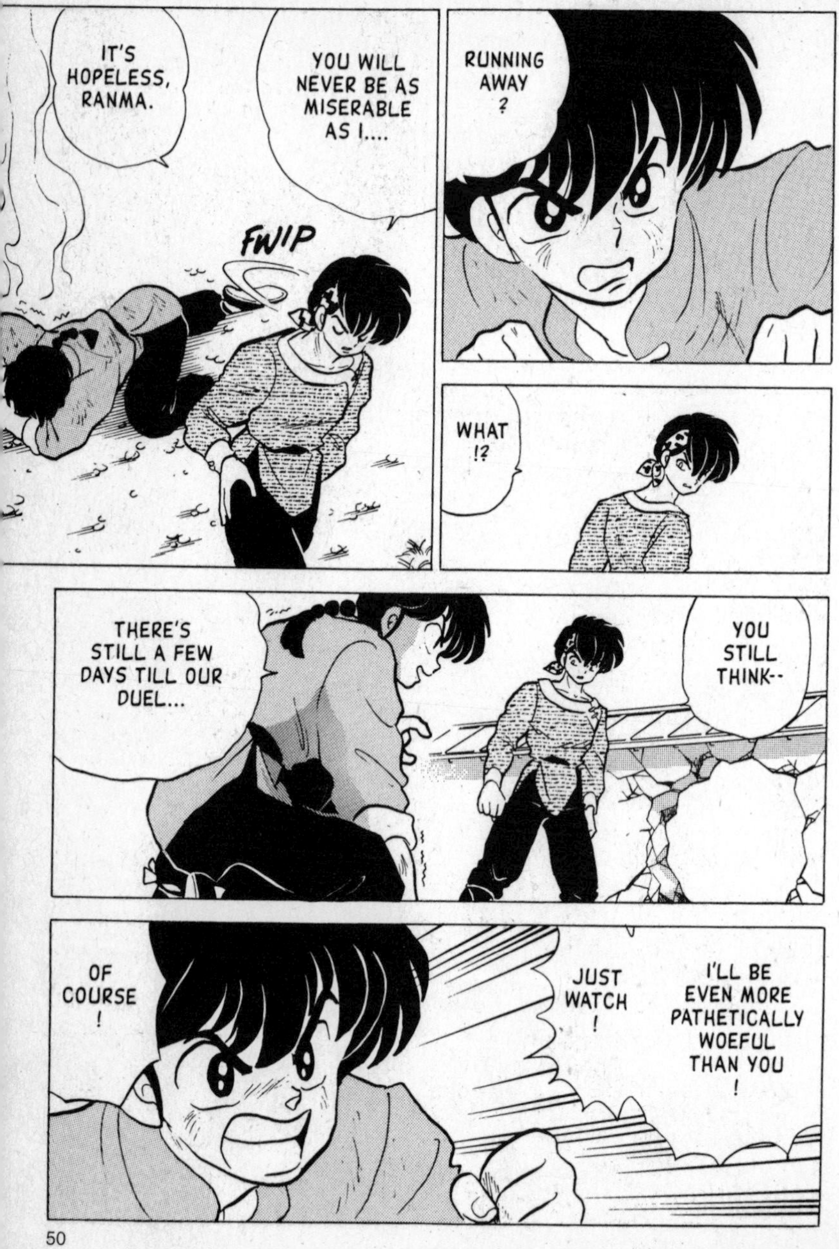
IT'S HOPELESS, RANMA.
YOU WILL NEVER BE AS MISERABLE AS I....
FWIP
RUNNING AWAY ?
WHAT !?
THERE'S STILL A FEW DAYS TILL OUR DUEL...
YOU STILL THINK--
OF COURSE !
JUST WATCH !
I'LL BE EVEN MORE PATHETICALLY WOEFUL THAN YOU !

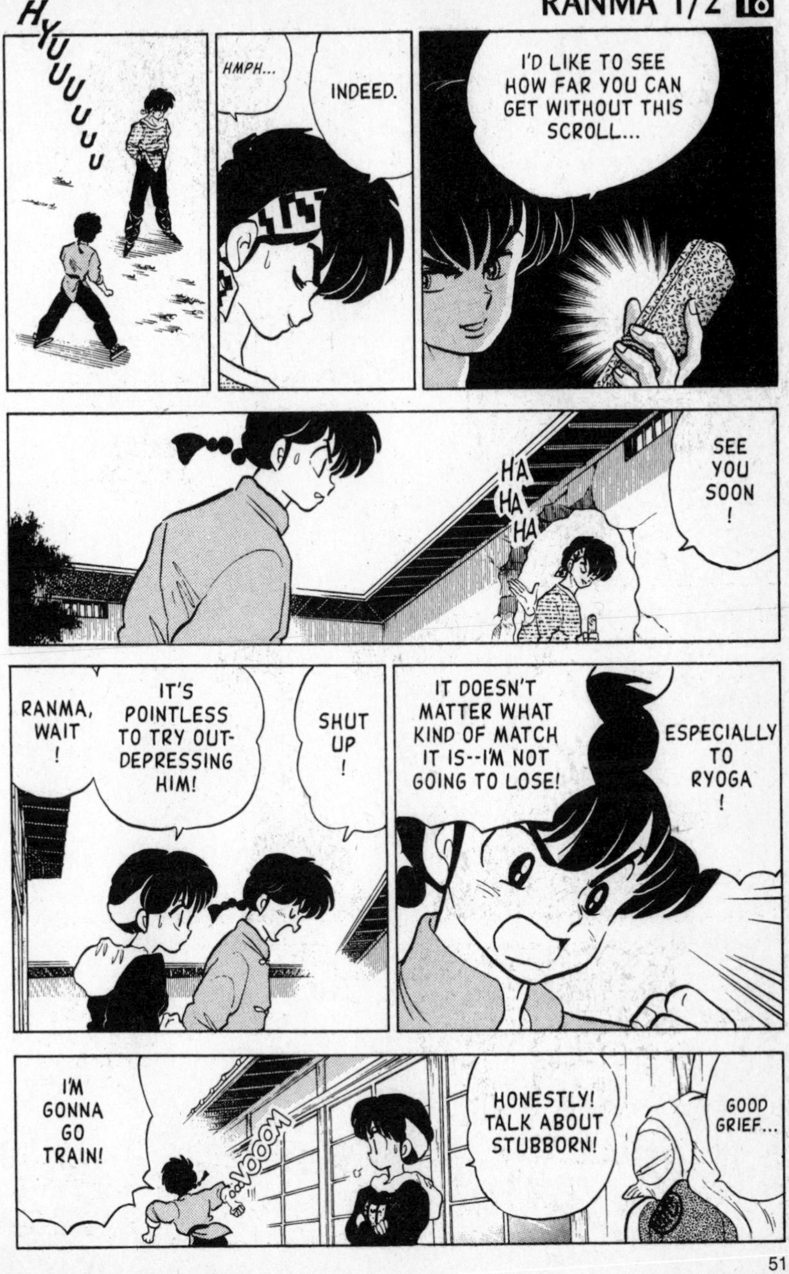
HYUUUUUUU
HMPH...
INDEED.
I'D LIKE TO SEE HOW FAR YOU CAN GET WITHOUT THIS SCROLL...
HA HA HA
SEE YOU SOON!
RANMA, WAIT!
IT'S POINTLESS TO TRY OUT-DEPRESSING HIM!
SHUT UP!
IT DOESN'T MATTER WHAT KIND OF MATCH IT IS--I'M NOT GOING TO LOSE!
ESPECIALLY TO RYOGA!
I'M GONNA GO TRAIN!
VOOOM
HONESTLY! TALK ABOUT STUBBORN!
GOOD GRIEF...

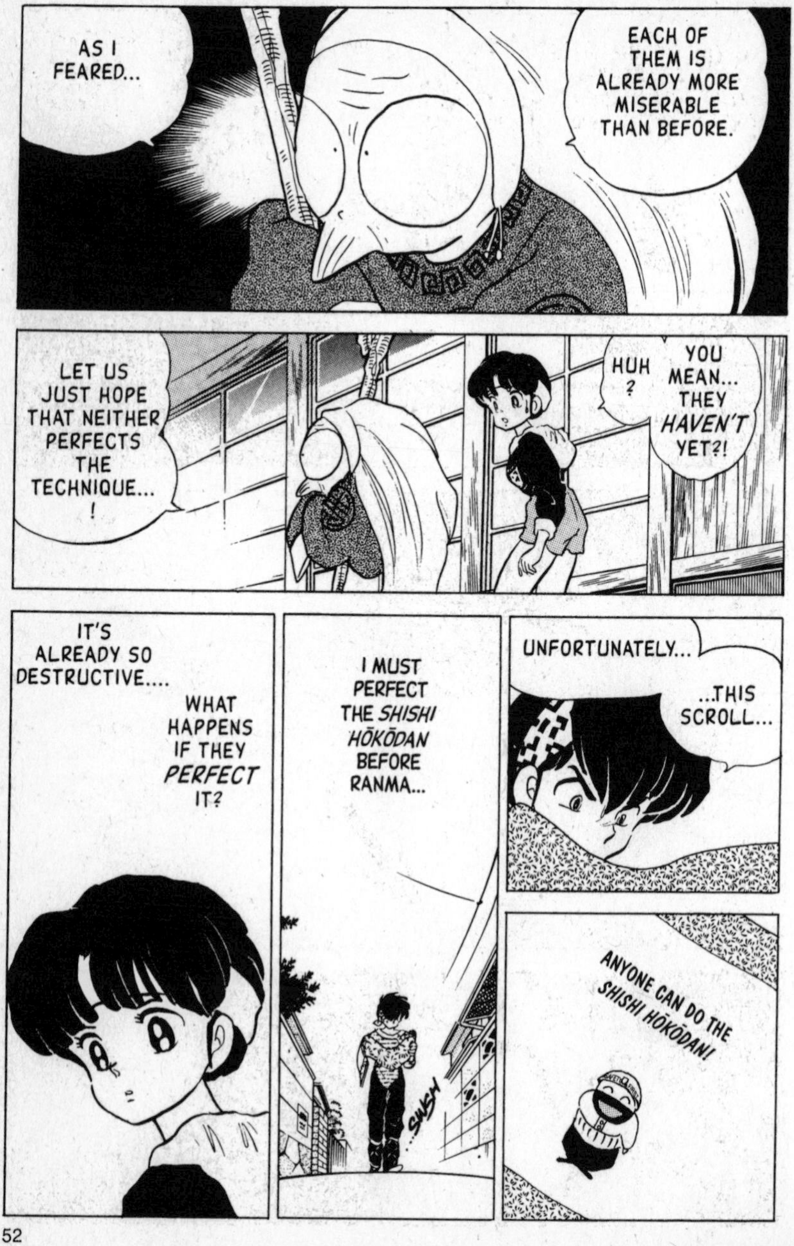
AS I FEARED...
EACH OF THEM IS ALREADY MORE MISERABLE THAN BEFORE.
LET US JUST HOPE THAT NEITHER PERFECTS THE TECHNIQUE... !
HUH?
YOU MEAN... THEY *HAVEN'T* YET?!
IT'S ALREADY SO DESTRUCTIVE....
WHAT HAPPENS IF THEY *PERFECT* IT?
I MUST PERFECT THE *SHISHI HŌKŌDAN* BEFORE RANMA...
...SHSH
UNFORTUNATELY...
...THIS SCROLL...
ANYONE CAN DO THE *SHISHI HŌKŌDAN!*

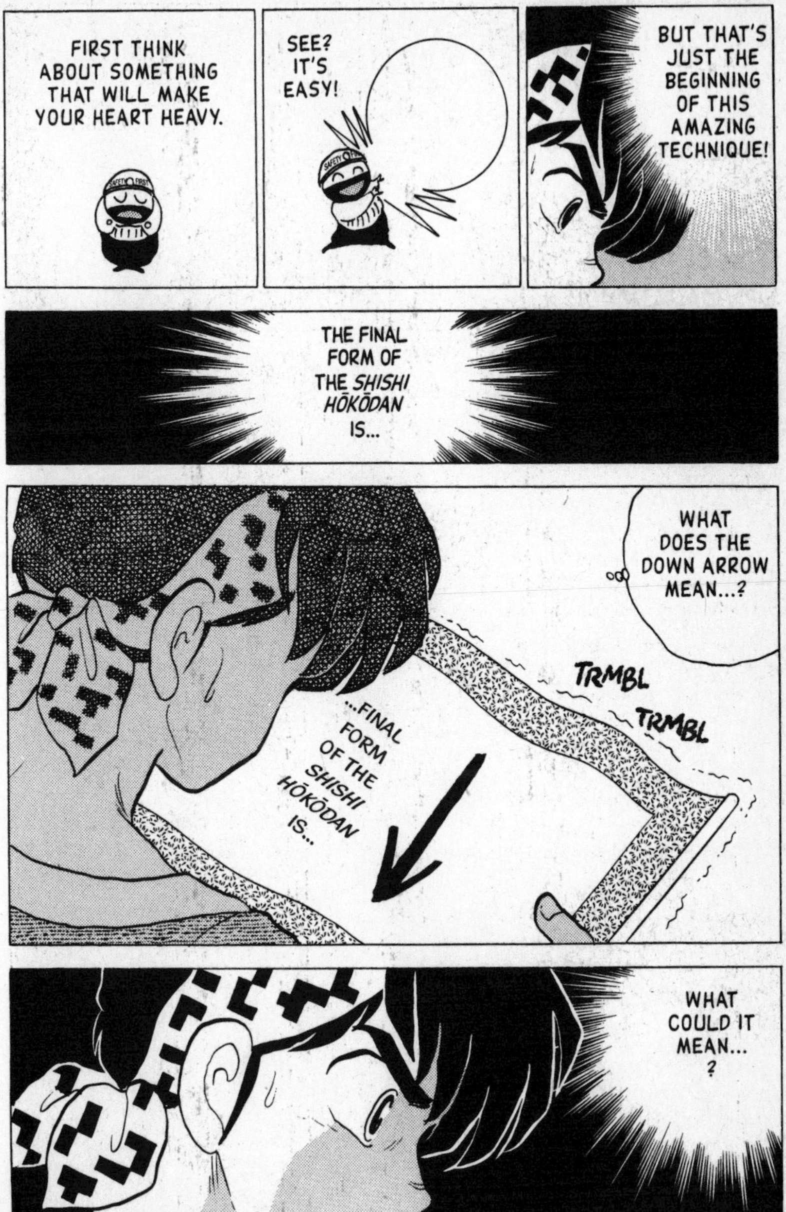
FIRST THINK ABOUT SOMETHING THAT WILL MAKE YOUR HEART HEAVY.
SEE? IT'S EASY!
SAFETY FIRST
BUT THAT'S JUST THE BEGINNING OF THIS AMAZING TECHNIQUE!
THE FINAL FORM OF THE SHISHI HŌKŌDAN IS...
WHAT DOES THE DOWN ARROW MEAN...?
TRMBL
TRMBL
...FINAL FORM OF THE SHISHI HŌKŌDAN IS...
WHAT COULD IT MEAN...?

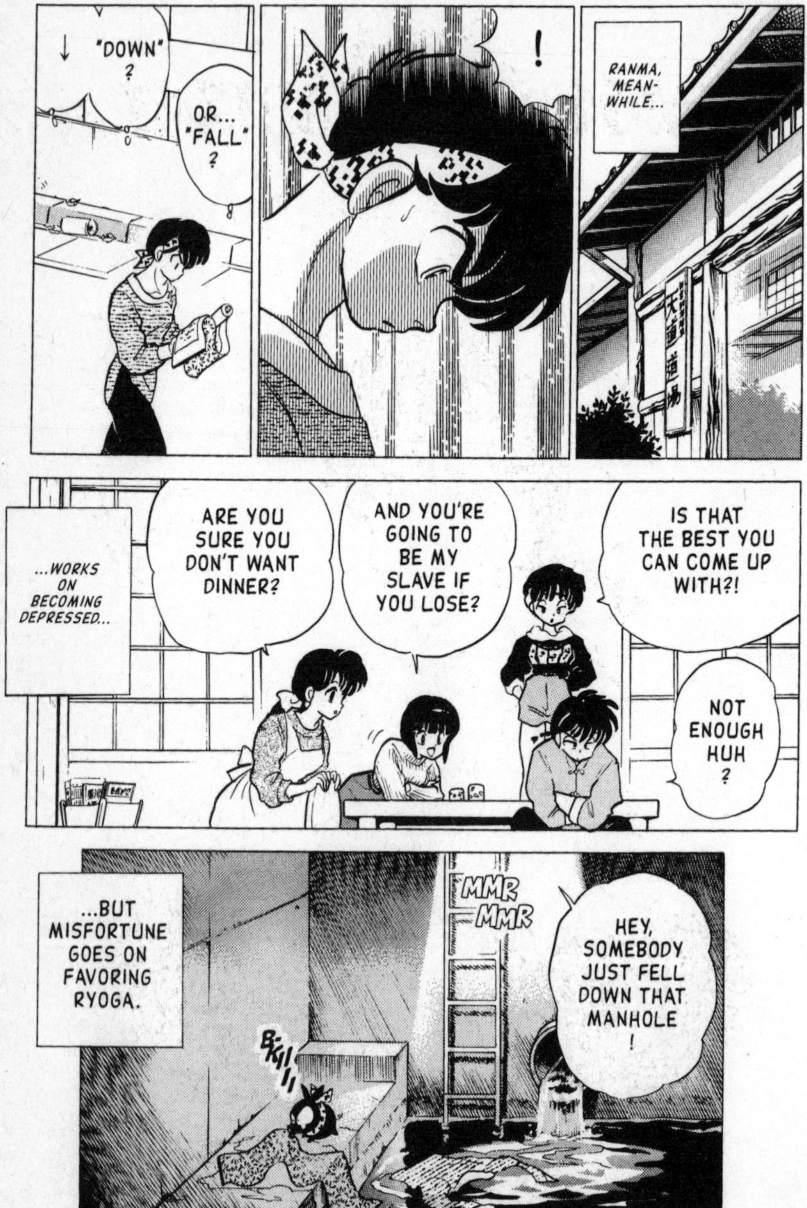
↓ "DOWN" ?
OR... "FALL" ?
!
RANMA, MEAN-WHILE...
...WORKS ON BECOMING DEPRESSED...
ARE YOU SURE YOU DON'T WANT DINNER?
AND YOU'RE GOING TO BE MY SLAVE IF YOU LOSE?
IS THAT THE BEST YOU CAN COME UP WITH?!
NOT ENOUGH HUH ?
...BUT MISFORTUNE GOES ON FAVORING RYOGA.
MMR MMR
BKIII
HEY, SOMEBODY JUST FELL DOWN THAT MANHOLE !

Part 4
EMOTIONAL IMPACT

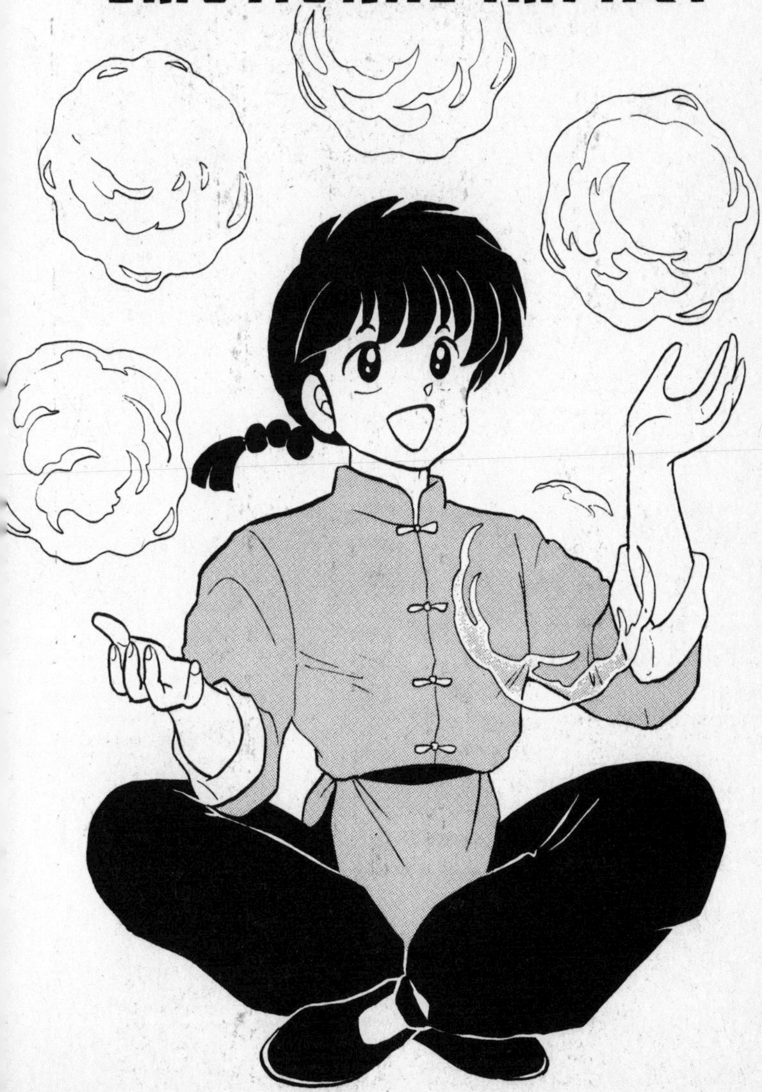

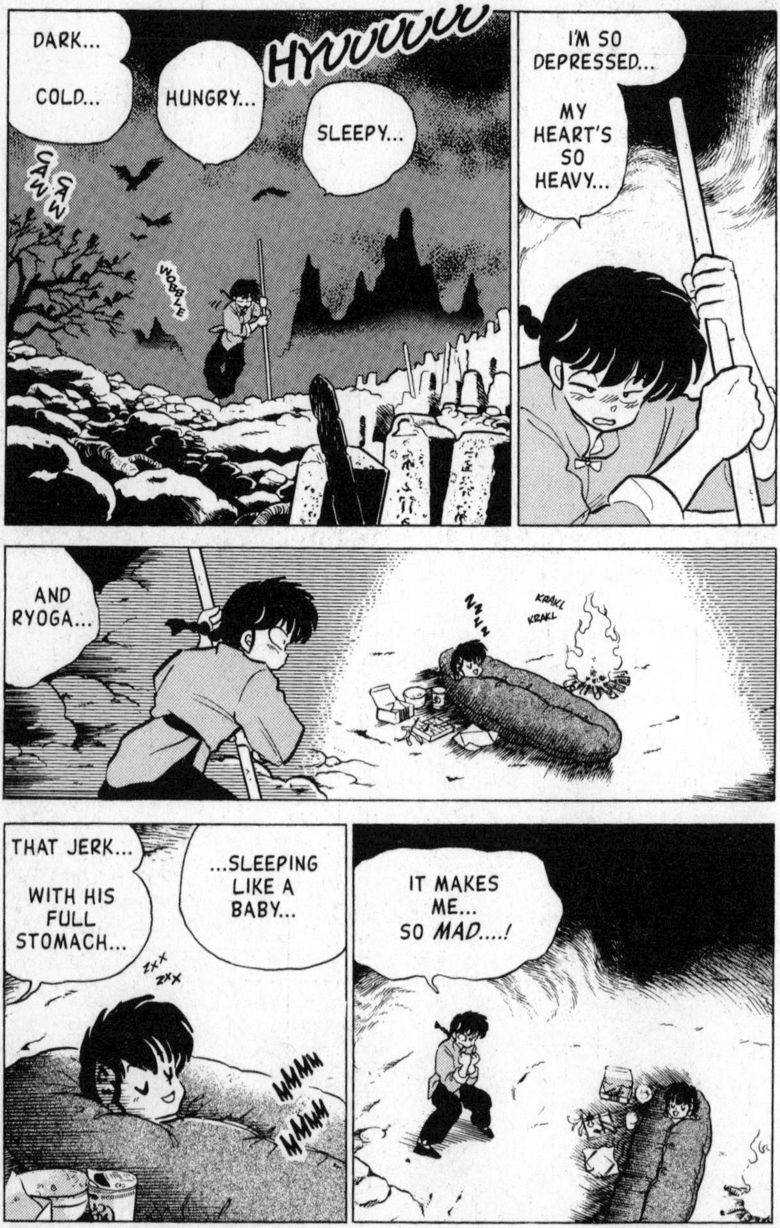
DARK...
COLD...
HUNGRY...
HYUUUUU
SLEEPY...
CAW CAW
WOBBLE
I'M SO DEPRESSED...
MY HEART'S SO HEAVY...
AND RYOGA...
ZZZZ
KRAKL KRAKL
THAT JERK...
WITH HIS FULL STOMACH...
...SLEEPING LIKE A BABY...
ZZZ ZZZ
MMMM MMMM
IT MAKES ME... SO MAD....!

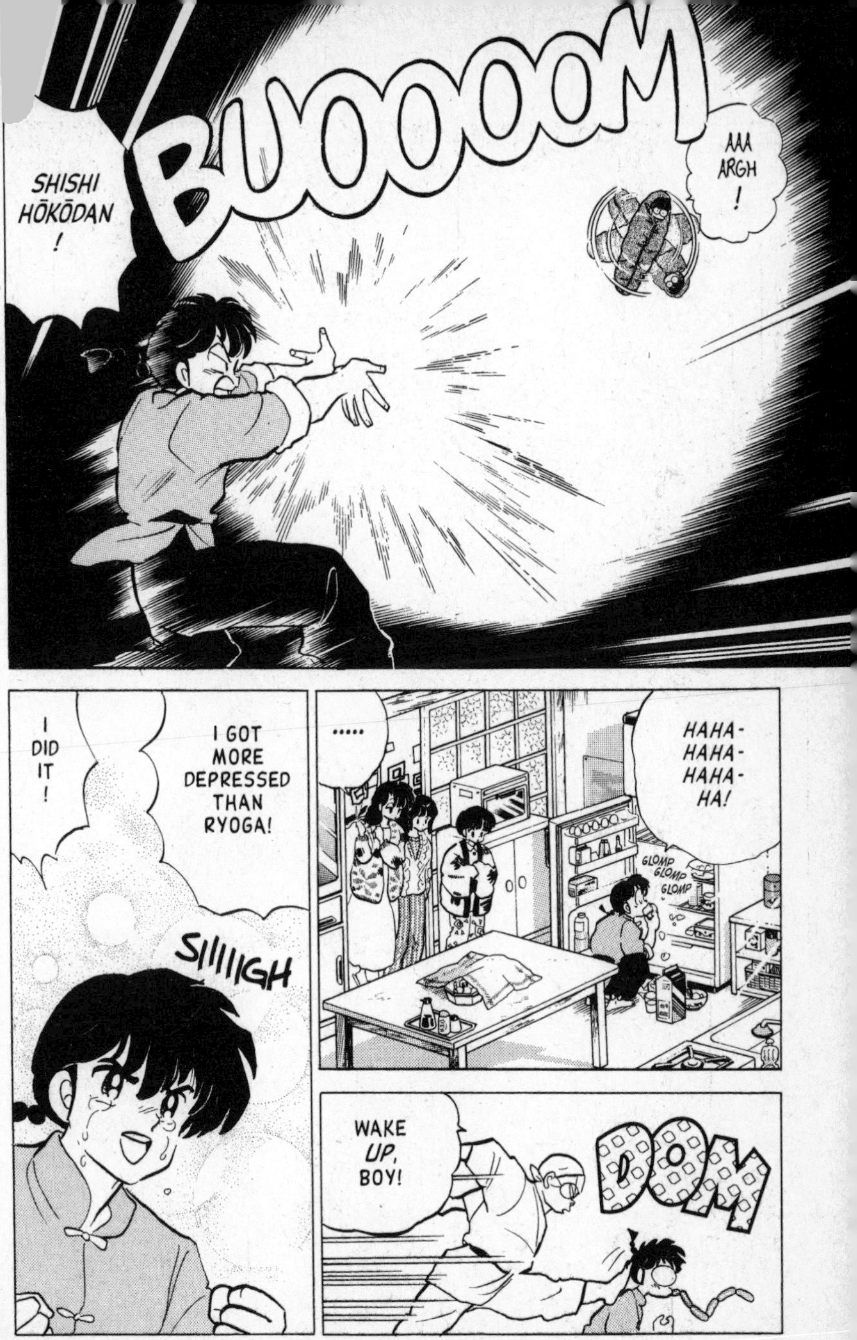
SHISHI HŌKŌDAN !
BUOOOOM
AAA ARGH !
I DID IT !
I GOT MORE DEPRESSED THAN RYOGA!
SIIIIGH
.....
HAHA-HAHA-HAHA-HA!
GLOMP GLOMP GLOMP
WAKE UP, BOY!
DOM

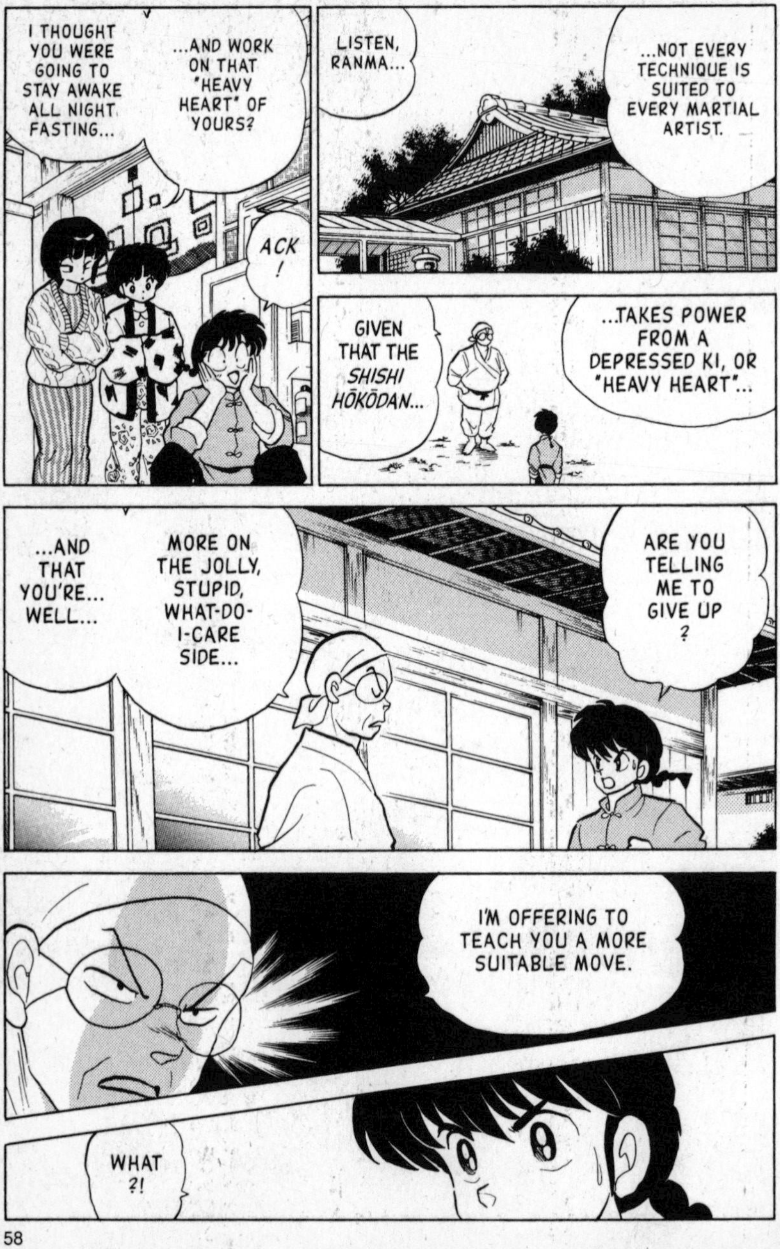
I THOUGHT YOU WERE GOING TO STAY AWAKE ALL NIGHT FASTING...
...AND WORK ON THAT "HEAVY HEART" OF YOURS?
ACK!
LISTEN, RANMA...
...NOT EVERY TECHNIQUE IS SUITED TO EVERY MARTIAL ARTIST.
GIVEN THAT THE SHISHI HŌKŌDAN...
...TAKES POWER FROM A DEPRESSED KI, OR "HEAVY HEART"...
...AND THAT YOU'RE... WELL...
MORE ON THE JOLLY, STUPID, WHAT-DO-I-CARE SIDE...
ARE YOU TELLING ME TO GIVE UP?
I'M OFFERING TO TEACH YOU A MORE SUITABLE MOVE.
WHAT?!

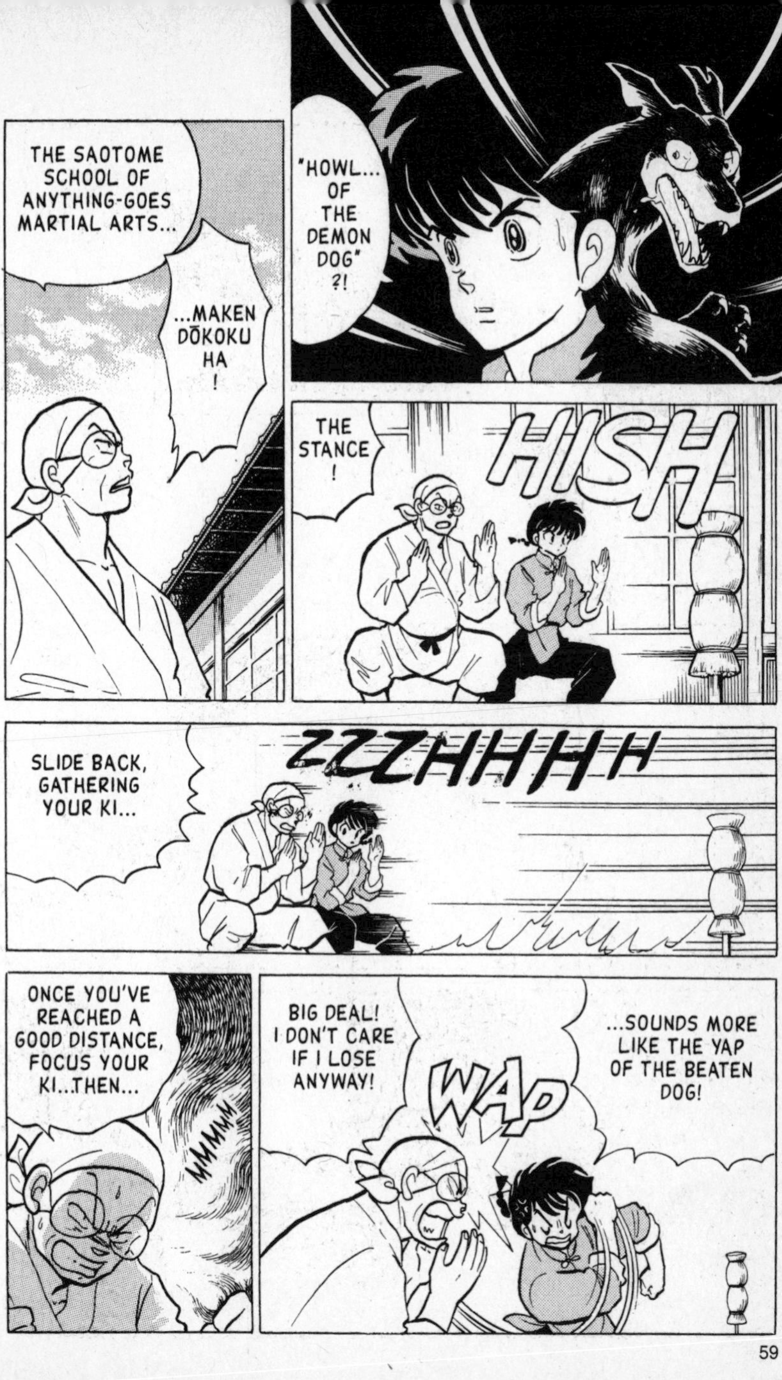
THE SAOTOME SCHOOL OF ANYTHING-GOES MARTIAL ARTS...
...MAKEN DŌKOKU HA!
"HOWL... OF THE DEMON DOG"?!
THE STANCE!
HISH
SLIDE BACK, GATHERING YOUR KI...
ZZZHHHHH
ONCE YOU'VE REACHED A GOOD DISTANCE, FOCUS YOUR KI...THEN...
MMMMM
BIG DEAL! I DON'T CARE IF I LOSE ANYWAY!
WAP
...SOUNDS MORE LIKE THE YAP OF THE BEATEN DOG!

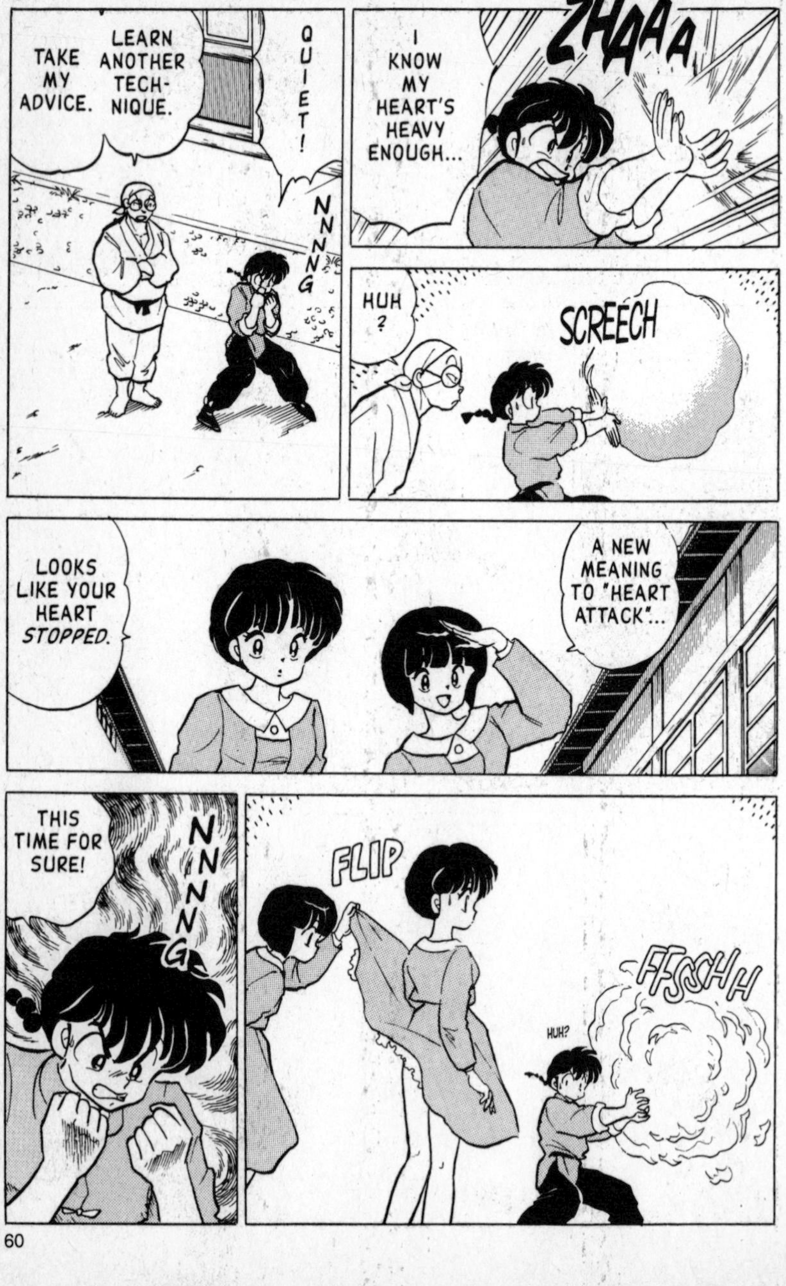
TAKE MY ADVICE. LEARN ANOTHER TECH-NIQUE.
QUIET!
NNNNG
I KNOW MY HEART'S HEAVY ENOUGH...
ZHAAAA
HUH?
SCREECH
LOOKS LIKE YOUR HEART *STOPPED.*
A NEW MEANING TO "HEART ATTACK"...
THIS TIME FOR SURE!
NNNNNG
FLIP
HUH?
FFSSHHH

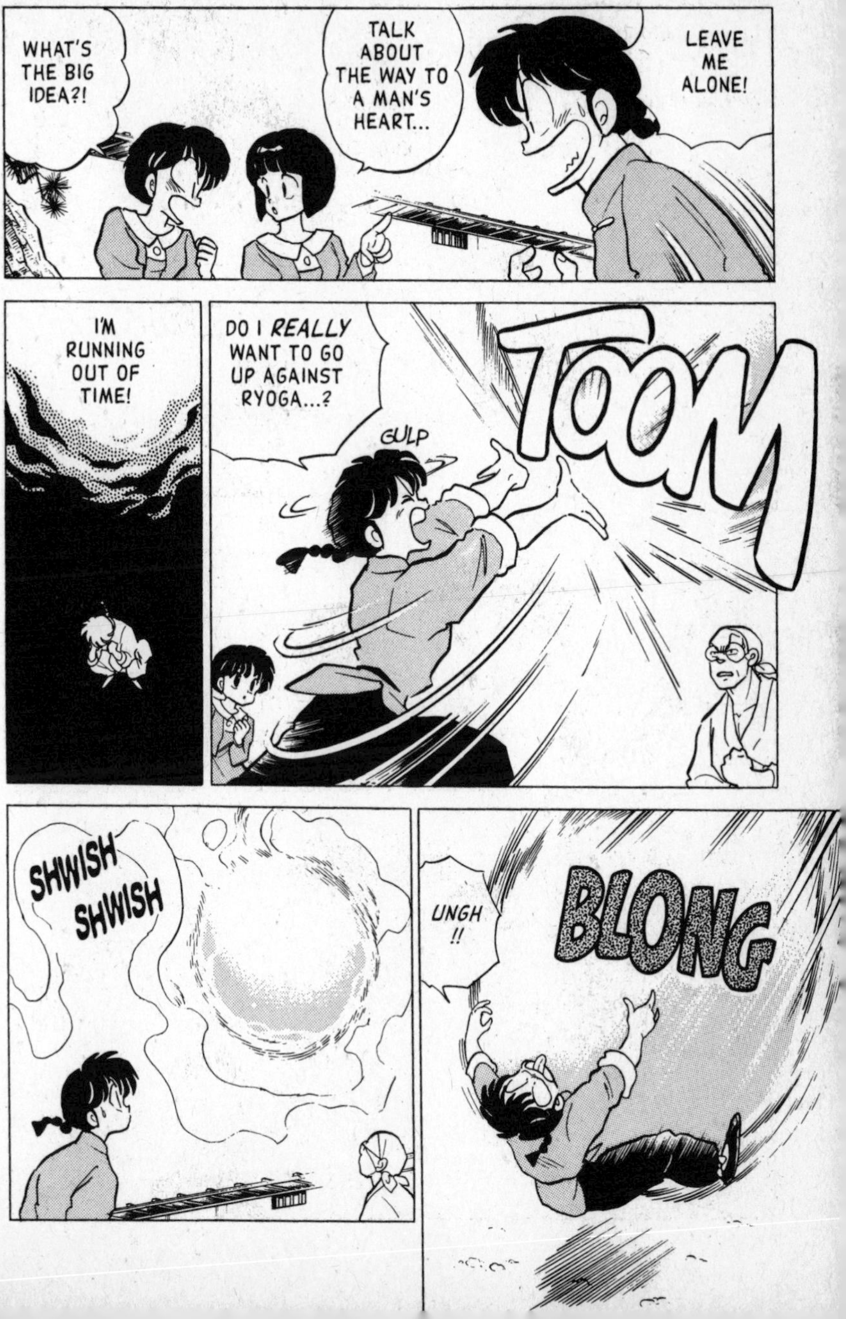
WHAT'S THE BIG IDEA?!
TALK ABOUT THE WAY TO A MAN'S HEART...
LEAVE ME ALONE!
I'M RUNNING OUT OF TIME!
DO I *REALLY* WANT TO GO UP AGAINST RYOGA...?
GULP
TOOM
SHWISH
SHWISH
UNGH !!
BLONG

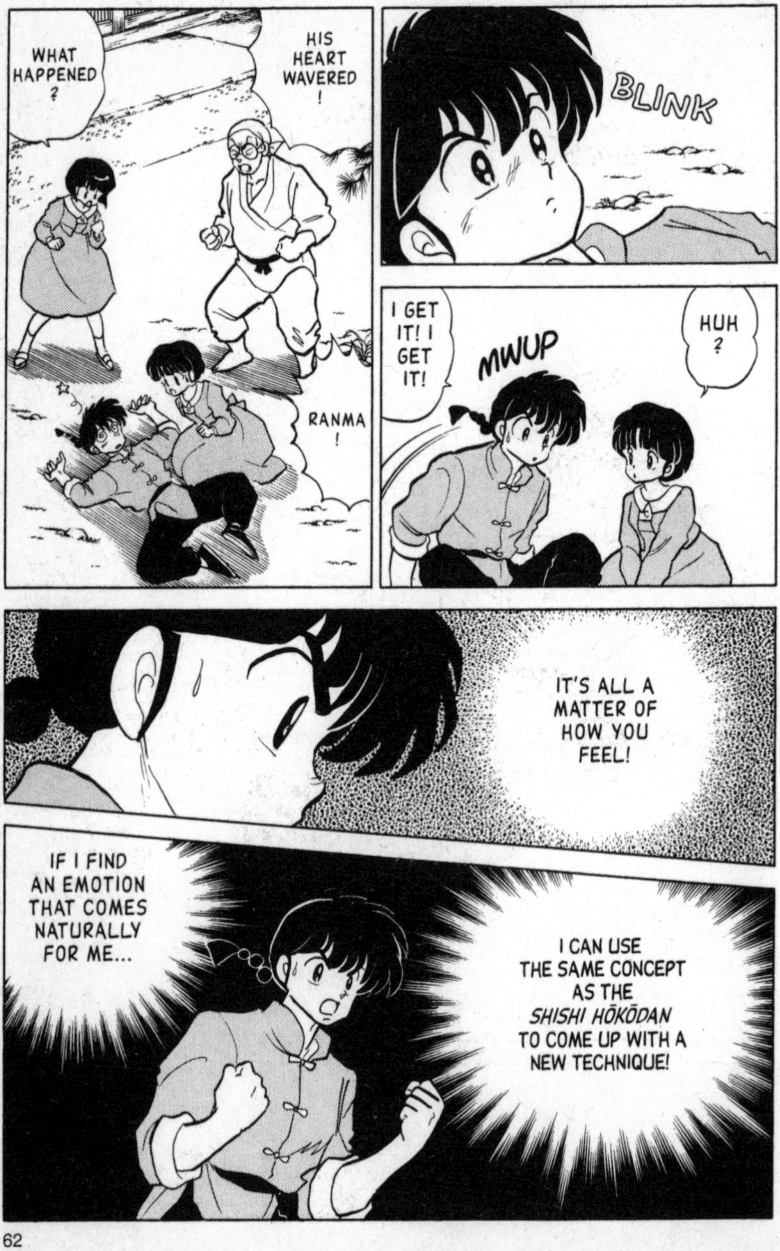
WHAT HAPPENED ?
HIS HEART WAVERED !
RANMA !
BLINK
I GET IT! I GET IT!
MWUP
HUH ?
IT'S ALL A MATTER OF HOW YOU FEEL!
IF I FIND AN EMOTION THAT COMES NATURALLY FOR ME...
I CAN USE THE SAME CONCEPT AS THE *SHISHI HŌKŌDAN* TO COME UP WITH A NEW TECHNIQUE!

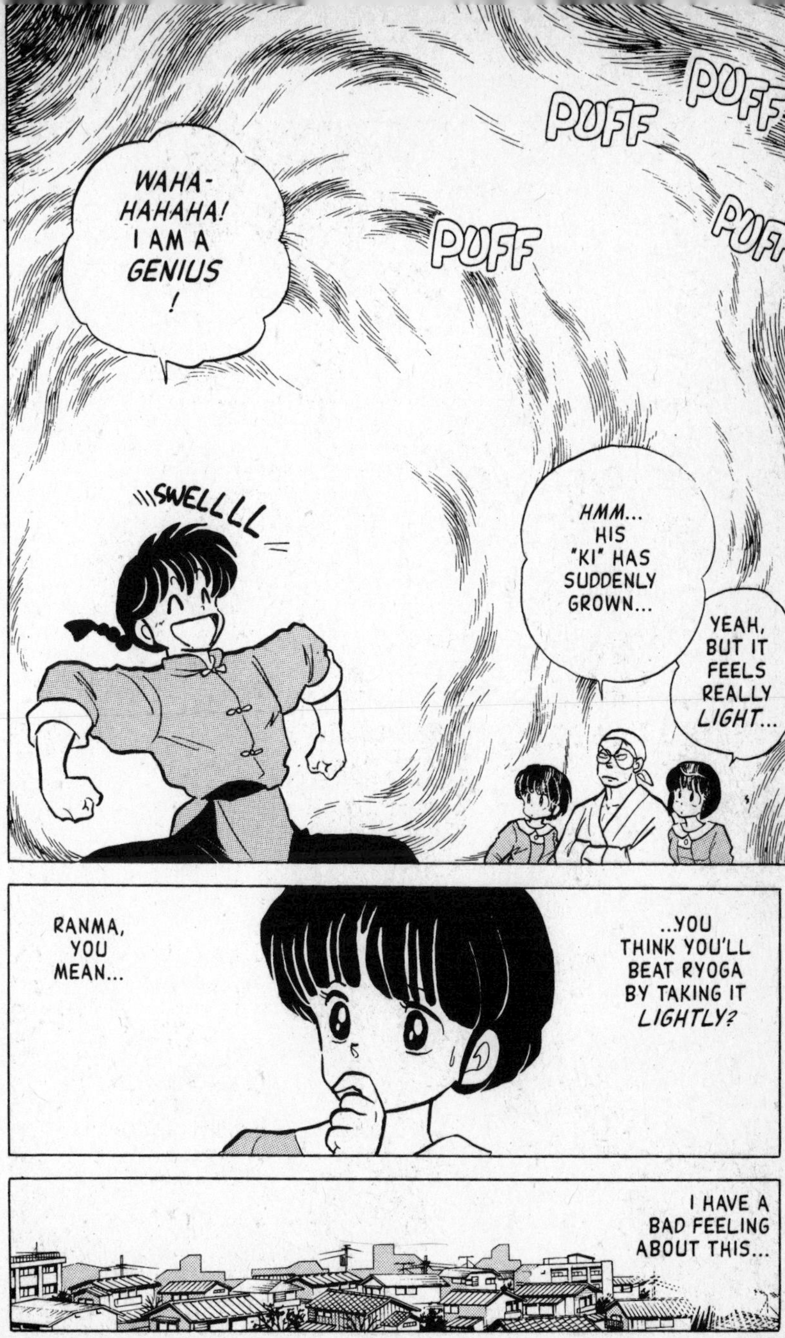
WAHA-HAHAHA! I AM A GENIUS !
PUFF
PUFF
PUFF
PUFF
SWELLLLL
HMM... HIS "KI" HAS SUDDENLY GROWN...
YEAH, BUT IT FEELS REALLY LIGHT...
RANMA, YOU MEAN...
...YOU THINK YOU'LL BEAT RYOGA BY TAKING IT LIGHTLY?
I HAVE A BAD FEELING ABOUT THIS...

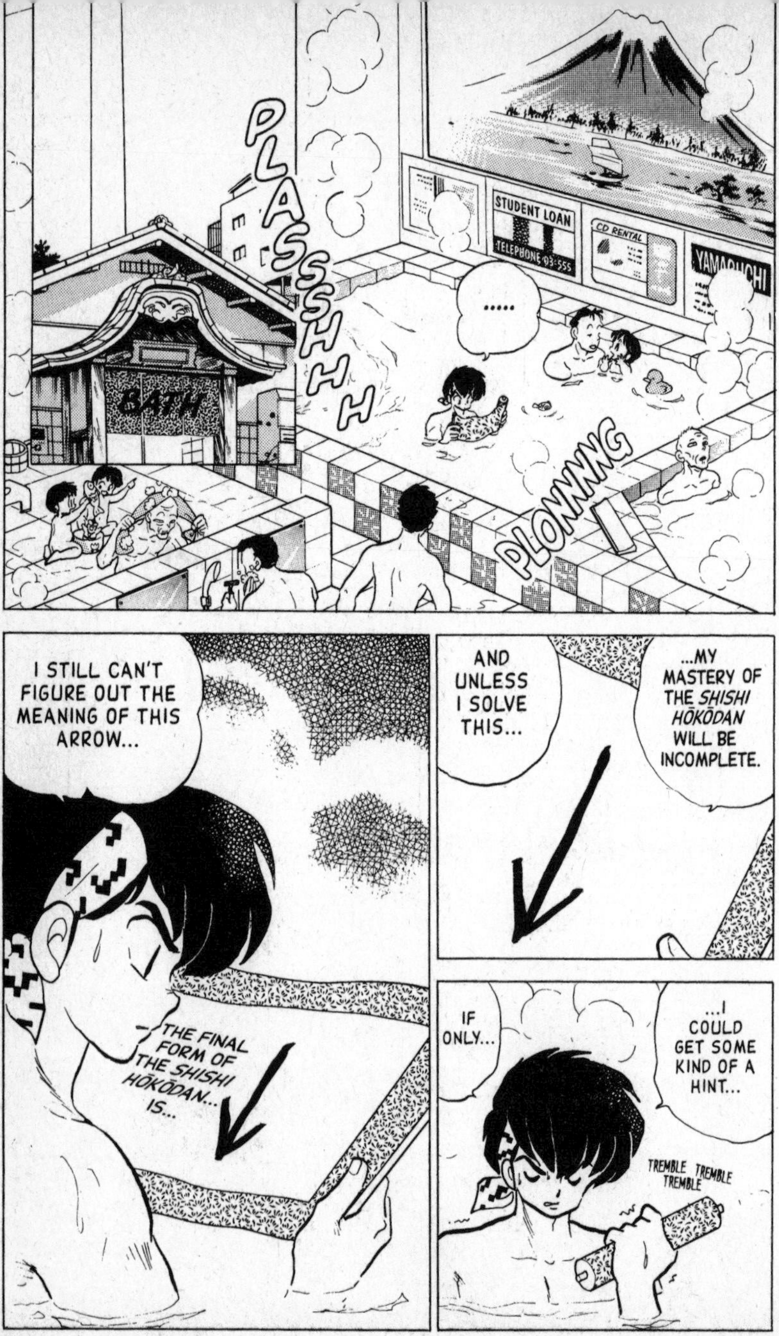
PLASSHHH
STUDENT LOAN
TELEPHONE 03-555
CD RENTAL
YAMAGUCHI
BATH
......
PLONNNG
I STILL CAN'T FIGURE OUT THE MEANING OF THIS ARROW...
THE FINAL FORM OF THE *SHISHI HŌKŌDAN*... IS...
AND UNLESS I SOLVE THIS...
...MY MASTERY OF THE *SHISHI HŌKŌDAN* WILL BE INCOMPLETE.
IF ONLY...
...I COULD GET SOME KIND OF A HINT...
TREMBLE TREMBLE TREMBLE

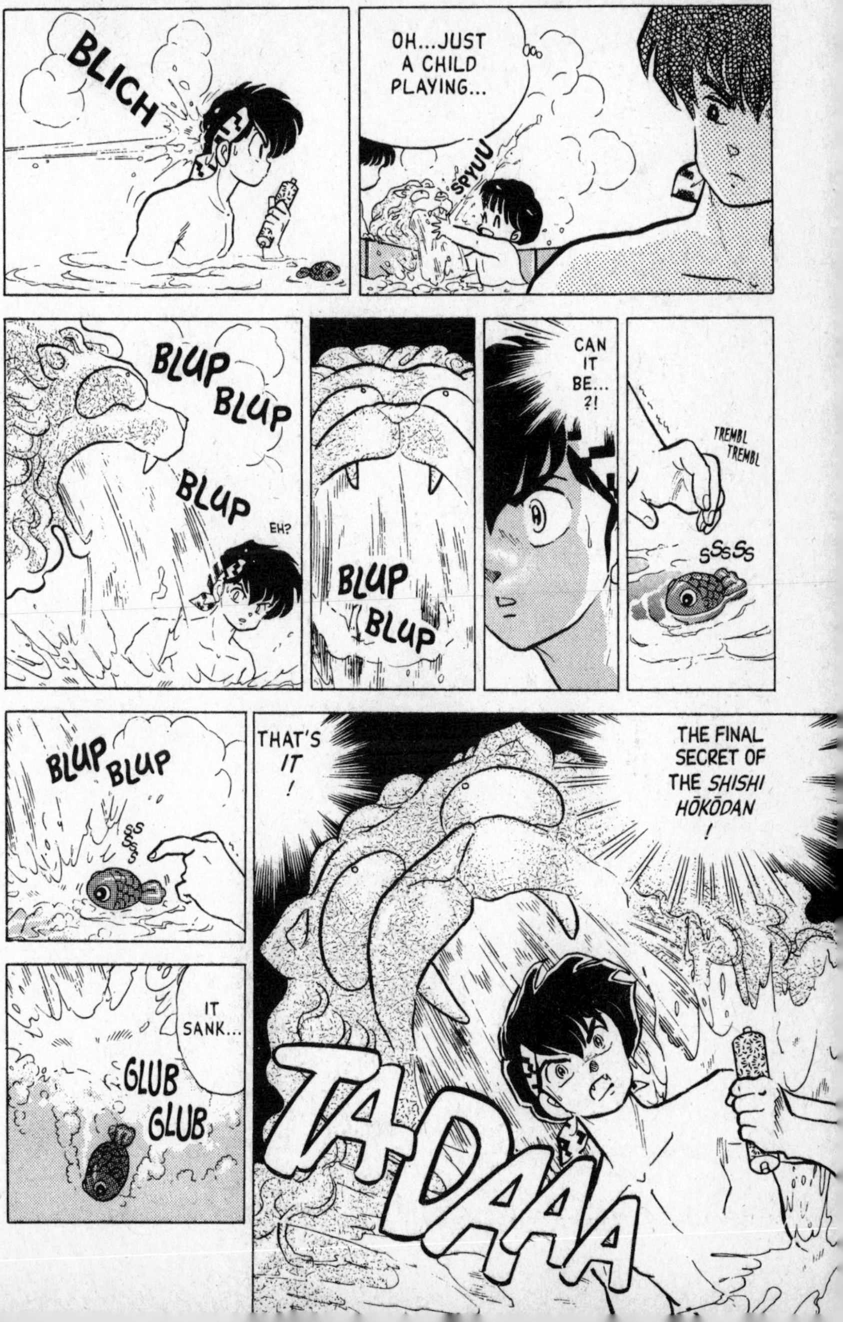
BLICH
OH...JUST A CHILD PLAYING...
SPYUU
BLUP BLUP
BLUP
EH?
BLUP BLUP
CAN IT BE... ?!
TREMBL TREMBL
SSSSS
BLUP BLUP
SSSSS
IT SANK...
GLUB GLUB
THAT'S *IT* !
THE FINAL SECRET OF THE *SHISHI HŌKŌDAN* !
TADAAA

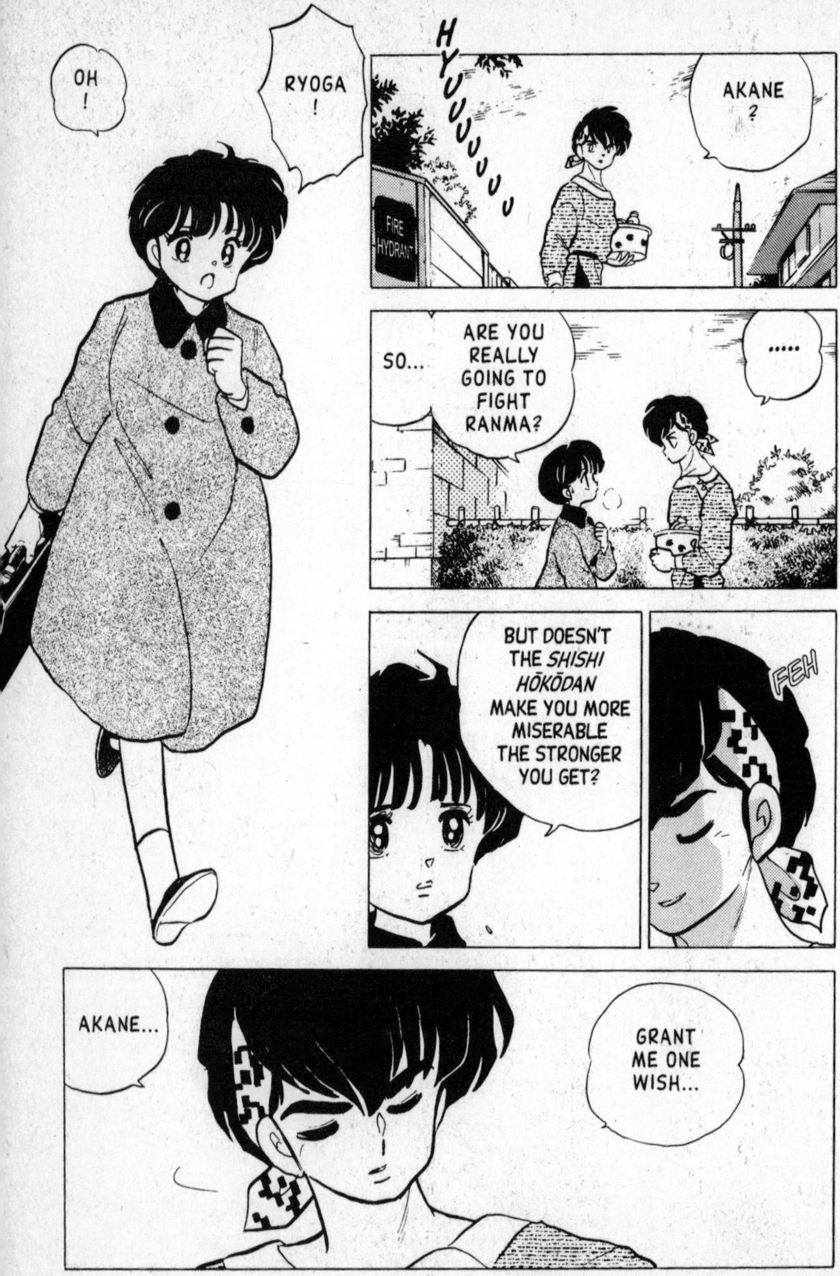

OH!
RYOGA!
HYUUUUUUUU
AKANE?
SO...
ARE YOU REALLY GOING TO FIGHT RANMA?
.....
BUT DOESN'T THE *SHISHI HŌKŌDAN* MAKE YOU MORE MISERABLE THE STRONGER YOU GET?
FEH
AKANE...
GRANT ME ONE WISH...

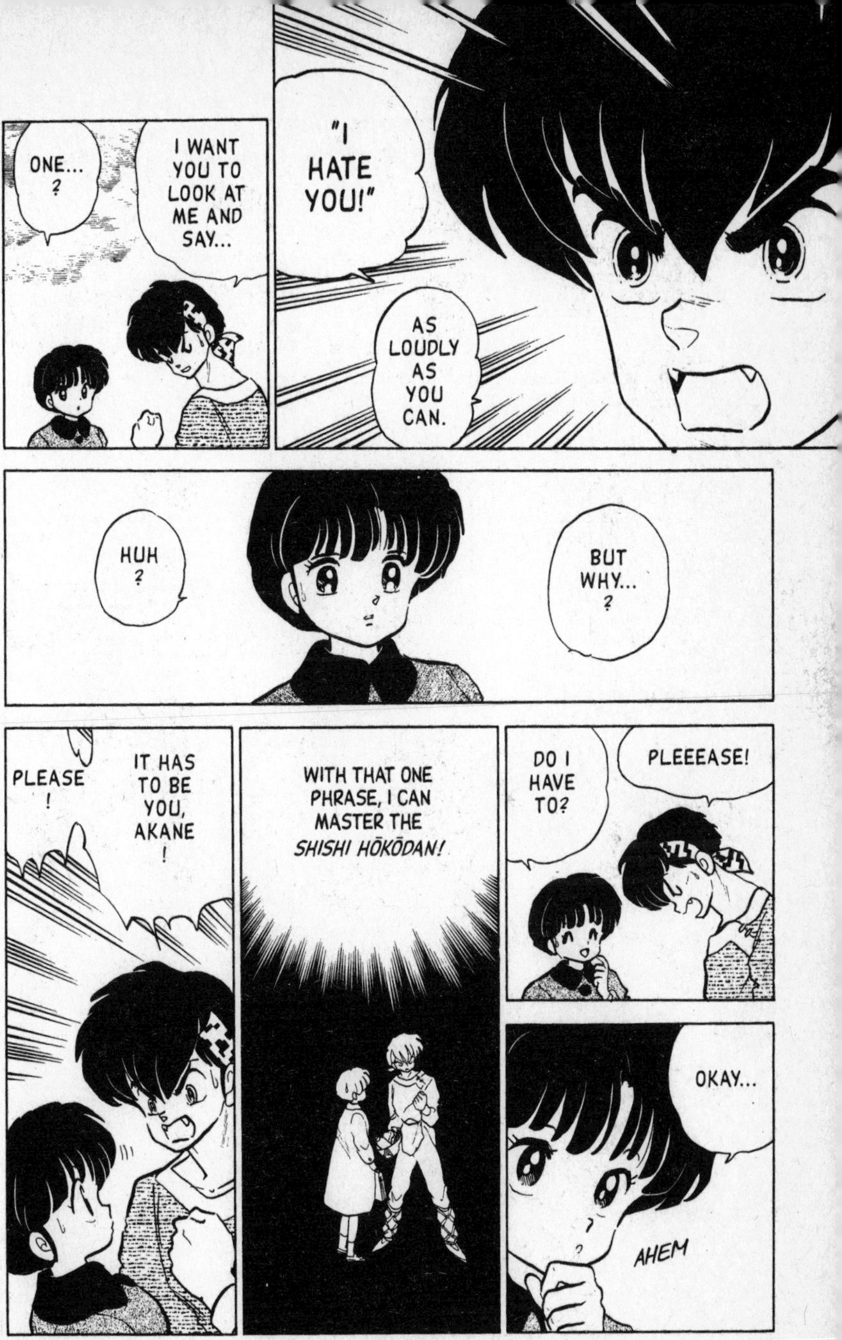
ONE... ?
I WANT YOU TO LOOK AT ME AND SAY...
"I HATE YOU!"
AS LOUDLY AS YOU CAN.
HUH ?
BUT WHY... ?
PLEASE !
IT HAS TO BE YOU, AKANE !
WITH THAT ONE PHRASE, I CAN MASTER THE *SHISHI HŌKŌDAN!*
DO I HAVE TO?
PLEEEASE!
OKAY...
AHEM

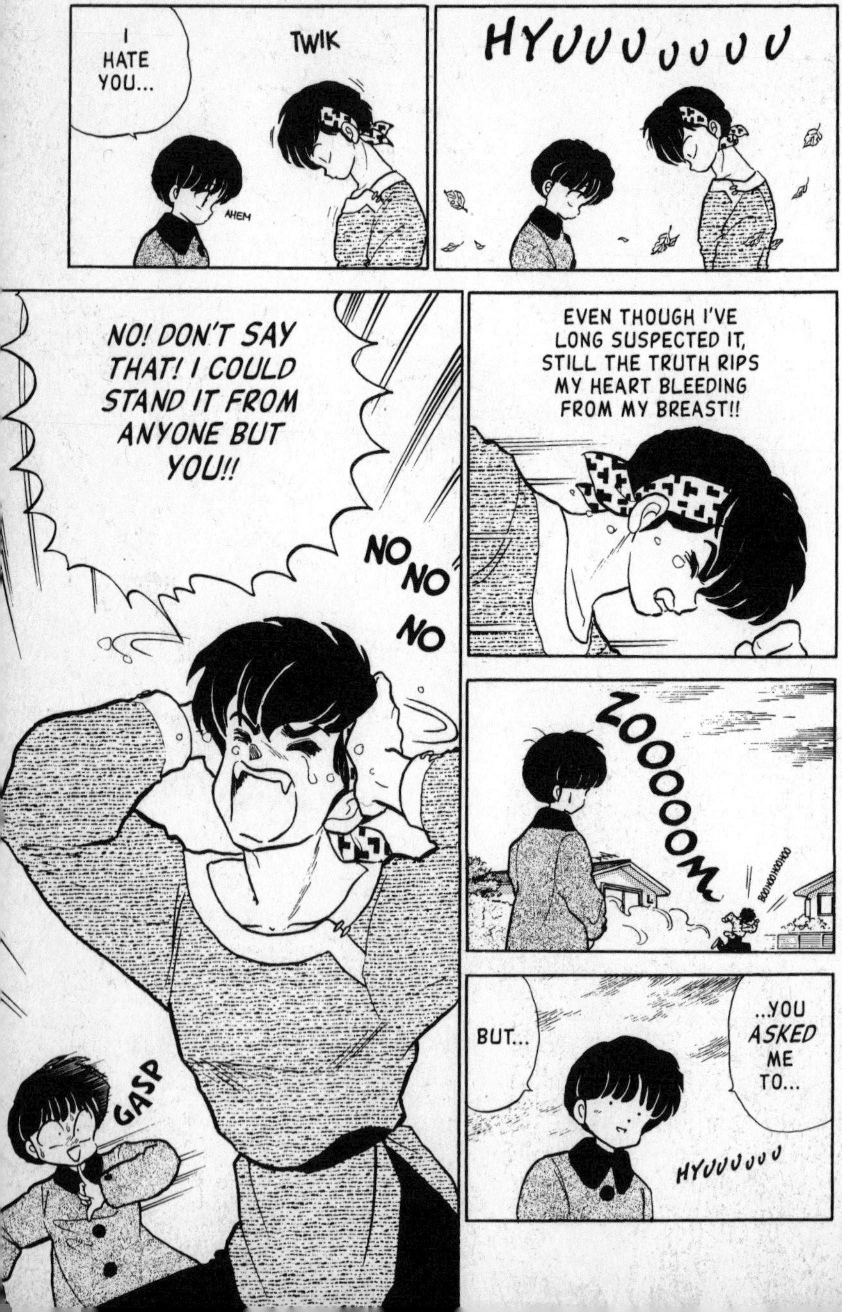
I HATE YOU...
TWIK
AHEM
HYUUUUUUUU
NO! DON'T SAY THAT! I COULD STAND IT FROM ANYONE BUT YOU!!
NO NO NO
GASP
EVEN THOUGH I'VE LONG SUSPECTED IT, STILL THE TRUTH RIPS MY HEART BLEEDING FROM MY BREAST!!
ZOOOOOM
BOOHOO HOOHOO
BUT...
...YOU ASKED ME TO...
HYUUUUUU

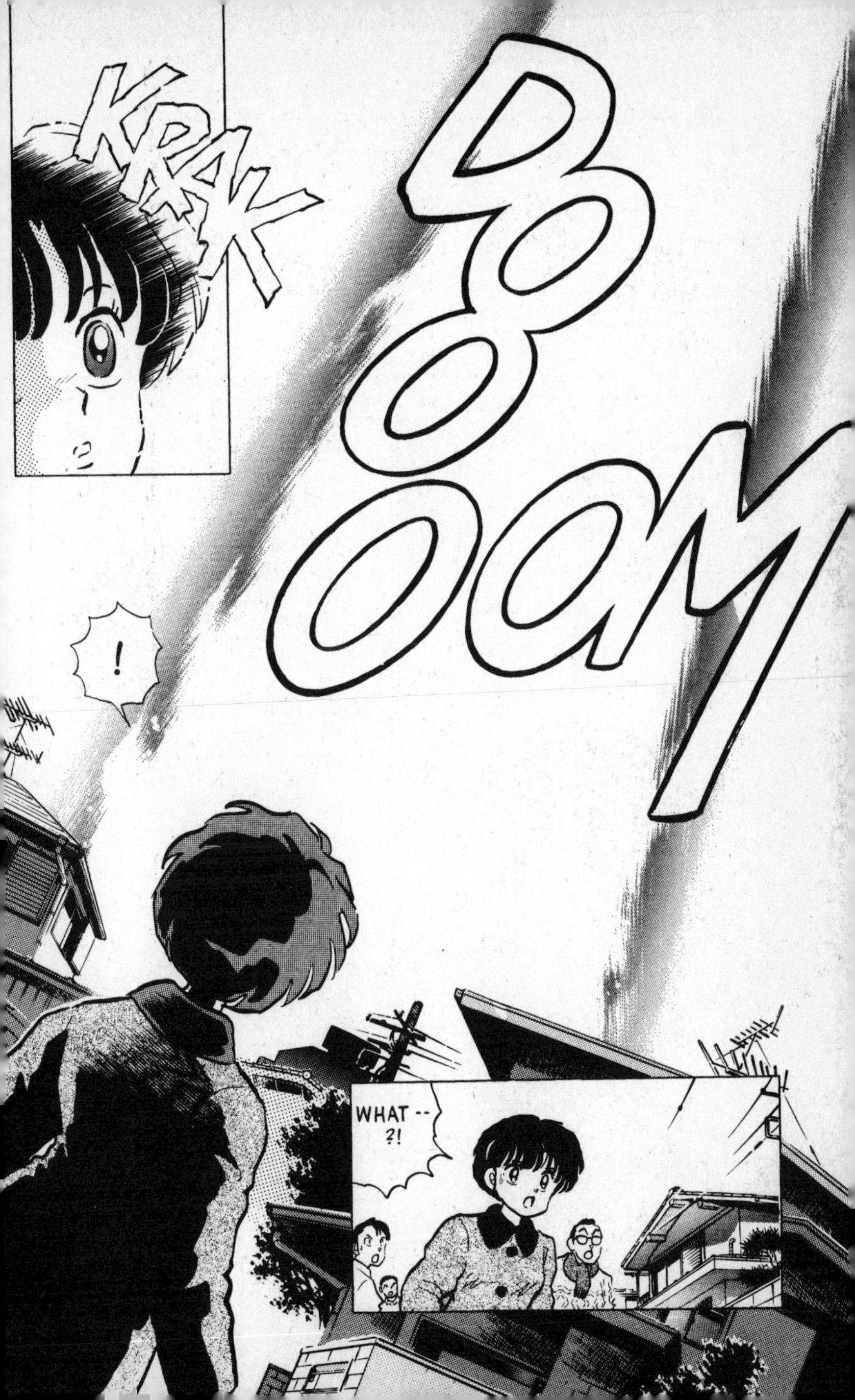
KRAK
BOOOOM
!
WHAT -- ?!

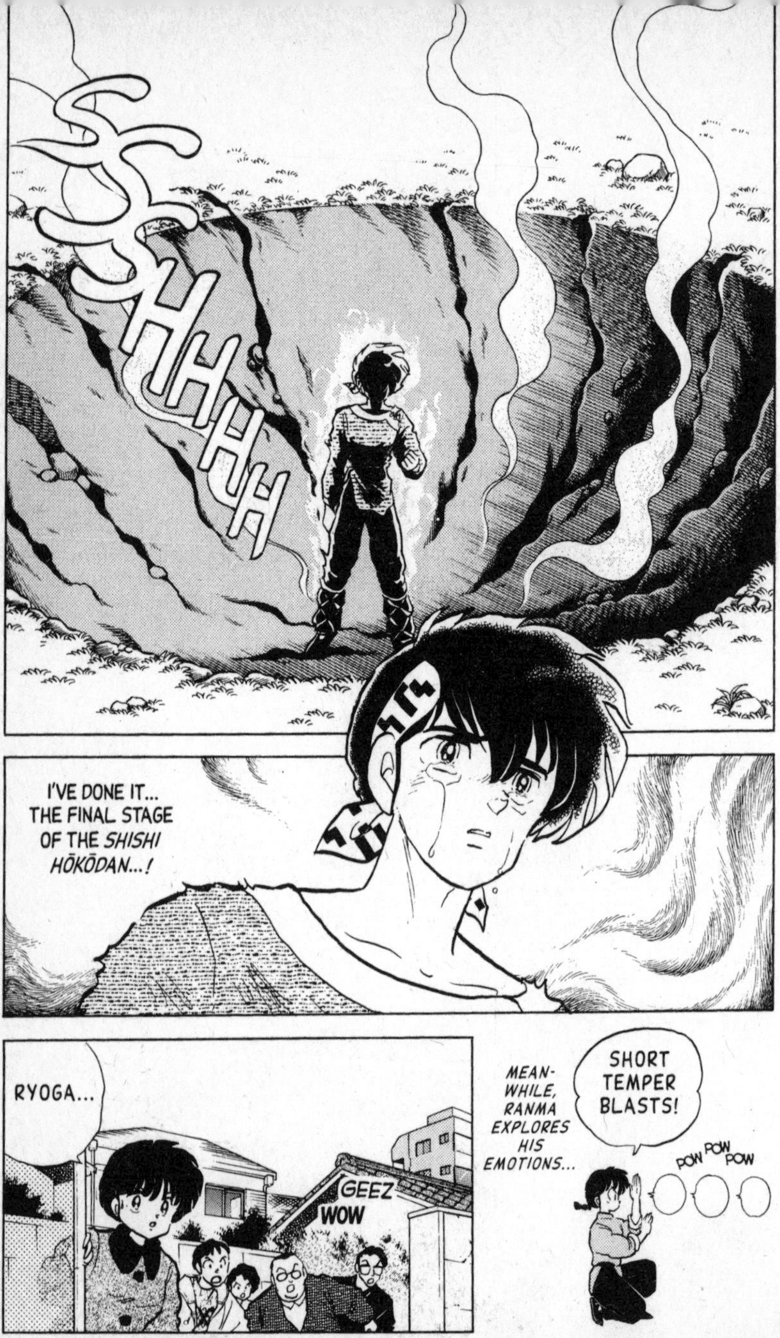
SHHHHHH
I'VE DONE IT... THE FINAL STAGE OF THE *SHISHI HŌKŌDAN*...!
RYOGA...
GEEZ
WOW
MEAN-WHILE, RANMA EXPLORES HIS EMOTIONS...
SHORT TEMPER BLASTS!
POW POW POW

Part 5
LION VERSUS TIGER!

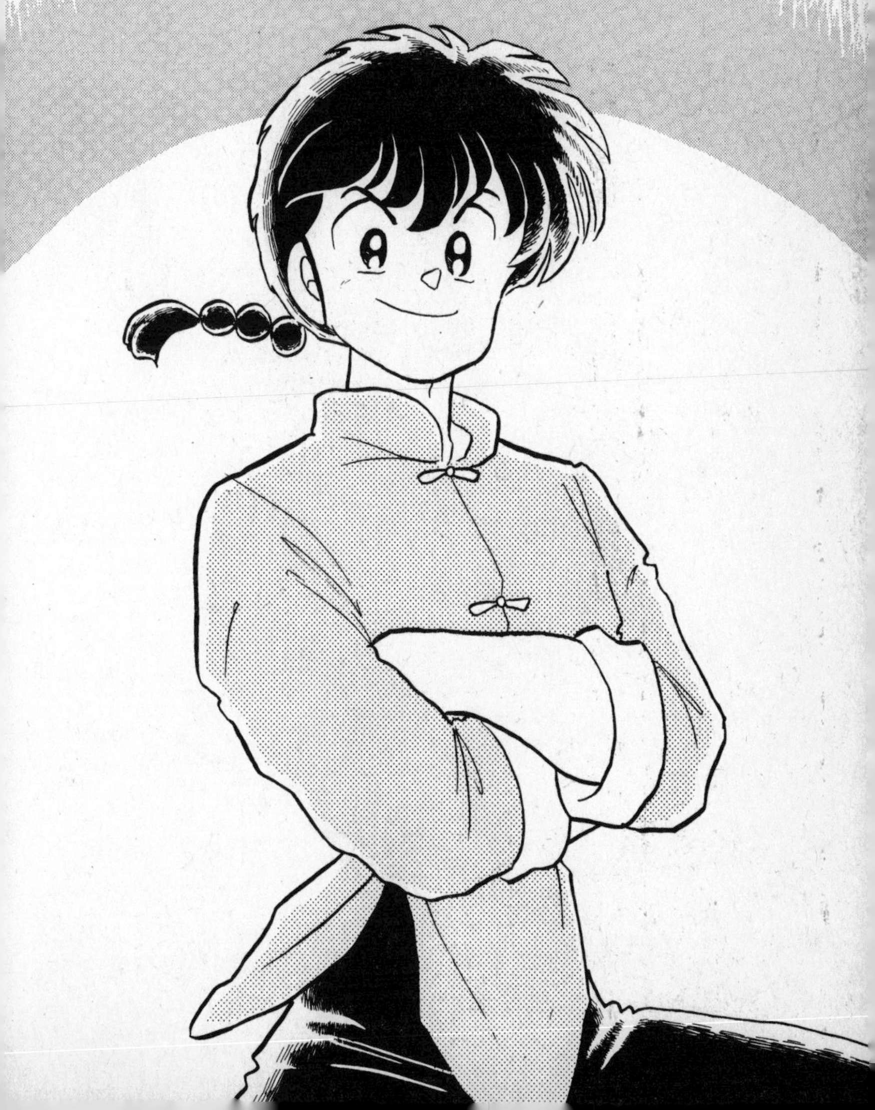

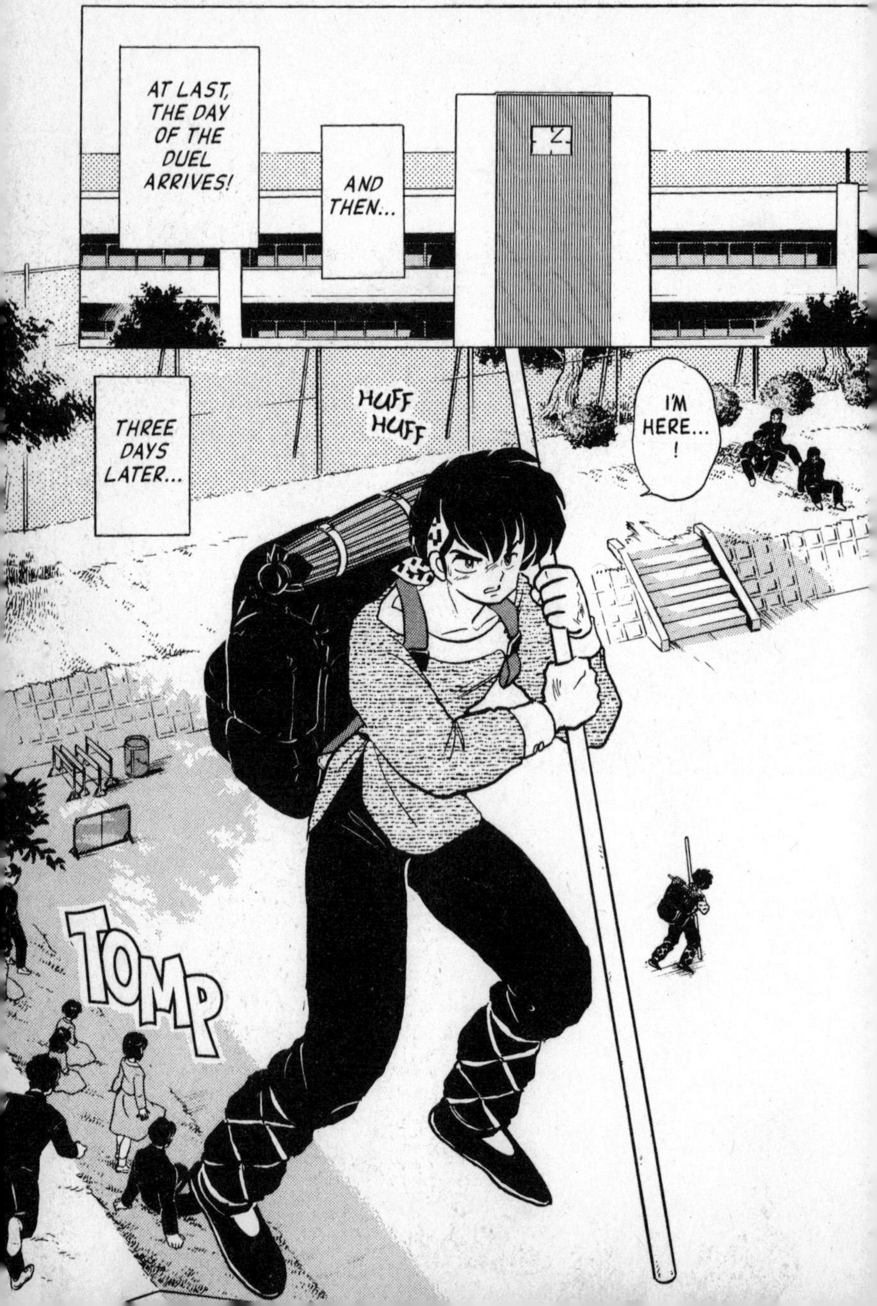
AT LAST, THE DAY OF THE DUEL ARRIVES!
AND THEN...
THREE DAYS LATER...
HUFF HUFF
I'M HERE... !
TOMP

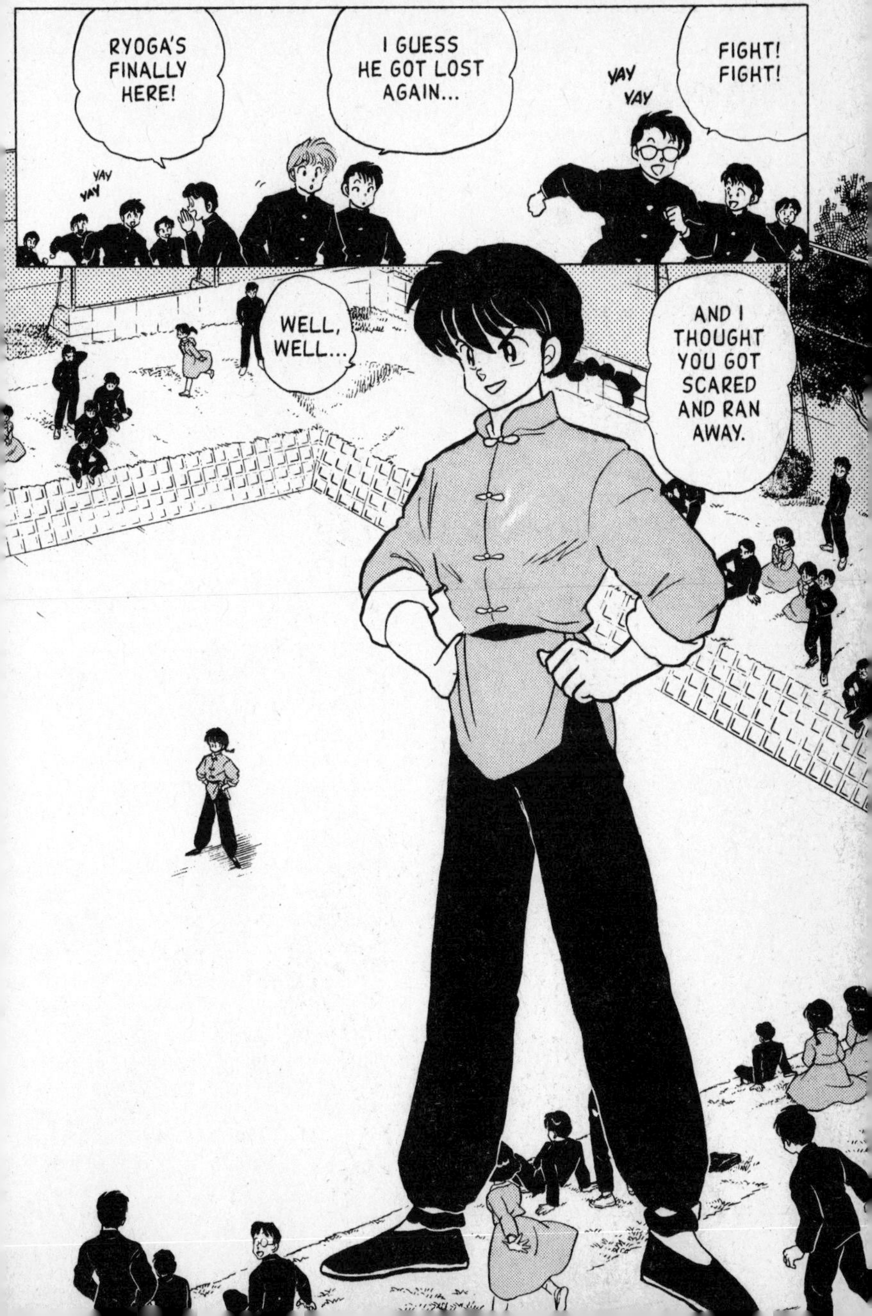
RYOGA'S FINALLY HERE!
YAY YAY
I GUESS HE GOT LOST AGAIN...
YAY YAY
FIGHT! FIGHT!
WELL, WELL...
AND I THOUGHT YOU GOT SCARED AND RAN AWAY.

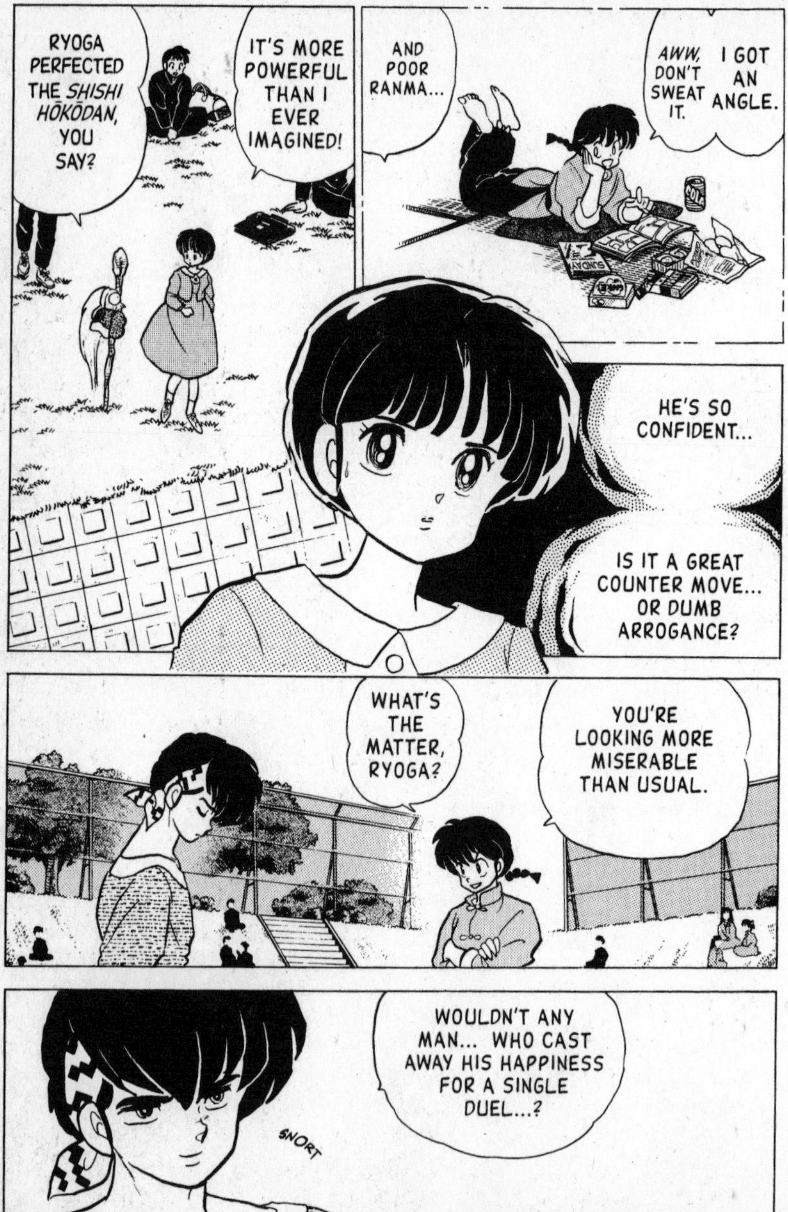
RYOGA PERFECTED THE *SHISHI HŌKŌDAN*, YOU SAY?
IT'S MORE POWERFUL THAN I EVER IMAGINED!
AND POOR RANMA...
AWW, DON'T SWEAT IT.
I GOT AN ANGLE.
HE'S SO CONFIDENT...
IS IT A GREAT COUNTER MOVE... OR DUMB ARROGANCE?
WHAT'S THE MATTER, RYOGA?
YOU'RE LOOKING MORE MISERABLE THAN USUAL.
SNORT
WOULDN'T ANY MAN... WHO CAST AWAY HIS HAPPINESS FOR A SINGLE DUEL...?

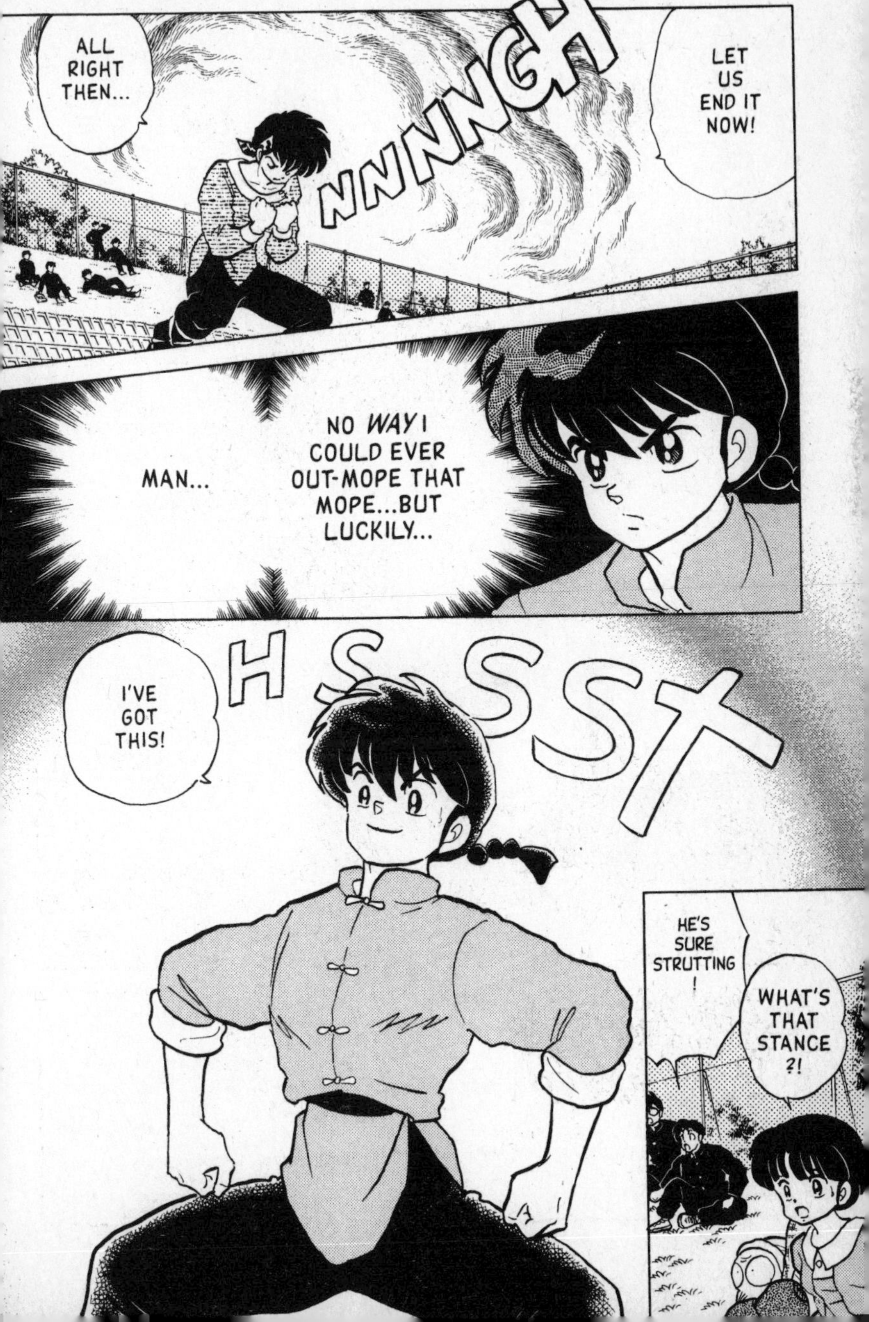
ALL RIGHT THEN...
NNNNCH
LET US END IT NOW!
MAN...
NO WAY I COULD EVER OUT-MOPE THAT MOPE...BUT LUCKILY...
I'VE GOT THIS!
HSSST
HE'S SURE STRUTTING!
WHAT'S THAT STANCE?!

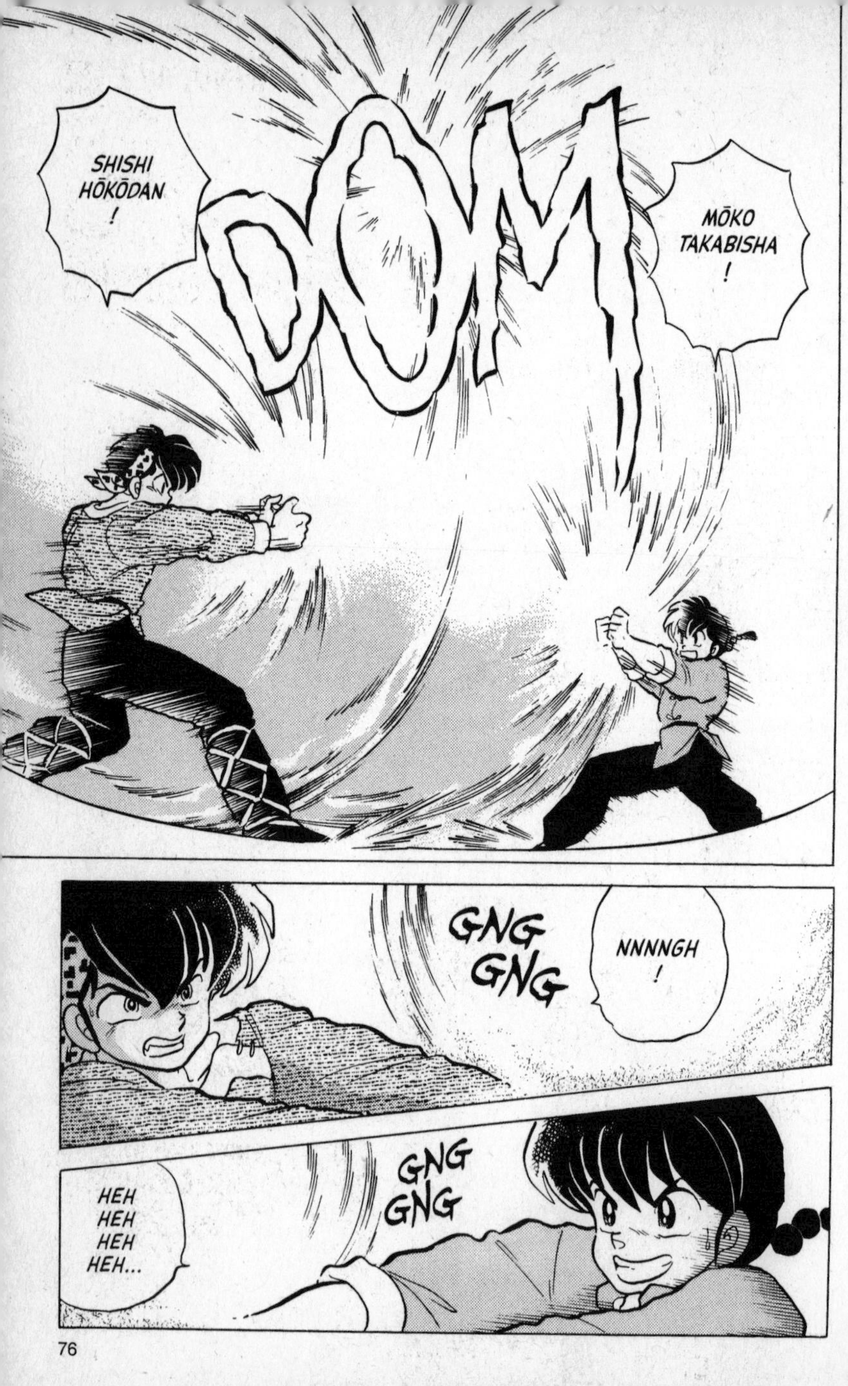
SHISHI HŌKŌDAN !
DOM
MŌKO TAKABISHA !
GNG GNG
NNNNGH !
HEH HEH HEH HEH...
GNG GNG

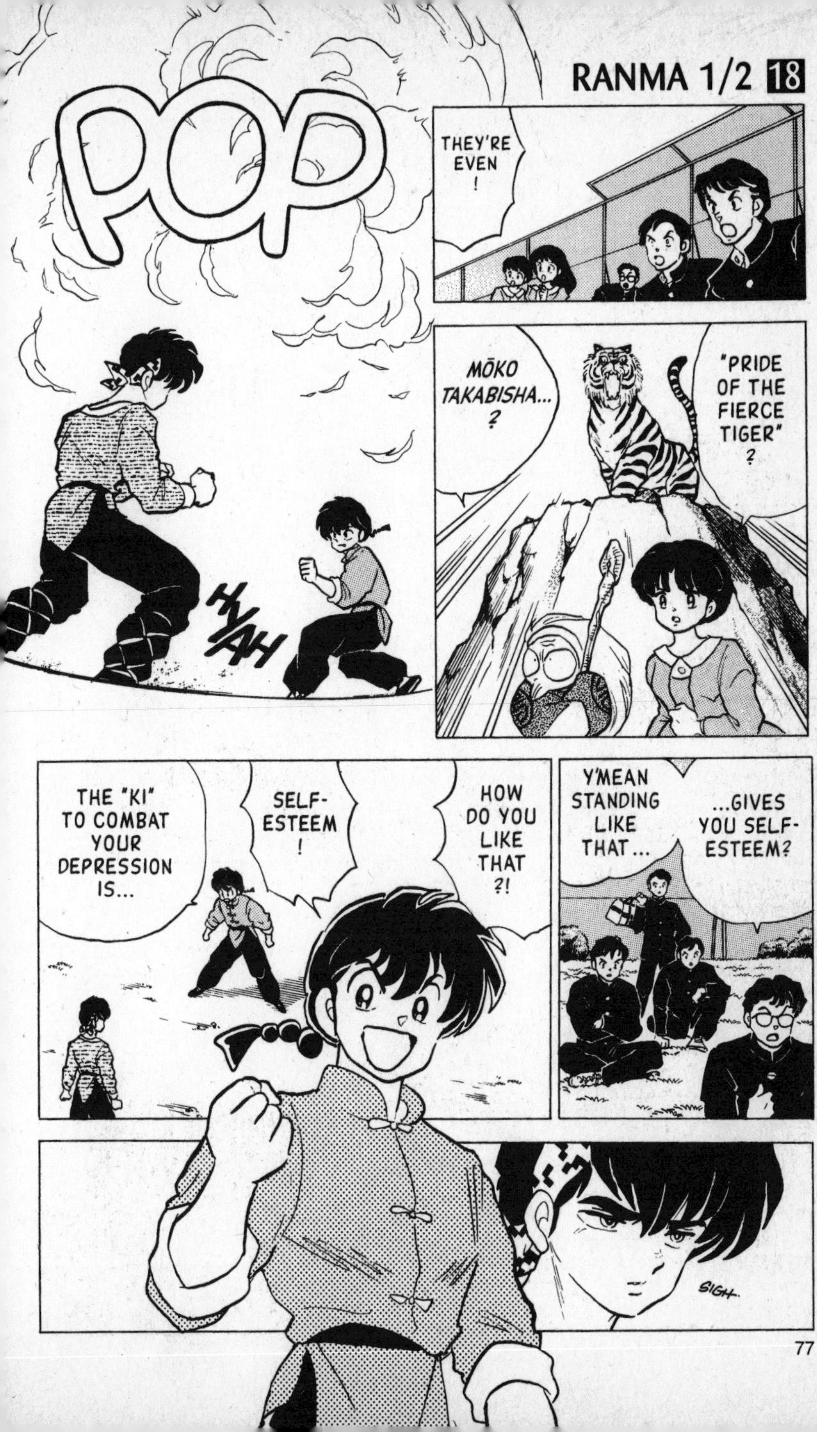
POP
HYAH
THEY'RE EVEN!
MŌKO TAKABISHA...?
"PRIDE OF THE FIERCE TIGER"?
THE "KI" TO COMBAT YOUR DEPRESSION IS...
SELF-ESTEEM!
HOW DO YOU LIKE THAT?!
Y'MEAN STANDING LIKE THAT...
...GIVES YOU SELF-ESTEEM?
SIGH

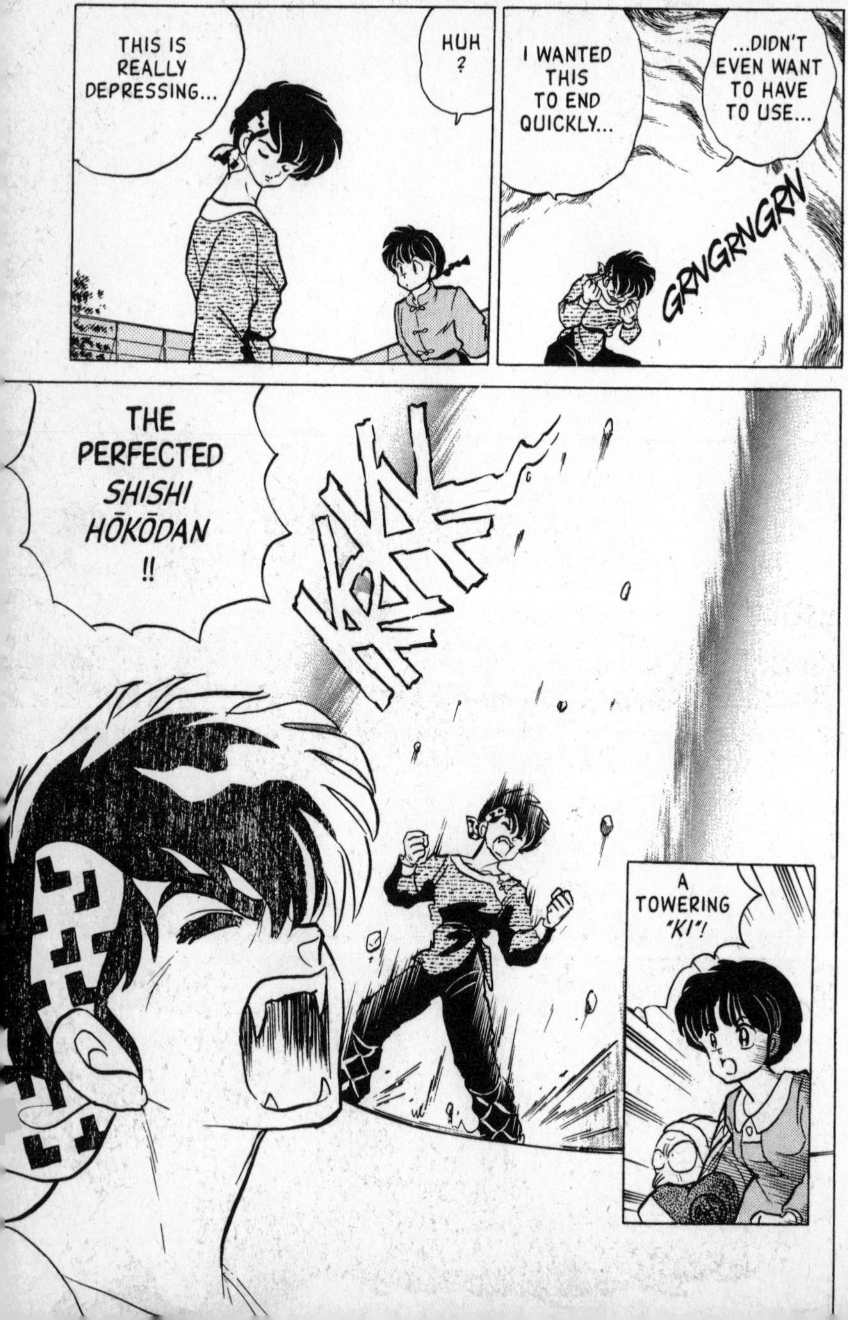
THIS IS REALLY DEPRESSING...
HUH?
I WANTED THIS TO END QUICKLY...
...DIDN'T EVEN WANT TO HAVE TO USE...
GRNGRNGRN
THE PERFECTED SHISHI HŌKŌDAN !!
A TOWERING "KI"!

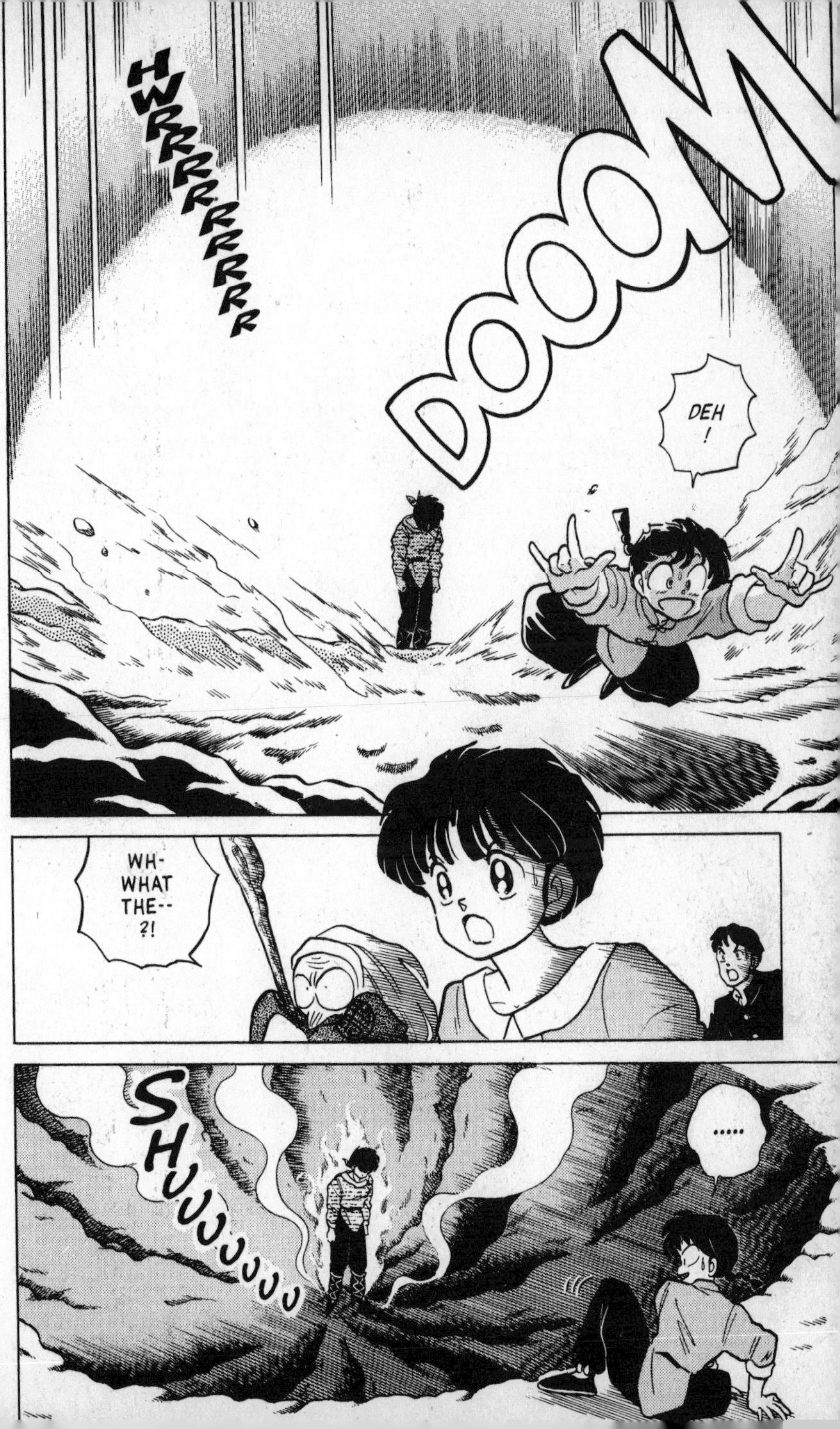
HWRRRRRRRRRR
DOOOM
DEH!
WH-WHAT THE--?!
SHUUUUUUU
.....

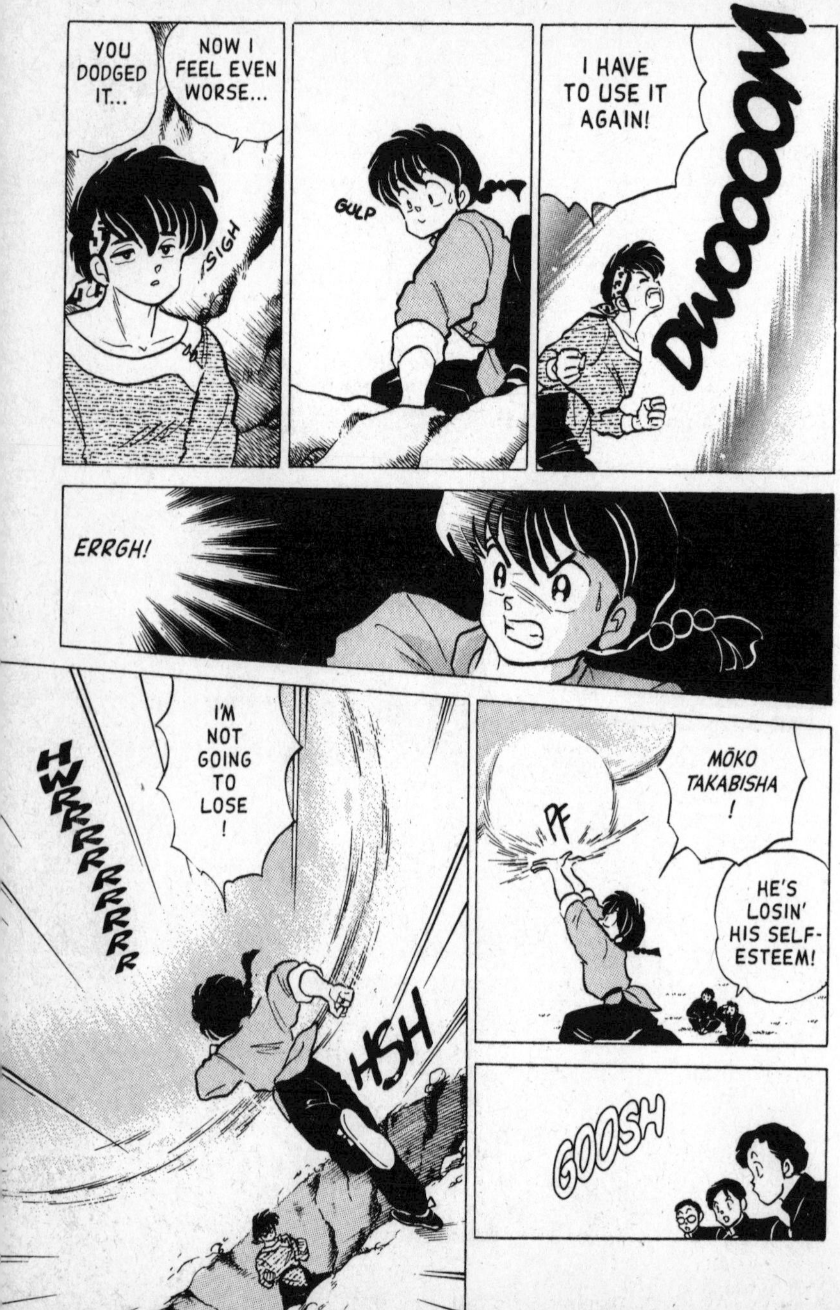

YOU DODGED IT...
NOW I FEEL EVEN WORSE...
SIGH
GULP
I HAVE TO USE IT AGAIN!
DWOOOOM
ERRGH!
HWRRRRRRRRR
I'M NOT GOING TO LOSE!
HSH
MŌKO TAKABISHA!
PF
HE'S LOSIN' HIS SELF-ESTEEM!
GOOSH

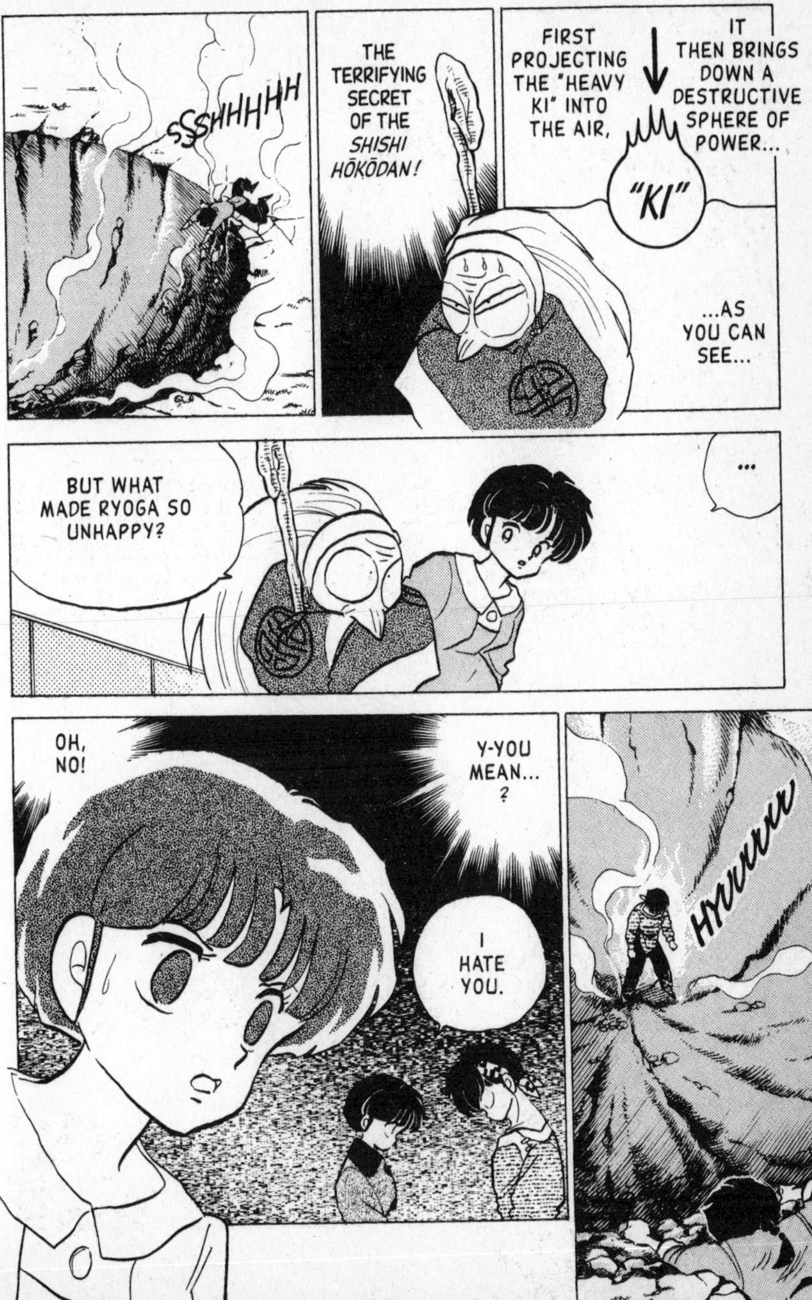
SSSHHHHHH
THE TERRIFYING SECRET OF THE SHISHI HŌKŌDAN!
FIRST PROJECTING THE "HEAVY KI" INTO THE AIR,
IT THEN BRINGS DOWN A DESTRUCTIVE SPHERE OF POWER...
"KI"
...AS YOU CAN SEE...
BUT WHAT MADE RYOGA SO UNHAPPY?
...
OH, NO!
Y-YOU MEAN...?
I HATE YOU.
HYUUUUU

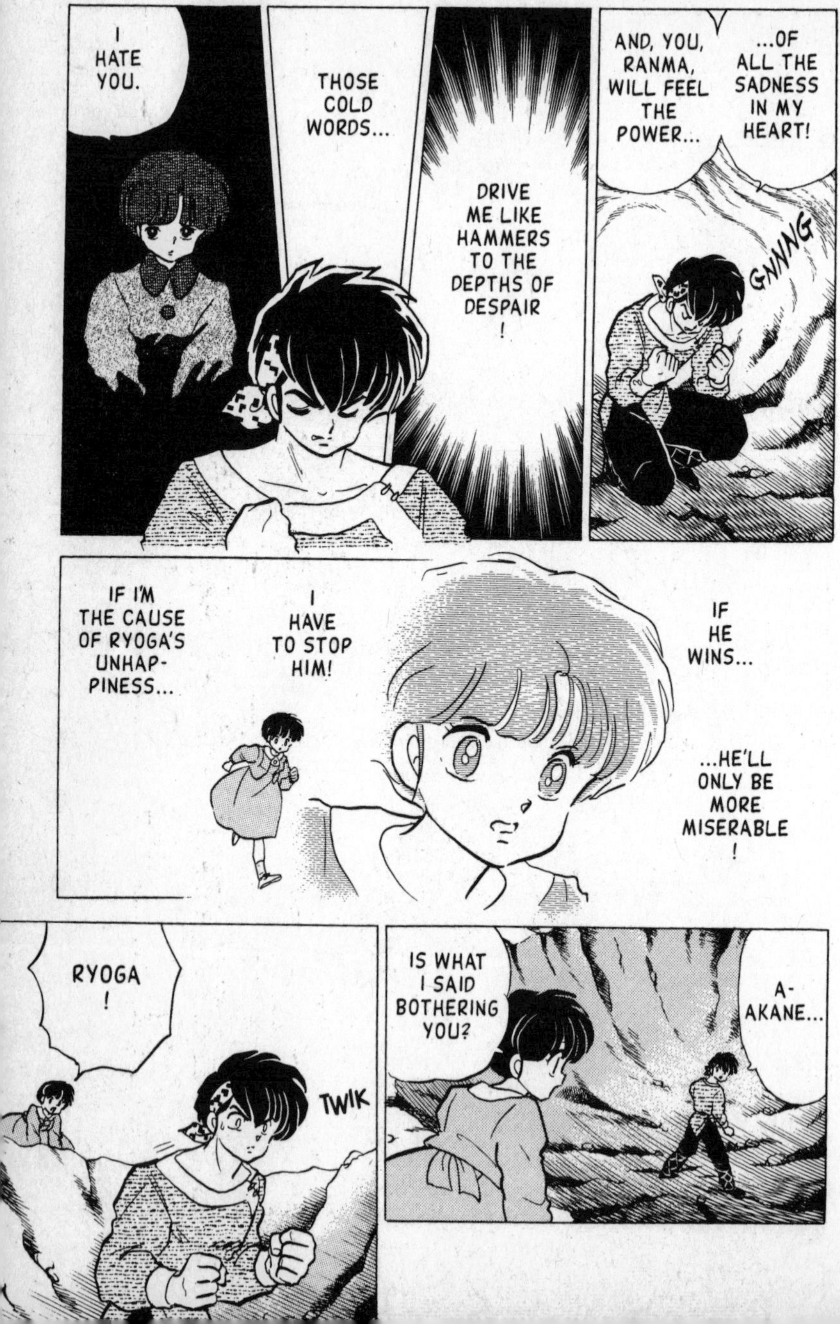
I HATE YOU.
THOSE COLD WORDS...
DRIVE ME LIKE HAMMERS TO THE DEPTHS OF DESPAIR!
AND, YOU, RANMA, WILL FEEL THE POWER...
...OF ALL THE SADNESS IN MY HEART!
GNNNG
IF I'M THE CAUSE OF RYOGA'S UNHAP-PINESS...
I HAVE TO STOP HIM!
IF HE WINS...
...HE'LL ONLY BE MORE MISERABLE!
RYOGA!
TWIK
IS WHAT I SAID BOTHERING YOU?
A-AKANE...

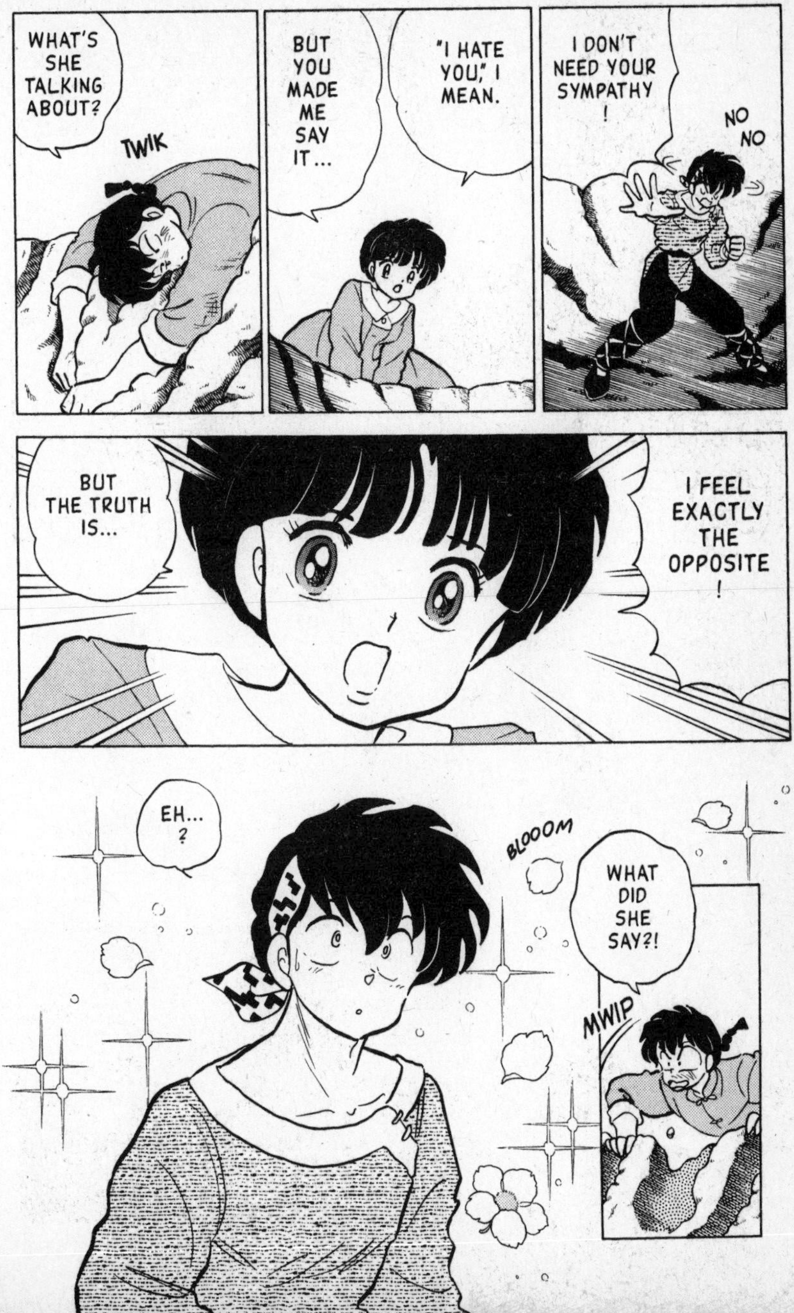
WHAT'S SHE TALKING ABOUT?
TWIK
BUT YOU MADE ME SAY IT...
"I HATE YOU," I MEAN.
I DON'T NEED YOUR SYMPATHY !
NO NO
BUT THE TRUTH IS...
I FEEL EXACTLY THE OPPOSITE !
EH... ?
BLOOOM
WHAT DID SHE SAY?!
MWIP

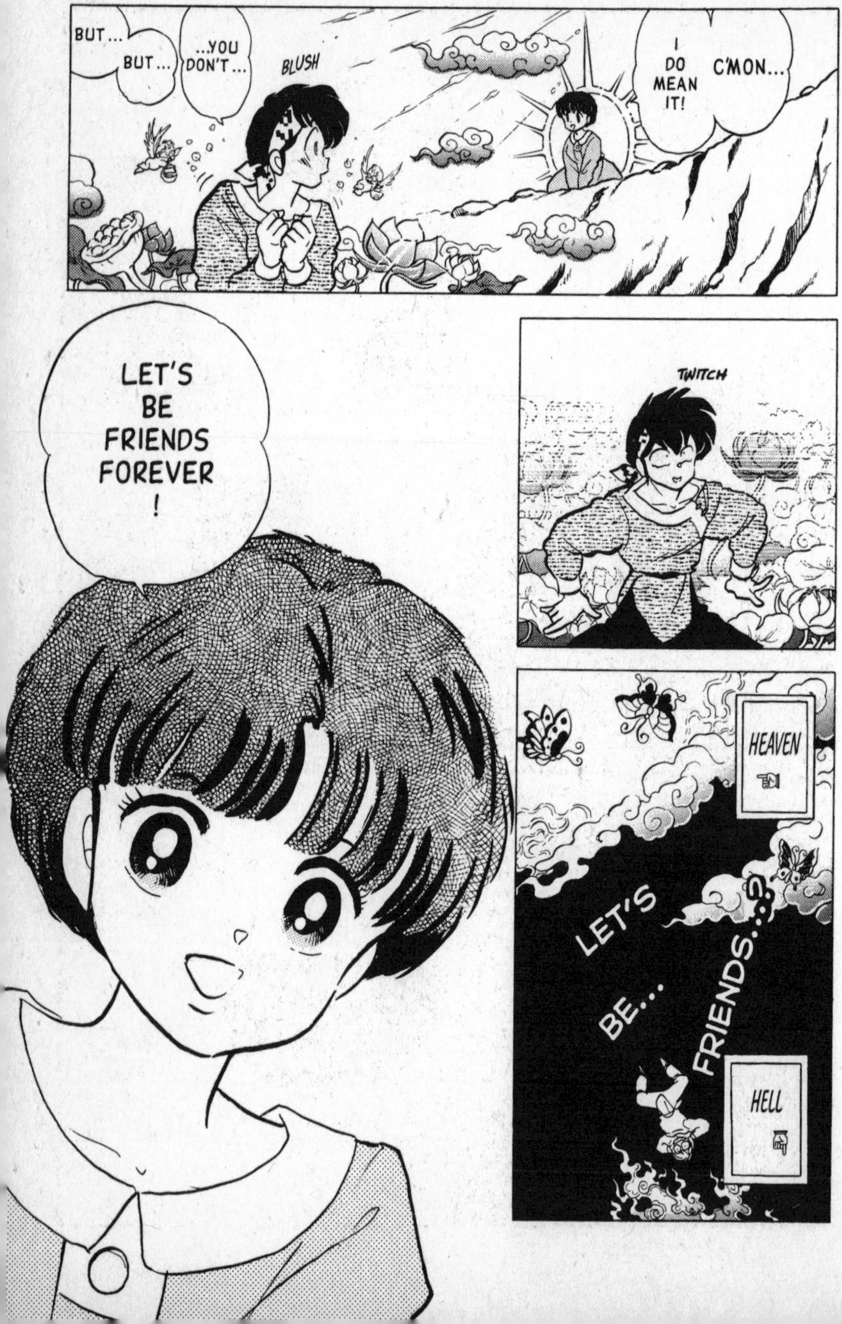
BUT...
BUT...
...YOU DON'T...
BLUSH
I DO MEAN IT!
C'MON...
LET'S BE FRIENDS FOREVER!
TWITCH
HEAVEN
LET'S BE... FRIENDS...?
HELL

OHO...

SO THAT'S HOW IT IS...!

WBBL...

THANK YOU, AKANE...FOR FINISHING ME OFF.

JUST BECAUSE AKANE DUMPED YOU?!

DOING THIS TO ME...

I HAVE NOTHING LEFT TO LOSE...

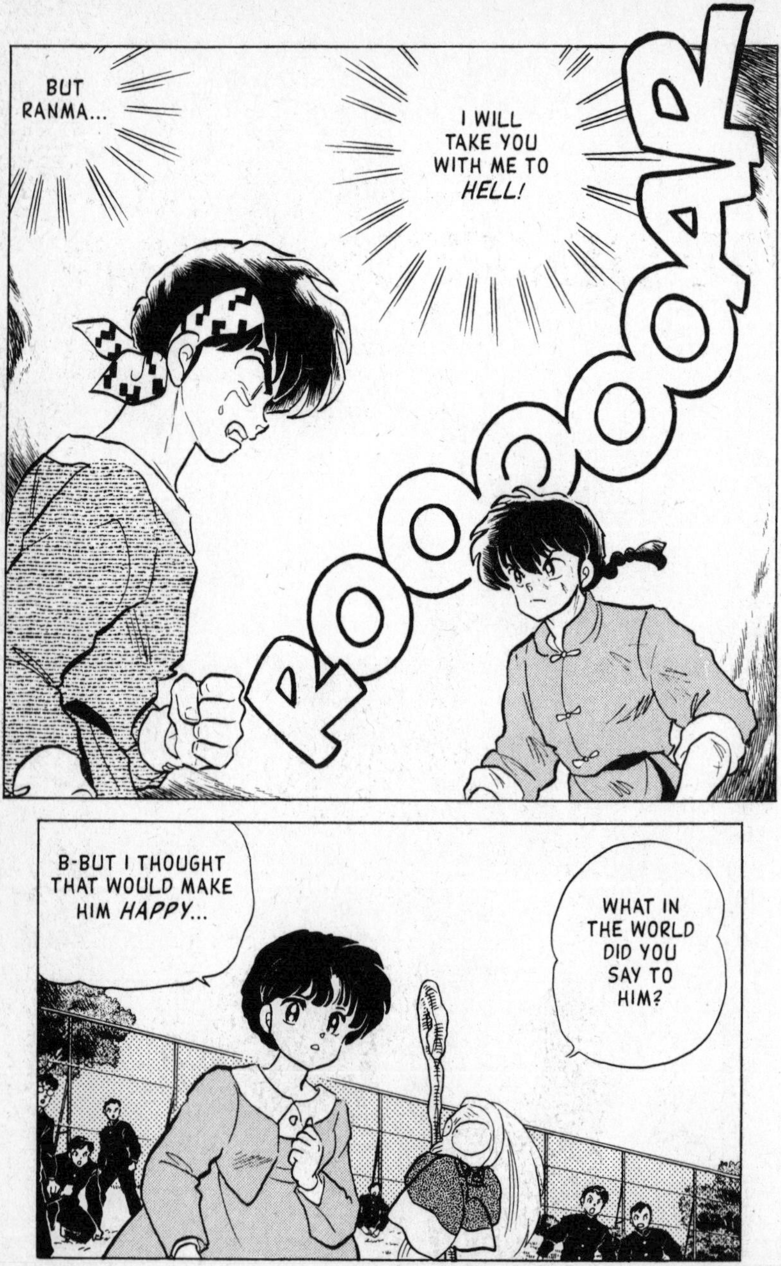
BUT RANMA...
I WILL TAKE YOU WITH ME TO *HELL!*
ROOOOOOAR
B-BUT I THOUGHT THAT WOULD MAKE HIM *HAPPY*...
WHAT IN THE WORLD DID YOU SAY TO HIM?

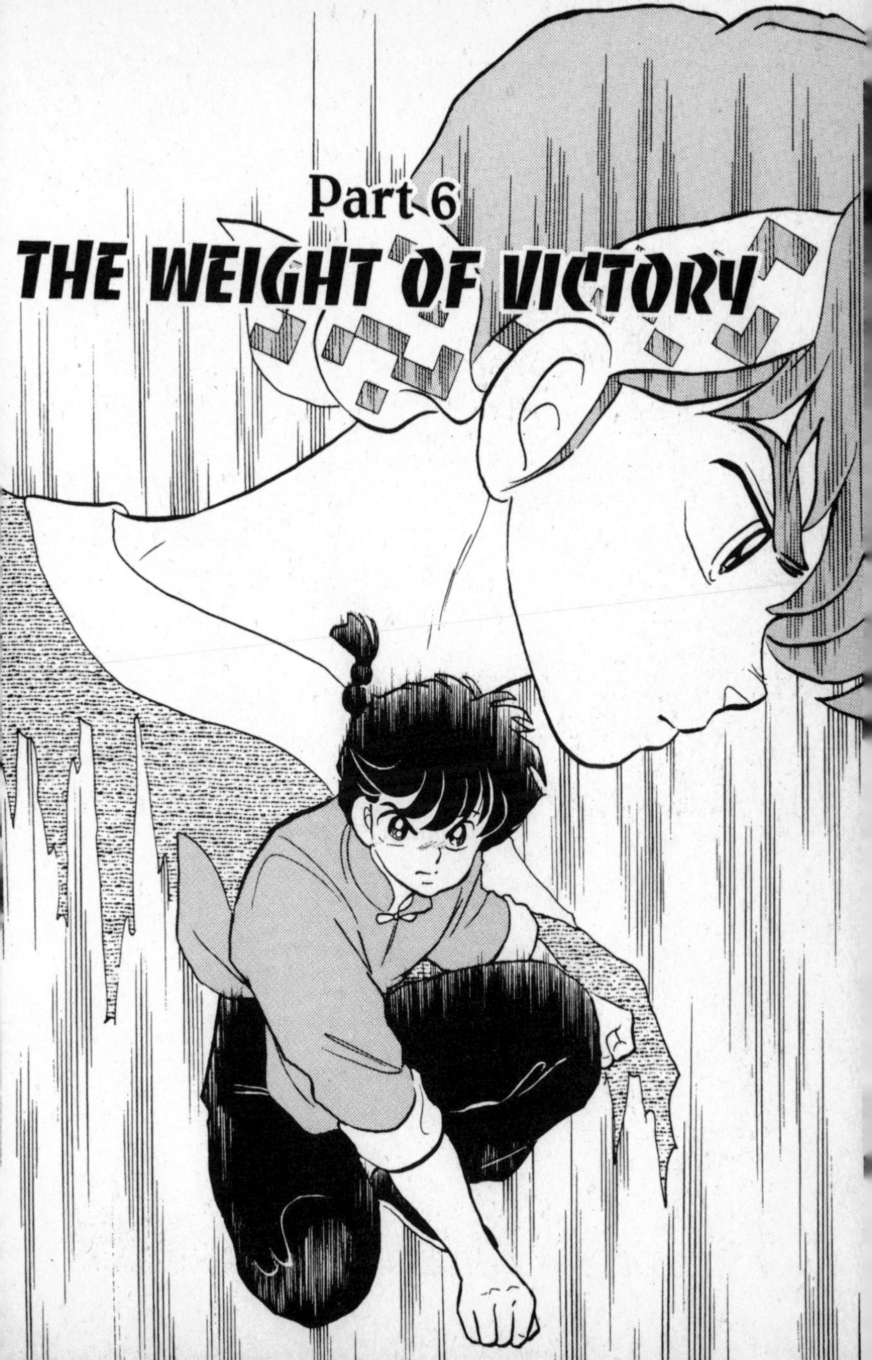
Part 6
THE WEIGHT OF VICTORY

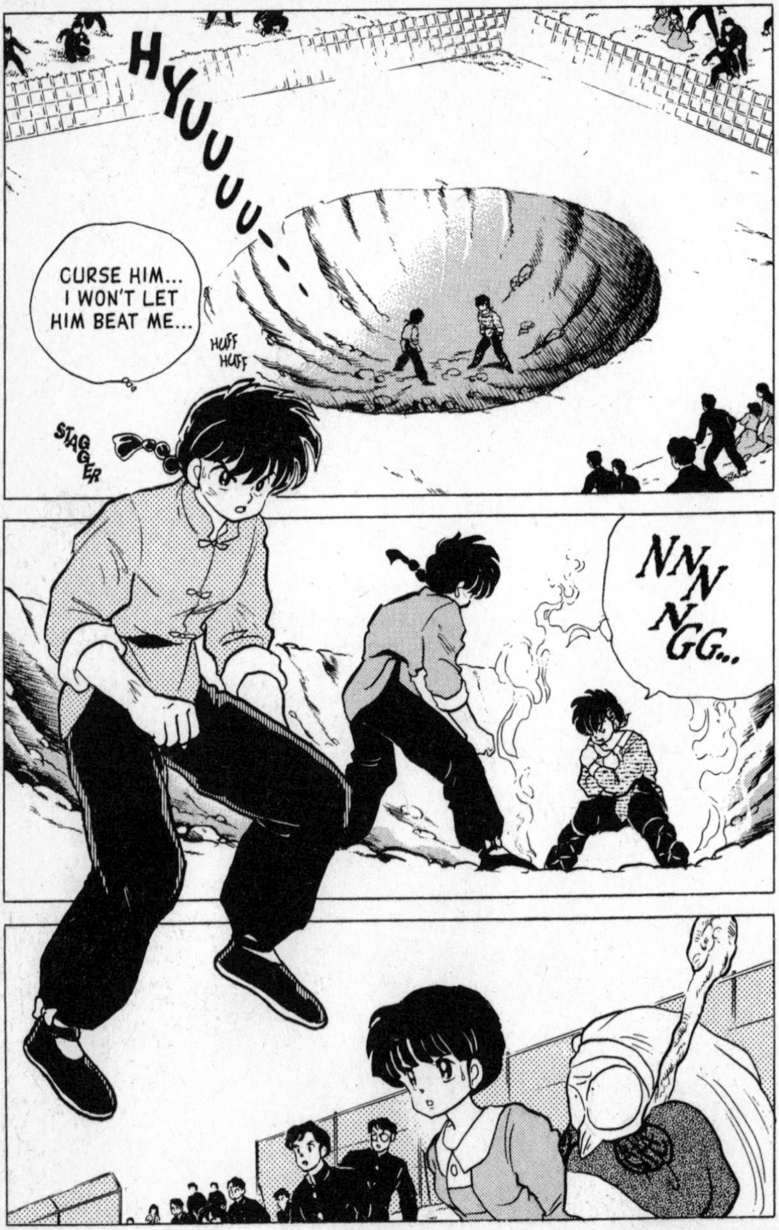
HYUUUUU--...
CURSE HIM... I WON'T LET HIM BEAT ME...
HUFF HUFF
STAGGER
NNNNGG...

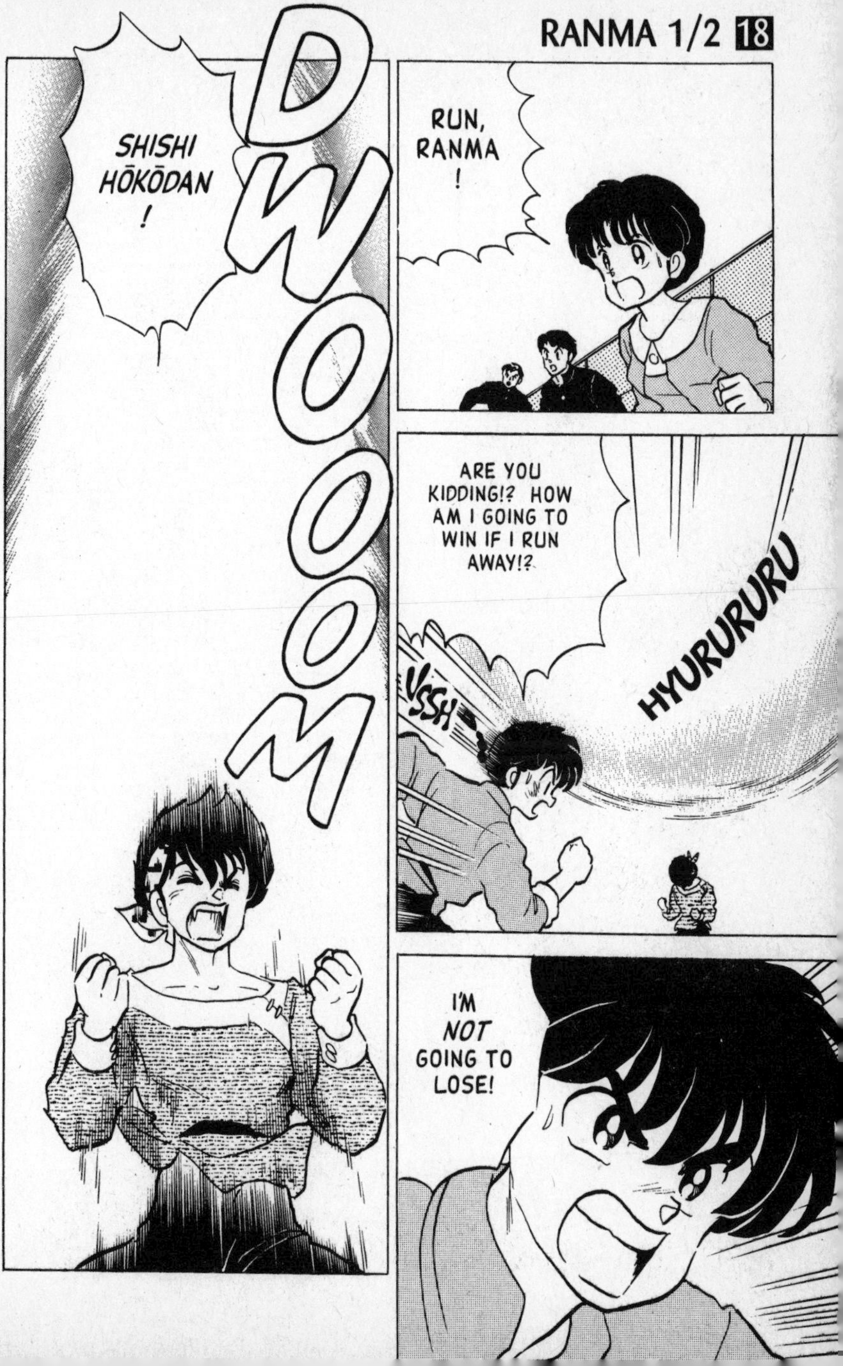
SHISHI HŌKŌDAN!
DWOOOM
RUN, RANMA!
ARE YOU KIDDING!? HOW AM I GOING TO WIN IF I RUN AWAY!?
VSSH
HYURURURU
I'M *NOT* GOING TO LOSE!

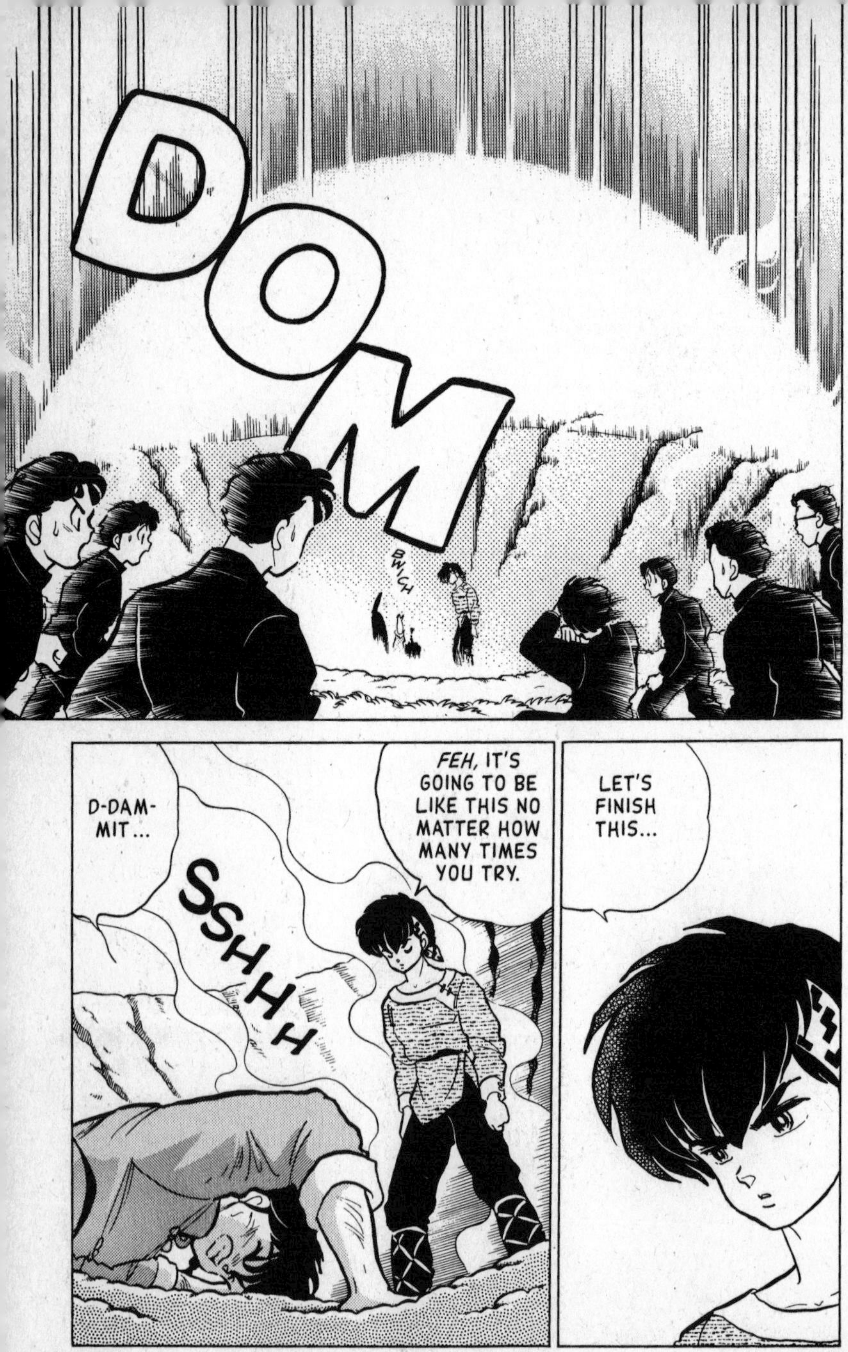
DOM
BWICH
D-DAM-MIT...
SSHHH
FEH, IT'S GOING TO BE LIKE THIS NO MATTER HOW MANY TIMES YOU TRY.
LET'S FINISH THIS...

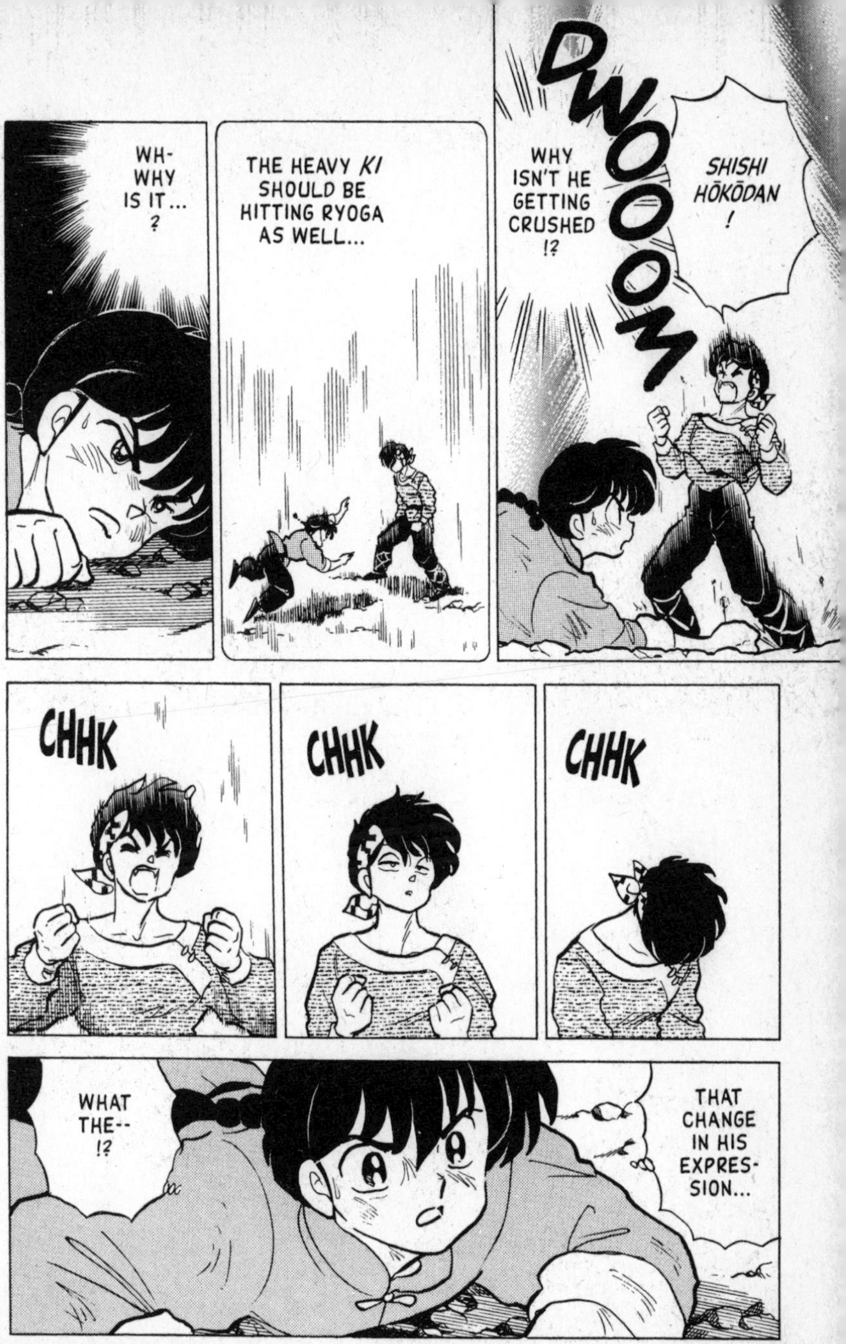

WH- WHY IS IT... ?
THE HEAVY *KI* SHOULD BE HITTING RYOGA AS WELL...
DWOOOOM
WHY ISN'T HE GETTING CRUSHED !?
SHISHI HŌKŌDAN !
CHHK
CHHK
CHHK
WHAT THE-- !?
THAT CHANGE IN HIS EXPRES- SION...

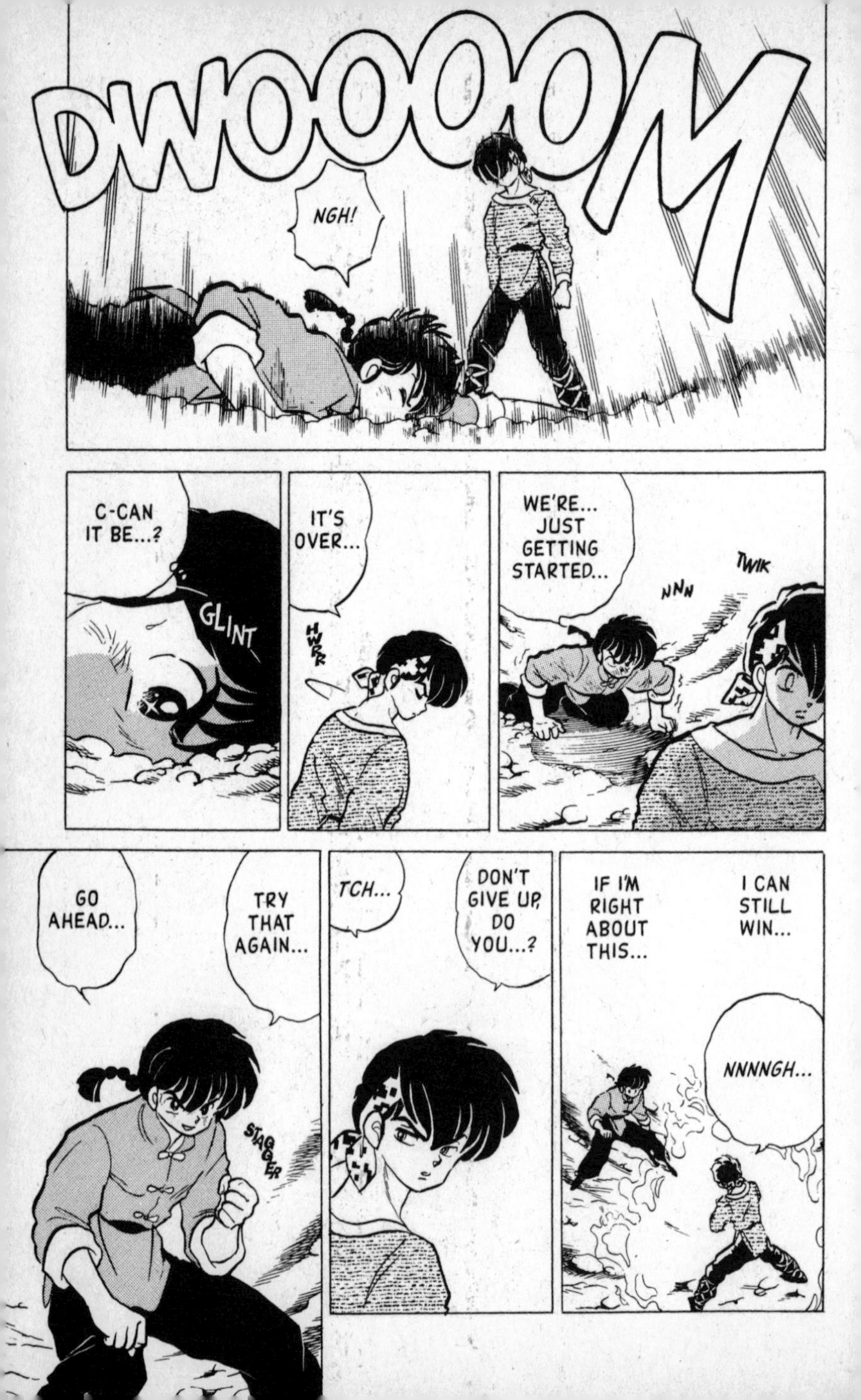
DWOOOOM
NGH!
C-CAN IT BE...?
GLINT
IT'S OVER...
HWRR
WE'RE... JUST GETTING STARTED...
NNN
TWIK
GO AHEAD...
TRY THAT AGAIN...
STAGGER
TCH...
DON'T GIVE UP, DO YOU...?
IF I'M RIGHT ABOUT THIS...
I CAN STILL WIN...
NNNNGH...

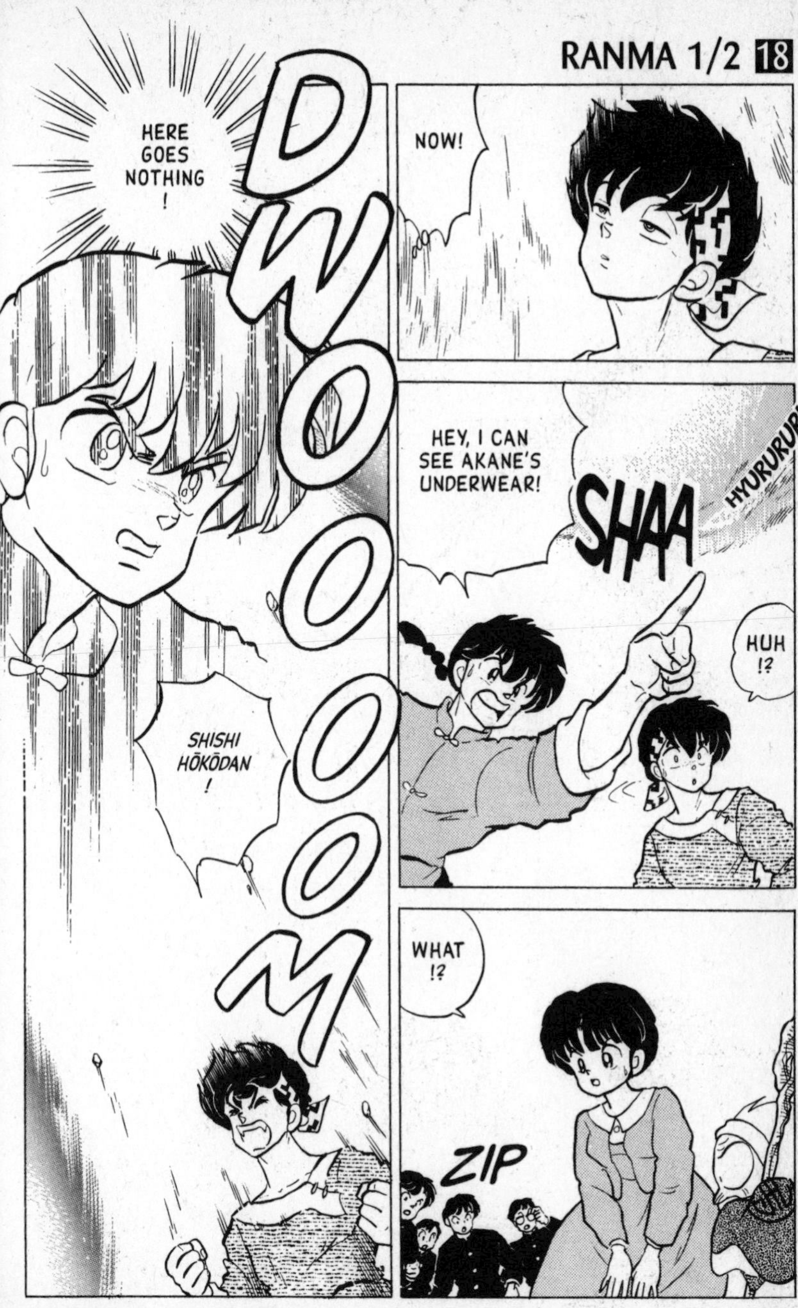
HERE GOES NOTHING!
DWOOOOOM
SHISHI HŌKŌDAN!
NOW!
HEY, I CAN SEE AKANE'S UNDERWEAR!
SHAA
HYURURURU
HUH!?
WHAT!?
ZIP

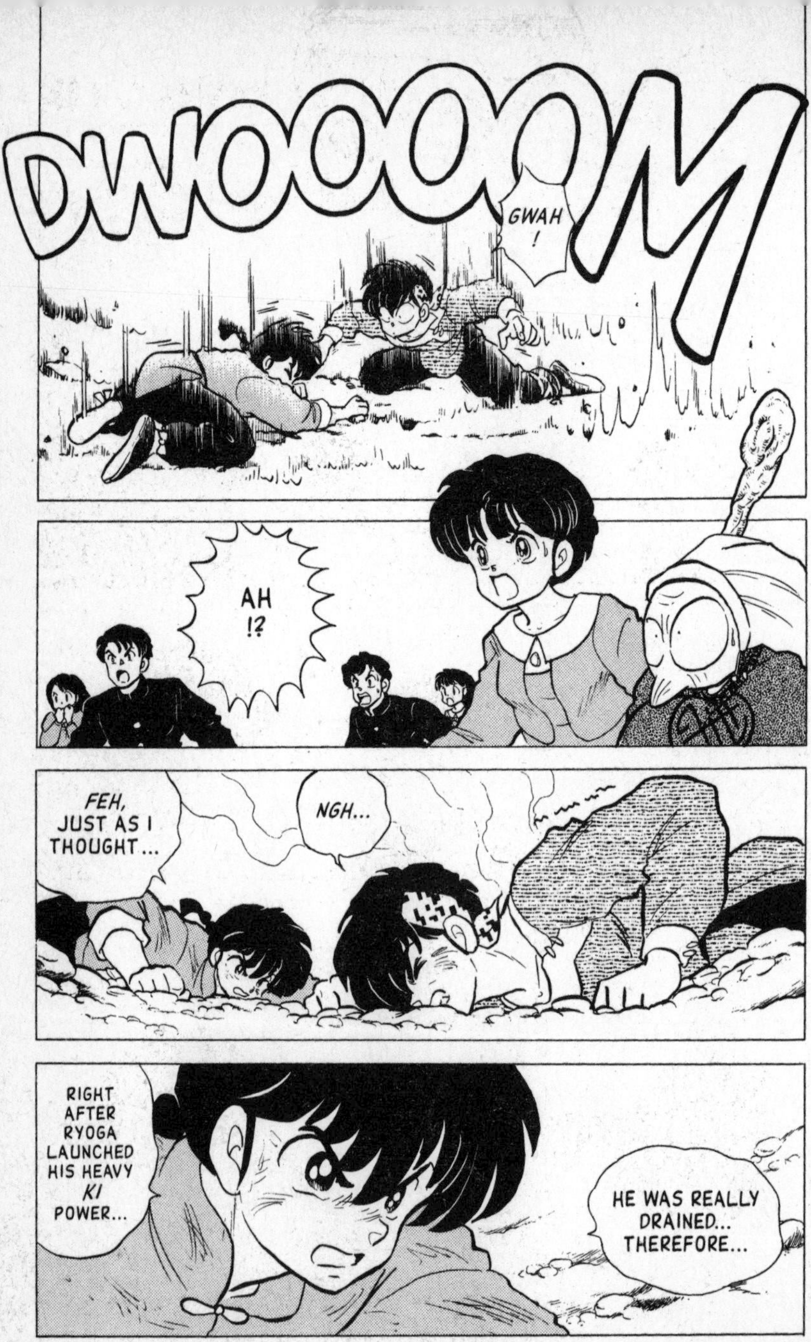
DWOOOOM
GWAH !
AH !?
FEH, JUST AS I THOUGHT...
NGH...
RIGHT AFTER RYOGA LAUNCHED HIS HEAVY *KI* POWER...
HE WAS REALLY DRAINED... THEREFORE...

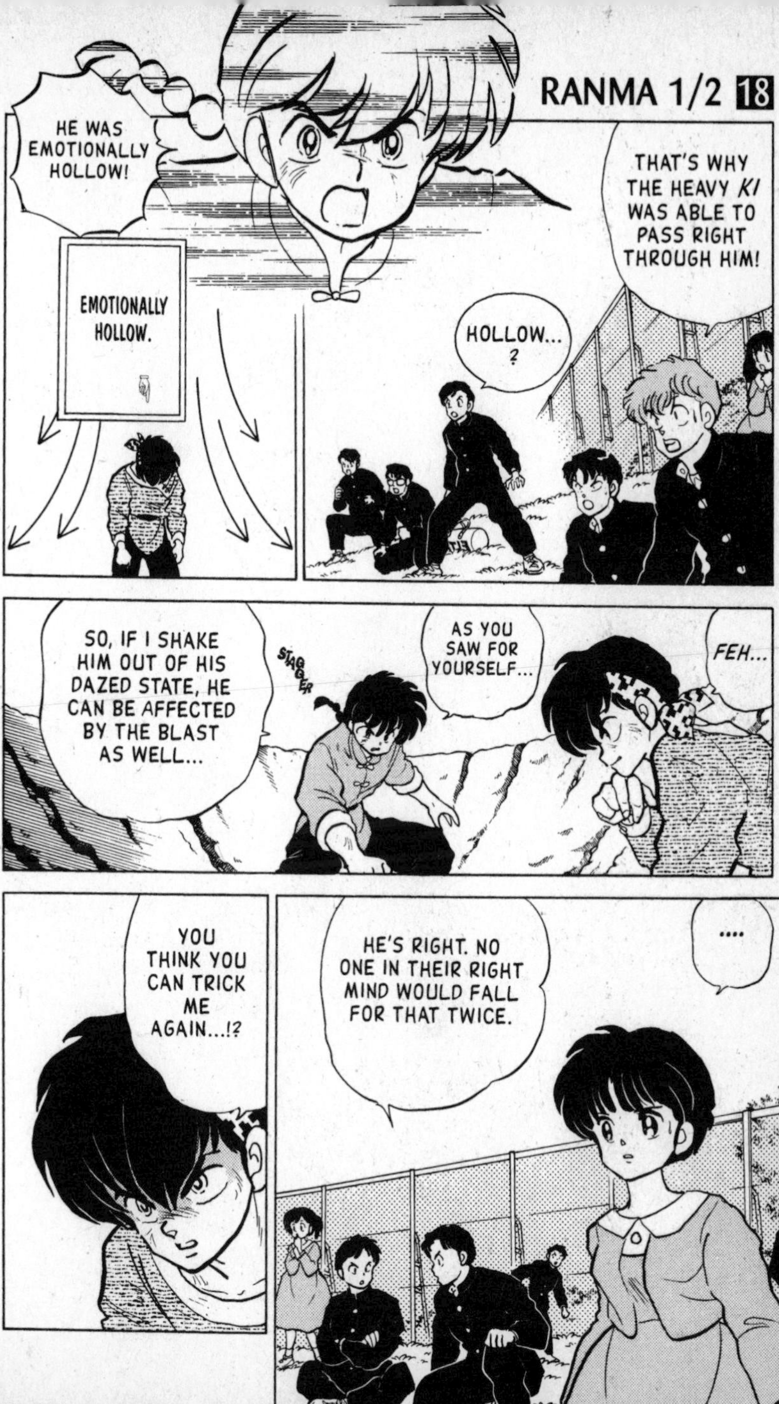
HE WAS EMOTIONALLY HOLLOW!
EMOTIONALLY HOLLOW.
THAT'S WHY THE HEAVY *KI* WAS ABLE TO PASS RIGHT THROUGH HIM!
HOLLOW...?
SO, IF I SHAKE HIM OUT OF HIS DAZED STATE, HE CAN BE AFFECTED BY THE BLAST AS WELL...
STAGGER
AS YOU SAW FOR YOURSELF...
FEH...
YOU THINK YOU CAN TRICK ME AGAIN...!?
HE'S RIGHT. NO ONE IN THEIR RIGHT MIND WOULD FALL FOR THAT TWICE.
....

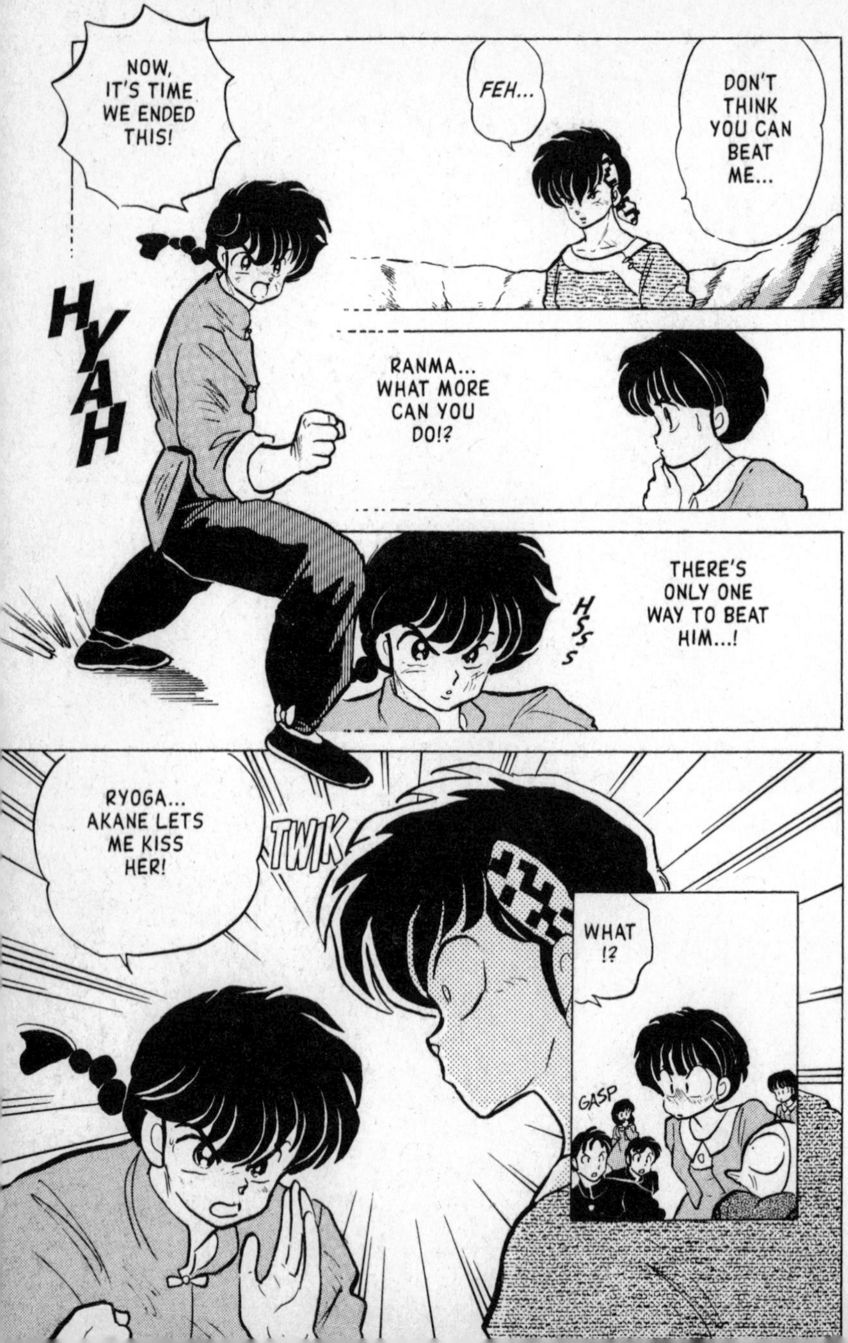
NOW, IT'S TIME WE ENDED THIS!
HYAH
FEH...
DON'T THINK YOU CAN BEAT ME...
RANMA... WHAT MORE CAN YOU DO!?
HSSS
THERE'S ONLY ONE WAY TO BEAT HIM...!
RYOGA... AKANE LETS ME KISS HER!
TWIK
WHAT !?
GASP

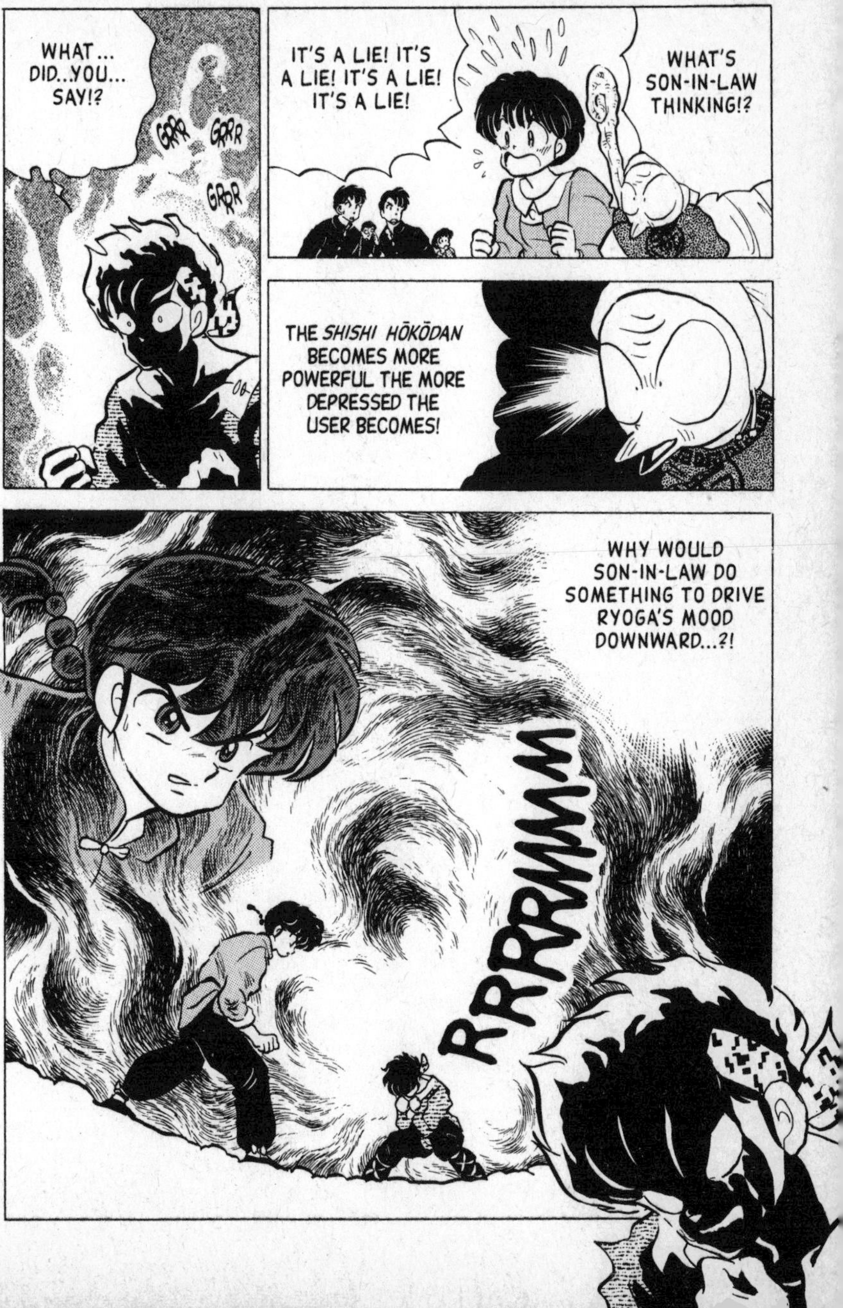
WHAT... DID...YOU... SAY!?
GRRR
GRRR
GRRR
IT'S A LIE! IT'S A LIE! IT'S A LIE! IT'S A LIE!
WHAT'S SON-IN-LAW THINKING!?
THE *SHISHI HŌKŌDAN* BECOMES MORE POWERFUL THE MORE DEPRESSED THE USER BECOMES!
WHY WOULD SON-IN-LAW DO SOMETHING TO DRIVE RYOGA'S MOOD DOWNWARD...?!
RRRRWMMM

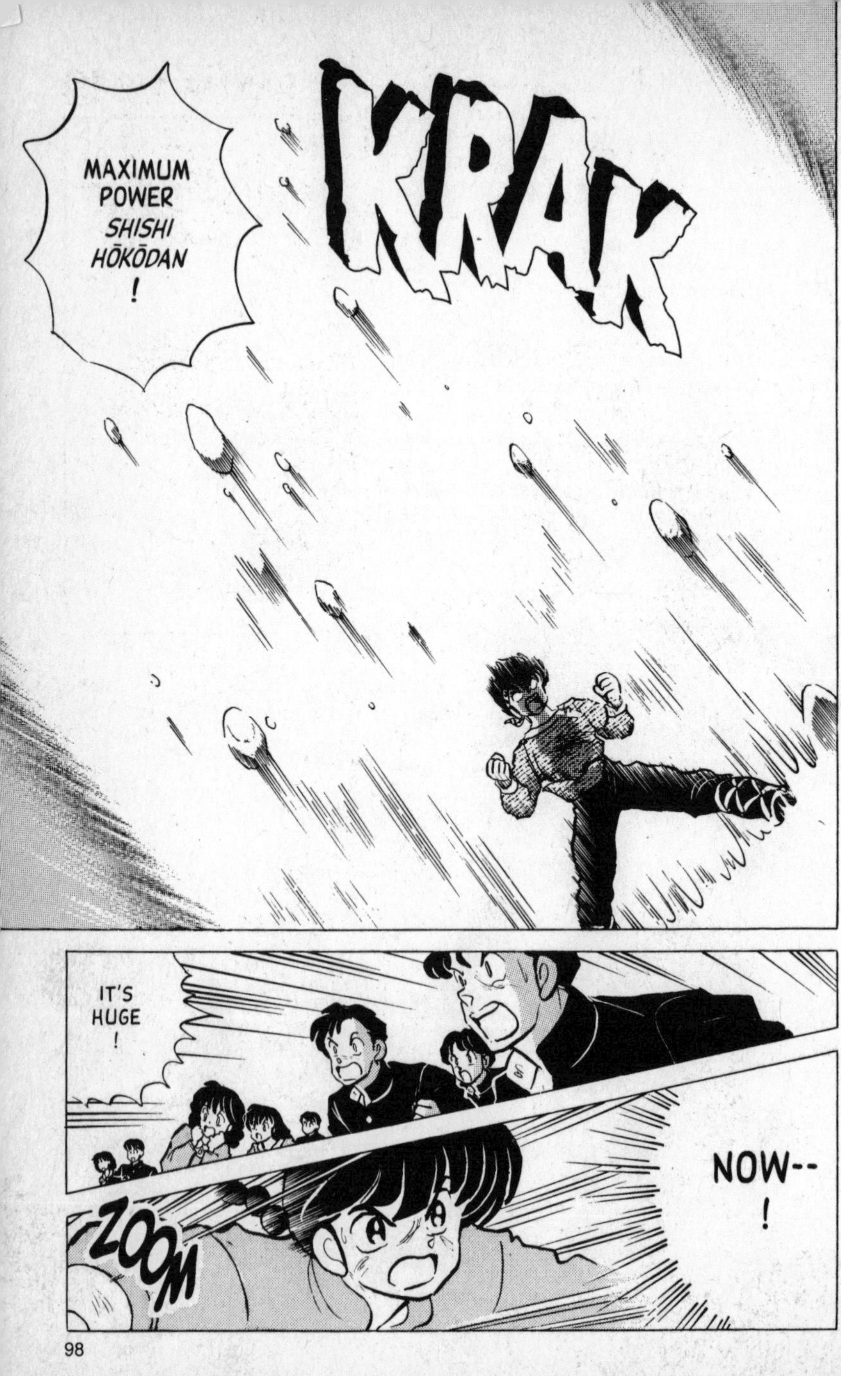
MAXIMUM POWER SHISHI HŌKŌDAN !
KRAK
IT'S HUGE !
NOW-- !
ZOOM

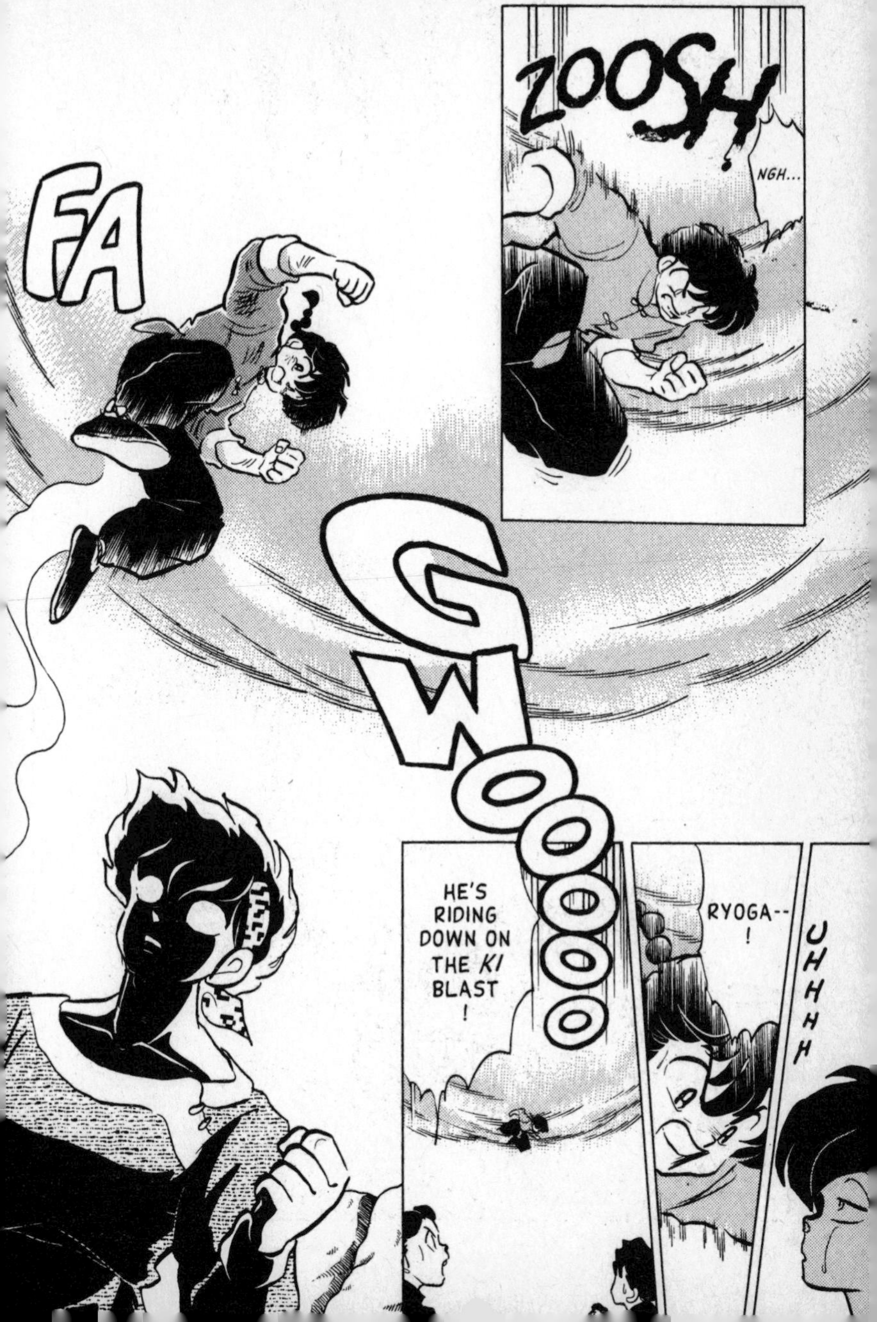
FA
ZOOSH
NGH...
GWOOOOO
HE'S RIDING DOWN ON THE *KI* BLAST!
RYOGA--!
UHHHHH

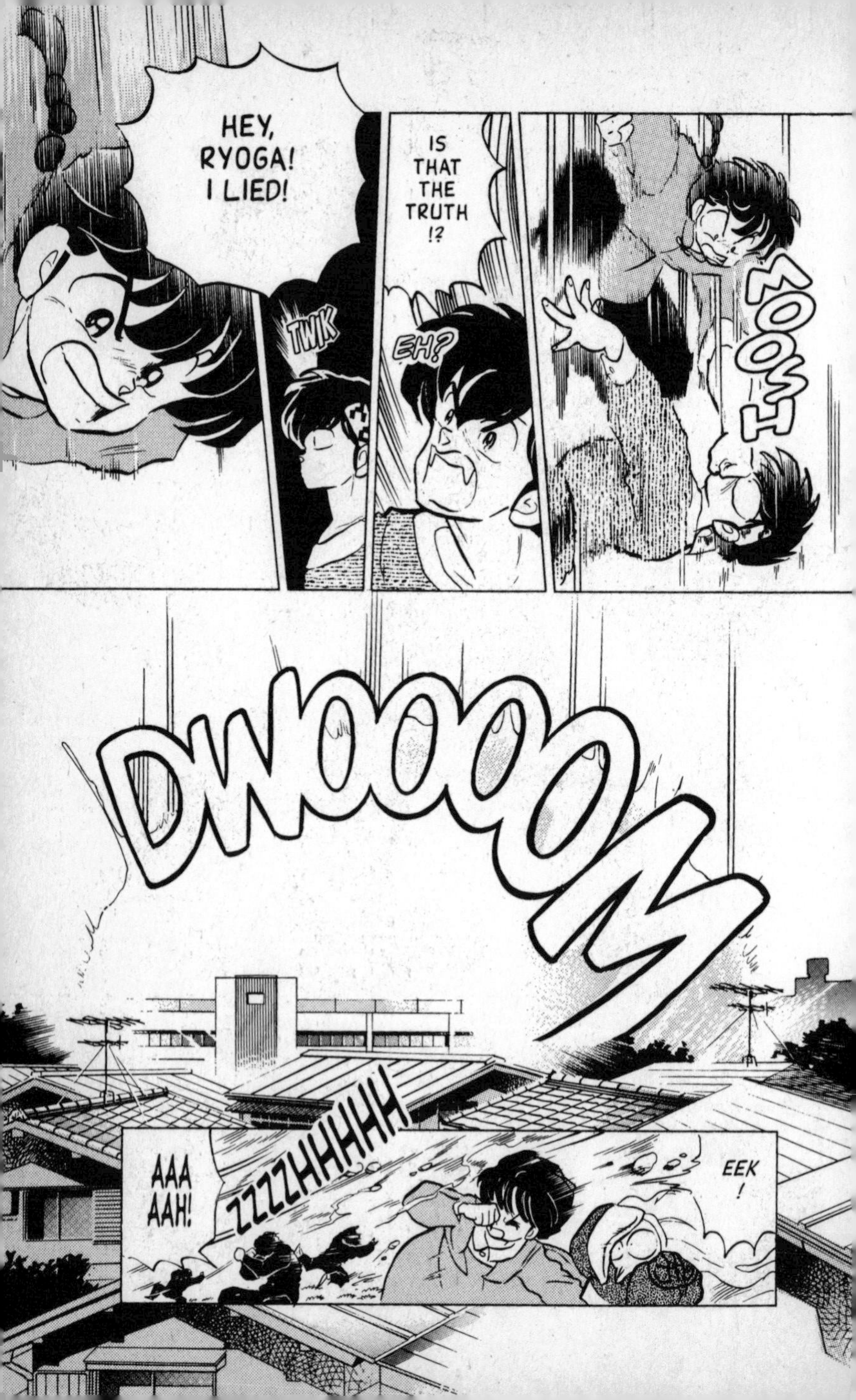
HEY, RYOGA! I LIED!
TWIK
IS THAT THE TRUTH !?
EH?
ZOOM!
DWOOOOM
AAA AAH!
ZZZZHHHHH
EEK !

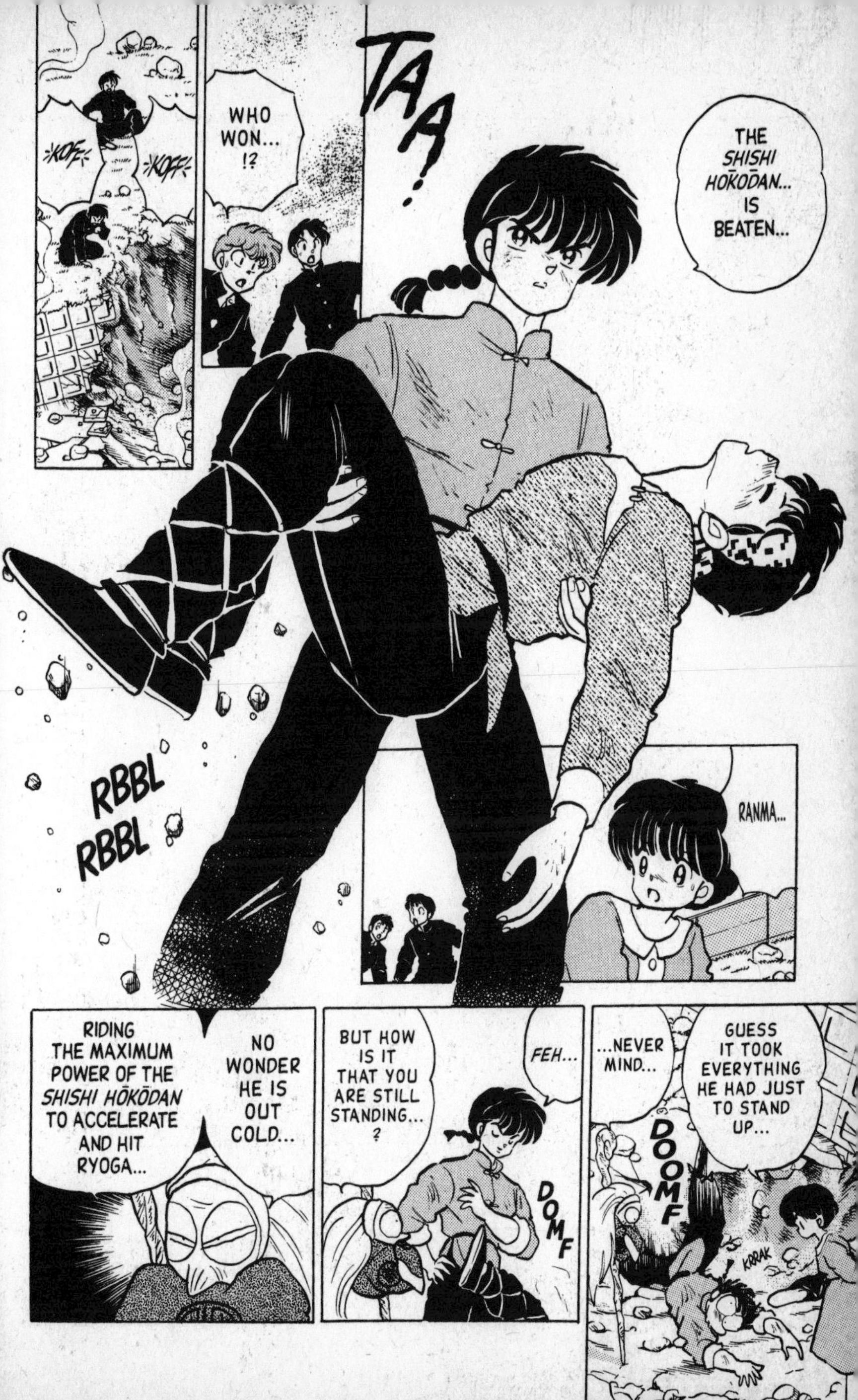
KOFF
KOFF
WHO WON... !?
TAA...!
THE SHISHI HŌKŌDAN... IS BEATEN...
RBBL RBBL
RANMA...
RIDING THE MAXIMUM POWER OF THE SHISHI HŌKŌDAN TO ACCELERATE AND HIT RYOGA...
NO WONDER HE IS OUT COLD...
BUT HOW IS IT THAT YOU ARE STILL STANDING...?
FEH...
DOMF
...NEVER MIND...
GUESS IT TOOK EVERYTHING HE HAD JUST TO STAND UP...
DOOOMF
KRRAK

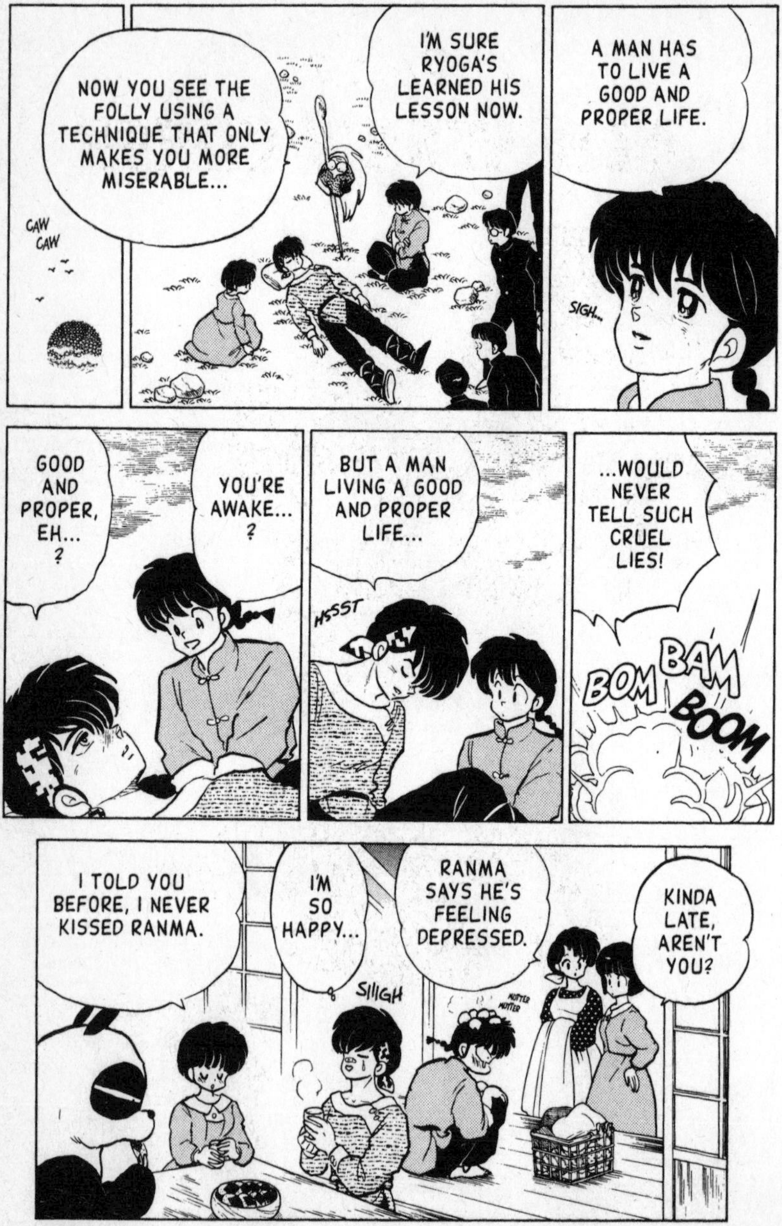
CAW CAW
NOW YOU SEE THE FOLLY USING A TECHNIQUE THAT ONLY MAKES YOU MORE MISERABLE...
I'M SURE RYOGA'S LEARNED HIS LESSON NOW.
A MAN HAS TO LIVE A GOOD AND PROPER LIFE.
SIGH...
GOOD AND PROPER, EH...?
YOU'RE AWAKE...?
BUT A MAN LIVING A GOOD AND PROPER LIFE...
HSSST
...WOULD NEVER TELL SUCH CRUEL LIES!
BOM BAM BOOM
I TOLD YOU BEFORE, I NEVER KISSED RANMA.
I'M SO HAPPY...
SIIGH
RANMA SAYS HE'S FEELING DEPRESSED.
MUTTER MUTTER
KINDA LATE, AREN'T YOU?

Part 7
NEW YEAR'S CURSE

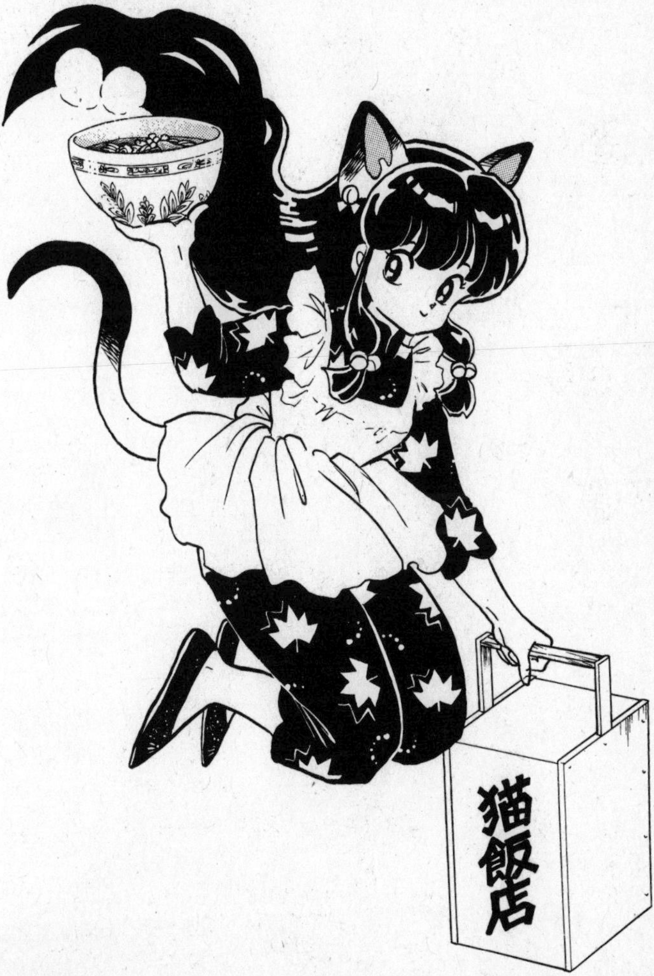
猫飯店

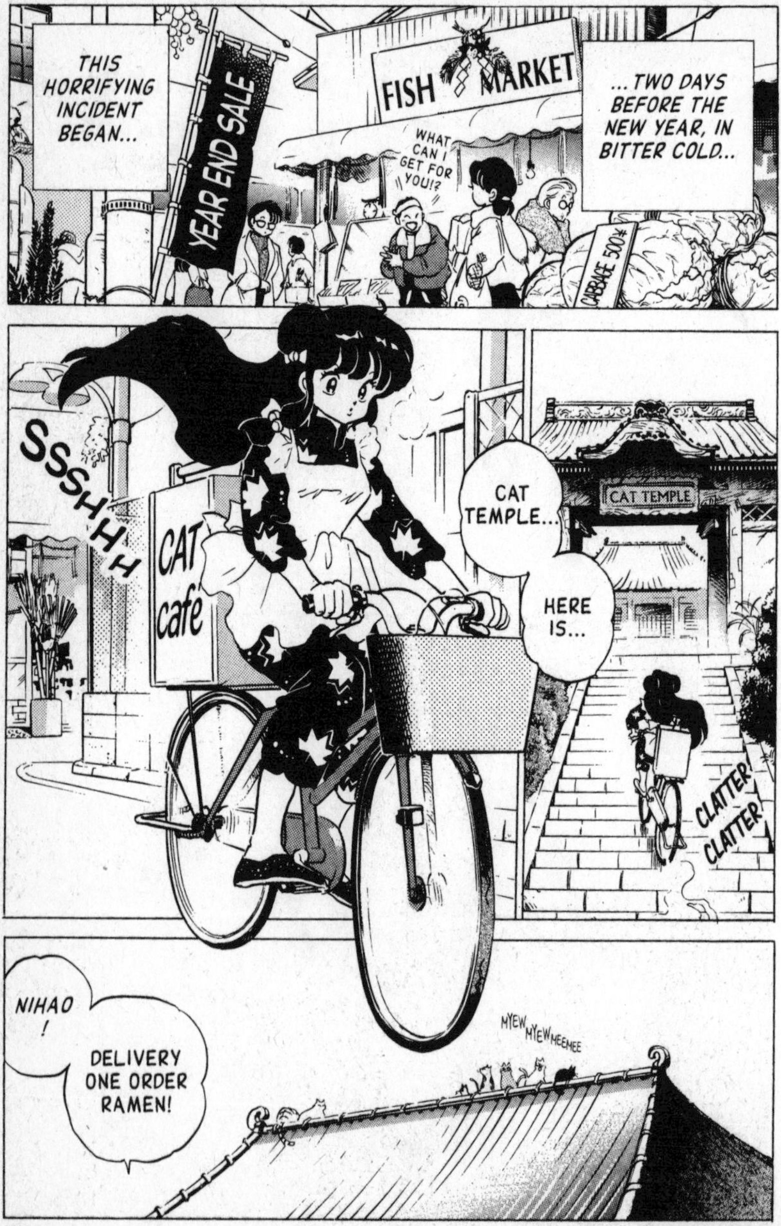
THIS HORRIFYING INCIDENT BEGAN...
YEAR END SALE
FISH MARKET
WHAT CAN I GET FOR YOU!?
...TWO DAYS BEFORE THE NEW YEAR, IN BITTER COLD...
CABBAGE 500¥
SSSHHHH
CAT cafe
CAT TEMPLE...
HERE IS...
CAT TEMPLE
CLATTER CLATTER
NIHAO! DELIVERY ONE ORDER RAMEN!
MYEW MYEW MEEMEE

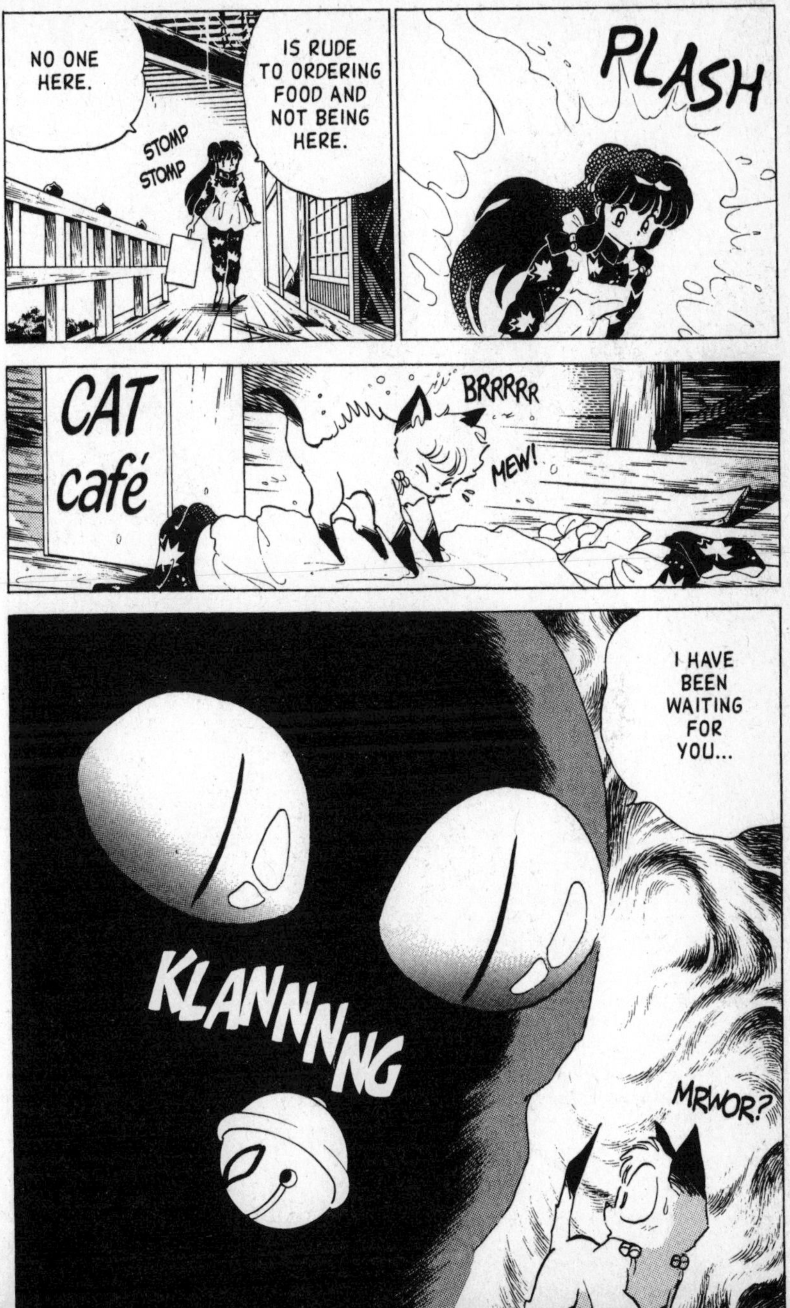
NO ONE HERE.
IS RUDE TO ORDERING FOOD AND NOT BEING HERE.
STOMP STOMP
PLASH
CAT café
BRRRRR
MEW!
I HAVE BEEN WAITING FOR YOU...
KLANNNNG
MRWOR?

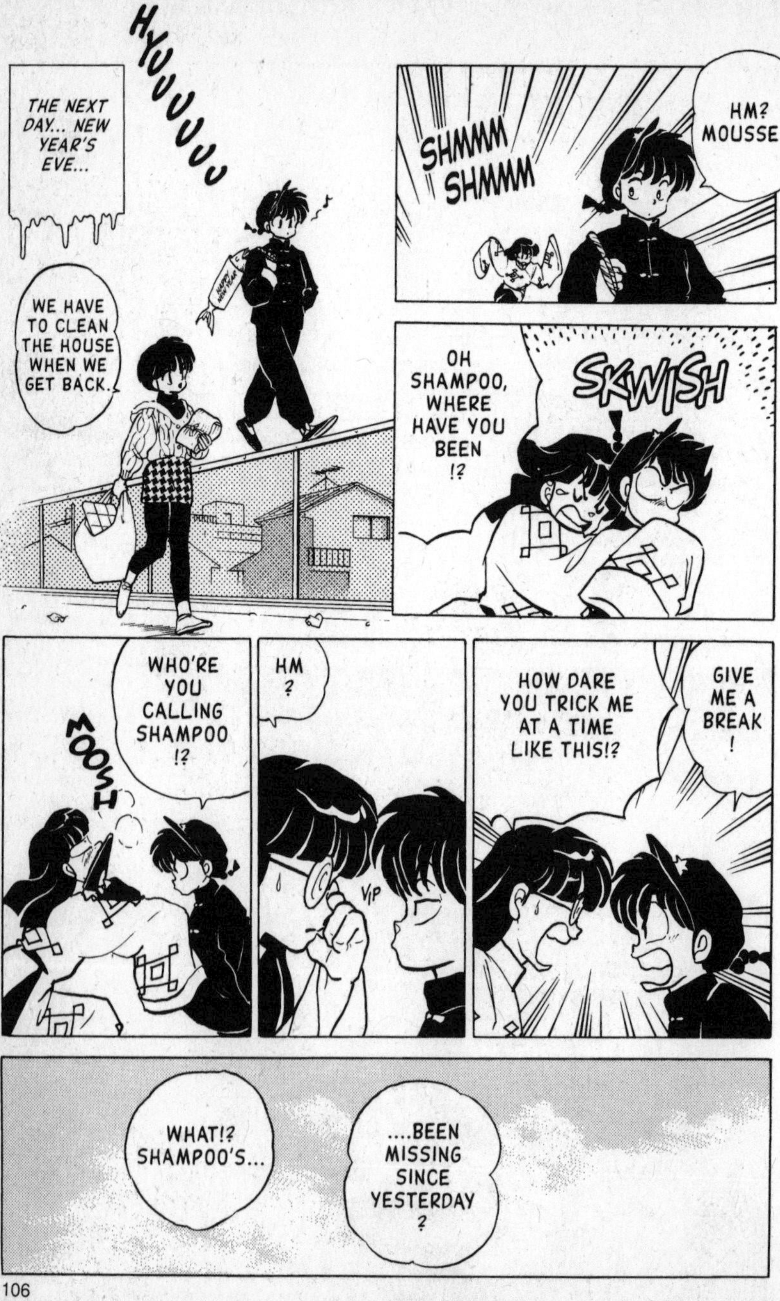
HYUUUUUUU
THE NEXT DAY... NEW YEAR'S EVE...
WE HAVE TO CLEAN THE HOUSE WHEN WE GET BACK.
SHMMM SHMMM
HM? MOUSSE...
OH SHAMPOO, WHERE HAVE YOU BEEN !?
SKWISH
WHO'RE YOU CALLING SHAMPOO !?
ZOOSH
HM ?
VIP
HOW DARE YOU TRICK ME AT A TIME LIKE THIS!?
GIVE ME A BREAK !
WHAT!? SHAMPOO'S...
....BEEN MISSING SINCE YESTERDAY ?

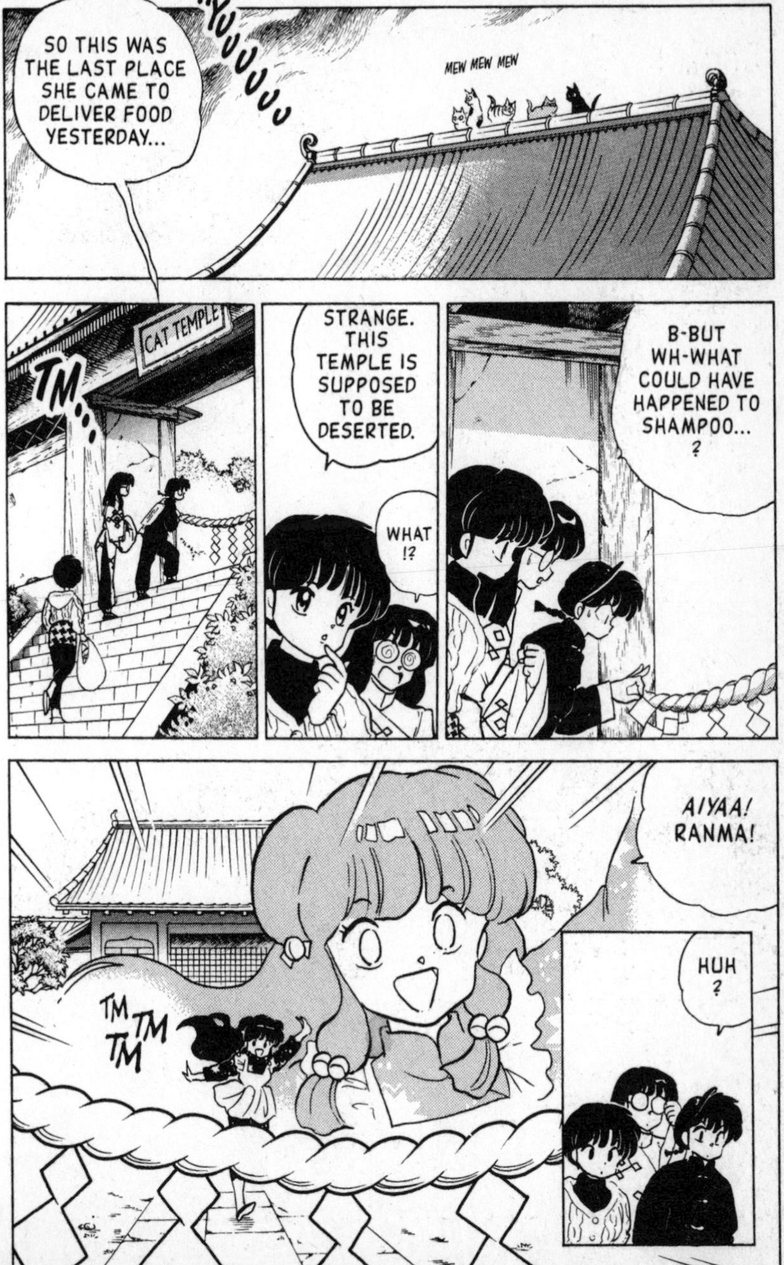
HYUUUUUU
SO THIS WAS THE LAST PLACE SHE CAME TO DELIVER FOOD YESTERDAY...
MEW MEW MEW
CAT TEMPLE
TM...
STRANGE. THIS TEMPLE IS SUPPOSED TO BE DESERTED.
WHAT !?
B-BUT WH-WHAT COULD HAVE HAPPENED TO SHAMPOO...?
AIYAA! RANMA!
TM TM TM
HUH?

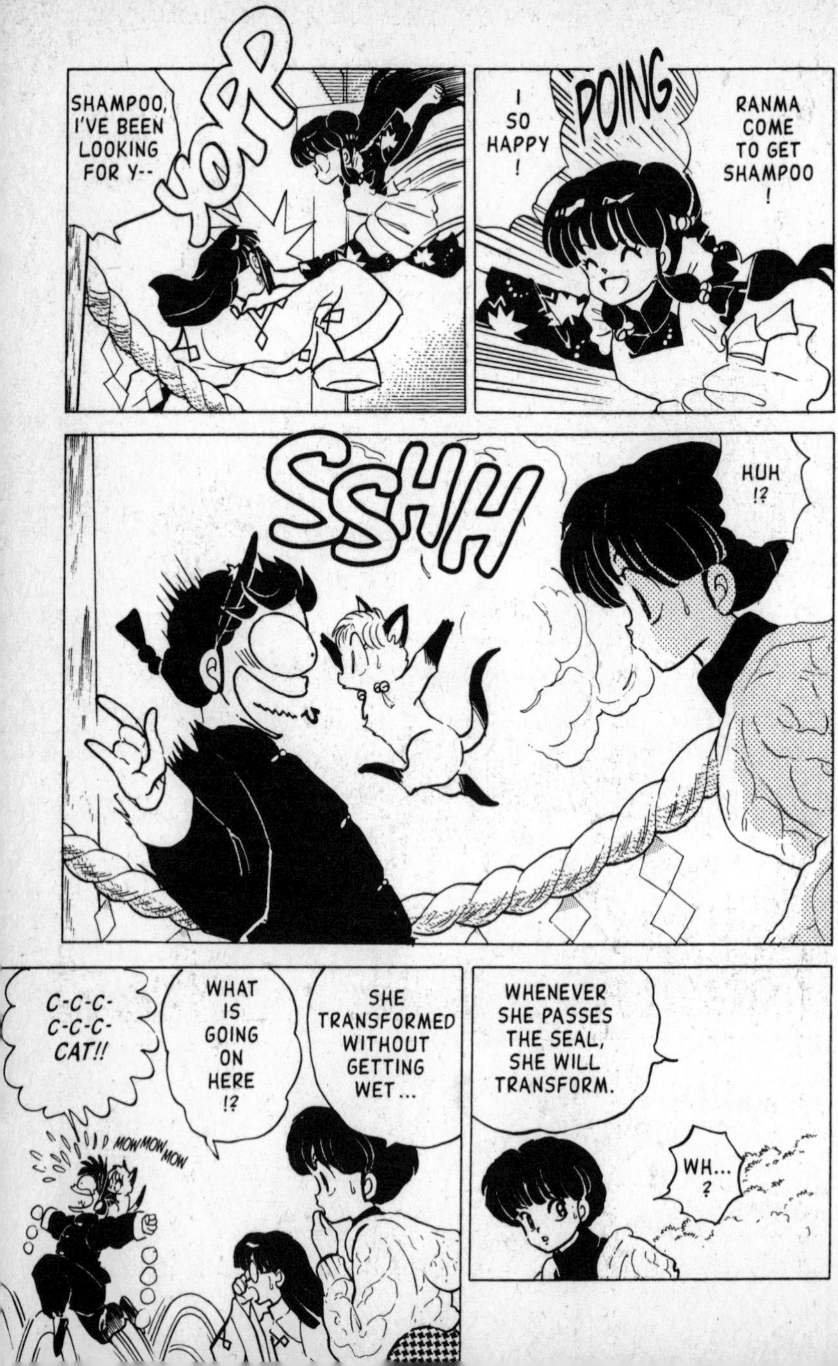
SHAMPOO, I'VE BEEN LOOKING FOR Y--
SOP
I SO HAPPY!
POING
RANMA COME TO GET SHAMPOO!
SSHH
HUH!?
C-C-C-C-C-C-CAT!!
MOWMOWMOW
WHAT IS GOING ON HERE!?
SHE TRANSFORMED WITHOUT GETTING WET...
WHENEVER SHE PASSES THE SEAL, SHE WILL TRANSFORM.
WH...?

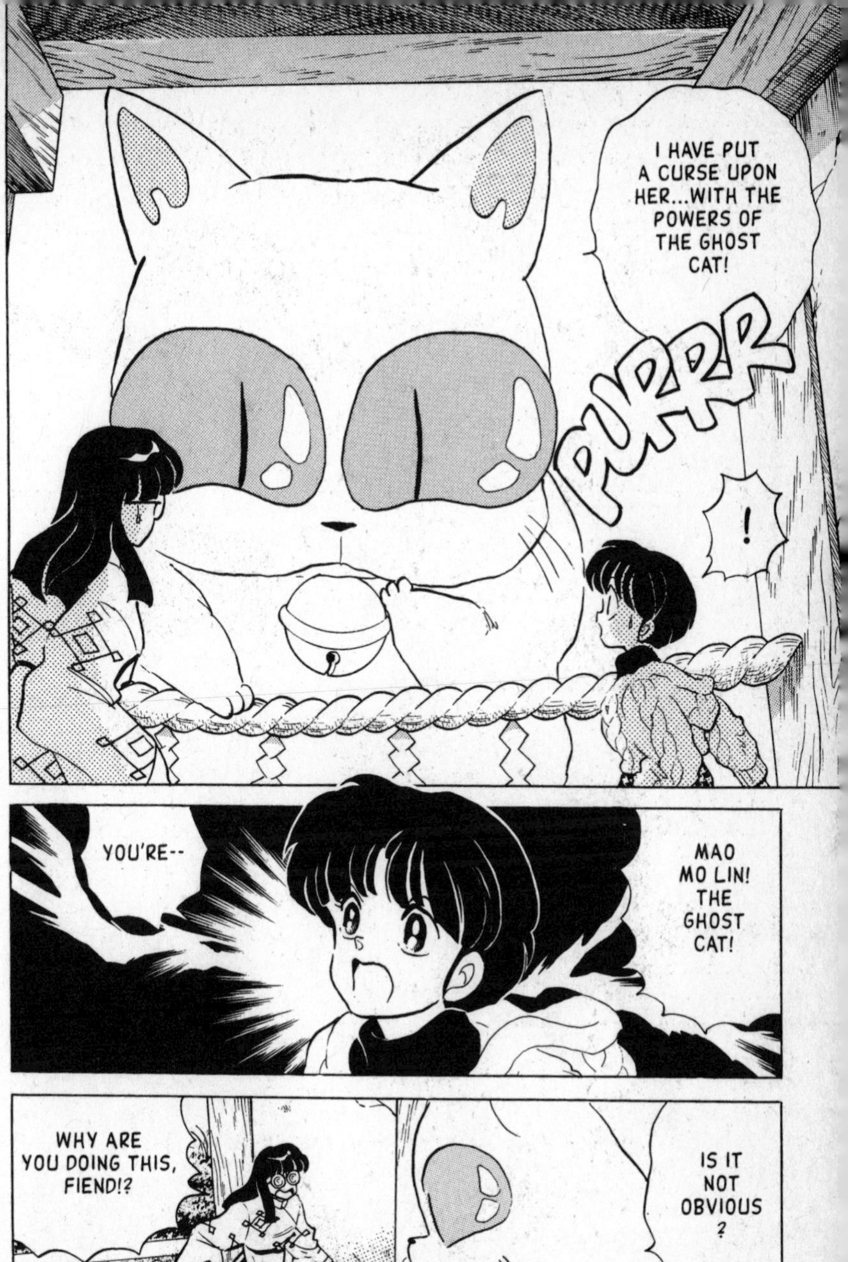
I HAVE PUT A CURSE UPON HER...WITH THE POWERS OF THE GHOST CAT!
PURRR
!
YOU'RE--
MAO MO LIN! THE GHOST CAT!
WHY ARE YOU DOING THIS, FIEND!?
IS IT NOT OBVIOUS?

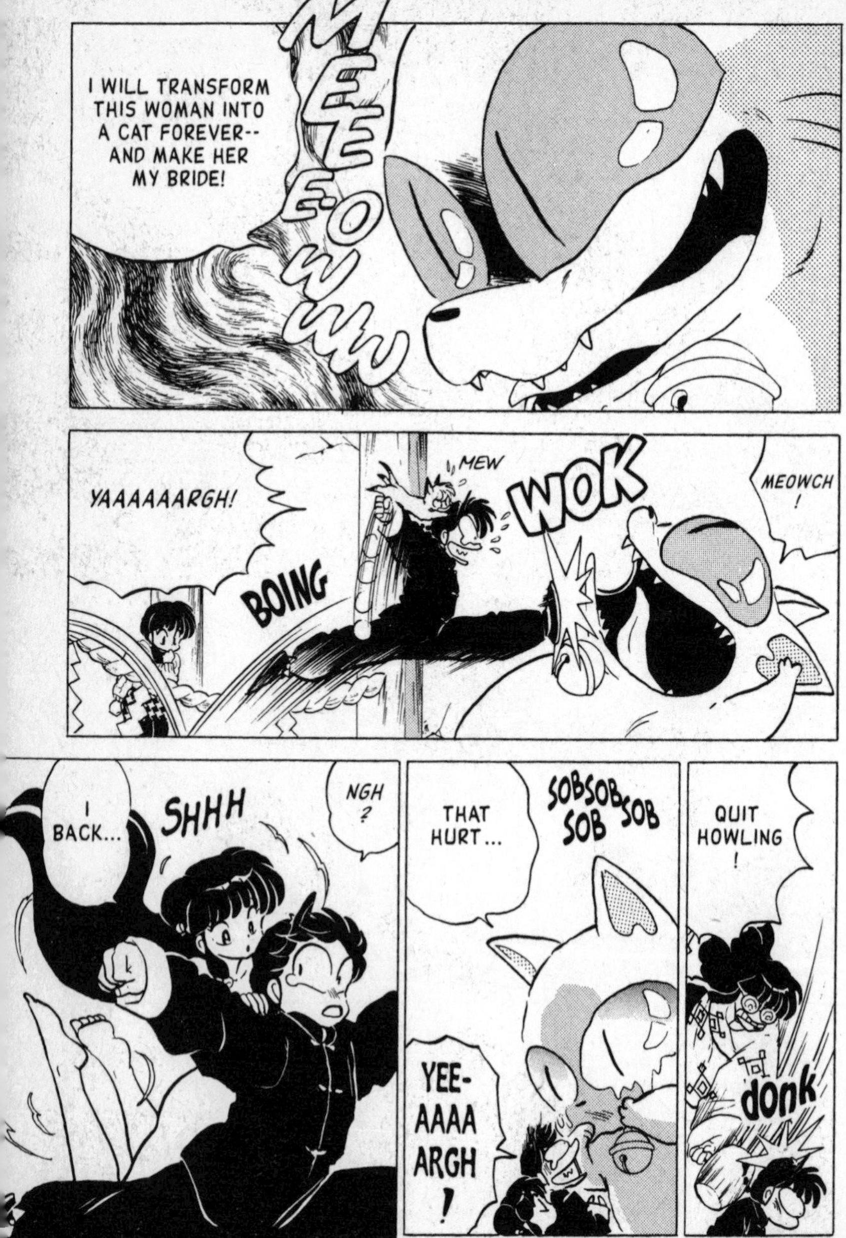
I WILL TRANSFORM THIS WOMAN INTO A CAT FOREVER-- AND MAKE HER MY BRIDE!
MEEEE-OWWW
YAAAAAARGH!
BOING
MEW
WOK
MEOWCH!
I BACK...
SHHH
NGH?
THAT HURT...
SOBSOB SOB SOB
YEE-AAAA ARGH!
QUIT HOWLING!
donk

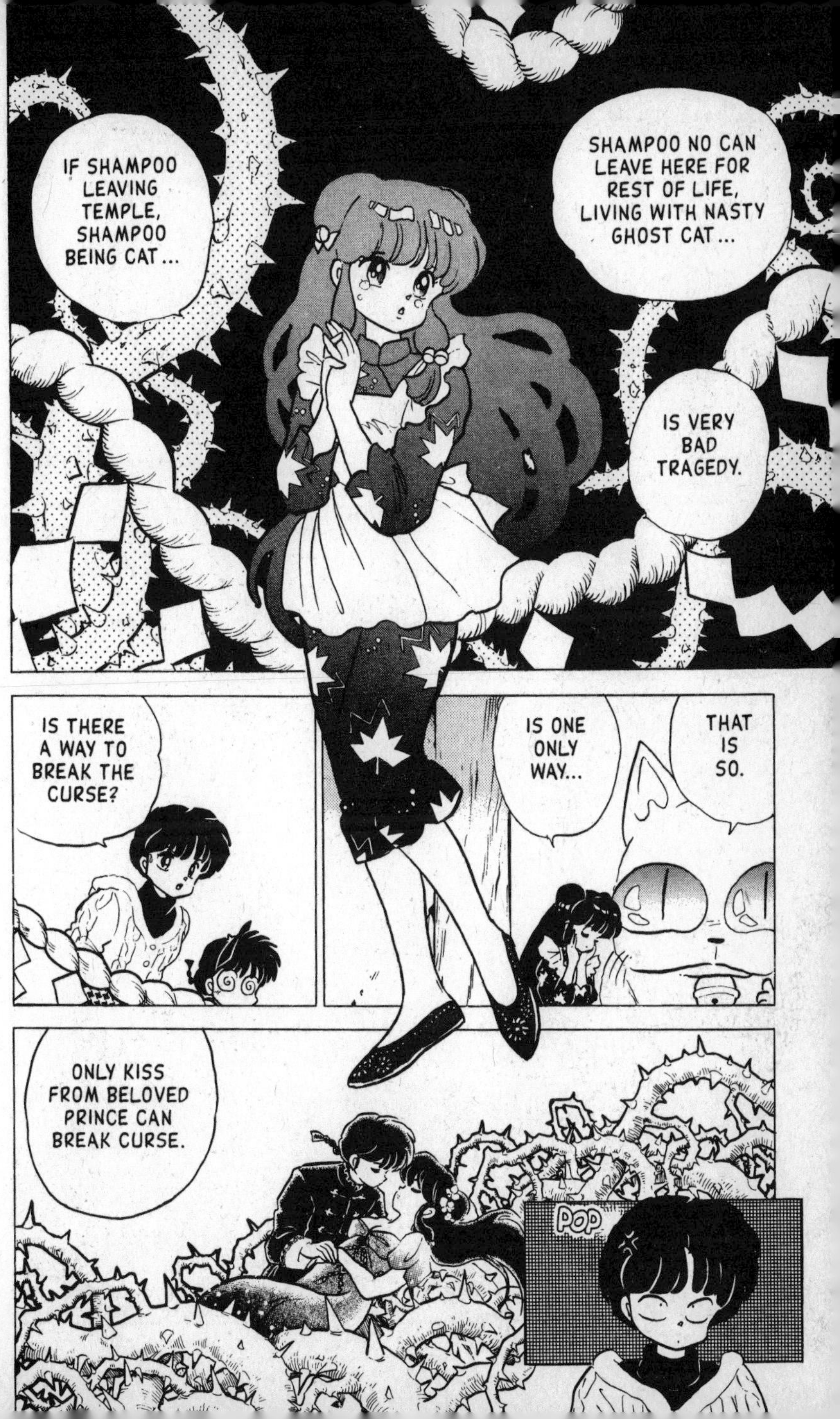
IF SHAMPOO LEAVING TEMPLE, SHAMPOO BEING CAT...
SHAMPOO NO CAN LEAVE HERE FOR REST OF LIFE, LIVING WITH NASTY GHOST CAT...
IS VERY BAD TRAGEDY.
IS THERE A WAY TO BREAK THE CURSE?
IS ONE ONLY WAY...
THAT IS SO.
ONLY KISS FROM BELOVED PRINCE CAN BREAK CURSE.
POP

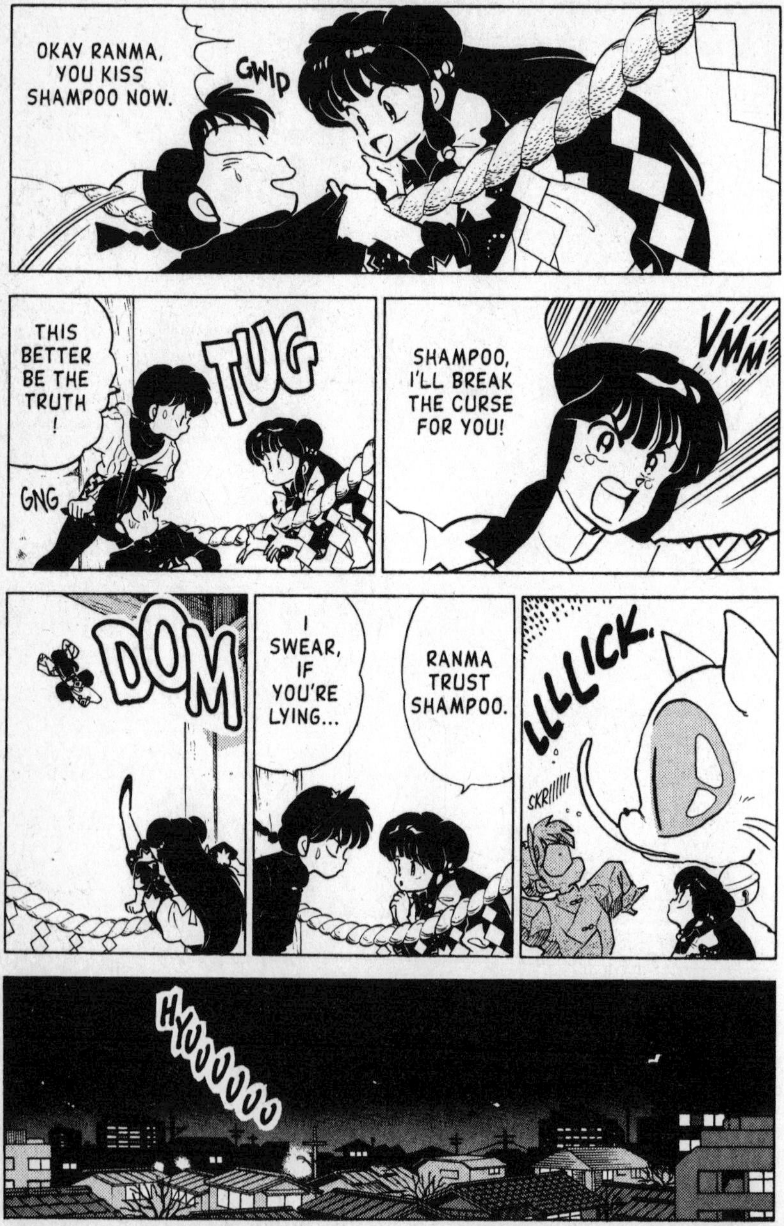
OKAY RANMA, YOU KISS SHAMPOO NOW.
GWIP
THIS BETTER BE THE TRUTH!
TUG
GNG
SHAMPOO, I'LL BREAK THE CURSE FOR YOU!
VMM
DOM
I SWEAR, IF YOU'RE LYING...
RANMA TRUST SHAMPOO.
LLLLICK
SKR!!!!!
HYUUUUUU

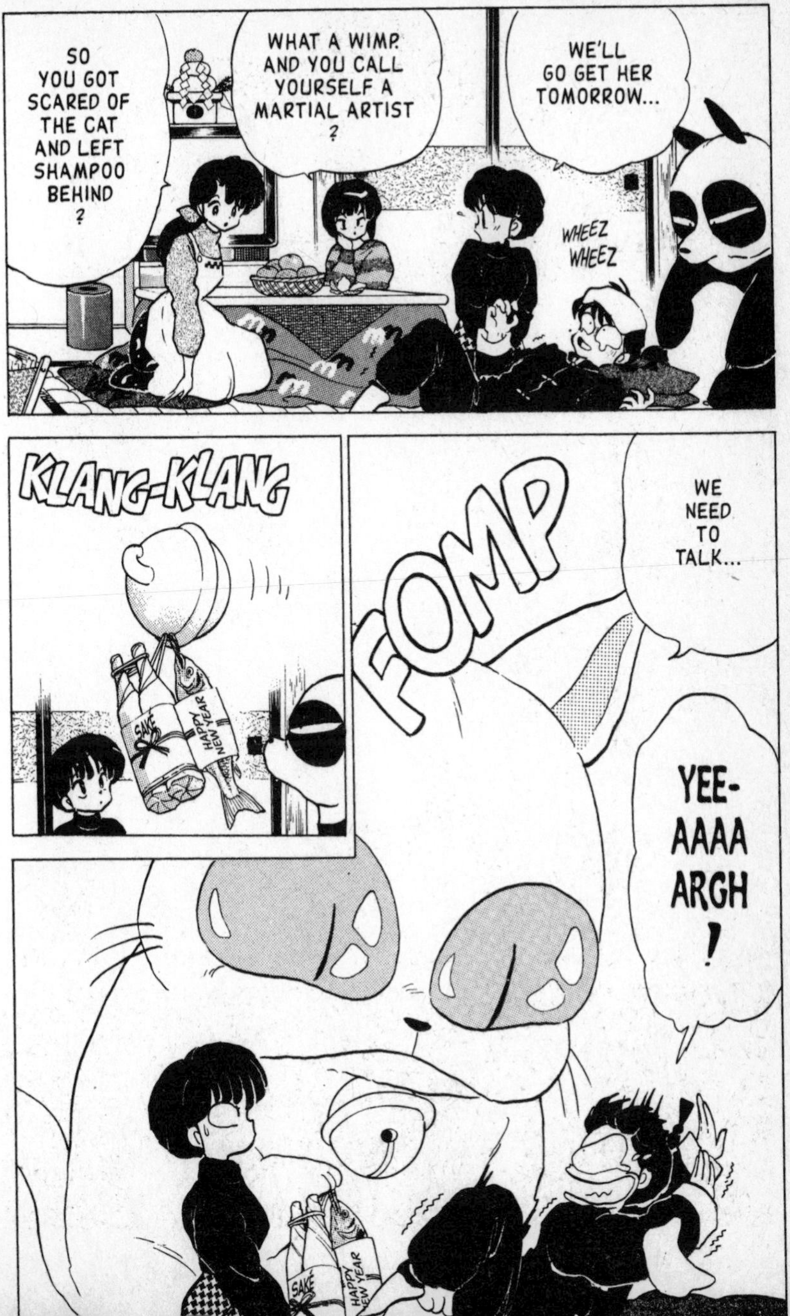
SO YOU GOT SCARED OF THE CAT AND LEFT SHAMPOO BEHIND?
WHAT A WIMP. AND YOU CALL YOURSELF A MARTIAL ARTIST?
WE'LL GO GET HER TOMORROW...
WHEEZ WHEEZ
KLANG-KLANG
SAKE
HAPPY NEW YEAR
FOMP
WE NEED TO TALK...
YEE-AAAA ARGH!
SAKE
HAPPY NEW YEAR

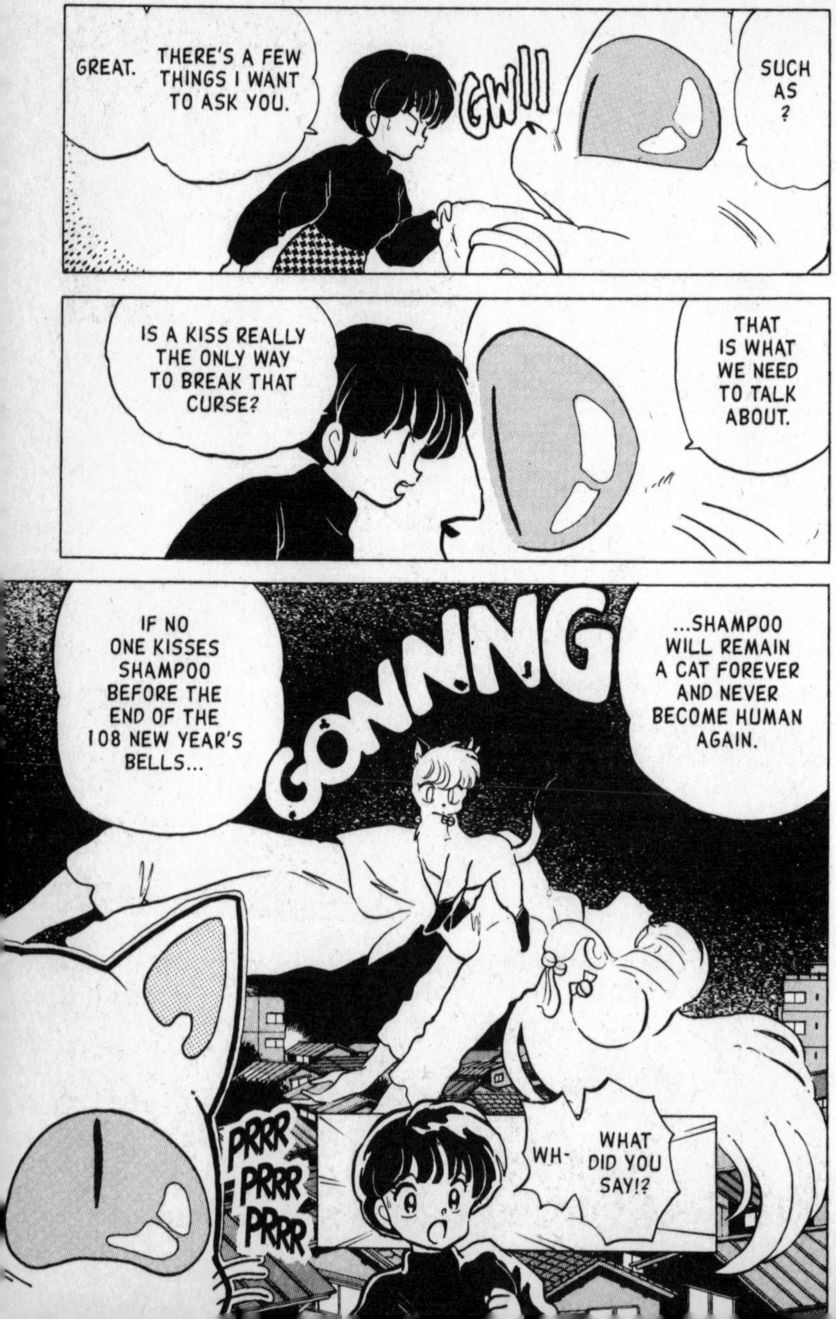
GREAT.
THERE'S A FEW THINGS I WANT TO ASK YOU.
GWII
SUCH AS?
IS A KISS REALLY THE ONLY WAY TO BREAK THAT CURSE?
THAT IS WHAT WE NEED TO TALK ABOUT.
IF NO ONE KISSES SHAMPOO BEFORE THE END OF THE 108 NEW YEAR'S BELLS...
GONNNG
...SHAMPOO WILL REMAIN A CAT FOREVER AND NEVER BECOME HUMAN AGAIN.
PRRR PRRR PRRR
WH-
WHAT DID YOU SAY!?

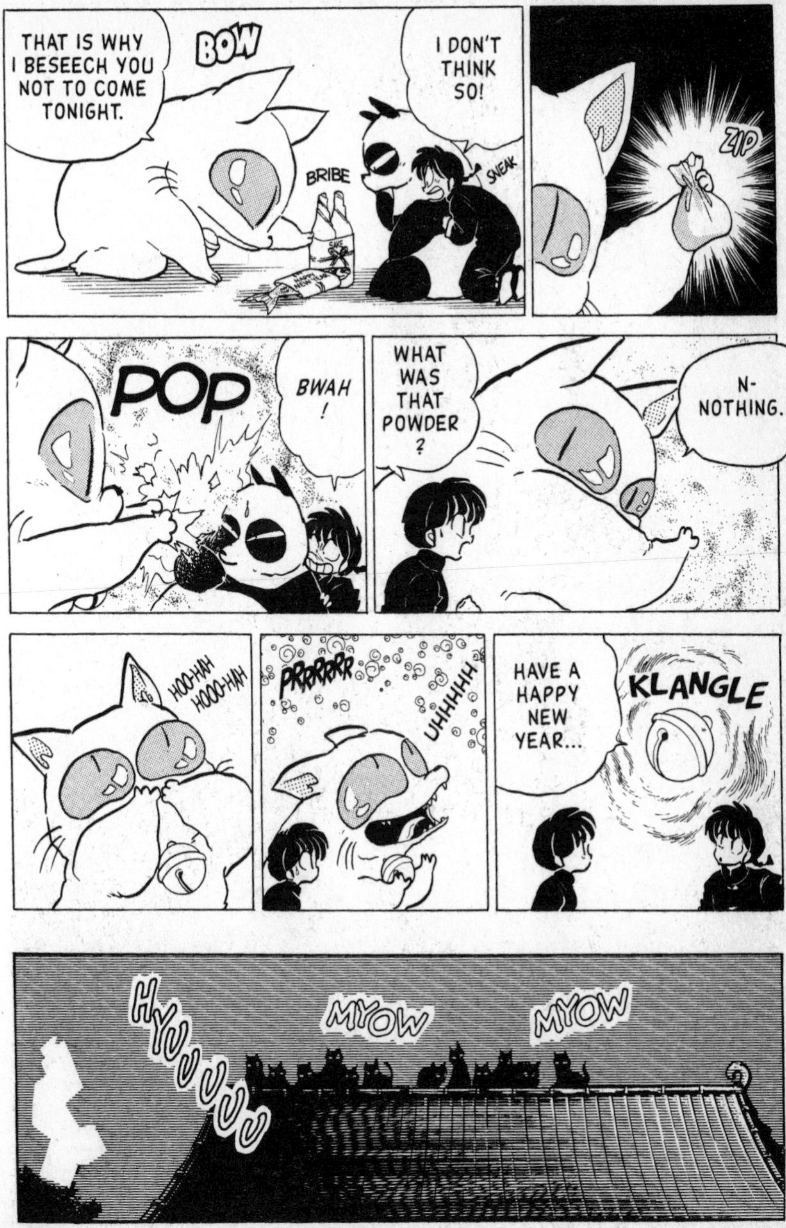
THAT IS WHY I BESEECH YOU NOT TO COME TONIGHT.
BOW
BRIBE
I DON'T THINK SO!
SNEAK
ZIP
POP
BWAH!
WHAT WAS THAT POWDER?
N-NOTHING...
HOO-HAH HOOO-HAH
PRRRRRR
UHHHHH
HAVE A HAPPY NEW YEAR...
KLANGLE
HYUUUUU
MYOW
MYOW

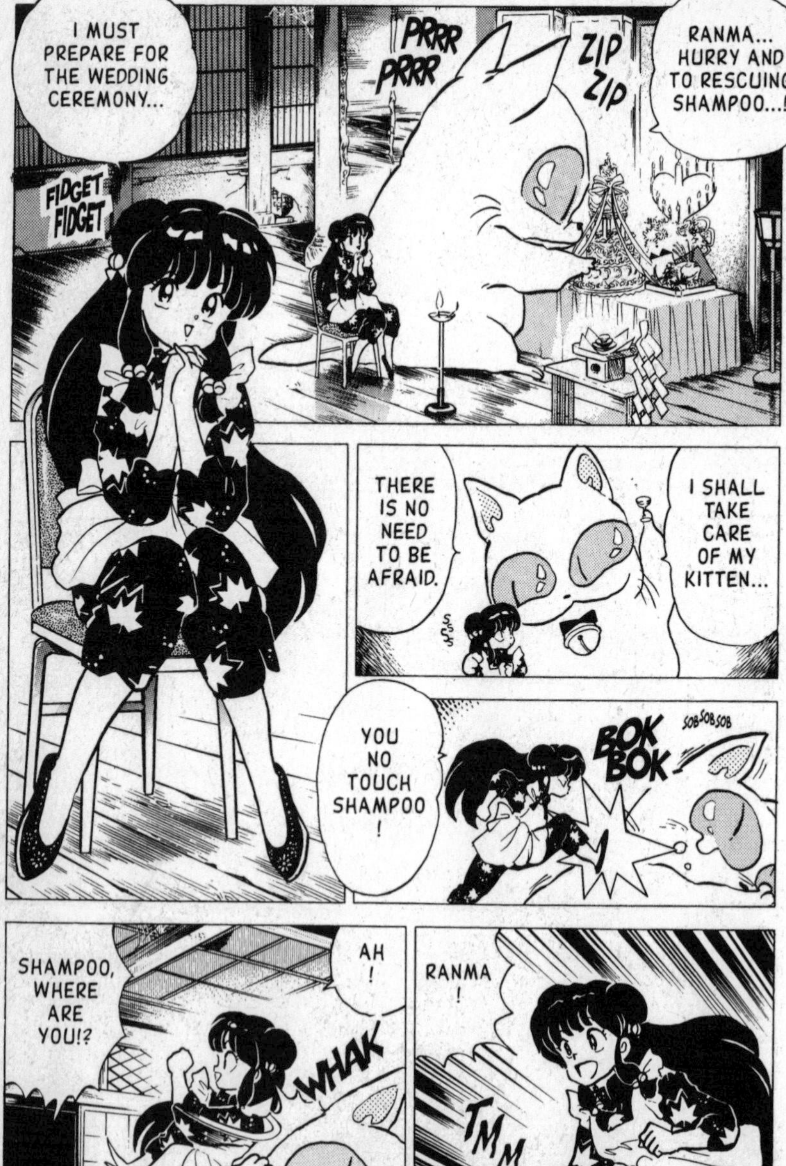

I MUST PREPARE FOR THE WEDDING CEREMONY...
FIDGET FIDGET
PRRR PRRR
ZIP ZIP
RANMA... HURRY AND TO RESCUING SHAMPOO...!
THERE IS NO NEED TO BE AFRAID.
I SHALL TAKE CARE OF MY KITTEN...
YOU NO TOUCH SHAMPOO!
BOK BOK
SOB SOB SOB
SHAMPOO, WHERE ARE YOU!?
AH!
WHAK
RANMA!
TMM

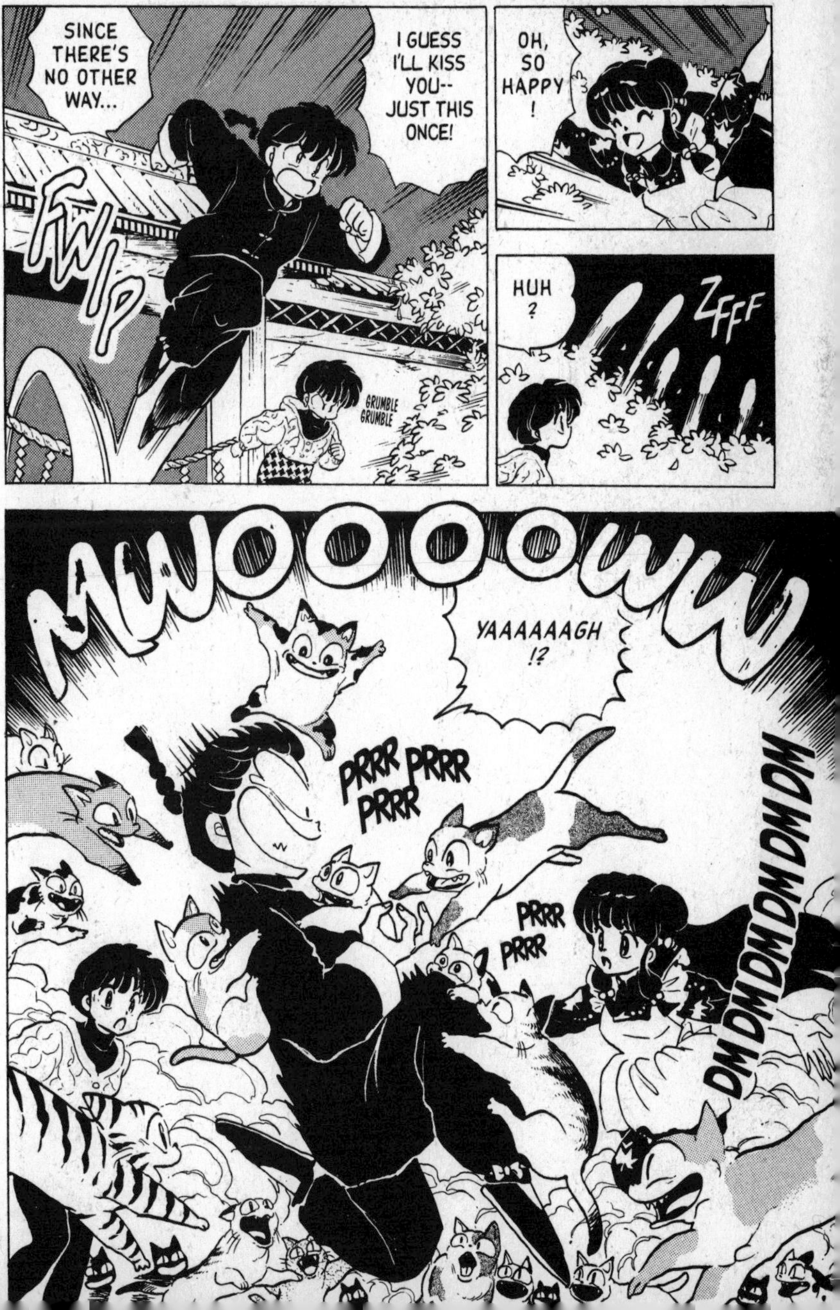
SINCE THERE'S NO OTHER WAY...
I GUESS I'LL KISS YOU-- JUST THIS ONCE!
FWIP
GRUMBLE GRUMBLE
OH, SO HAPPY!
HUH?
ZFFF
MWOOOOWW
YAAAAAAGH !?
PRRR PRRR PRRR
PRRR PRRR
DM DM DM DM DM DM

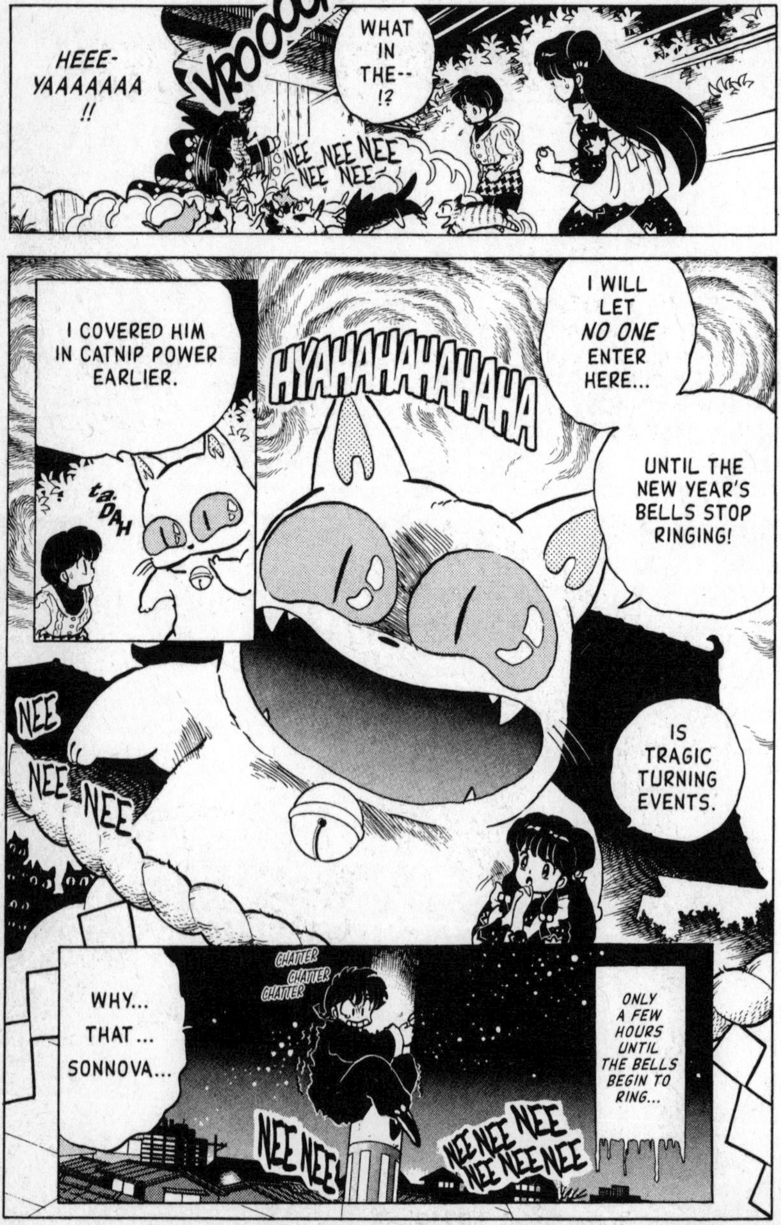
HEEE-YAAAAAAA!!
VROOOOM
WHAT IN THE--!?
NEE NEE NEE NEE NEE
I COVERED HIM IN CATNIP POWER EARLIER.
ta-DAH
HYAHAHAHAHAHA
I WILL LET NO ONE ENTER HERE...
UNTIL THE NEW YEAR'S BELLS STOP RINGING!
NEE
NEE NEE
IS TRAGIC TURNING EVENTS.
WHY... THAT... SONNOVA...
CHATTER CHATTER CHATTER
NEE NEE
NEE NEE NEE NEE NEE NEE
ONLY A FEW HOURS UNTIL THE BELLS BEGIN TO RING...

Part 8
RING PROPOSAL

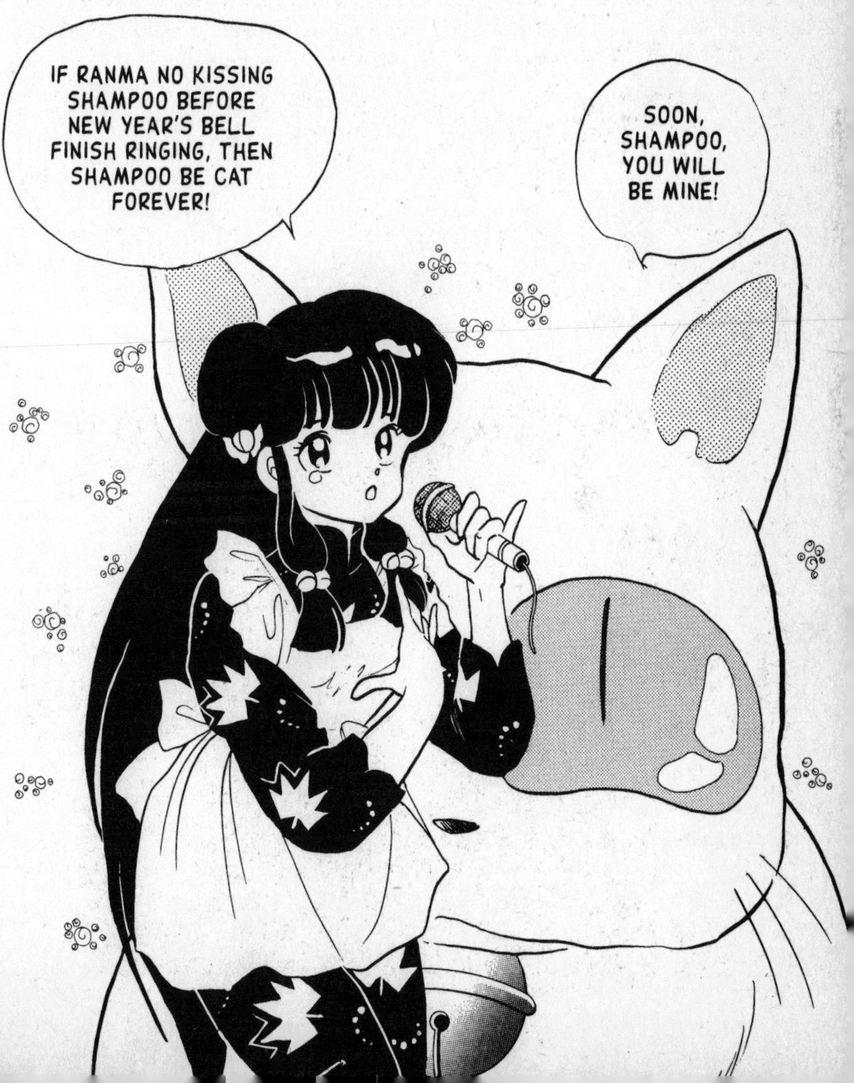
IF RANMA NO KISSING SHAMPOO BEFORE NEW YEAR'S BELL FINISH RINGING, THEN SHAMPOO BE CAT FOREVER!
SOON, SHAMPOO, YOU WILL BE MINE!

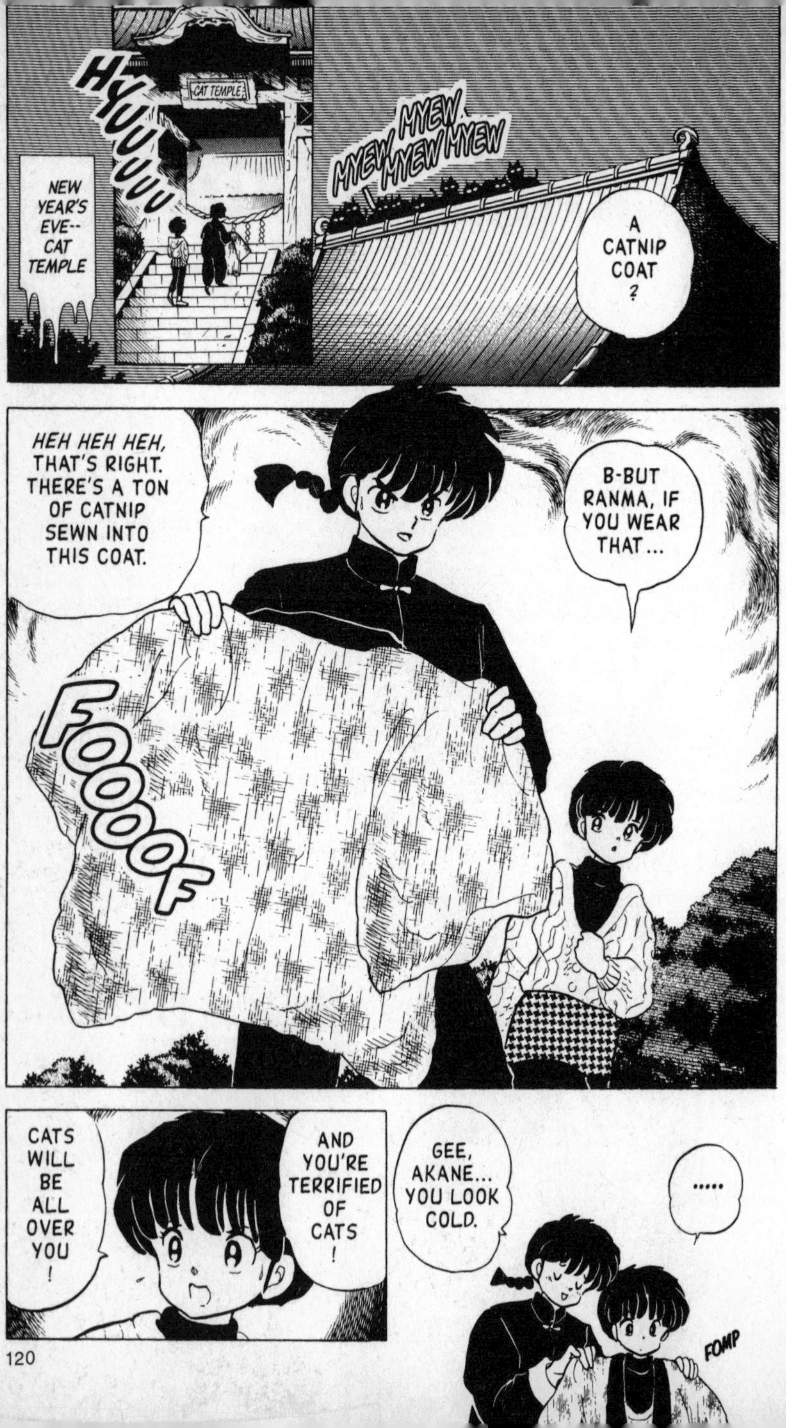
HYUUUUU
CAT TEMPLE
NEW YEAR'S EVE-- CAT TEMPLE
MYEW MYEW MYEW MYEW MYEW
A CATNIP COAT ?
HEH HEH HEH, THAT'S RIGHT. THERE'S A TON OF CATNIP SEWN INTO THIS COAT.
FOOOOOF
B-BUT RANMA, IF YOU WEAR THAT...
CATS WILL BE ALL OVER YOU !
AND YOU'RE TERRIFIED OF CATS !
GEE, AKANE... YOU LOOK COLD.
.....
FOMP

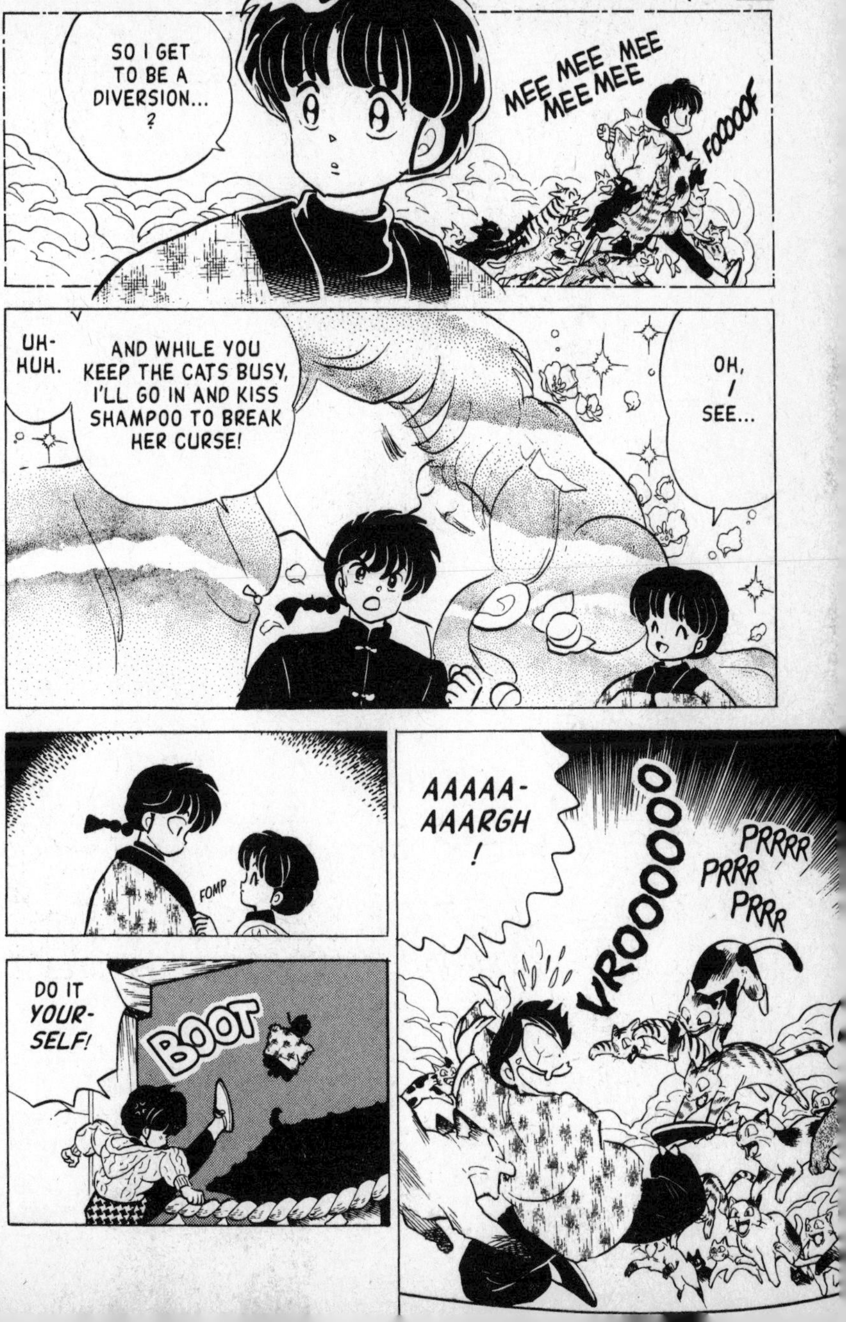
SO I GET TO BE A DIVERSION... ?
MEE MEE MEE MEE MEE
FOOOOOF
UH-HUH.
AND WHILE YOU KEEP THE CATS BUSY, I'LL GO IN AND KISS SHAMPOO TO BREAK HER CURSE!
OH, I SEE...
FOMP
DO IT *YOURSELF!*
BOOT
AAAAA-AAARGH!
VROOOOOOO
PRRRR
PRRR
PRRR

EE! EE! EE!

TUP TUP

PRRR PRRR

PRRR PRRR

BAD KITTY !!!

ZOP

HIYAA!

MEEE-YOWW

VROOOM

BRRRR

SHAMPOO!

WHRRR WHRRR

TA-DA

NOW, ACCEPT A KISS FROM ME!

MOOSH

WHY MUST YOU *ALWAYS* INTERFERE WITH ME!?

LOOK WHO'S *TALKING*!

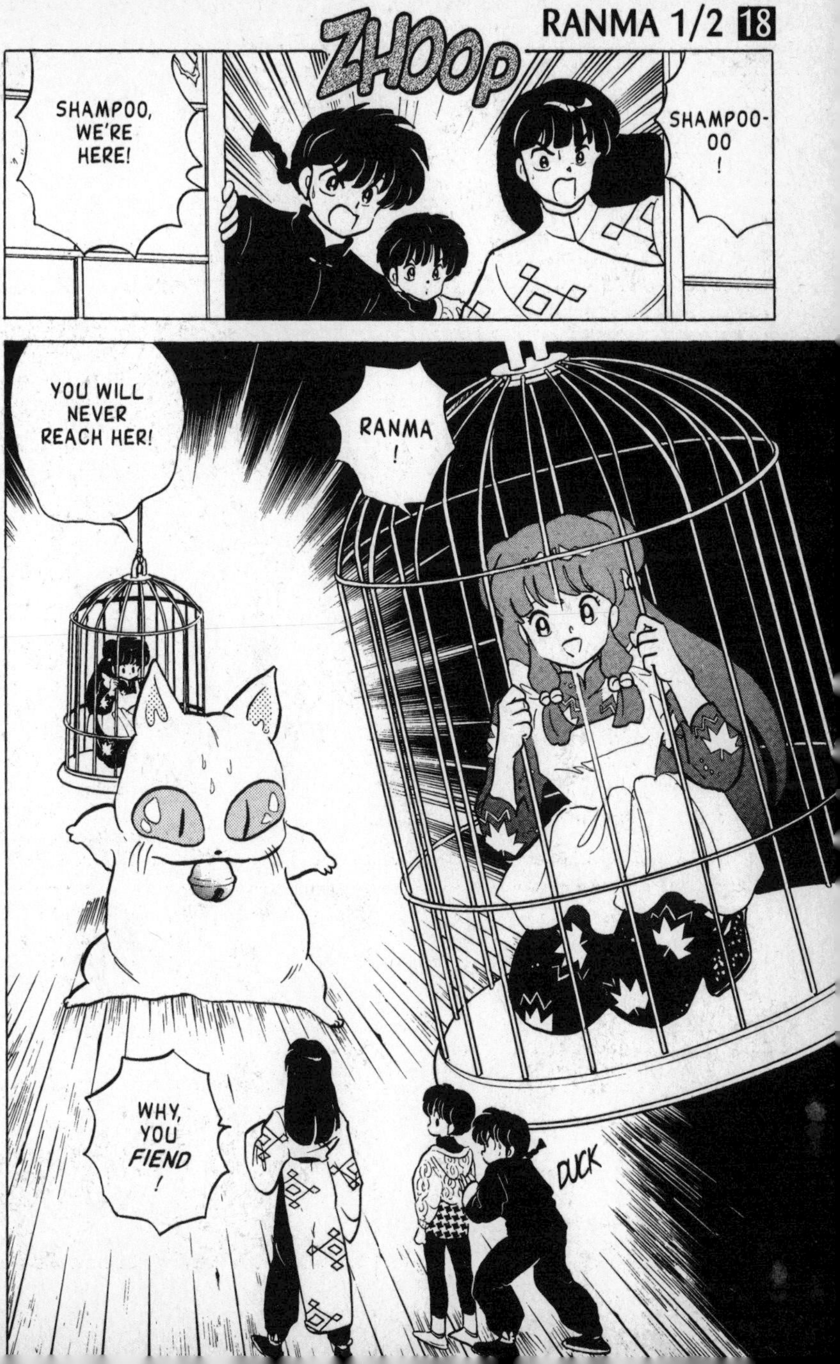
ZHOOP
SHAMPOO, WE'RE HERE!
SHAMPOO-OO!
YOU WILL NEVER REACH HER!
RANMA!
WHY, YOU FIEND!
DUCK

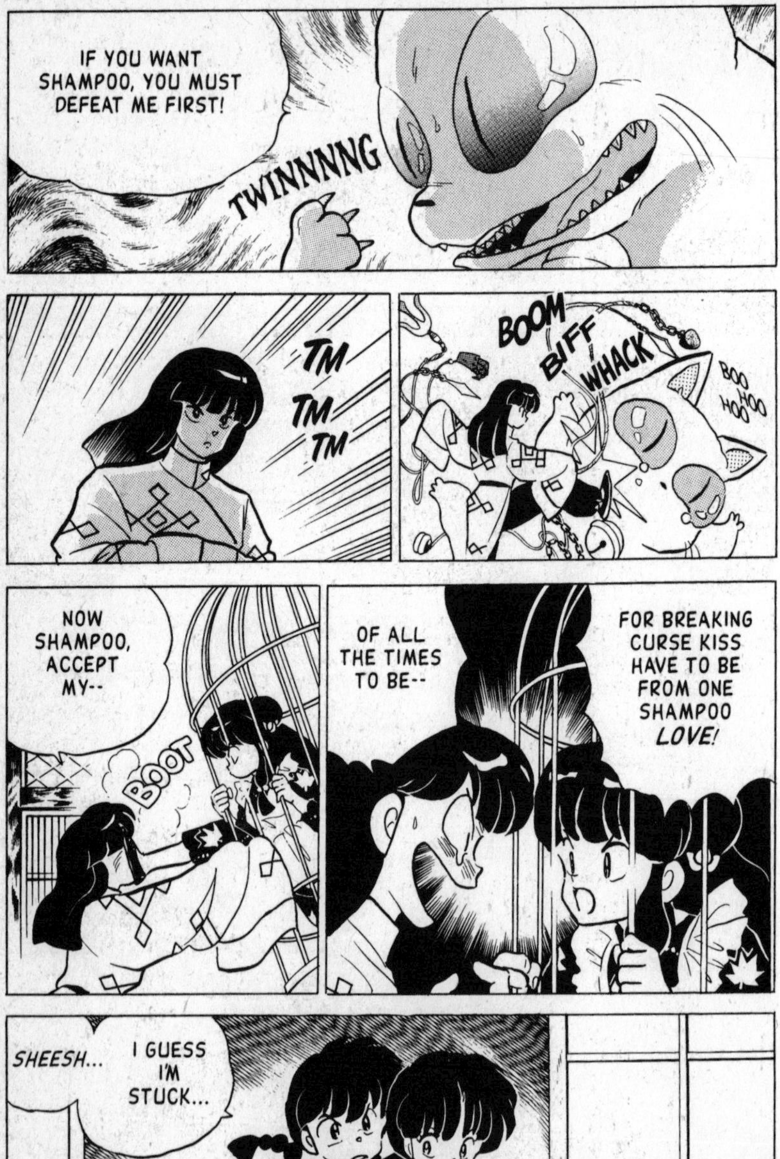
IF YOU WANT SHAMPOO, YOU MUST DEFEAT ME FIRST!
TWINNNNG
TM
TM
TM
BOOM
BIFF
WHACK
BOO HOO HOO
NOW SHAMPOO, ACCEPT MY--
BOOT
OF ALL THE TIMES TO BE--
FOR BREAKING CURSE KISS HAVE TO BE FROM ONE SHAMPOO *LOVE!*
SHEESH...
I GUESS I'M STUCK...

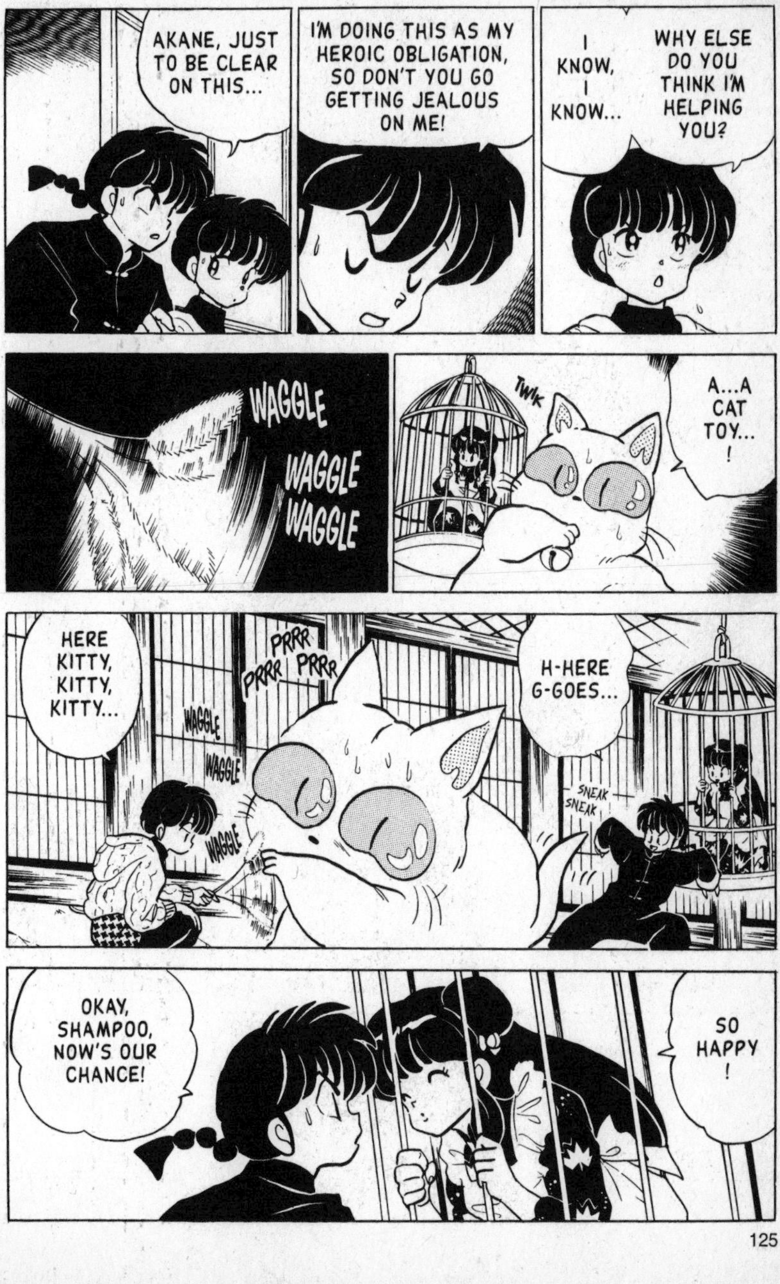
AKANE, JUST TO BE CLEAR ON THIS...
I'M DOING THIS AS MY HEROIC OBLIGATION, SO DON'T YOU GO GETTING JEALOUS ON ME!
I KNOW, I KNOW...
WHY ELSE DO YOU THINK I'M HELPING YOU?
WAGGLE
WAGGLE
WAGGLE
TWIK
A...A CAT TOY...!
HERE KITTY, KITTY, KITTY...
PRRR PRRR PRRR
WAGGLE
WAGGLE
WAGGLE
H-HERE G-GOES...
SNEAK SNEAK
OKAY, SHAMPOO, NOW'S OUR CHANCE!
SO HAPPY!

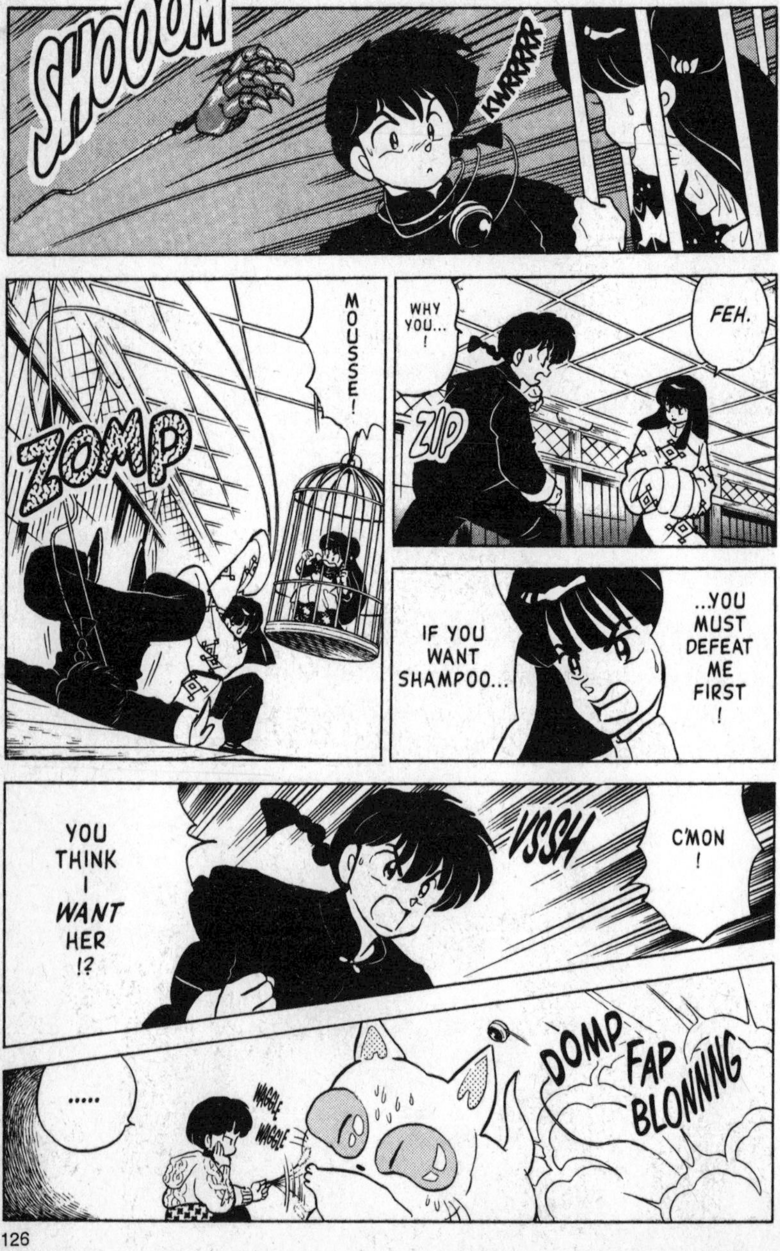
SHOOOM
KWRRRRRR
ZOMP
MOUSSE!
WHY YOU...!
ZIP
FEH.
IF YOU WANT SHAMPOO...
...YOU MUST DEFEAT ME FIRST!
YOU THINK I *WANT* HER!?
VSSH
C'MON!
......
WAGGLE WAGGLE
DOMP
FAP
BLONNNG

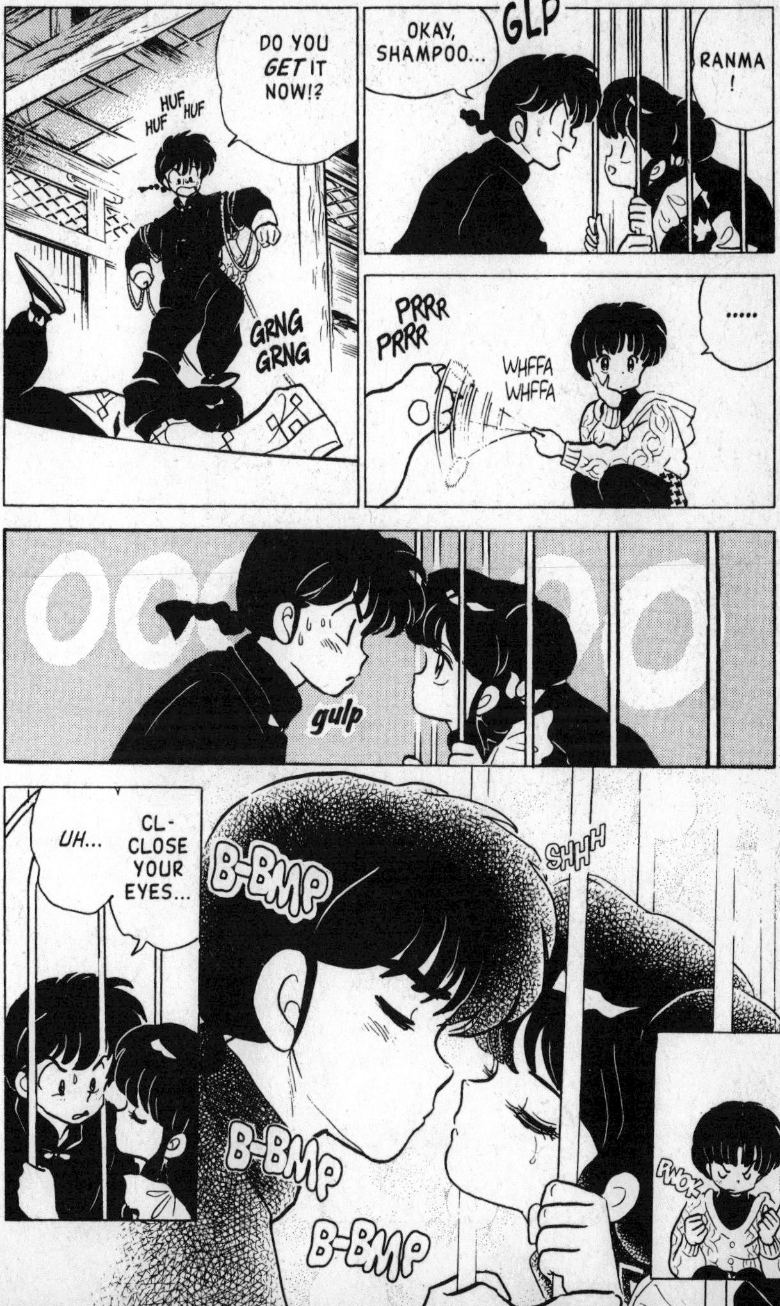
HUF HUF HUF
DO YOU GET IT NOW!?
GRNG GRNG
OKAY, SHAMPOO...
GLP
RANMA!
PRRR PRRR
WHFFA WHFFA
......
gulp
UH... CL- CLOSE YOUR EYES...
B-BMP
SHHH
B-BMP
B-BMP
PWOK

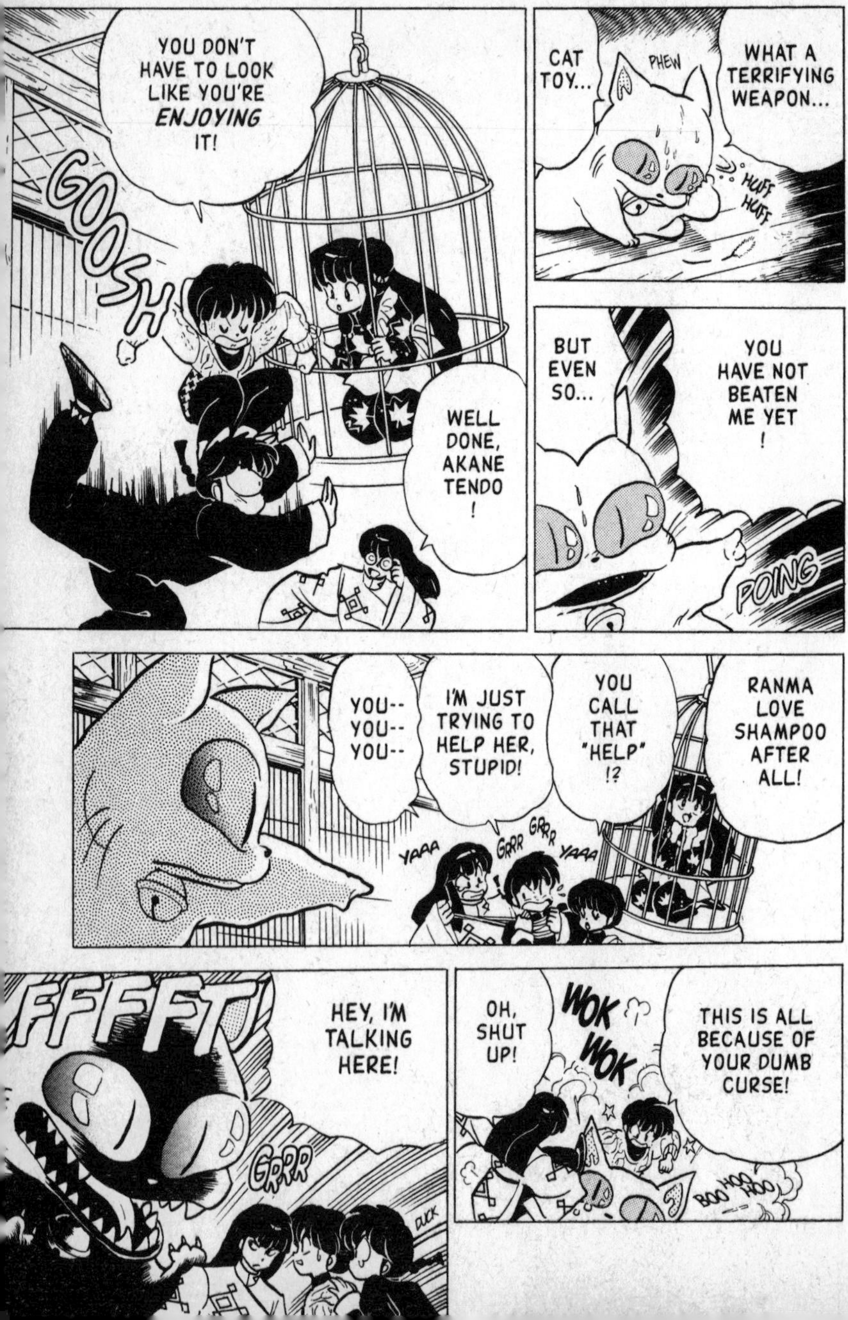
YOU DON'T HAVE TO LOOK LIKE YOU'RE *ENJOYING* IT!
GOOSH
WELL DONE, AKANE TENDO !
CAT TOY...
PHEW
WHAT A TERRIFYING WEAPON...
HUFF HUFF
BUT EVEN SO...
YOU HAVE NOT BEATEN ME YET !
POING
YOU-- YOU-- YOU--
I'M JUST TRYING TO HELP HER, STUPID!
YOU CALL THAT "HELP" !?
RANMA LOVE SHAMPOO AFTER ALL!
YAAA
GRRR
GRRR
YAAA
FFFFT!
HEY, I'M TALKING HERE!
GRRR
DUCK
OH, SHUT UP!
WOK WOK
THIS IS ALL BECAUSE OF YOUR DUMB CURSE!
BOO HOO HOO

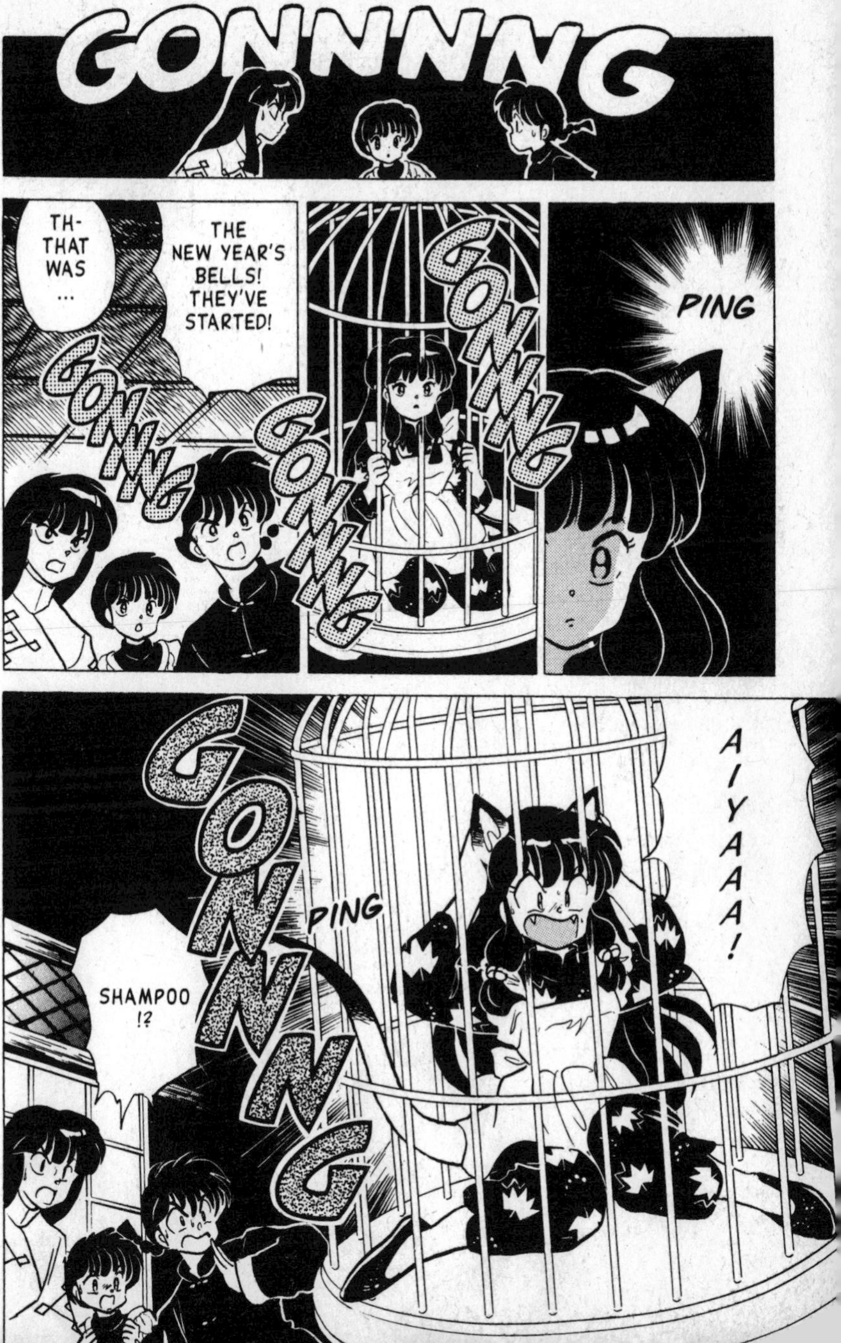
GONNNNG
TH- THAT WAS ...
THE NEW YEAR'S BELLS! THEY'VE STARTED!
GONNNG
GONNNG
GONNNG
PING
GONNNNG
PING
SHAMPOO !?
AIYAAAA!

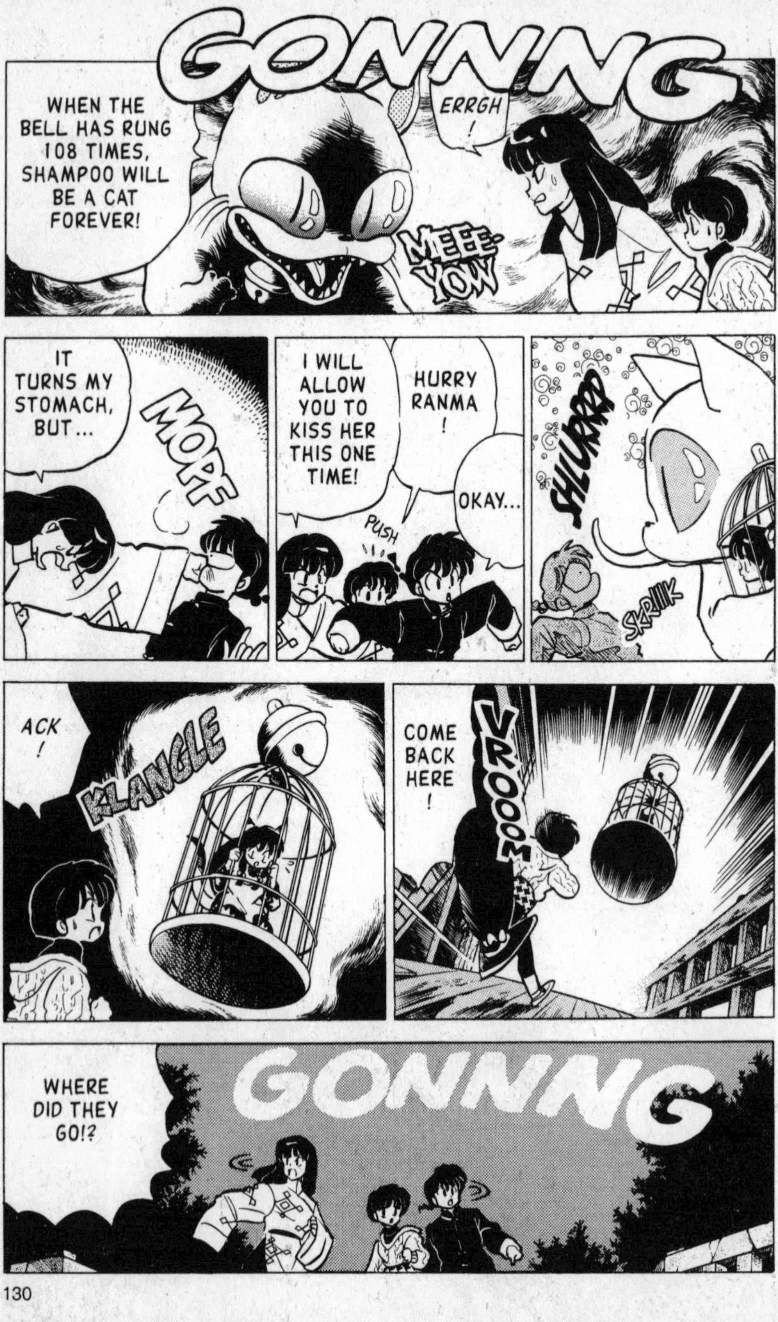
GONNNG
WHEN THE BELL HAS RUNG 108 TIMES, SHAMPOO WILL BE A CAT FOREVER!
ERRGH!
MEEE-YOW
IT TURNS MY STOMACH, BUT...
MOPF
I WILL ALLOW YOU TO KISS HER THIS ONE TIME!
HURRY RANMA!
PUSH
OKAY...
SHLURRRP
SKRIIIK
ACK!
KLANGLE
COME BACK HERE!
VROOOOM
WHERE DID THEY GO!?
GONNNG

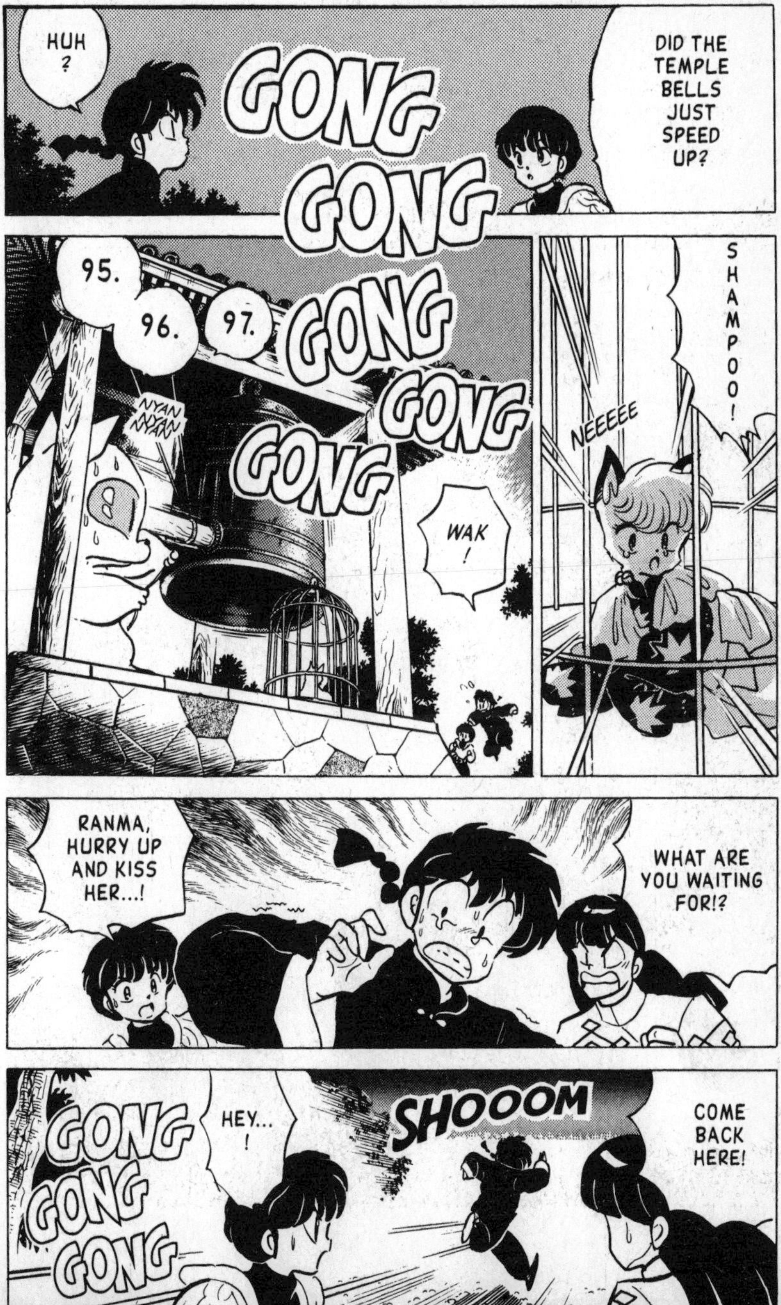
HUH?
GONG
GONG
DID THE TEMPLE BELLS JUST SPEED UP?
95.
96.
97.
NYAN NYAN NYAN
GONG
GONG
GONG
WAK!
SHAMPOO!
NEEEEE
RANMA, HURRY UP AND KISS HER...!
WHAT ARE YOU WAITING FOR!?
GONG
GONG
GONG
HEY...!
SHOOOM
COME BACK HERE!

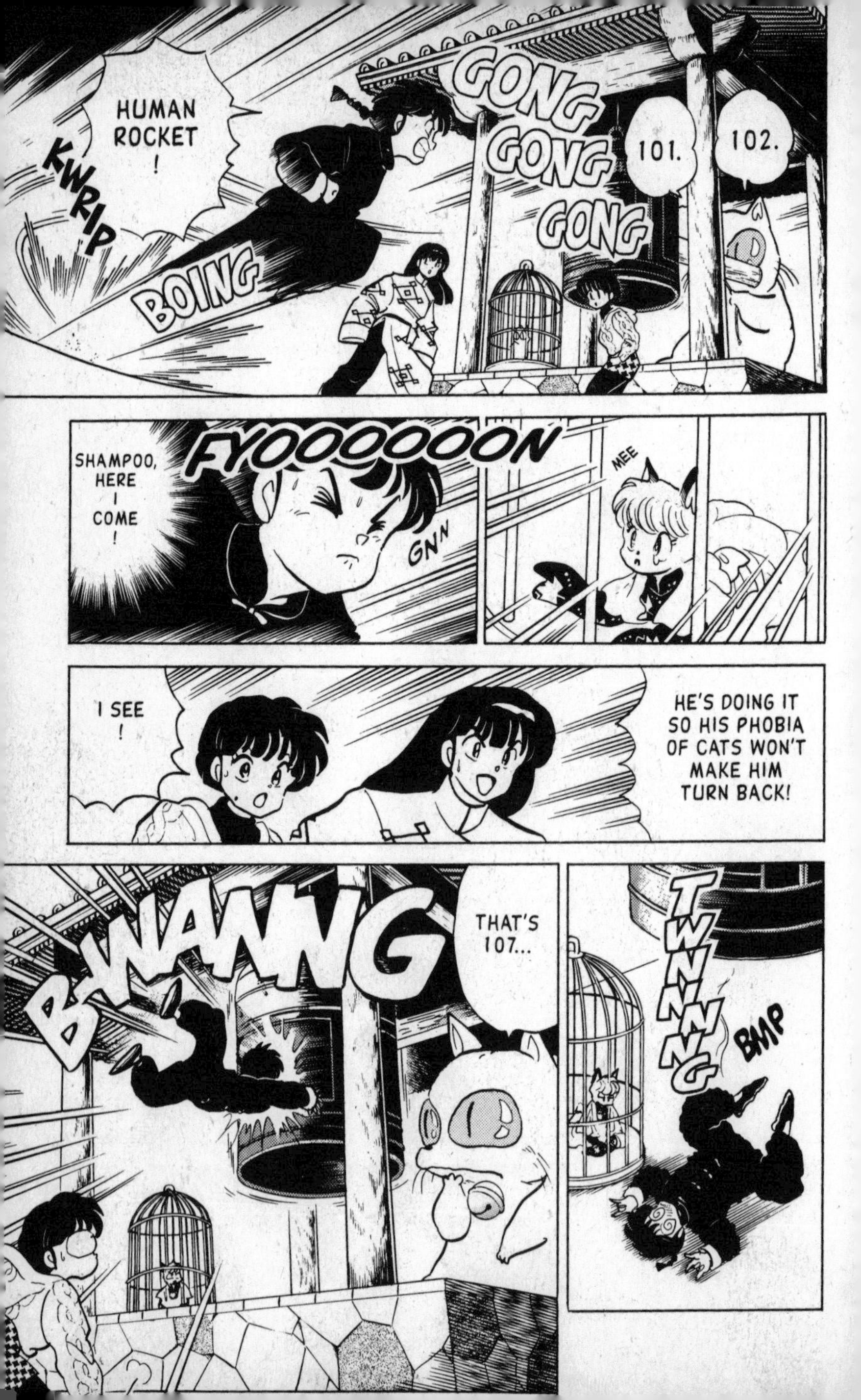
HUMAN ROCKET !
KWRIP
BOING
GONG GONG GONG
101.
102.
SHAMPOO, HERE I COME !
FYOOOOOOON
GNN
MEE
I SEE !
HE'S DOING IT SO HIS PHOBIA OF CATS WON'T MAKE HIM TURN BACK!
BWANNG
THAT'S 107...
TWNNNG
BMP

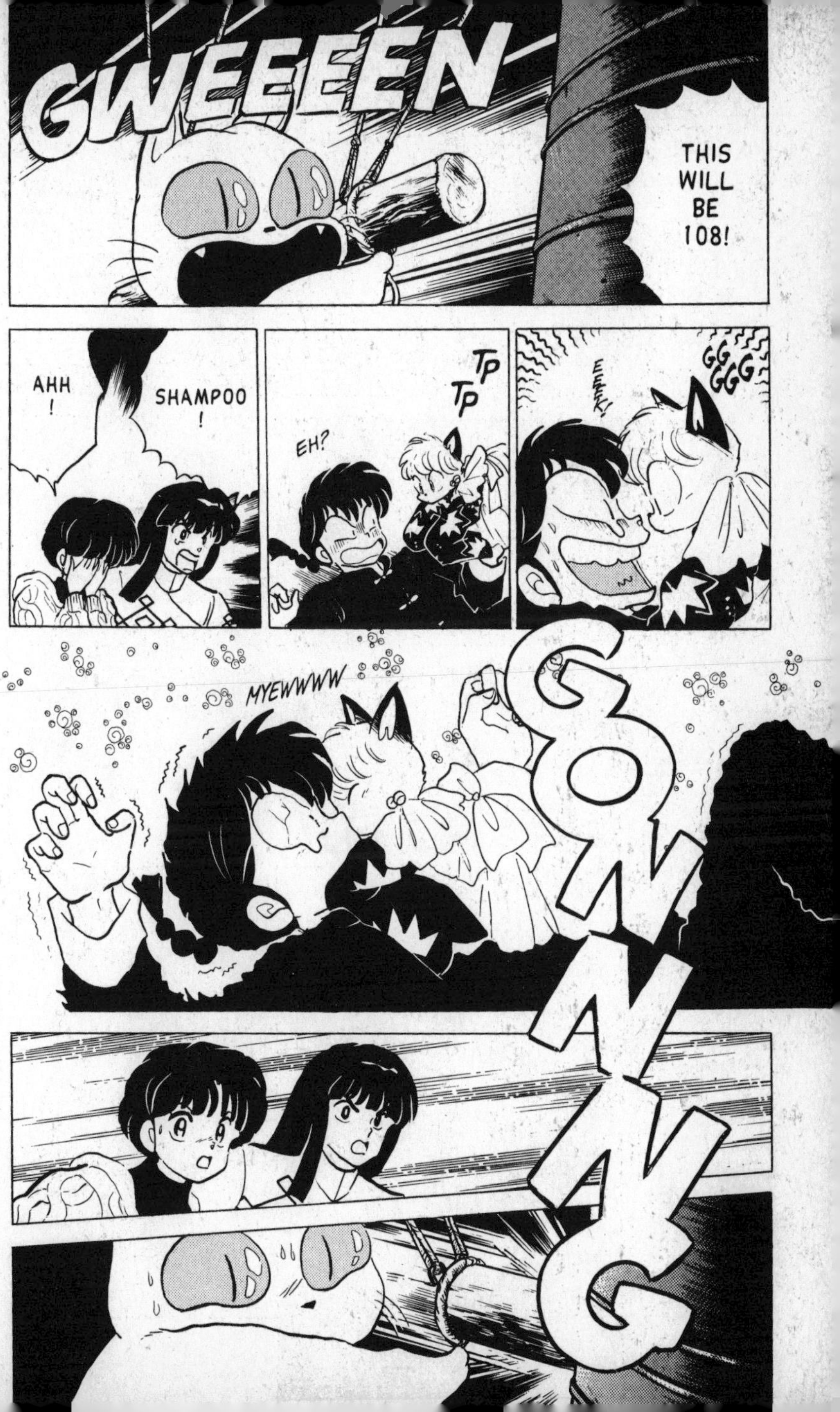
GWEEEEN
THIS WILL BE 108!
AHH!
SHAMPOO!
EH?
TP TP
EEEK!
GGGG GGG
MYEWWWW
GONNNG

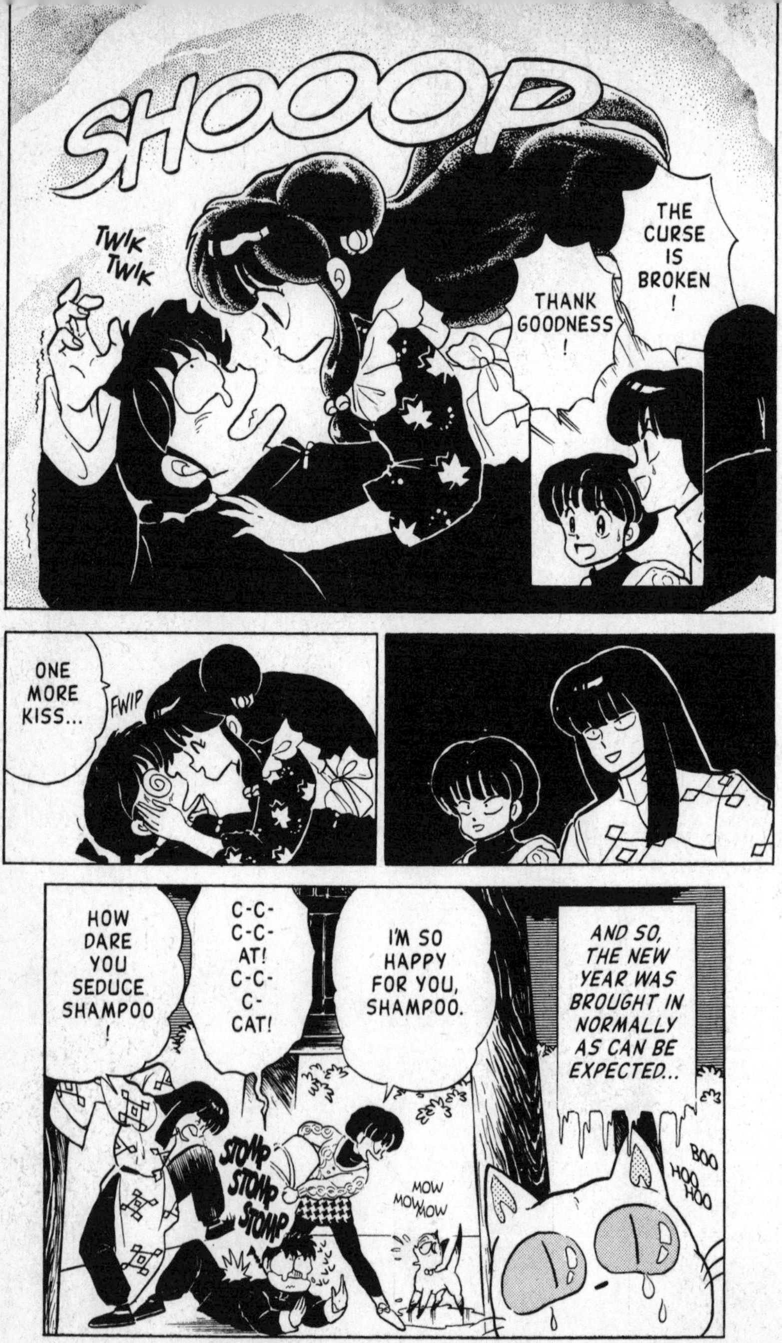
SHOOOP
TWIK TWIK
THANK GOODNESS!
THE CURSE IS BROKEN!
ONE MORE KISS...
FWIP
HOW DARE YOU SEDUCE SHAMPOO!
C-C-C-C-AT! C-C-C-CAT!
I'M SO HAPPY FOR YOU, SHAMPOO.
AND SO, THE NEW YEAR WAS BROUGHT IN NORMALLY AS CAN BE EXPECTED...
STOMP STOMP STOMP
MOW MOW MOW
BOO HOO HOO

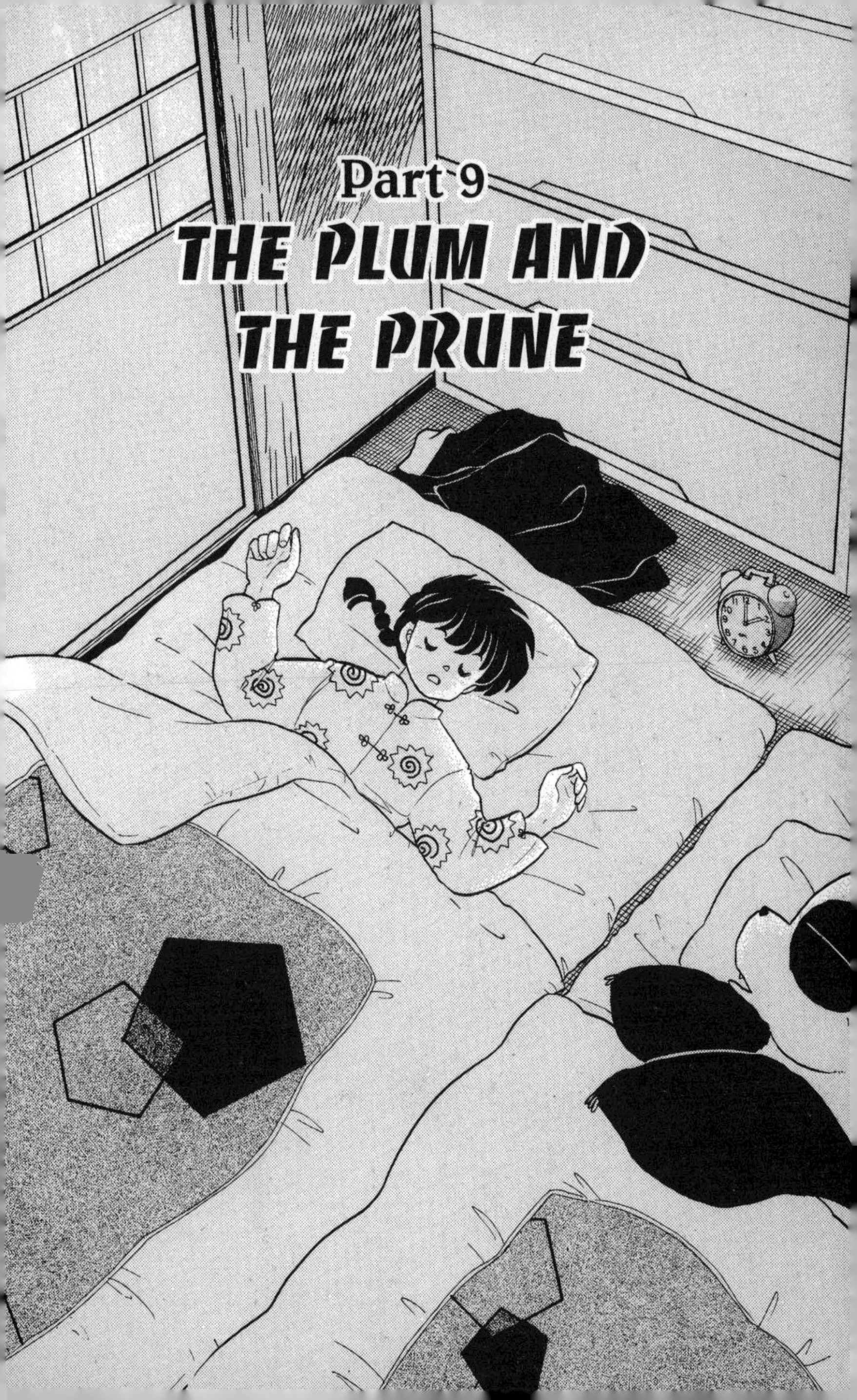
Part 9
THE PLUM AND
THE PRUNE

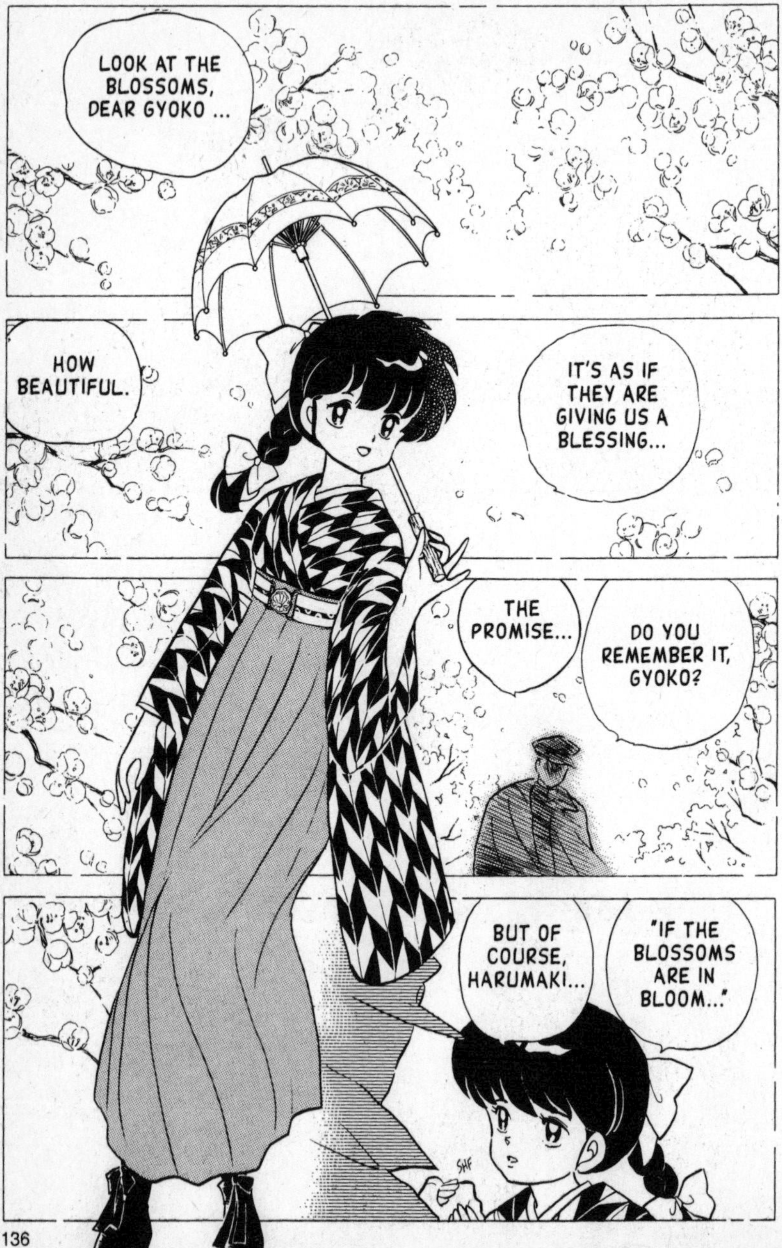
LOOK AT THE BLOSSOMS, DEAR GYOKO ...
HOW BEAUTIFUL.
IT'S AS IF THEY ARE GIVING US A BLESSING...
THE PROMISE...
DO YOU REMEMBER IT, GYOKO?
BUT OF COURSE, HARUMAKI...
"IF THE BLOSSOMS ARE IN BLOOM..."
SHF

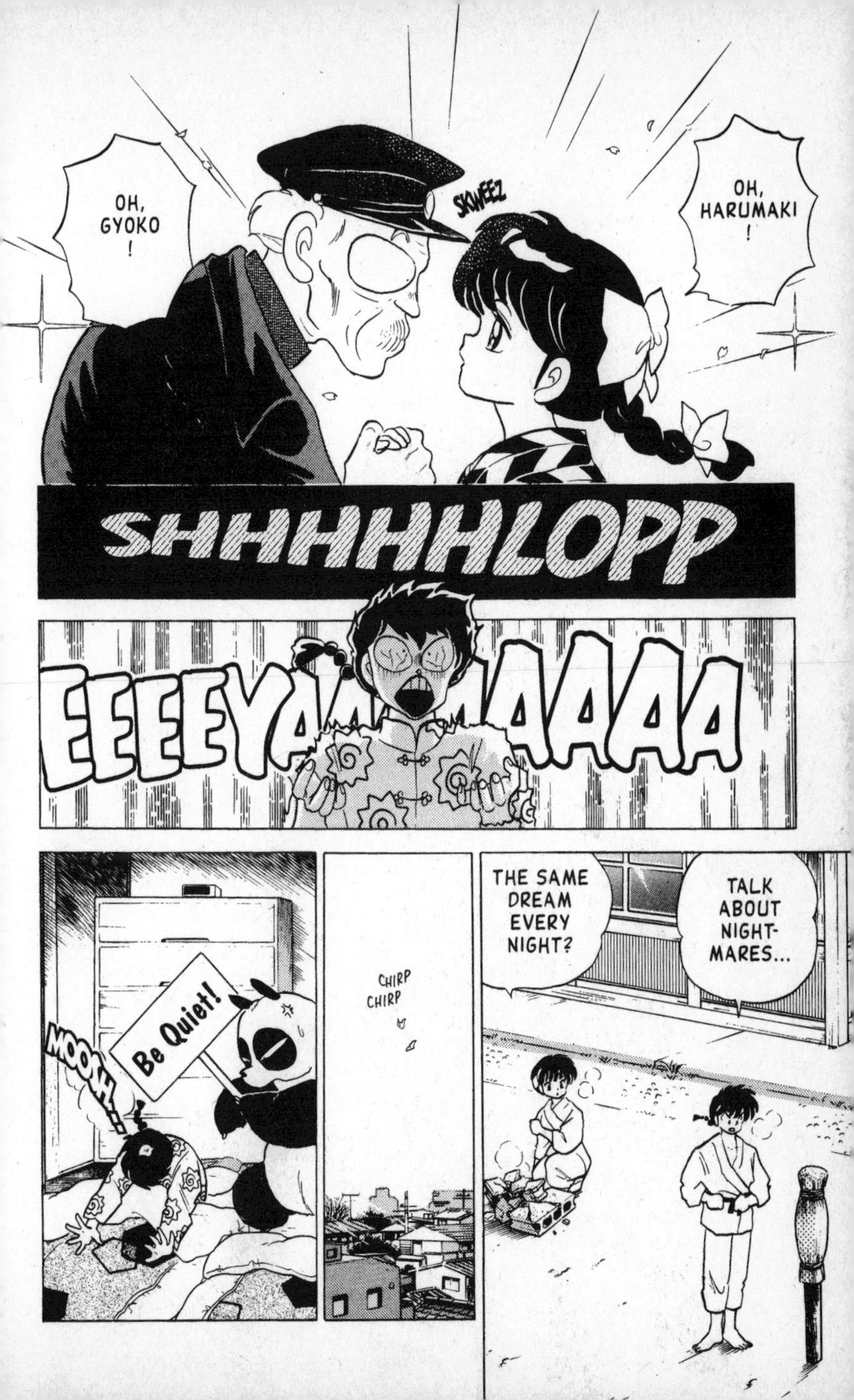
OH, GYOKO!
SKWEEZ
OH, HARUMAKI!
SHHHHHLOPP
EEEEYAAAAAAAA
MOOSH...
Be Quiet!
CHIRP CHIRP
THE SAME DREAM EVERY NIGHT?
TALK ABOUT NIGHT-MARES...

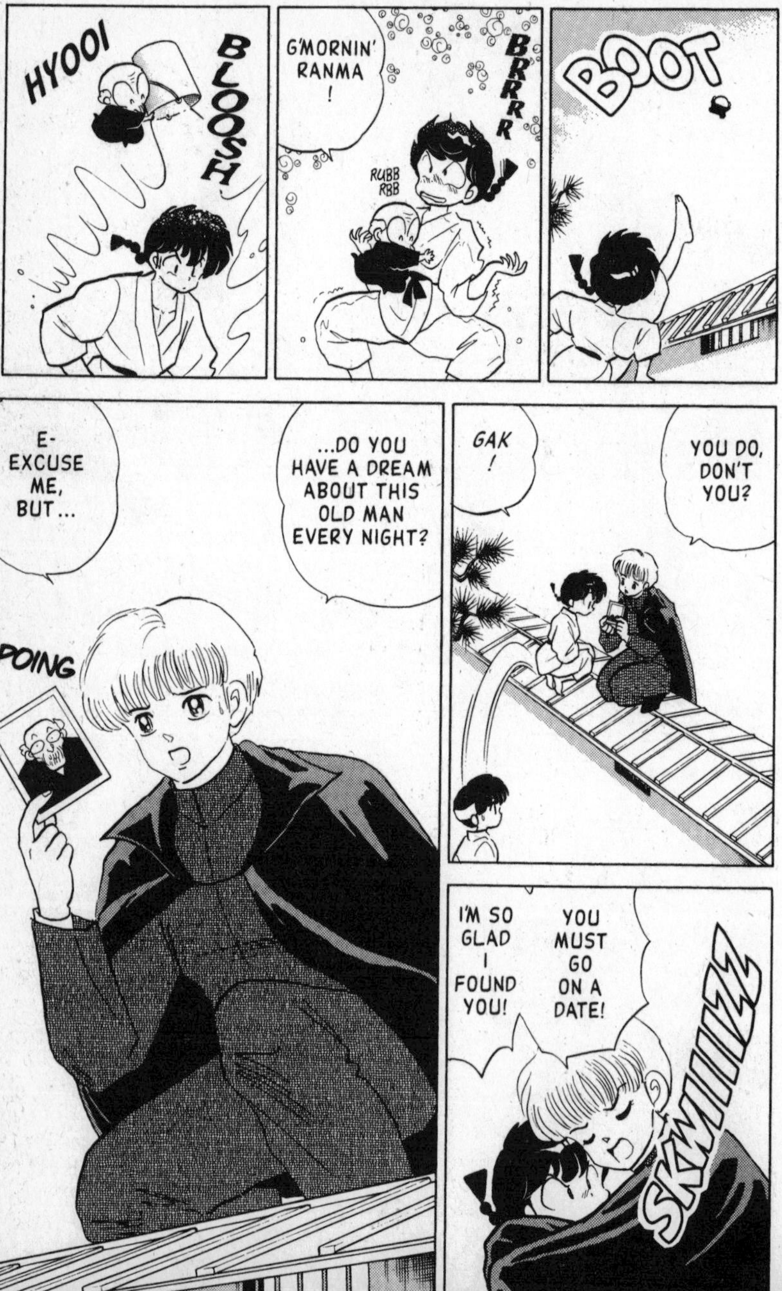
HYOOI
BLOOSH
G'MORNIN' RANMA !
BRRRR
RUBB RBB
BOOT
E- EXCUSE ME, BUT ...
...DO YOU HAVE A DREAM ABOUT THIS OLD MAN EVERY NIGHT?
POING
GAK !
YOU DO, DON'T YOU?
I'M SO GLAD I FOUND YOU!
YOU MUST GO ON A DATE!
SKWIIIZZ

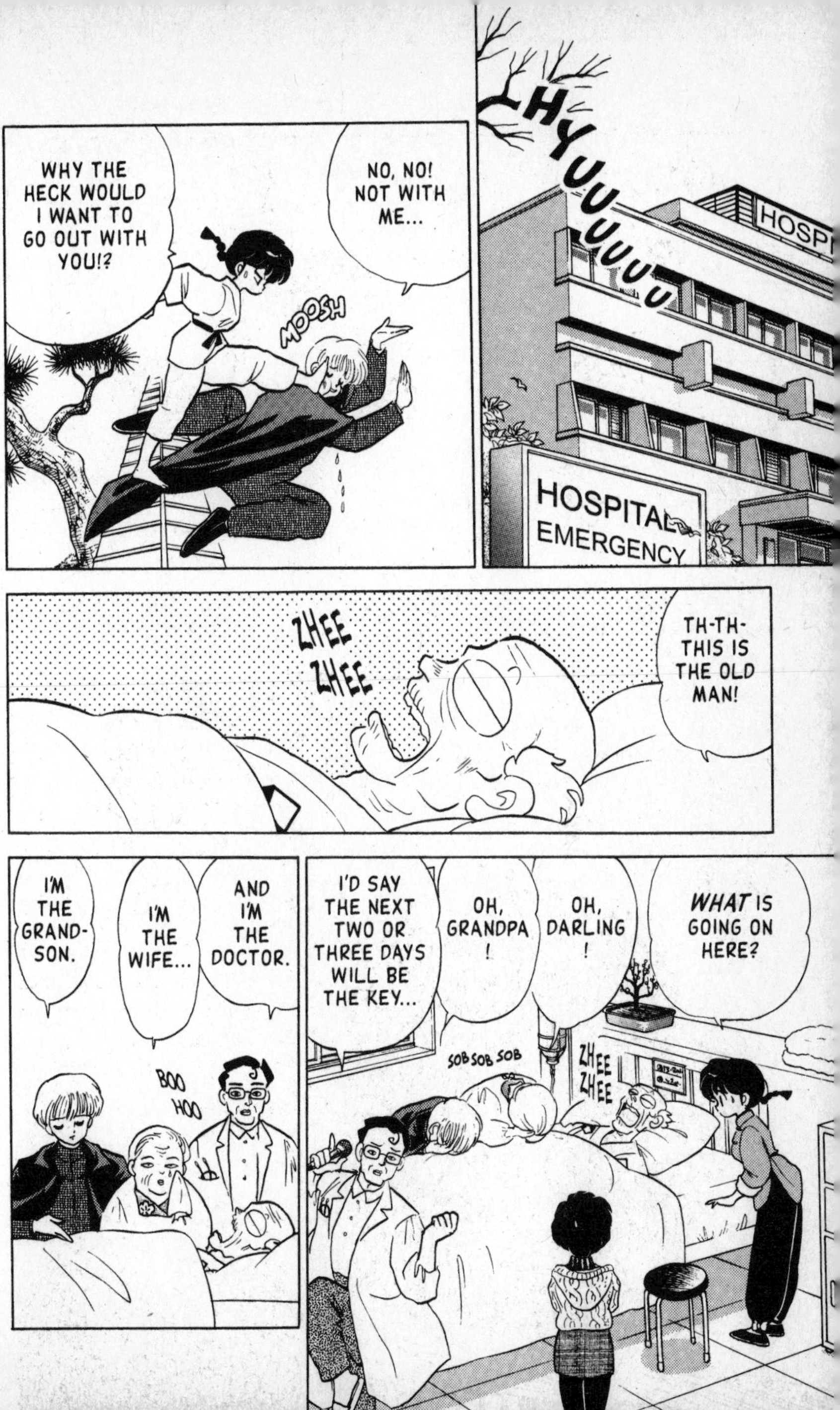

WHY THE HECK WOULD I WANT TO GO OUT WITH YOU!?
NO, NO! NOT WITH ME...
MOOSH
HYUUUUUUU
HOSPI
HOSPITAL
EMERGENCY
ZHEE ZHEE
TH-TH-THIS IS THE OLD MAN!
I'M THE GRAND-SON.
I'M THE WIFE...
AND I'M THE DOCTOR.
BOO HOO
I'D SAY THE NEXT TWO OR THREE DAYS WILL BE THE KEY...
OH, GRANDPA!
OH, DARLING!
WHAT IS GOING ON HERE?
SOB SOB SOB
ZHEE ZHEE

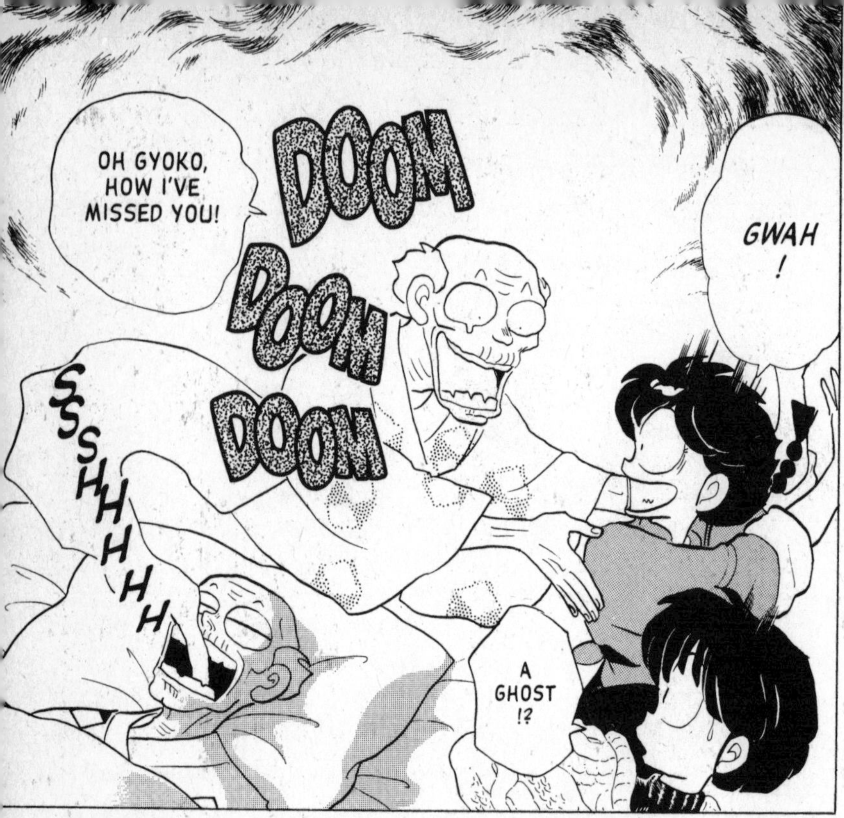
OH GYOKO, HOW I'VE MISSED YOU!
DOOM
DOOM
DOOM
GWAH!
SSHHHHH
A GHOST!?

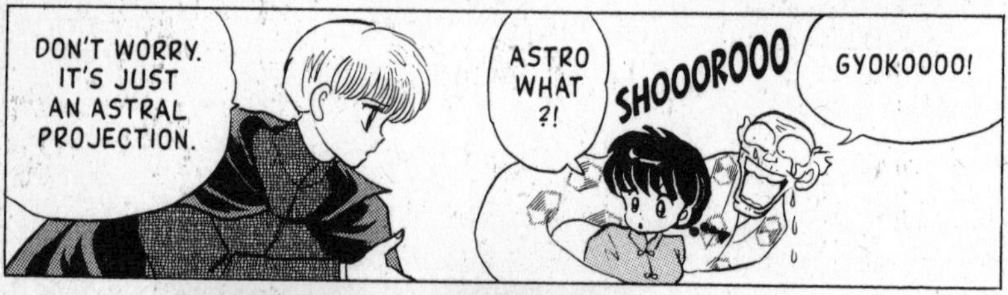
DON'T WORRY. IT'S JUST AN ASTRAL PROJECTION.
ASTRO WHAT?!
SHOOOROOO
GYOKOOOO!

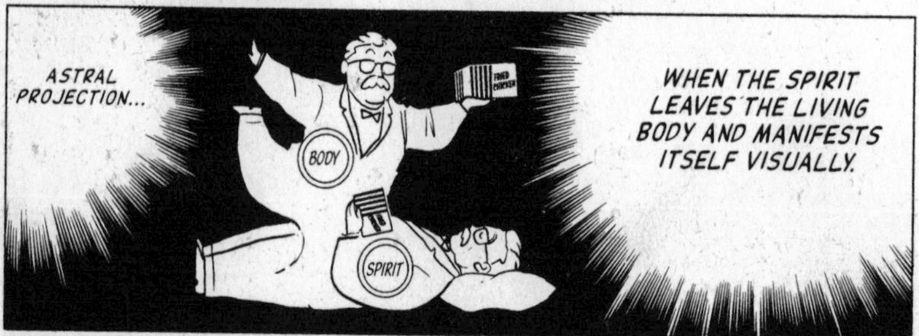
ASTRAL PROJECTION...
BODY
SPIRIT
WHEN THE SPIRIT LEAVES THE LIVING BODY AND MANIFESTS ITSELF VISUALLY.

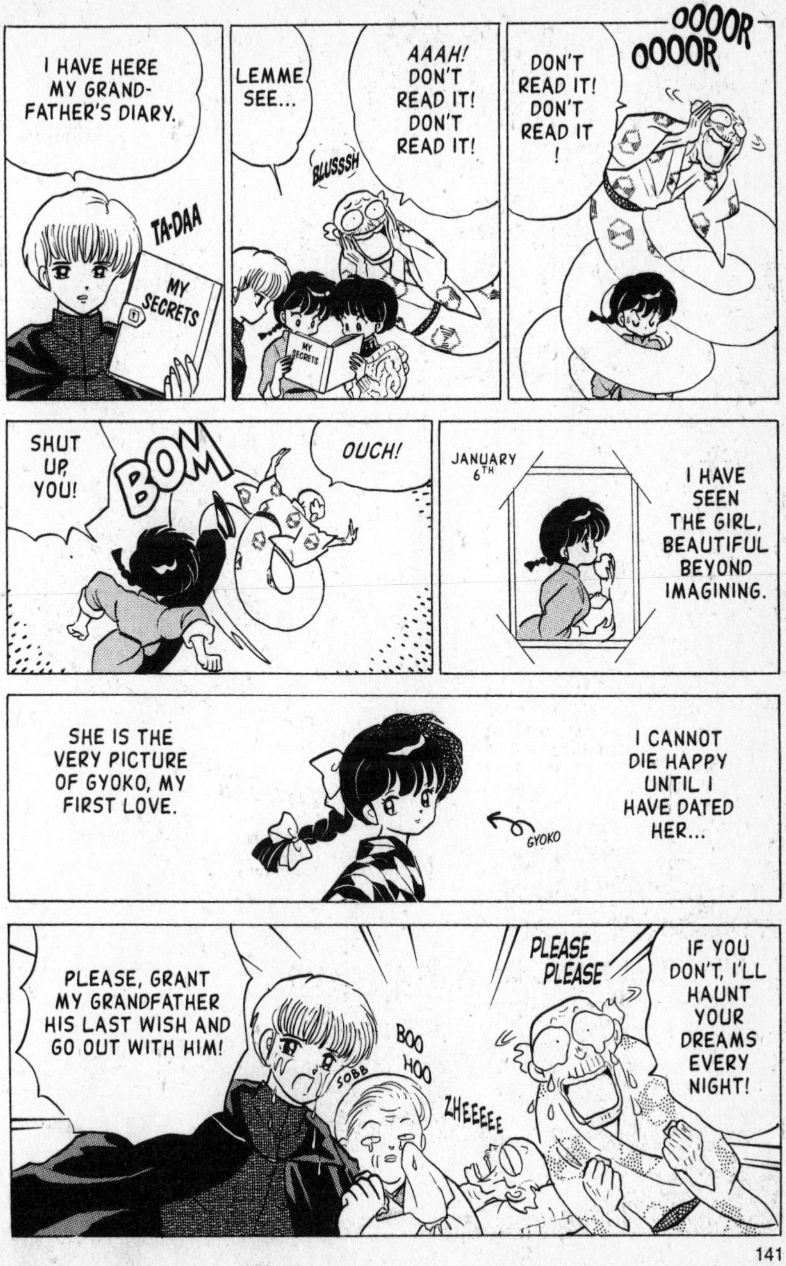
I HAVE HERE MY GRAND-FATHER'S DIARY.
TA-DAA
MY SECRETS
LEMME SEE...
AAAH! DON'T READ IT! DON'T READ IT!
BLUSSSH
MY SECRETS
DON'T READ IT! DON'T READ IT !
OOOOR OOOOR
SHUT UP, YOU!
BOM
OUCH!
JANUARY 6TH
I HAVE SEEN THE GIRL, BEAUTIFUL BEYOND IMAGINING.
SHE IS THE VERY PICTURE OF GYOKO, MY FIRST LOVE.
GYOKO
I CANNOT DIE HAPPY UNTIL I HAVE DATED HER...
PLEASE, GRANT MY GRANDFATHER HIS LAST WISH AND GO OUT WITH HIM!
BOO HOO
SOBB
ZHEEEEEE
PLEASE PLEASE
IF YOU DON'T, I'LL HAUNT YOUR DREAMS EVERY NIGHT!

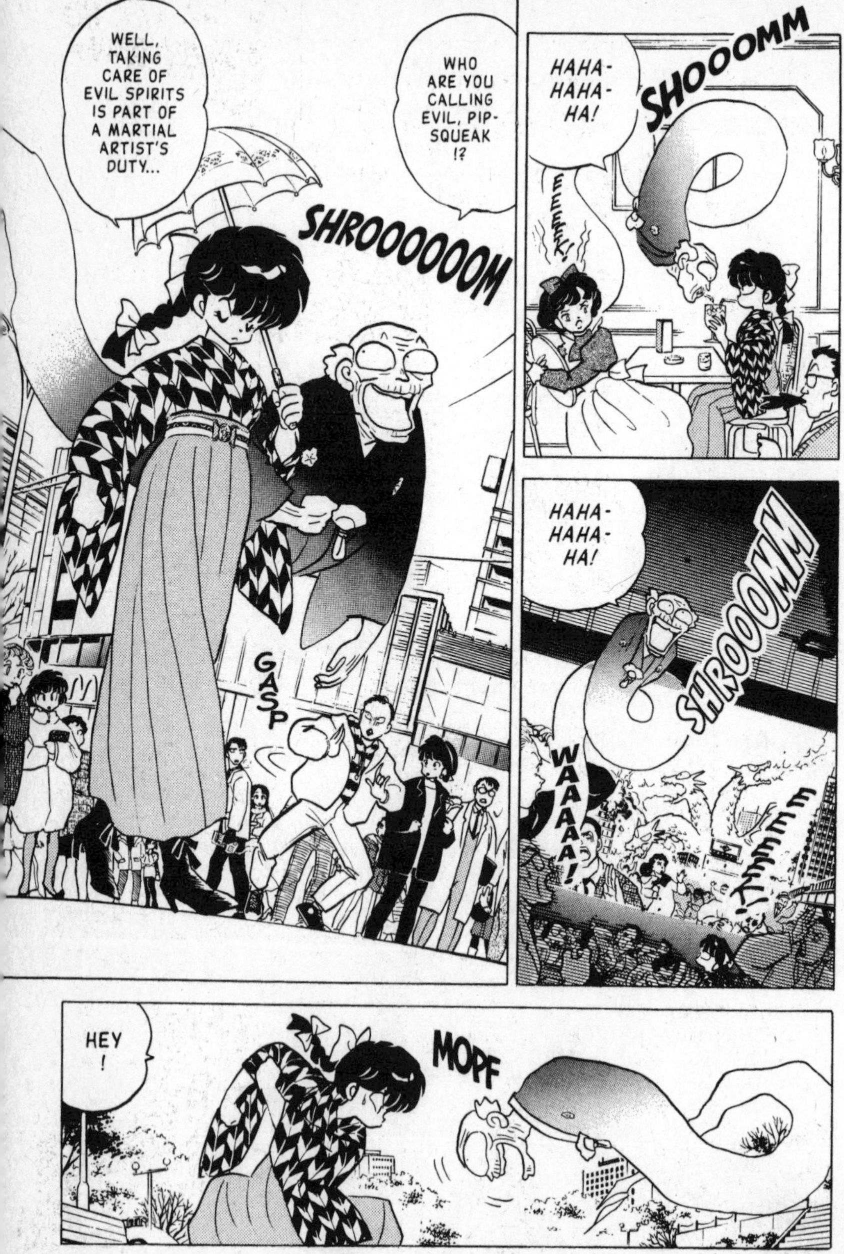
WELL, TAKING CARE OF EVIL SPIRITS IS PART OF A MARTIAL ARTIST'S DUTY...
WHO ARE YOU CALLING EVIL, PIP-SQUEAK!?
SHROOOOOOOM
GASP
HAHA-HAHA-HA!
SHOOOMM
EEEEK!
HAHA-HAHA-HA!
SHROOOMM
WAAAAA!
EEEEEEK!
HEY!
MOPF

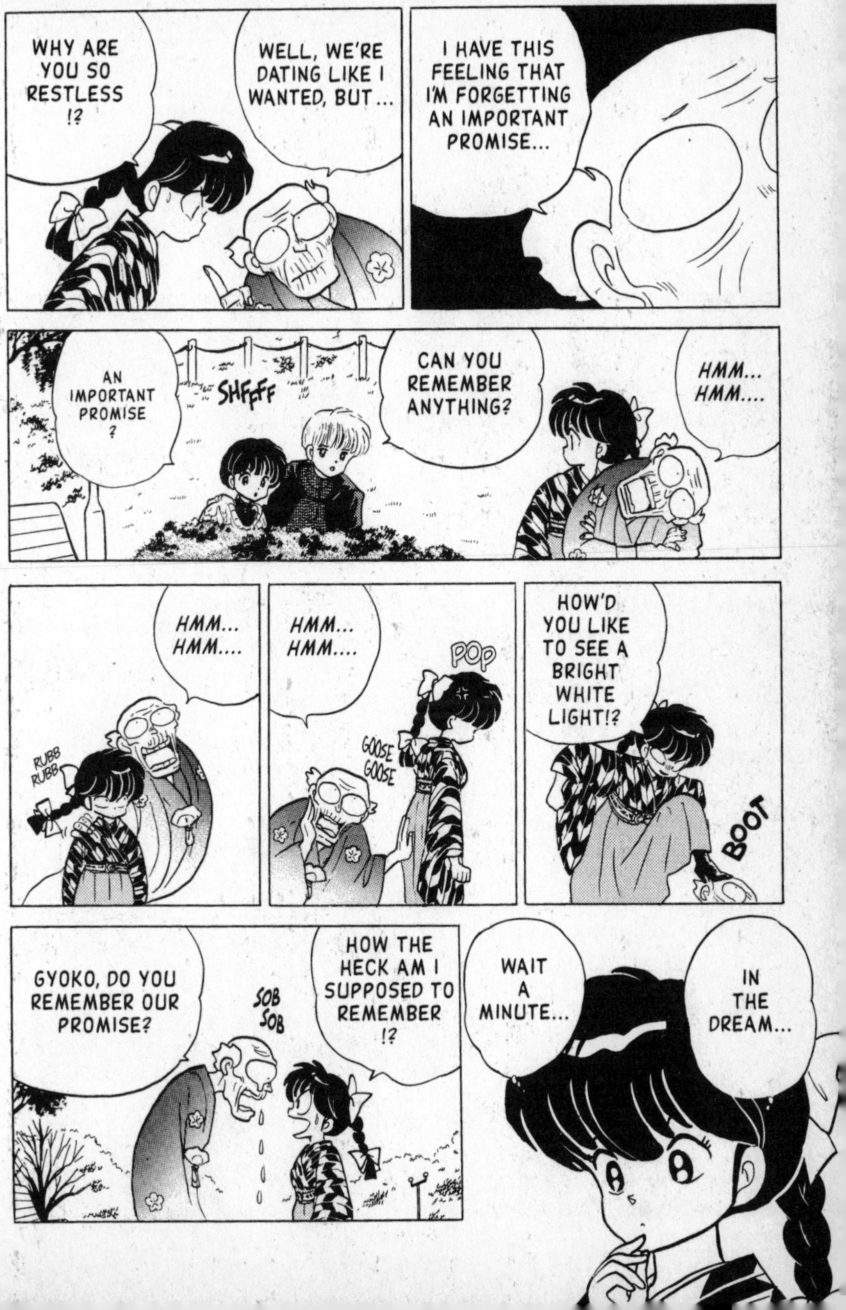
WHY ARE YOU SO RESTLESS !?
WELL, WE'RE DATING LIKE I WANTED, BUT...
I HAVE THIS FEELING THAT I'M FORGETTING AN IMPORTANT PROMISE...
AN IMPORTANT PROMISE ?
SHFFFF
CAN YOU REMEMBER ANYTHING?
HMM... HMM....
RUBB RUBB
HMM... HMM....
POP
HMM... HMM....
GOOSE GOOSE
HOW'D YOU LIKE TO SEE A BRIGHT WHITE LIGHT!?
BOOT
GYOKO, DO YOU REMEMBER OUR PROMISE?
SOB SOB
HOW THE HECK AM I SUPPOSED TO REMEMBER !?
WAIT A MINUTE...
IN THE DREAM...

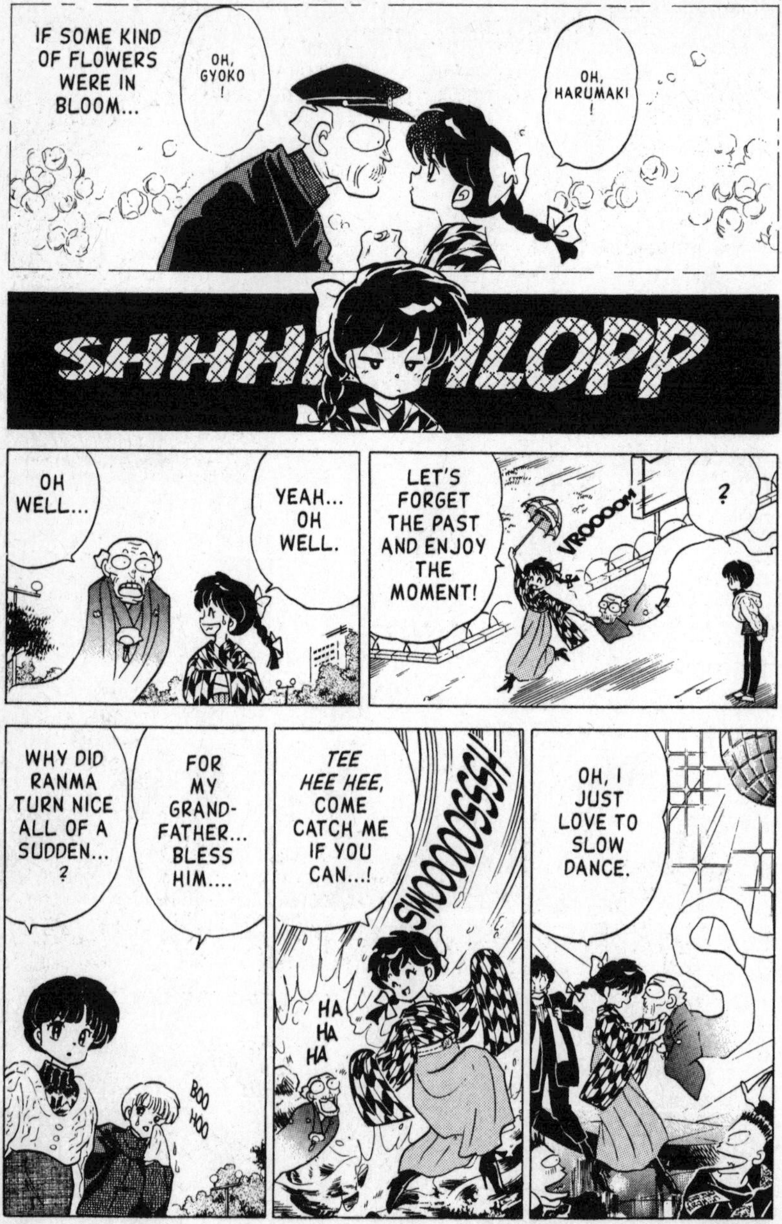
IF SOME KIND OF FLOWERS WERE IN BLOOM...
OH, GYOKO !
OH, HARUMAKI !
SHHHHHLOPP
OH WELL...
YEAH... OH WELL.
LET'S FORGET THE PAST AND ENJOY THE MOMENT!
VROOOOM
?
WHY DID RANMA TURN NICE ALL OF A SUDDEN... ?
FOR MY GRANDFATHER... BLESS HIM....
BOO HOO
TEE HEE HEE, COME CATCH ME IF YOU CAN...!
SWOOOOSSSH
HA HA HA
OH, I JUST LOVE TO SLOW DANCE.

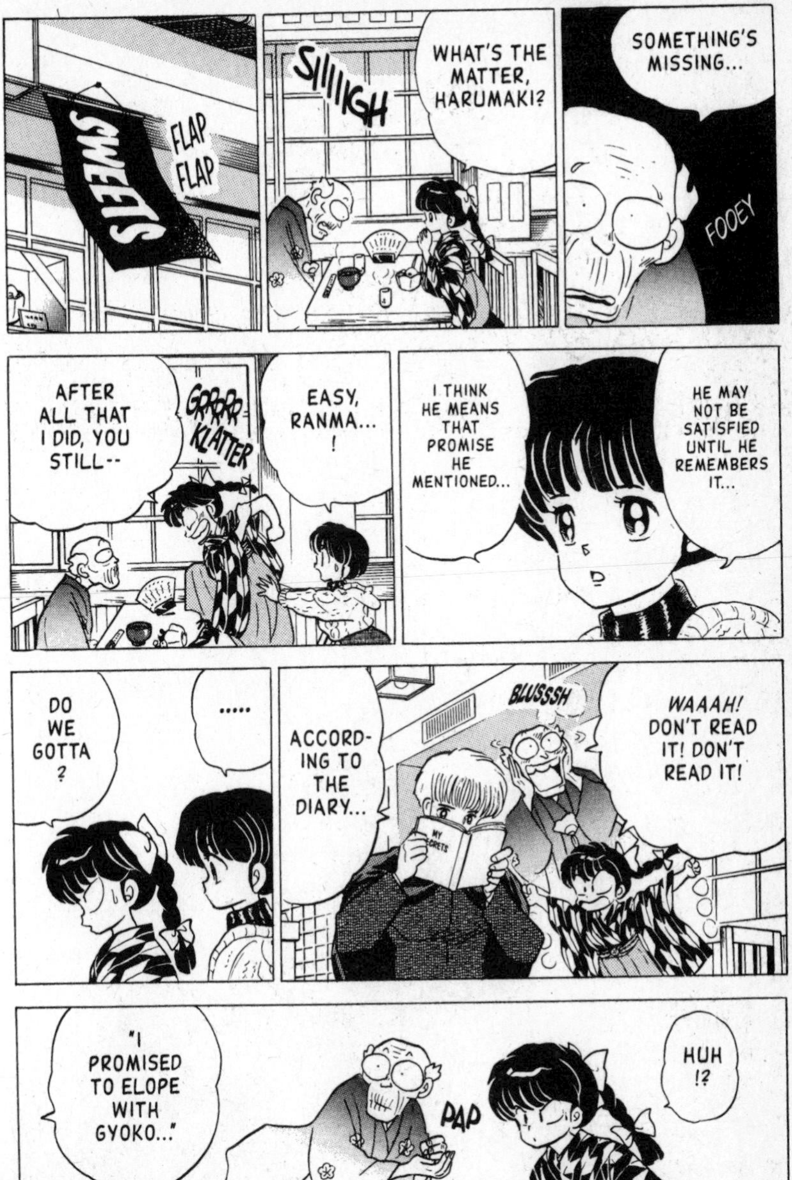
SWEETS
FLAP FLAP
SIIIIGH
WHAT'S THE MATTER, HARUMAKI?
SOMETHING'S MISSING...
FOOEY
AFTER ALL THAT I DID, YOU STILL--
GRRRRR
KLATTER
EASY, RANMA...!
I THINK HE MEANS THAT PROMISE HE MENTIONED...
HE MAY NOT BE SATISFIED UNTIL HE REMEMBERS IT...
DO WE GOTTA?
.....
ACCORDING TO THE DIARY...
BLUSSSH
WAAAH! DON'T READ IT! DON'T READ IT!
"I PROMISED TO ELOPE WITH GYOKO..."
PAP
HUH!?

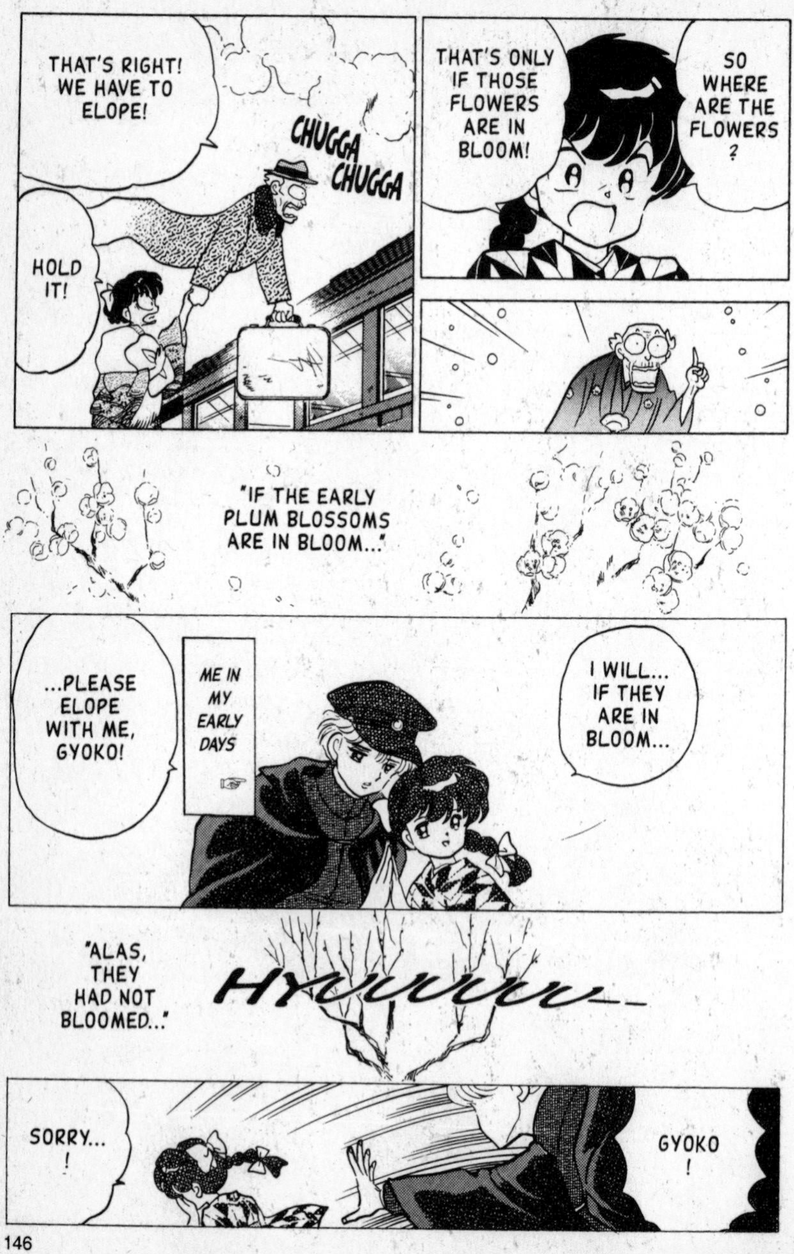
THAT'S RIGHT! WE HAVE TO ELOPE!
CHUGGA CHUGGA
HOLD IT!
THAT'S ONLY IF THOSE FLOWERS ARE IN BLOOM!
SO WHERE ARE THE FLOWERS ?
"IF THE EARLY PLUM BLOSSOMS ARE IN BLOOM..."
...PLEASE ELOPE WITH ME, GYOKO!
ME IN MY EARLY DAYS
I WILL... IF THEY ARE IN BLOOM...
"ALAS, THEY HAD NOT BLOOMED..."
HYUUUUU--
SORRY... !
GYOKO !

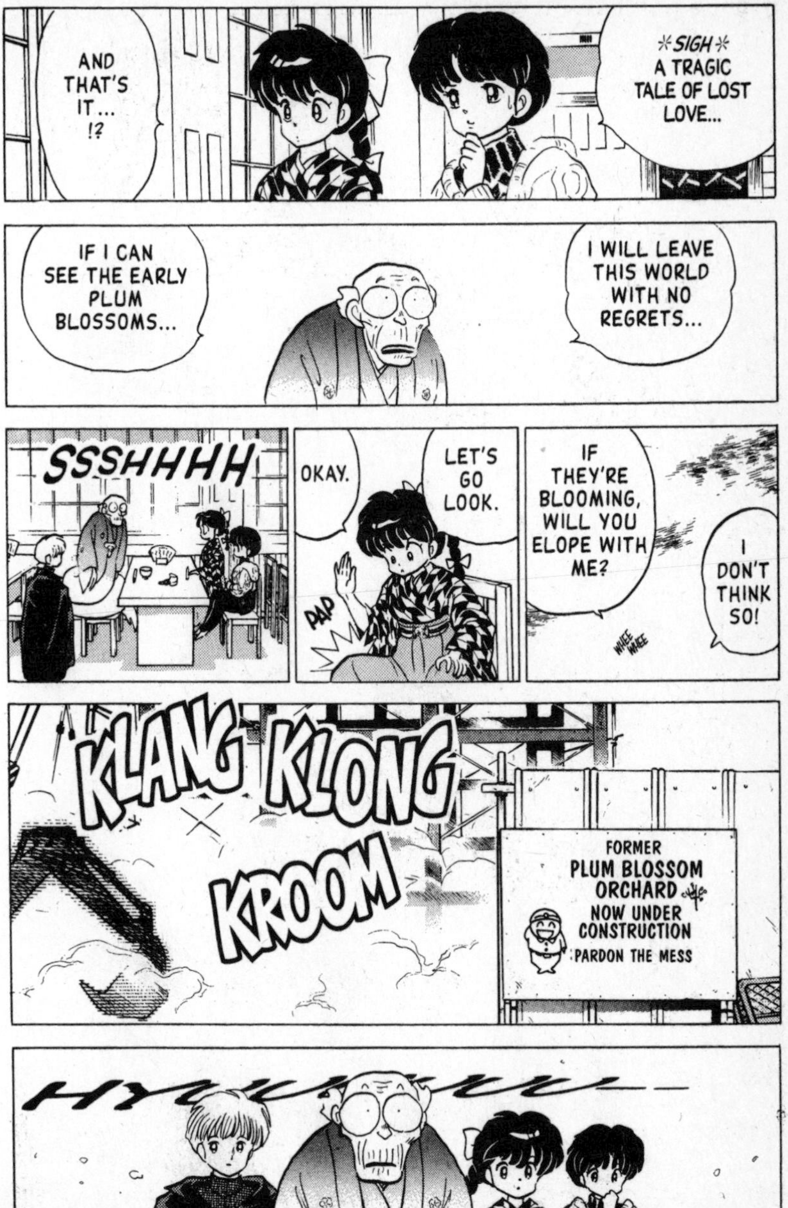
AND THAT'S IT... !?
SIGH A TRAGIC TALE OF LOST LOVE...
IF I CAN SEE THE EARLY PLUM BLOSSOMS...
I WILL LEAVE THIS WORLD WITH NO REGRETS...
SSSHHHH
OKAY.
LET'S GO LOOK.
PAP
IF THEY'RE BLOOMING, WILL YOU ELOPE WITH ME?
I DON'T THINK SO!
WHEE WHEE
KLANG KLONG
KROOM
FORMER
PLUM BLOSSOM ORCHARD
NOW UNDER CONSTRUCTION
PARDON THE MESS
HYUUUUU

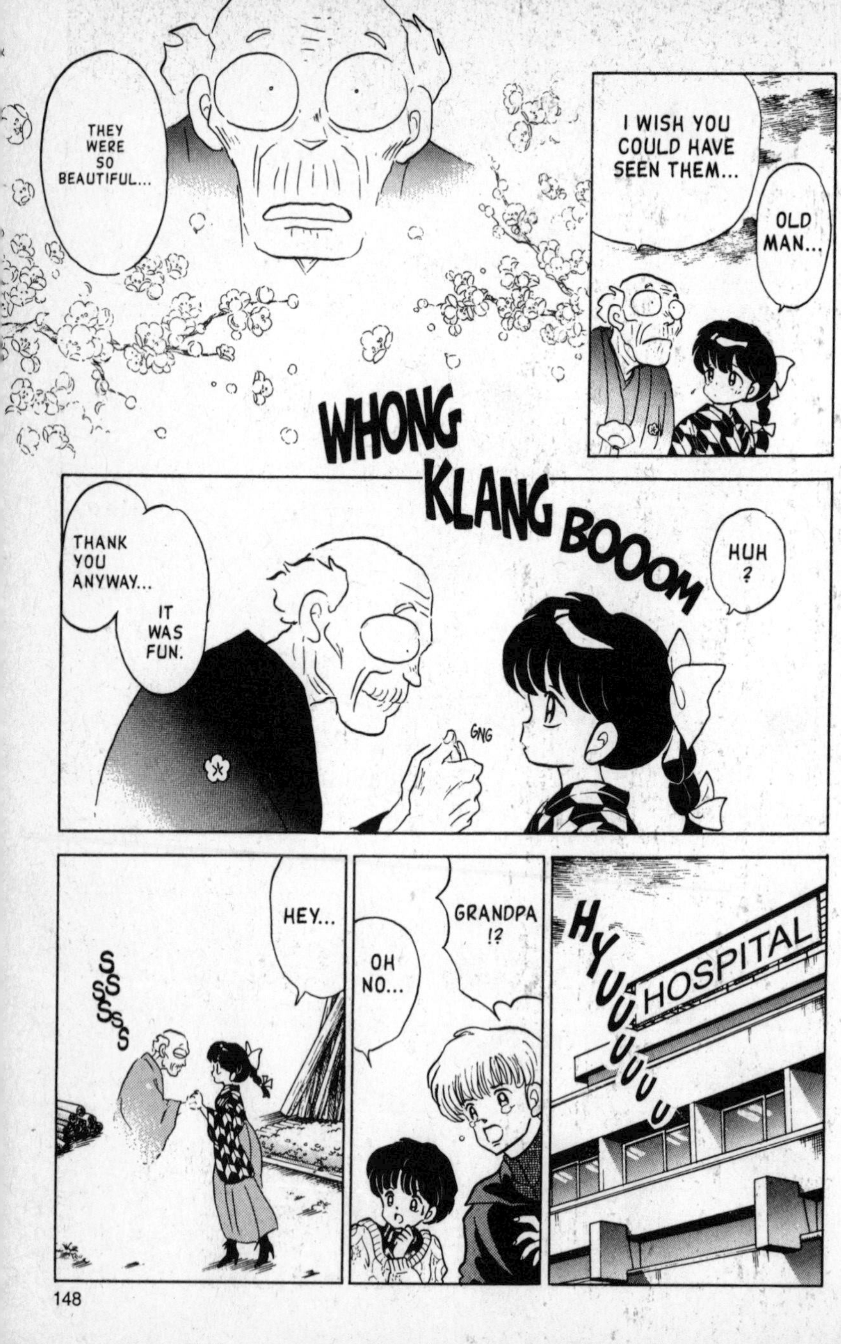
THEY WERE SO BEAUTIFUL...
I WISH YOU COULD HAVE SEEN THEM...
OLD MAN...
WHONG
KLANG
BOOOM
THANK YOU ANYWAY...
IT WAS FUN.
GNG
HUH ?
SSSSSS
HEY...
GRANDPA !?
OH NO...
HYUUUUUUUU
HOSPITAL

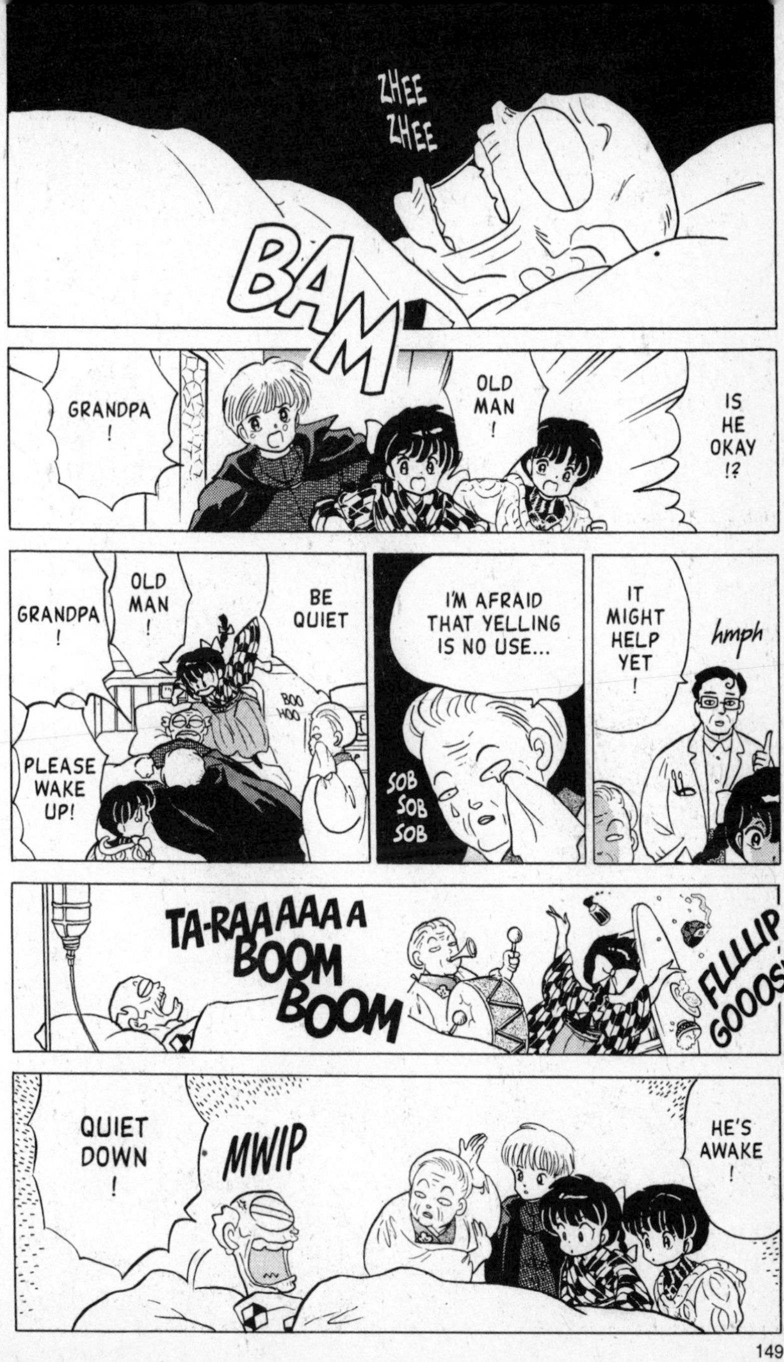

ZHEE
ZHEE
BAM
GRANDPA!
OLD MAN!
IS HE OKAY!?
GRANDPA!
OLD MAN!
BE QUIET
BOO HOO
PLEASE WAKE UP!
I'M AFRAID THAT YELLING IS NO USE...
SOB SOB SOB
IT MIGHT HELP YET!
hmph
TA-RAAAAAA
BOOM
BOOM
FLLLLIP
GOOOSH
QUIET DOWN!
MWIP
HE'S AWAKE!

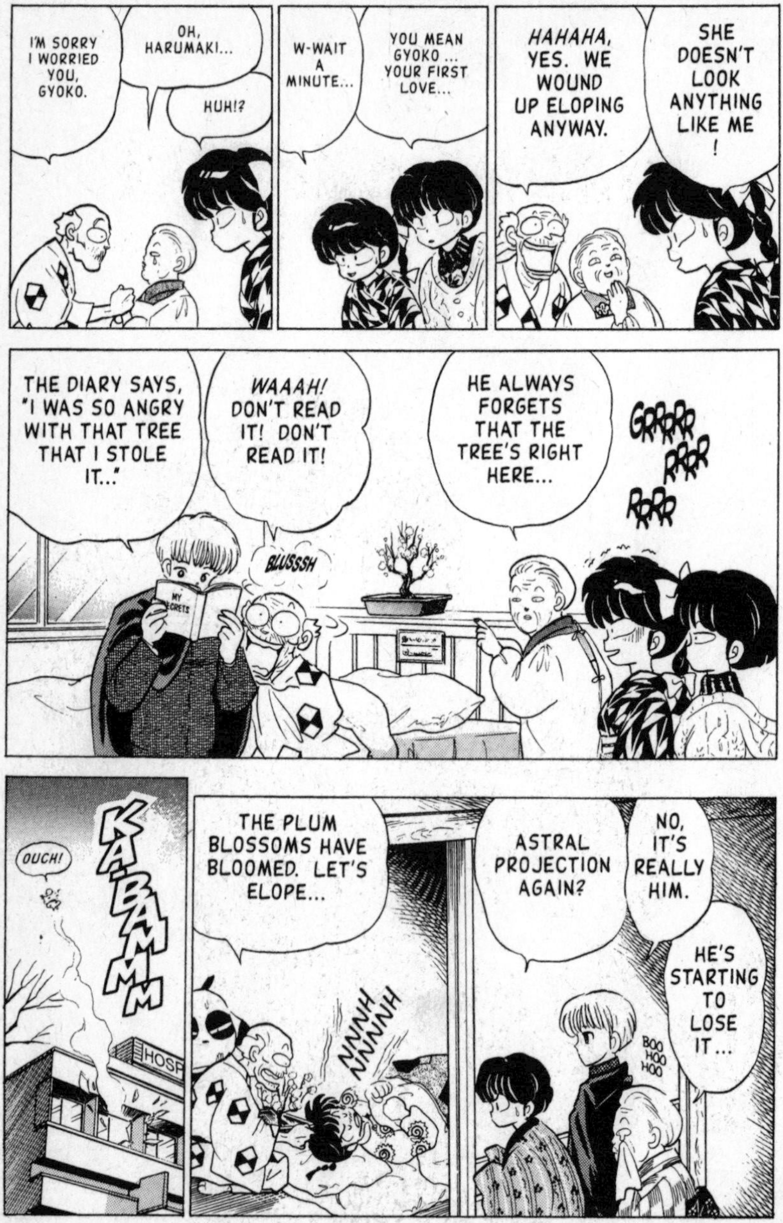
I'M SORRY I WORRIED YOU, GYOKO.
OH, HARUMAKI...
HUH!?
W-WAIT A MINUTE...
YOU MEAN GYOKO ... YOUR FIRST LOVE...
HAHAHA, YES. WE WOUND UP ELOPING ANYWAY.
SHE DOESN'T LOOK ANYTHING LIKE ME !
THE DIARY SAYS, "I WAS SO ANGRY WITH THAT TREE THAT I STOLE IT..."
WAAAH! DON'T READ IT! DON'T READ IT!
MY SECRETS
BLUSSSH
HE ALWAYS FORGETS THAT THE TREE'S RIGHT HERE...
GRRRRR RRRR RRRR
OUCH!
KA-BAMMM
HOSP
THE PLUM BLOSSOMS HAVE BLOOMED. LET'S ELOPE...
NNNNH NNNNH
ASTRAL PROJECTION AGAIN?
NO, IT'S REALLY HIM.
HE'S STARTING TO LOSE IT...
BOO HOO HOO

Part 10
SIBLING WARFARE

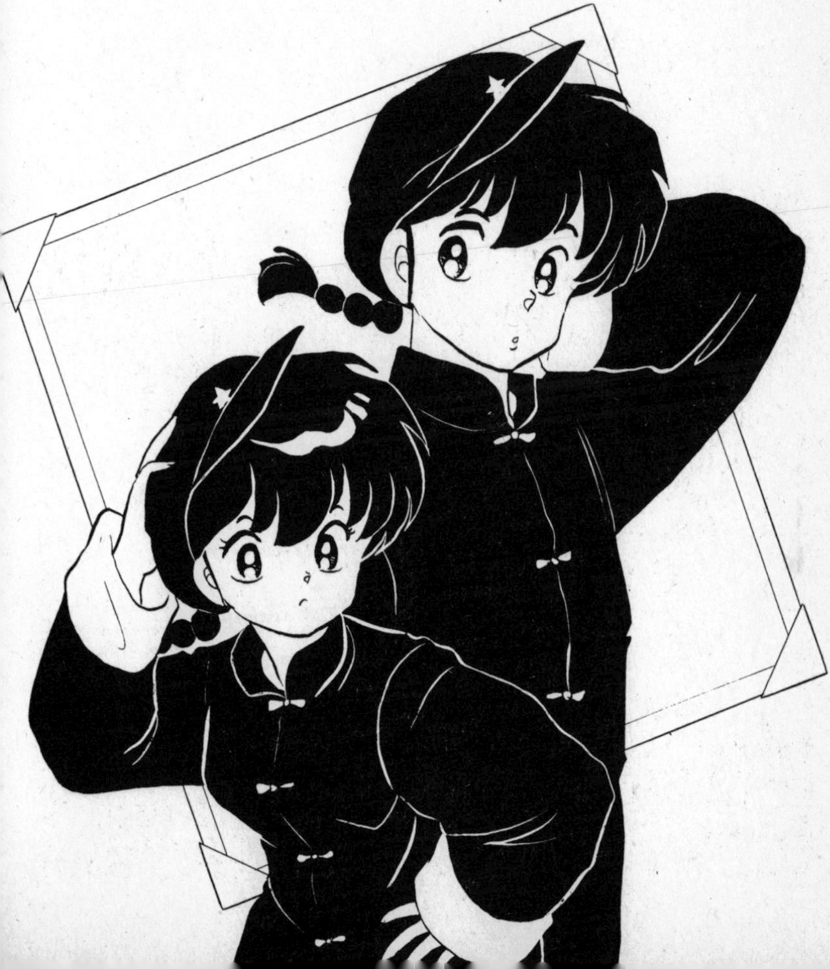

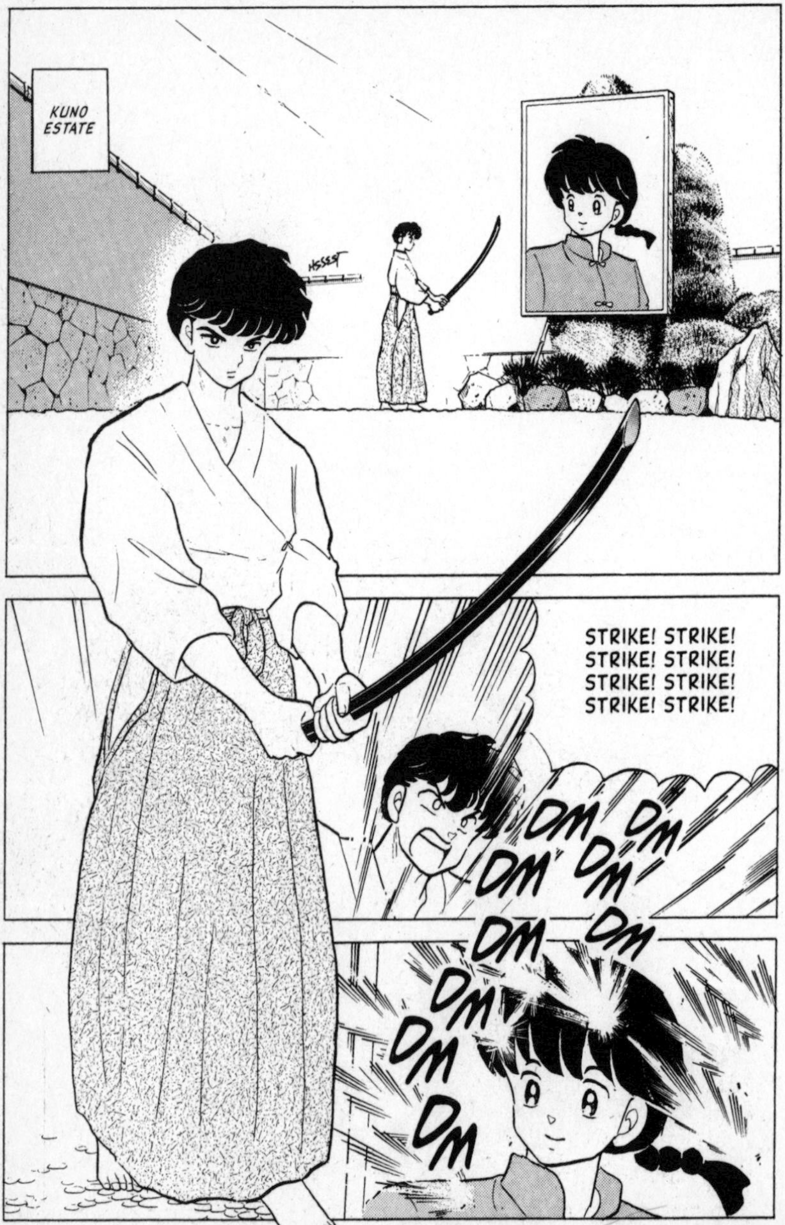
KUNO
ESTATE
HSSSST
STRIKE! STRIKE!
STRIKE! STRIKE!
STRIKE! STRIKE!
STRIKE! STRIKE!
DM DM
DM DM
DM DM
DM DM
DM
DM
DM
DM

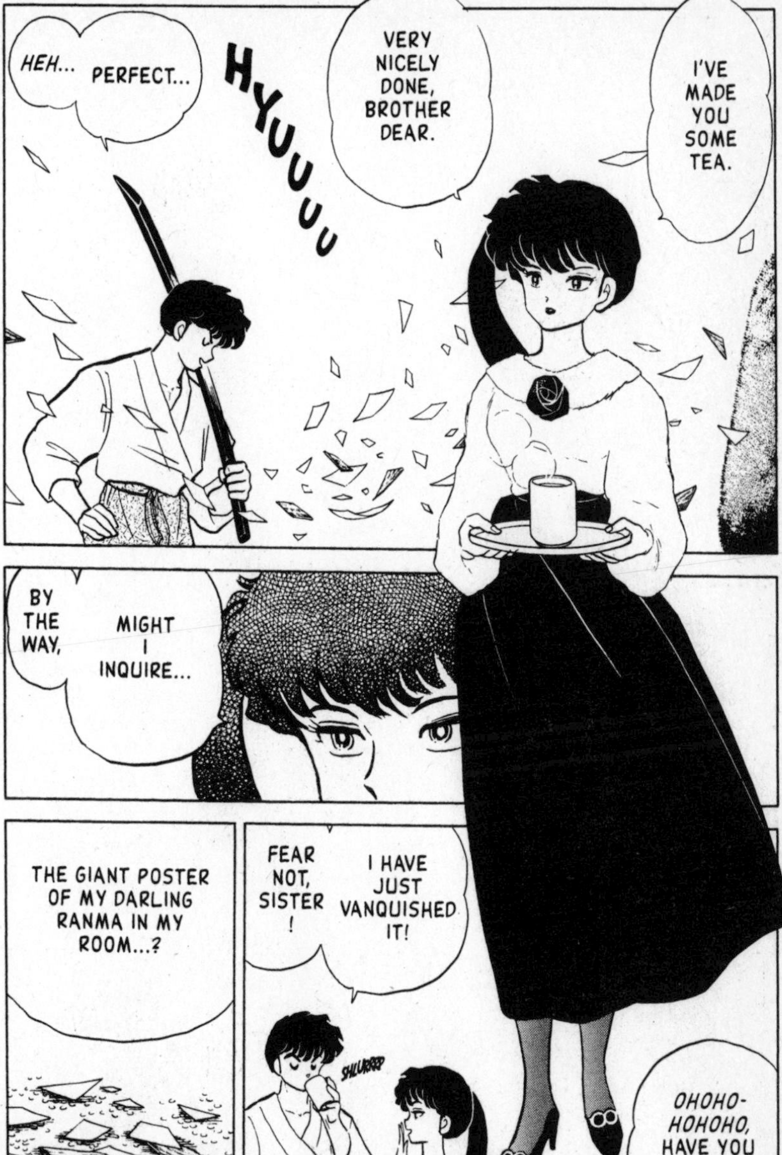
HEH... PERFECT...
HYUUUUU
VERY NICELY DONE, BROTHER DEAR.
I'VE MADE YOU SOME TEA.
BY THE WAY, MIGHT I INQUIRE...
THE GIANT POSTER OF MY DARLING RANMA IN MY ROOM...?
FEAR NOT, SISTER! I HAVE JUST VANQUISHED IT!
SHLURRP
OHOHO-HOHOHO, HAVE YOU NOW

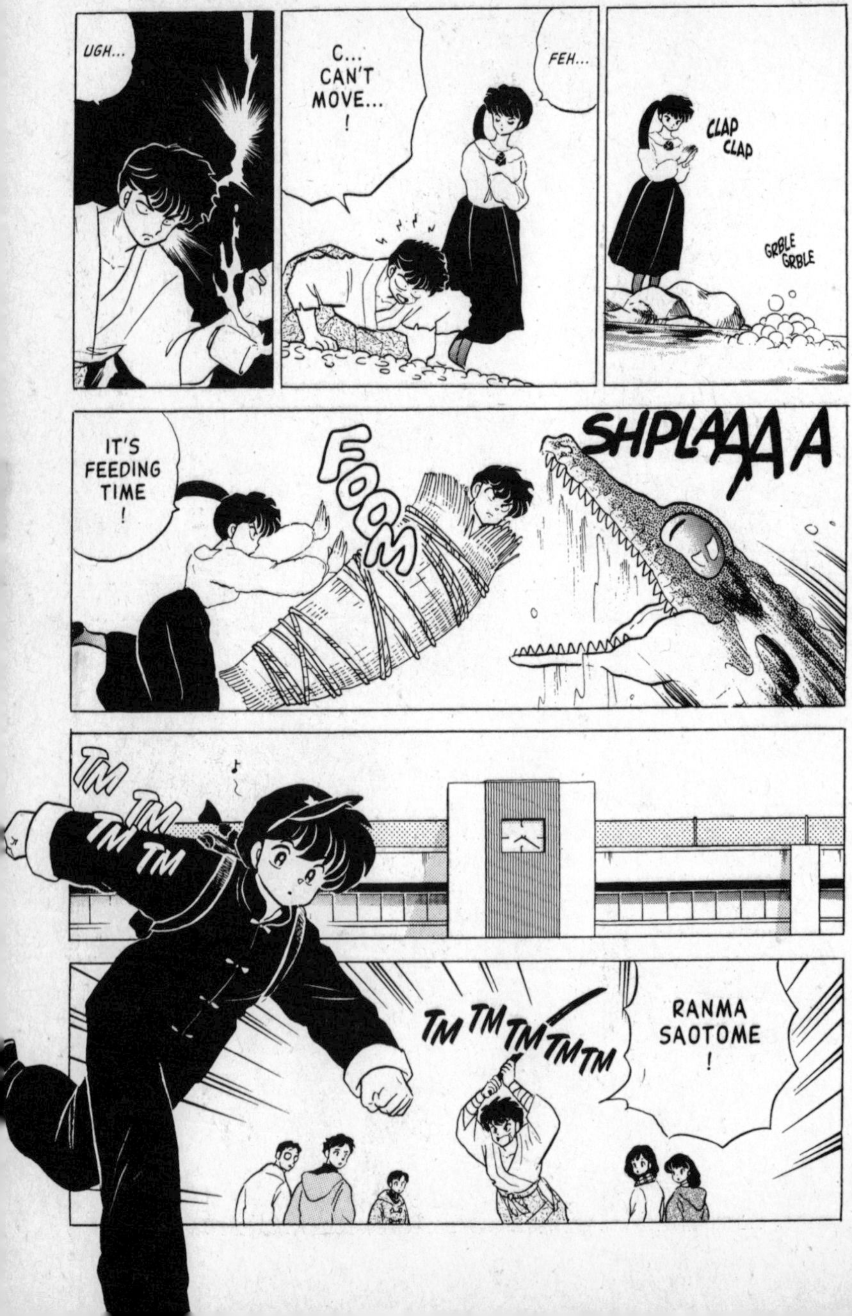
UGH...
C... CAN'T MOVE... !
FEH...
CLAP CLAP
GRBLE GRBLE
IT'S FEEDING TIME !
FOOM
SHPLAAAAA
TM TM TM TM
TM TM TM TM TM TM
RANMA SAOTOME !

WHAT DID YOU DO THAT FOR ?!

HSS HSS

THAT'S MY LINE !

A FIGHT WITH YOUR SISTER, HUH?

CORRECT.

NOW I NEED TO MAKE PEACE WITH HER...

AND SO...

I WILL HAND YOU OVER TO MY TWISTED SISTER AS HER SLAVE, AND ALL WILL BE FORGIVEN!

WELL, IN THAT CASE...

DREAM ON, STUPID !

IN THAT CASE...

155

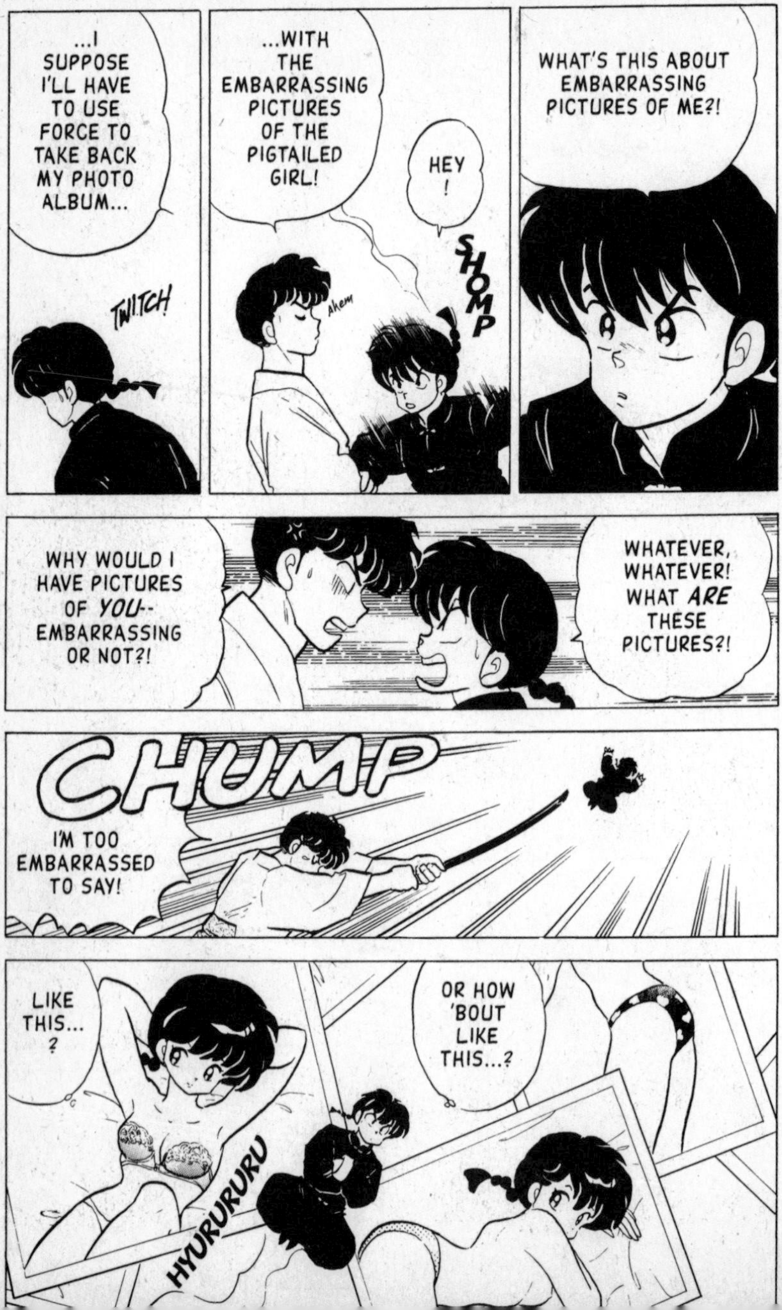
...I SUPPOSE I'LL HAVE TO USE FORCE TO TAKE BACK MY PHOTO ALBUM...
TWITCH
...WITH THE EMBARRASSING PICTURES OF THE PIGTAILED GIRL!
Ahem
HEY!
SHOMP
WHAT'S THIS ABOUT EMBARRASSING PICTURES OF ME?!
WHY WOULD I HAVE PICTURES OF *YOU*-- EMBARRASSING OR NOT?!
WHATEVER, WHATEVER! WHAT *ARE* THESE PICTURES?!
CHUMP
I'M TOO EMBARRASSED TO SAY!
LIKE THIS...?
OR HOW 'BOUT LIKE THIS...?
HYURURURU

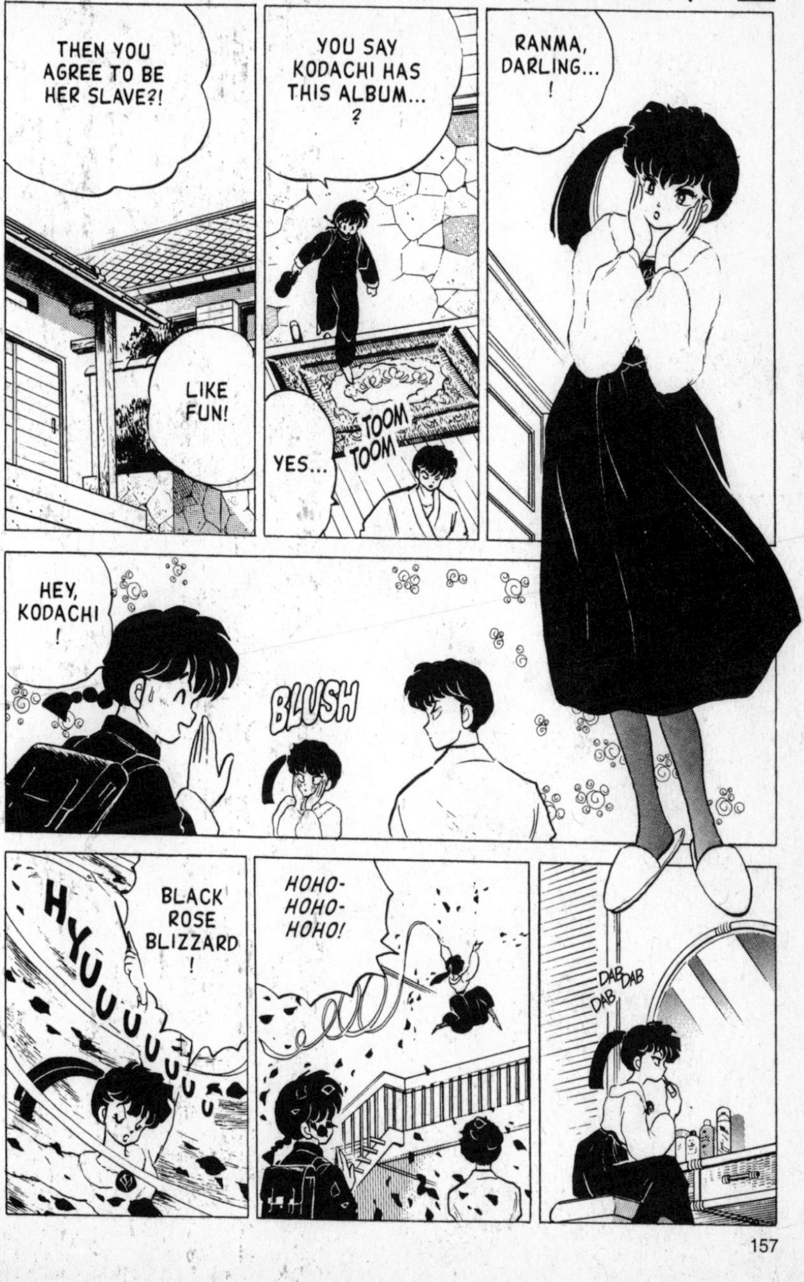
THEN YOU AGREE TO BE HER SLAVE?!
LIKE FUN!
YOU SAY KODACHI HAS THIS ALBUM...?
YES...
TOOM TOOM
RANMA, DARLING...!
HEY, KODACHI!
BLUSH
BLACK ROSE BLIZZARD!
HYUUUUUUUU
HOHO-HOHO-HOHO!
DAB DAB DAB

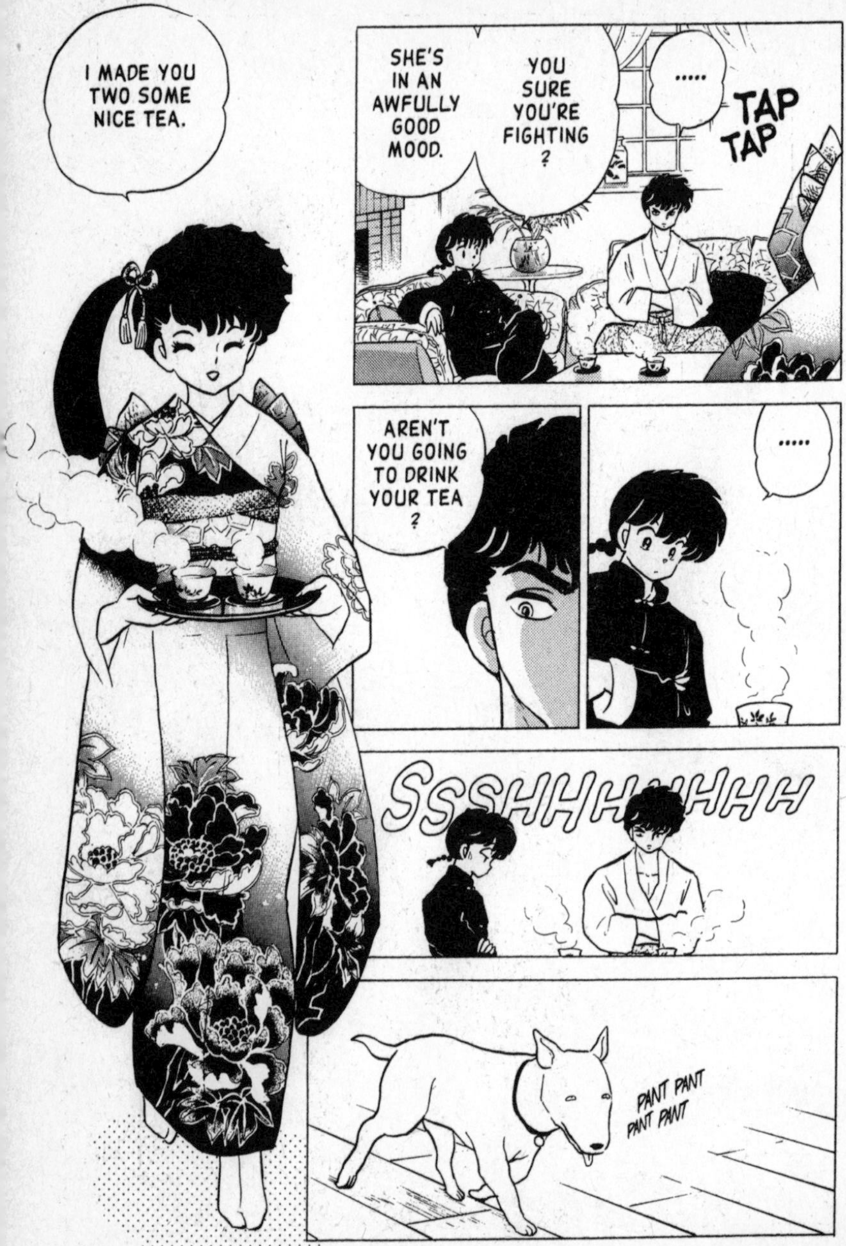
I MADE YOU TWO SOME NICE TEA.
SHE'S IN AN AWFULLY GOOD MOOD.
YOU SURE YOU'RE FIGHTING?
.....
TAP TAP
AREN'T YOU GOING TO DRINK YOUR TEA?
.....
SSSHHHHHHH
PANT PANT PANT PANT

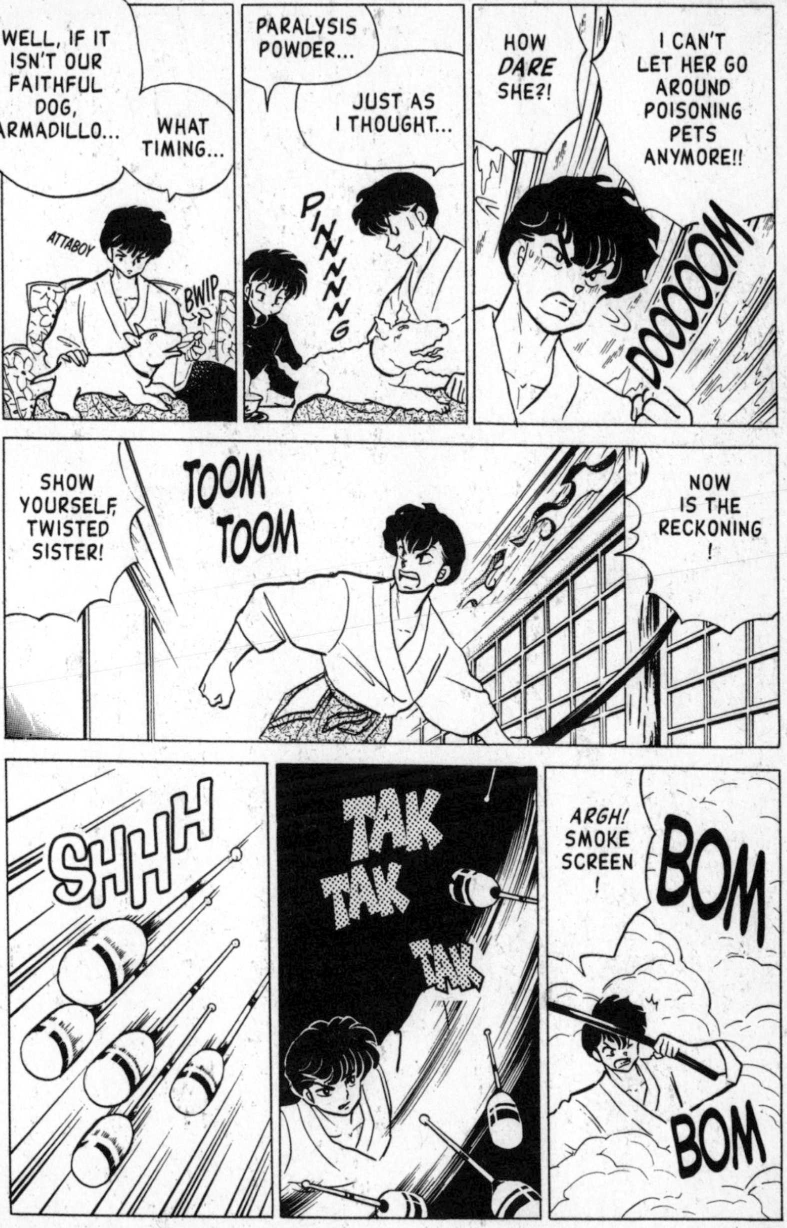
WELL, IF IT ISN'T OUR FAITHFUL DOG, ARMADILLO...
WHAT TIMING...
ATTABOY
BWIP
PARALYSIS POWDER...
JUST AS I THOUGHT...
PINNNNG
HOW DARE SHE?!
I CAN'T LET HER GO AROUND POISONING PETS ANYMORE!!
DOOOOOM
SHOW YOURSELF, TWISTED SISTER!
TOOM TOOM
NOW IS THE RECKONING!
SHHH
TAK TAK TAK
ARGH! SMOKE SCREEN!
BOM
BOM

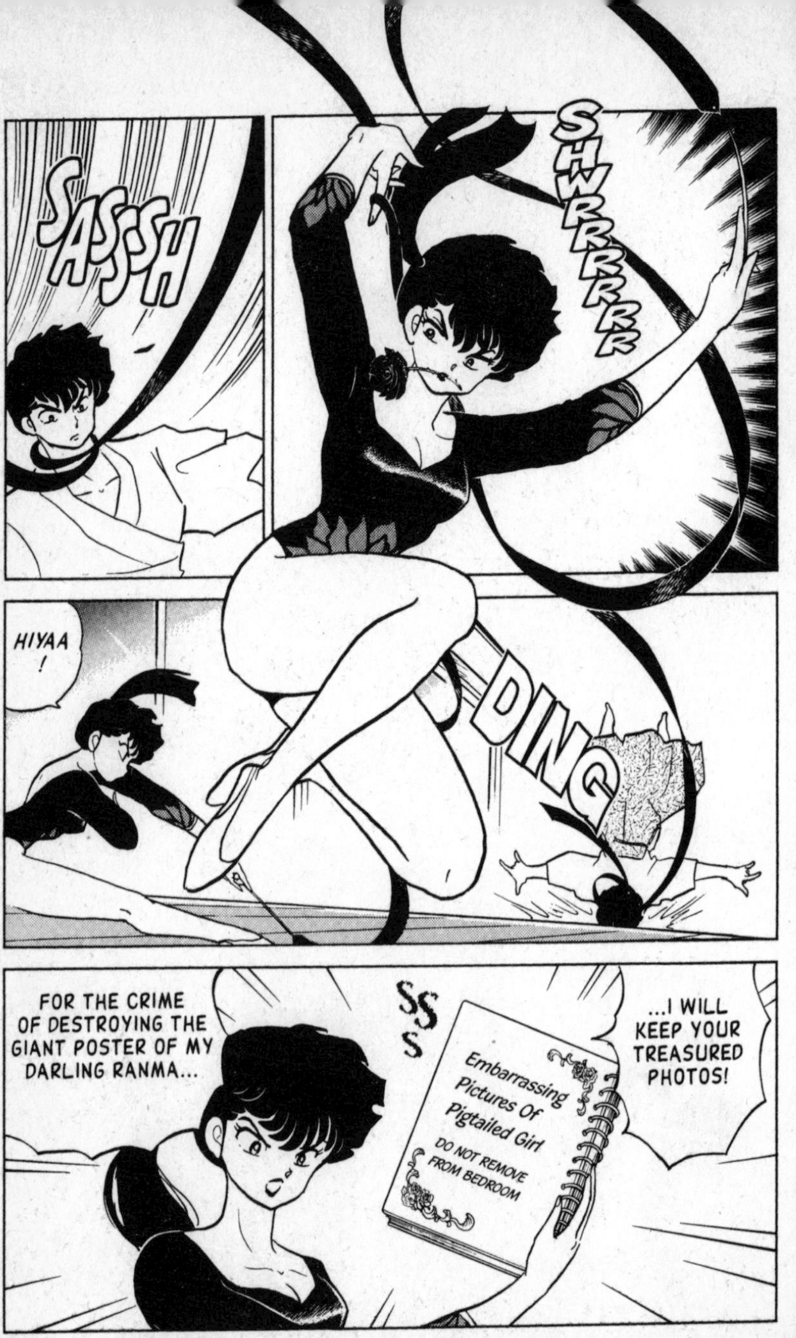
SASSSH
SHWRRRRRR
HIYAA!
DING
FOR THE CRIME OF DESTROYING THE GIANT POSTER OF MY DARLING RANMA...
SSS
Embarrassing Pictures Of Pigtailed Girl
DO NOT REMOVE FROM BEDROOM
...I WILL KEEP YOUR TREASURED PHOTOS!

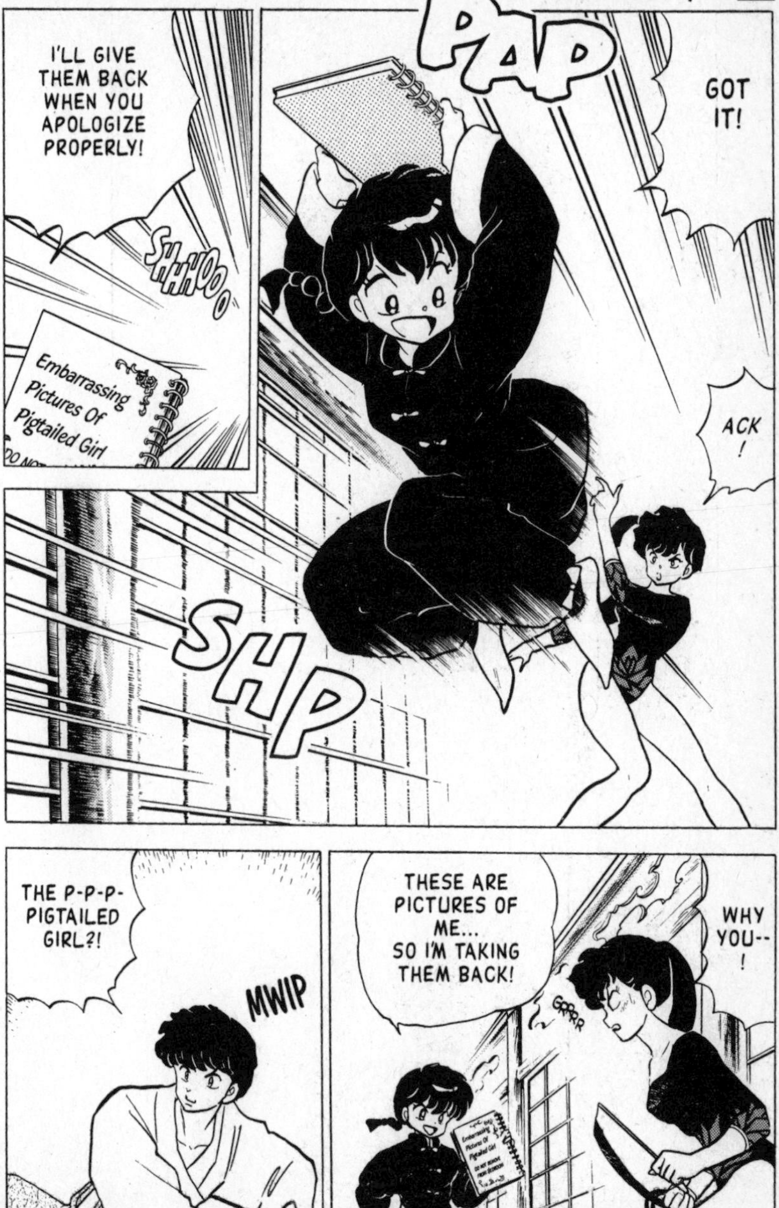
I'LL GIVE THEM BACK WHEN YOU APOLOGIZE PROPERLY!
SHHHOOO
Embarrassing Pictures Of Pigtailed Girl
PAP
GOT IT!
ACK!
SHP
THE P-P-P-PIGTAILED GIRL?!
MWIP
THESE ARE PICTURES OF ME... SO I'M TAKING THEM BACK!
GRRRR
WHY YOU--!

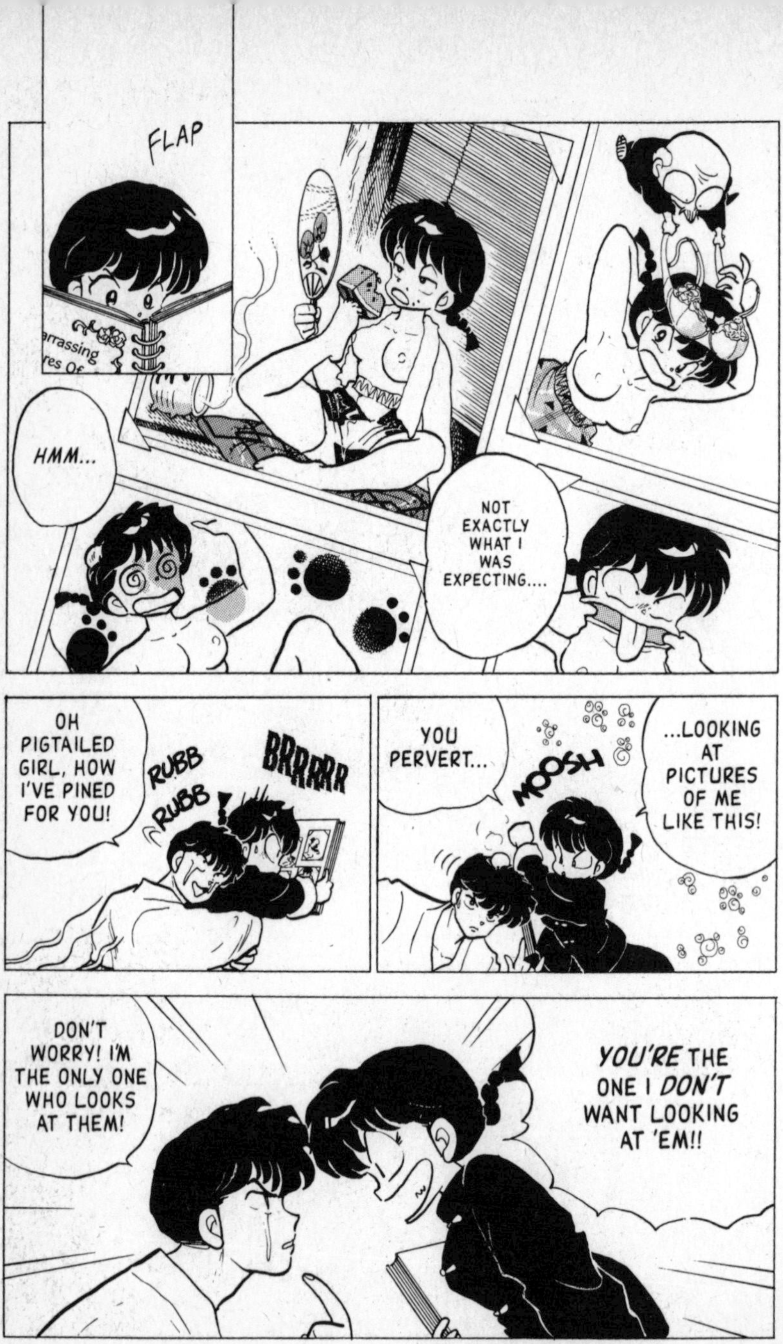

FLAP
HMM...
NOT EXACTLY WHAT I WAS EXPECTING....
OH PIGTAILED GIRL, HOW I'VE PINED FOR YOU!
RUBB RUBB
BRRRRRR
YOU PERVERT...
MOOSH
...LOOKING AT PICTURES OF ME LIKE THIS!
DON'T WORRY! I'M THE ONLY ONE WHO LOOKS AT THEM!
YOU'RE THE ONE I *DON'T* WANT LOOKING AT 'EM!!

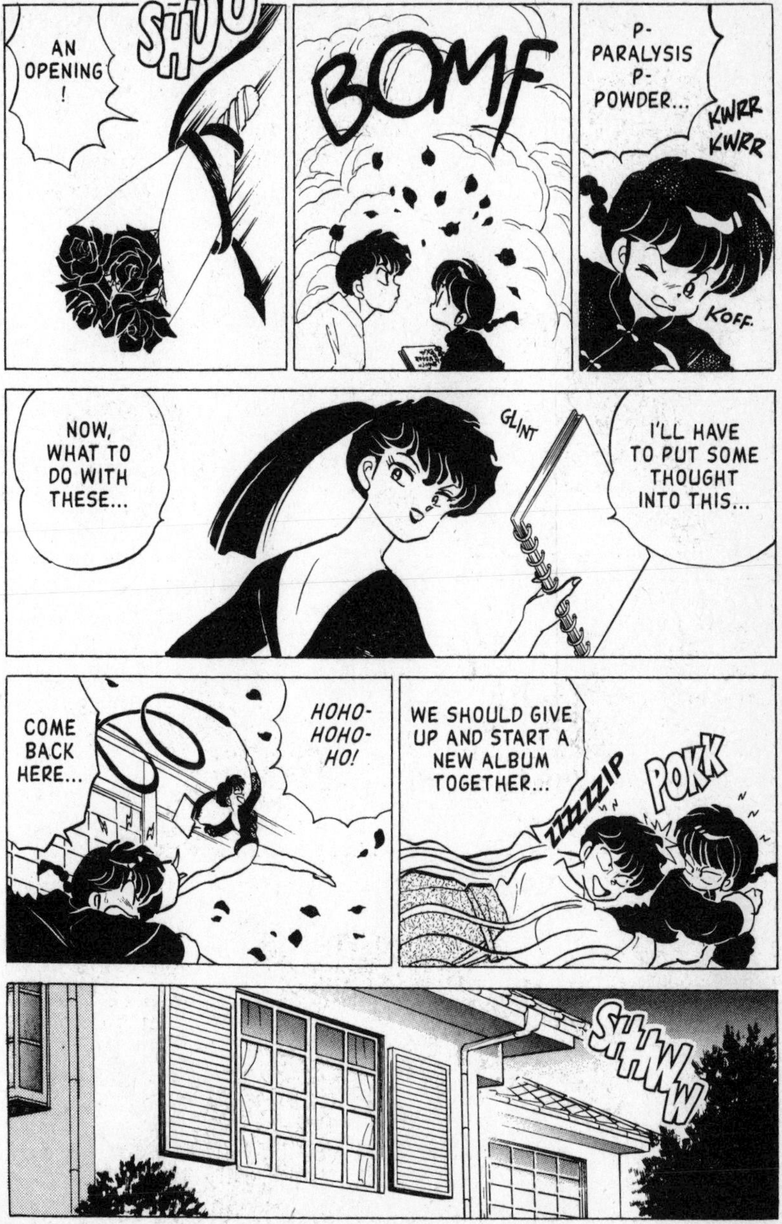
AN OPENING !
SHUU
BOMF
P- PARALYSIS P- POWDER...
KWRR KWRR
KOFF.
NOW, WHAT TO DO WITH THESE...
GLINT
I'LL HAVE TO PUT SOME THOUGHT INTO THIS...
COME BACK HERE...
HOHO-HOHO-HO!
WE SHOULD GIVE UP AND START A NEW ALBUM TOGETHER...
ZZZZZZIP
POKK
SHHWW

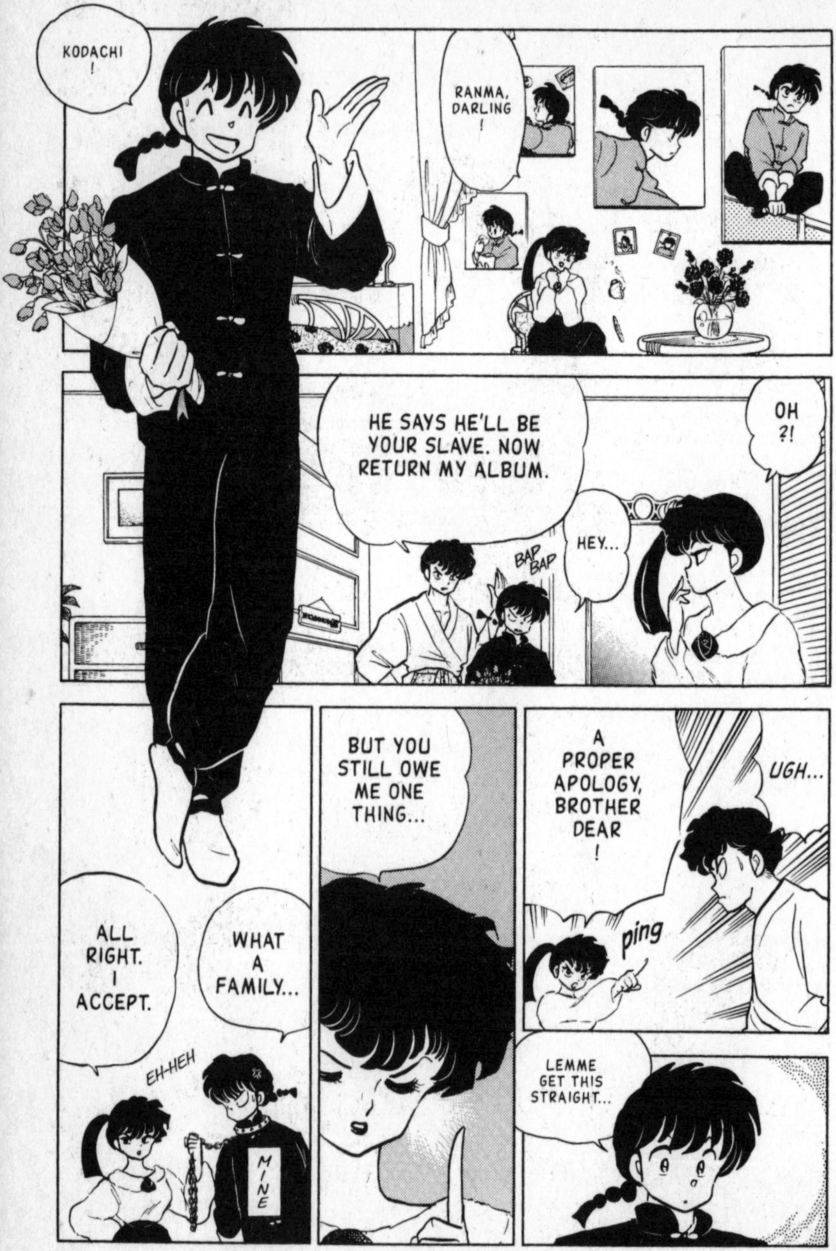
KODACHI!
RANMA, DARLING!
HE SAYS HE'LL BE YOUR SLAVE. NOW RETURN MY ALBUM.
BAP BAP
HEY...
OH ?!
ALL RIGHT. I ACCEPT.
WHAT A FAMILY...
EH-HEH
MINE
BUT YOU STILL OWE ME ONE THING...
A PROPER APOLOGY, BROTHER DEAR!
UGH...
ping
LEMME GET THIS STRAIGHT...

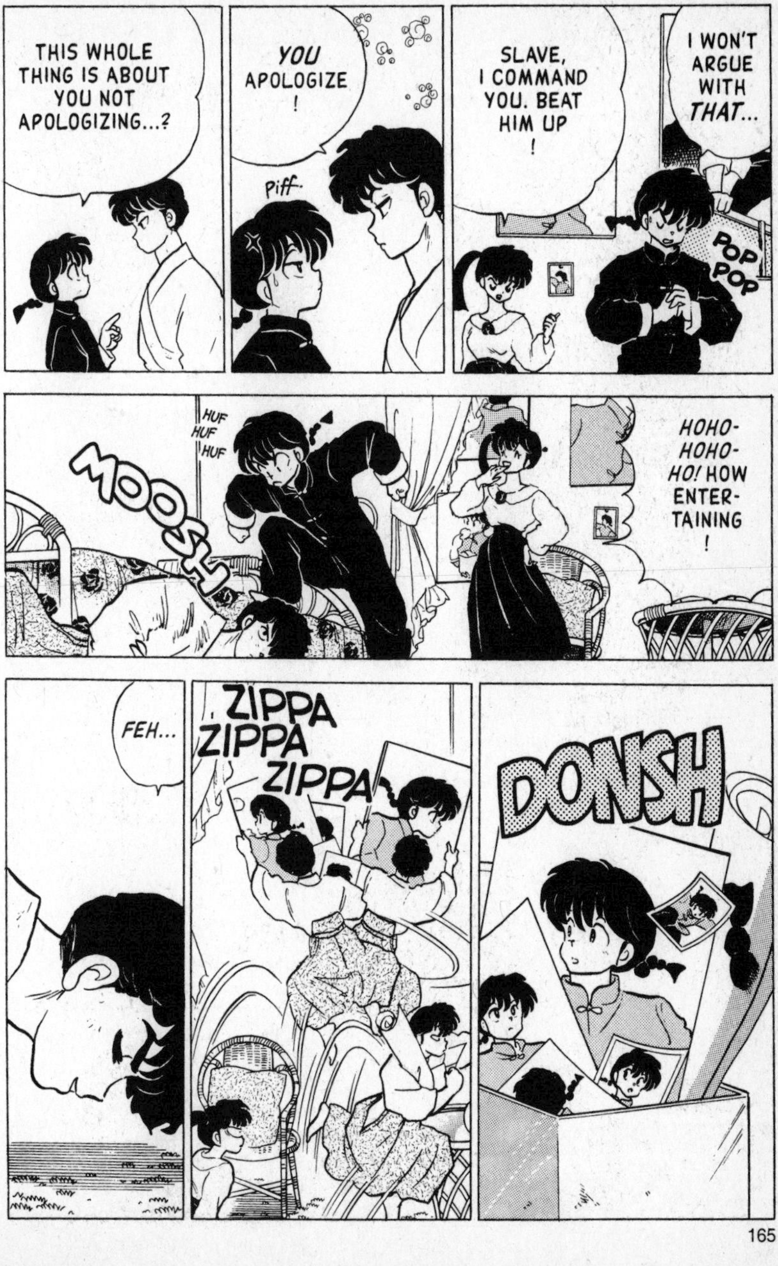
THIS WHOLE THING IS ABOUT YOU NOT APOLOGIZING...?
YOU APOLOGIZE!
Piff
SLAVE, I COMMAND YOU. BEAT HIM UP!
I WON'T ARGUE WITH THAT...
POP POP
MOOSH
HUF HUF HUF
HOHO-HOHO-HO! HOW ENTERTAINING!
FEH...
ZIPPA ZIPPA ZIPPA
DONSH

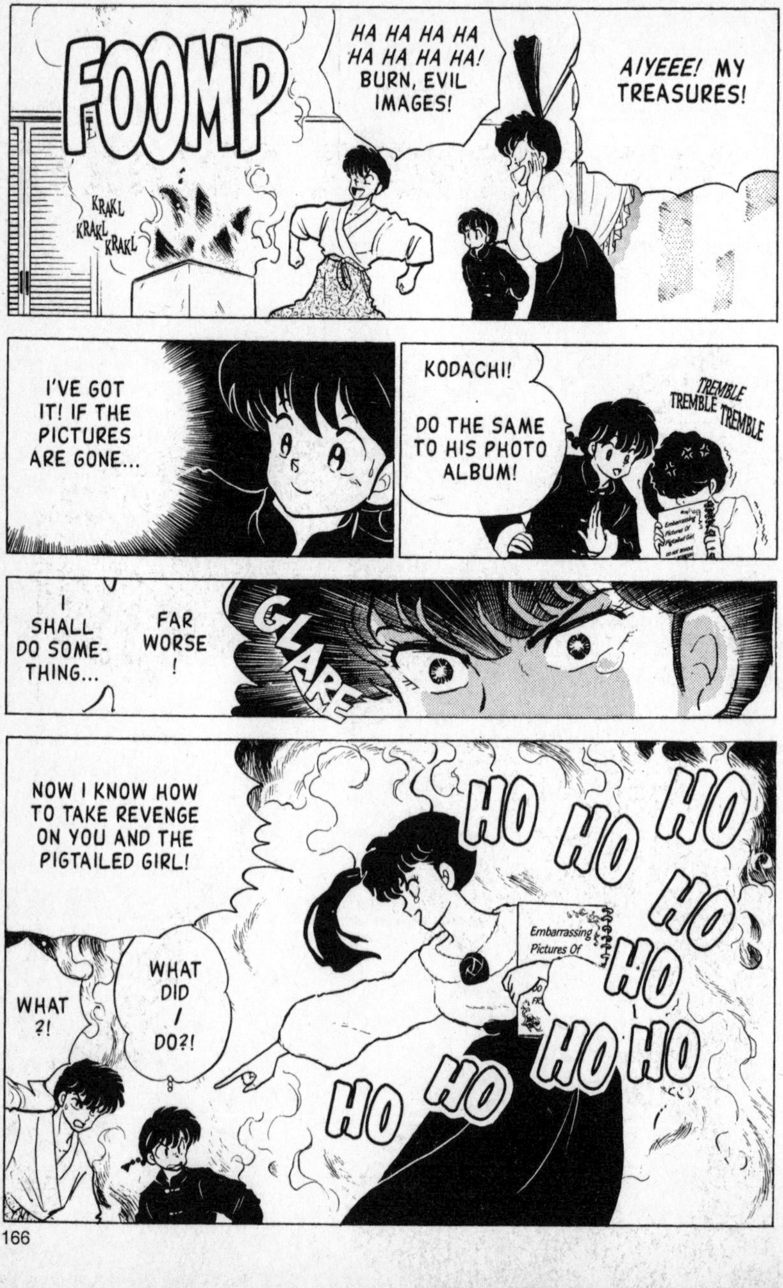

FOOMP
KRAKL KRAKL KRAKL
HA HA HA HA HA HA HA HA! BURN, EVIL IMAGES!
AIYEEE! MY TREASURES!
I'VE GOT IT! IF THE PICTURES ARE GONE...
KODACHI!
DO THE SAME TO HIS PHOTO ALBUM!
TREMBLE TREMBLE TREMBLE
I SHALL DO SOMETHING...
FAR WORSE!
GLARE
NOW I KNOW HOW TO TAKE REVENGE ON YOU AND THE PIGTAILED GIRL!
Embarrassing Pictures Of
HO HO HO HO HO HO HO HO HO HO
WHAT?!
WHAT DID I DO?!

Part 11

THE SCANDAL BREAKS!

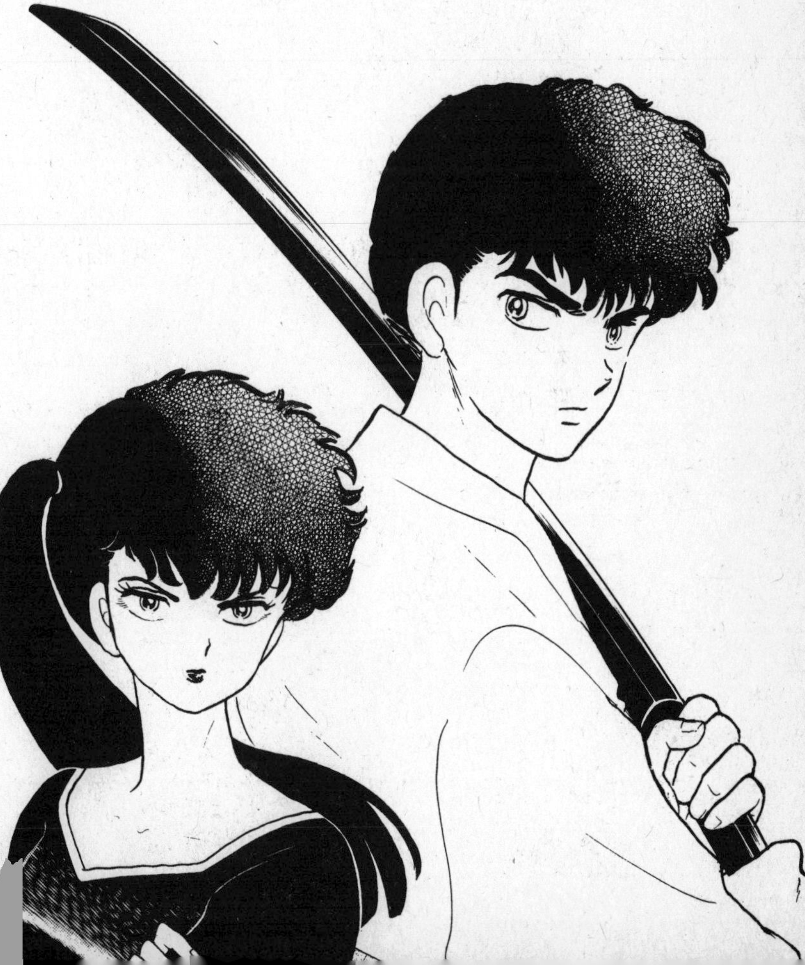

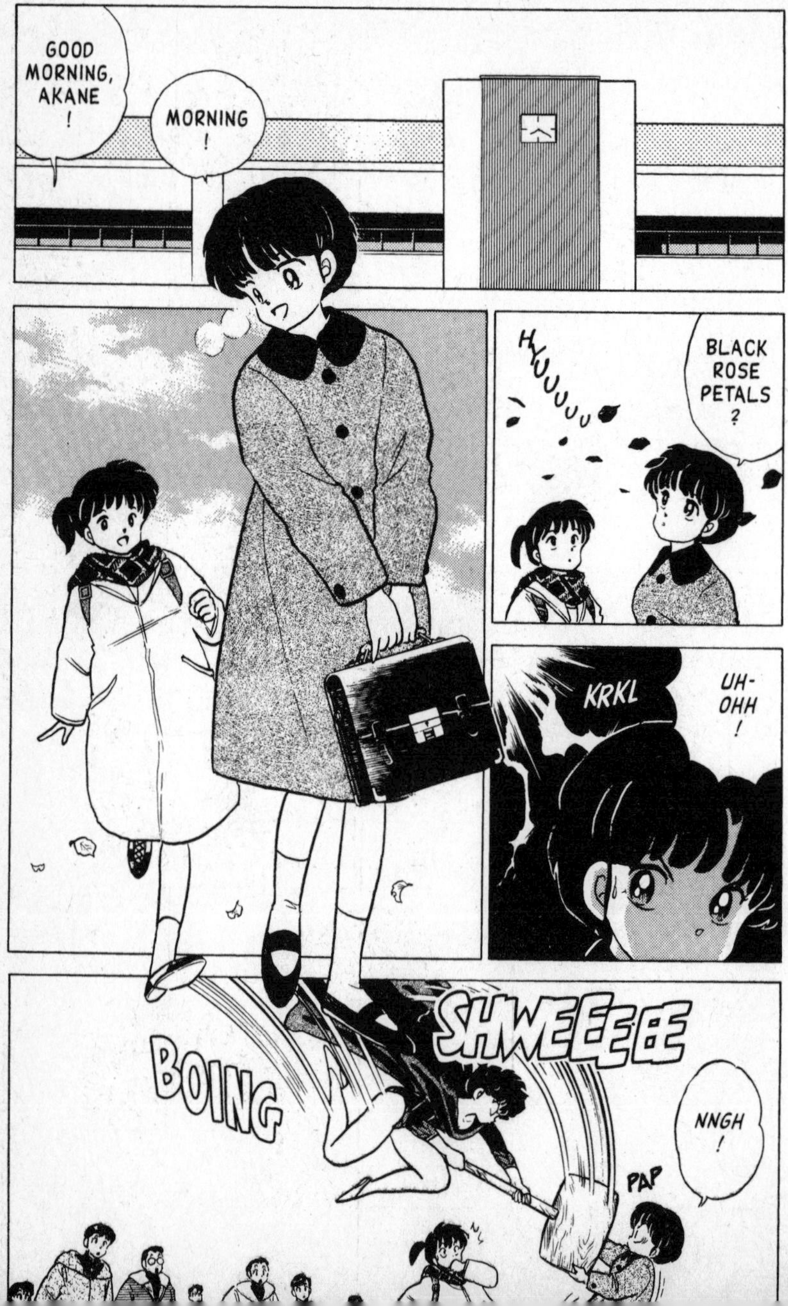
GOOD MORNING, AKANE!
MORNING!
HYUUUUU
BLACK ROSE PETALS?
KRKL
UH-OHH!
BOING
SHWEEEEE
NNGH!
PAP

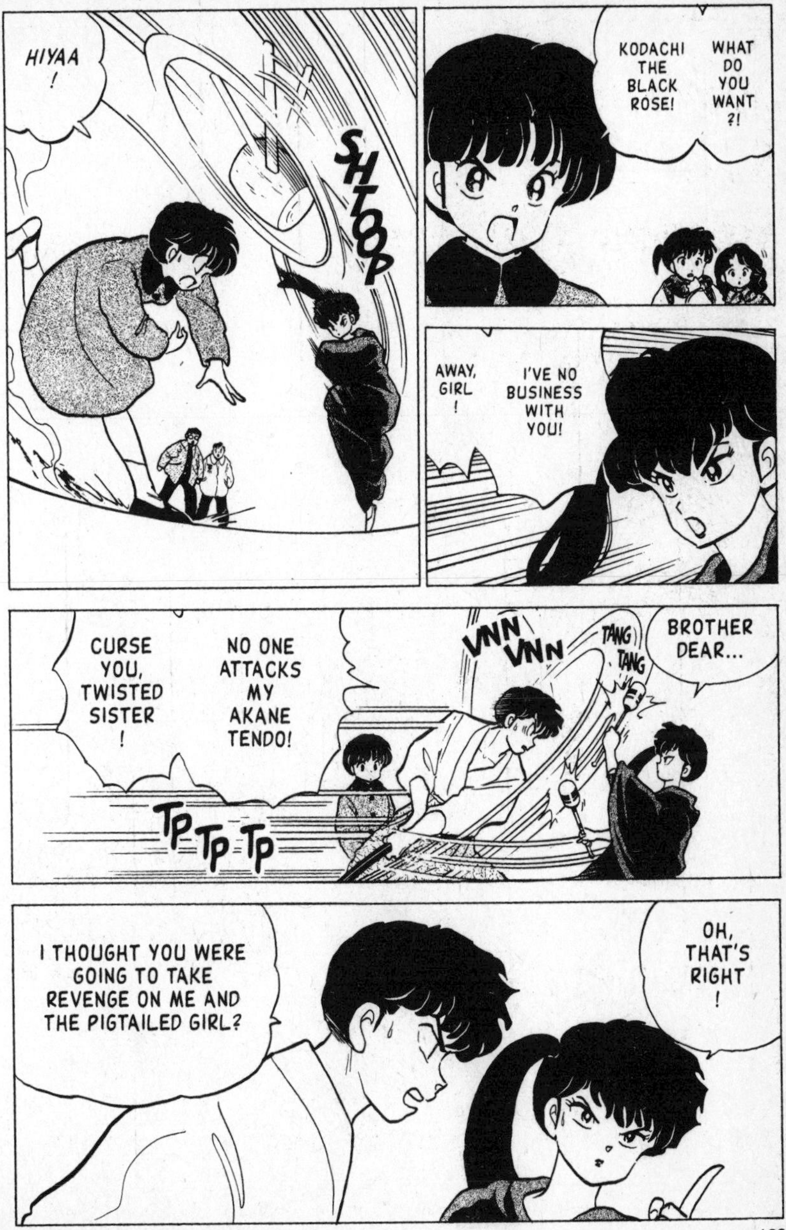
HIYAA!
SHTOOP
KODACHI THE BLACK ROSE!
WHAT DO YOU WANT?!
AWAY, GIRL!
I'VE NO BUSINESS WITH YOU!
CURSE YOU, TWISTED SISTER!
NO ONE ATTACKS MY AKANE TENDO!
TP TP TP
VNN VNN
TANG TANG
BROTHER DEAR...
I THOUGHT YOU WERE GOING TO TAKE REVENGE ON ME AND THE PIGTAILED GIRL?
OH, THAT'S RIGHT!

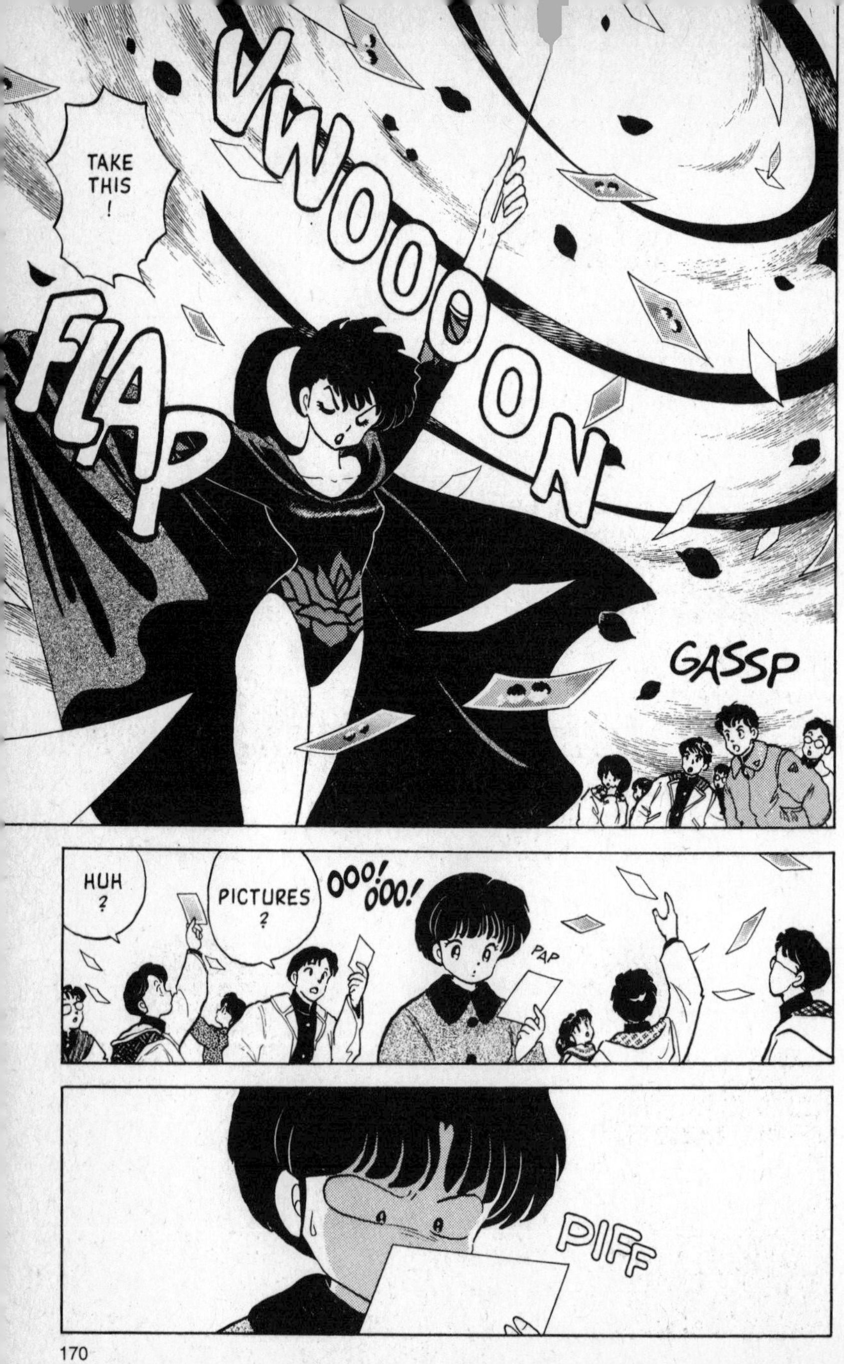
TAKE THIS!
VWOOOOON
FLAP
GASSP
HUH?
PICTURES?
OOO! OOO!
PAP
PIFF

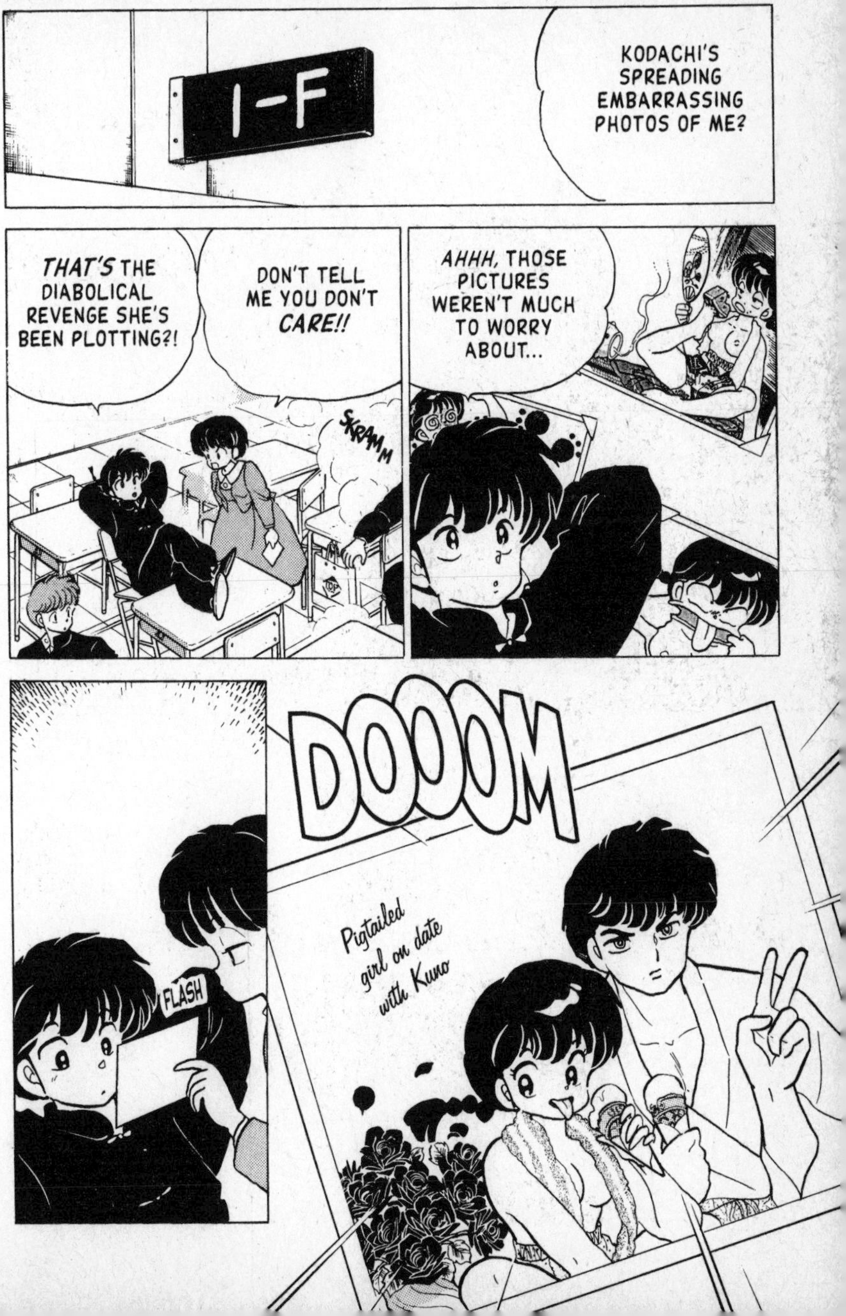
I-F
KODACHI'S SPREADING EMBARRASSING PHOTOS OF ME?
THAT'S THE DIABOLICAL REVENGE SHE'S BEEN PLOTTING?!
DON'T TELL ME YOU DON'T CARE!!
SKRAMM
AHHH, THOSE PICTURES WEREN'T MUCH TO WORRY ABOUT...
DOOOM
FLASH
Pigtailed girl on date with Kuno

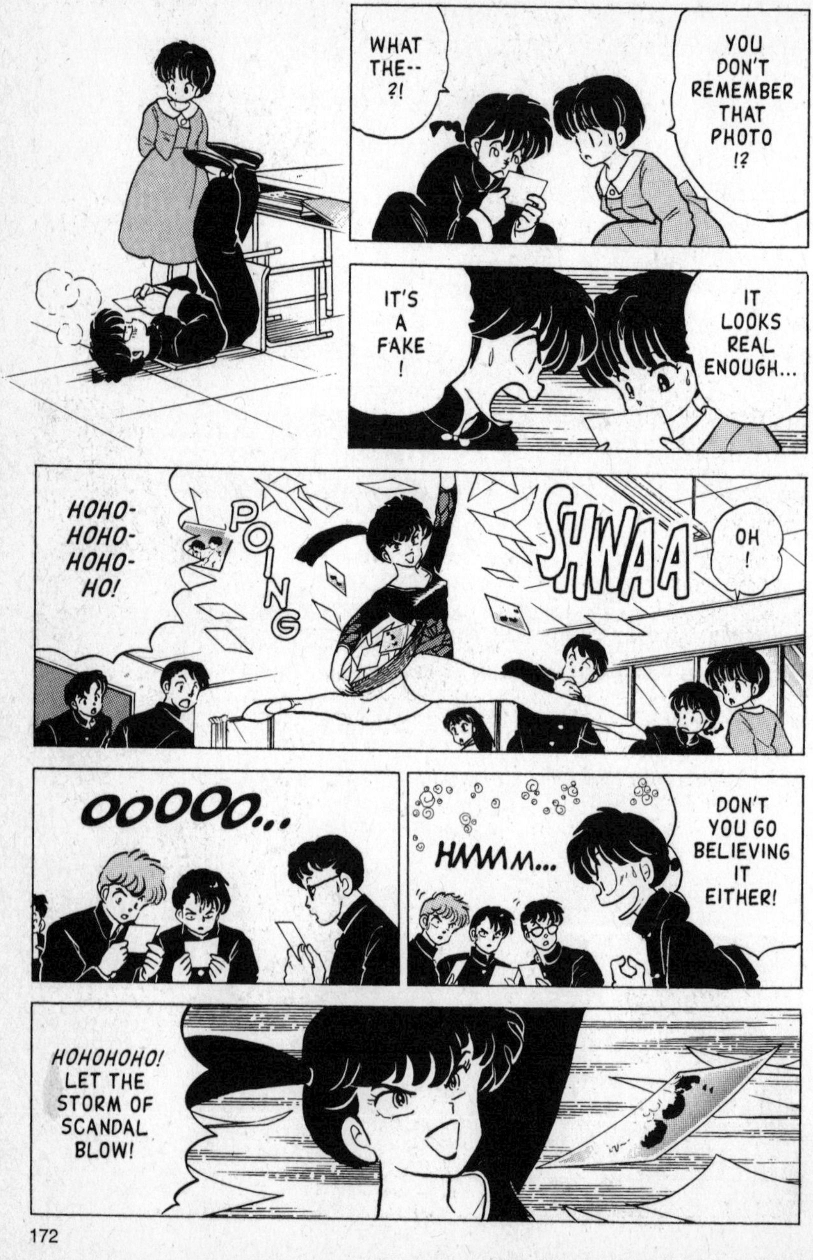
WHAT THE-- ?!
YOU DON'T REMEMBER THAT PHOTO !?
IT'S A FAKE !
IT LOOKS REAL ENOUGH...
HOHO-HOHO-HOHO-HO!
POING
SHWAA
OH !
OOOOO...
HMMM...
DON'T YOU GO BELIEVING IT EITHER!
HOHOHOHO! LET THE STORM OF SCANDAL BLOW!

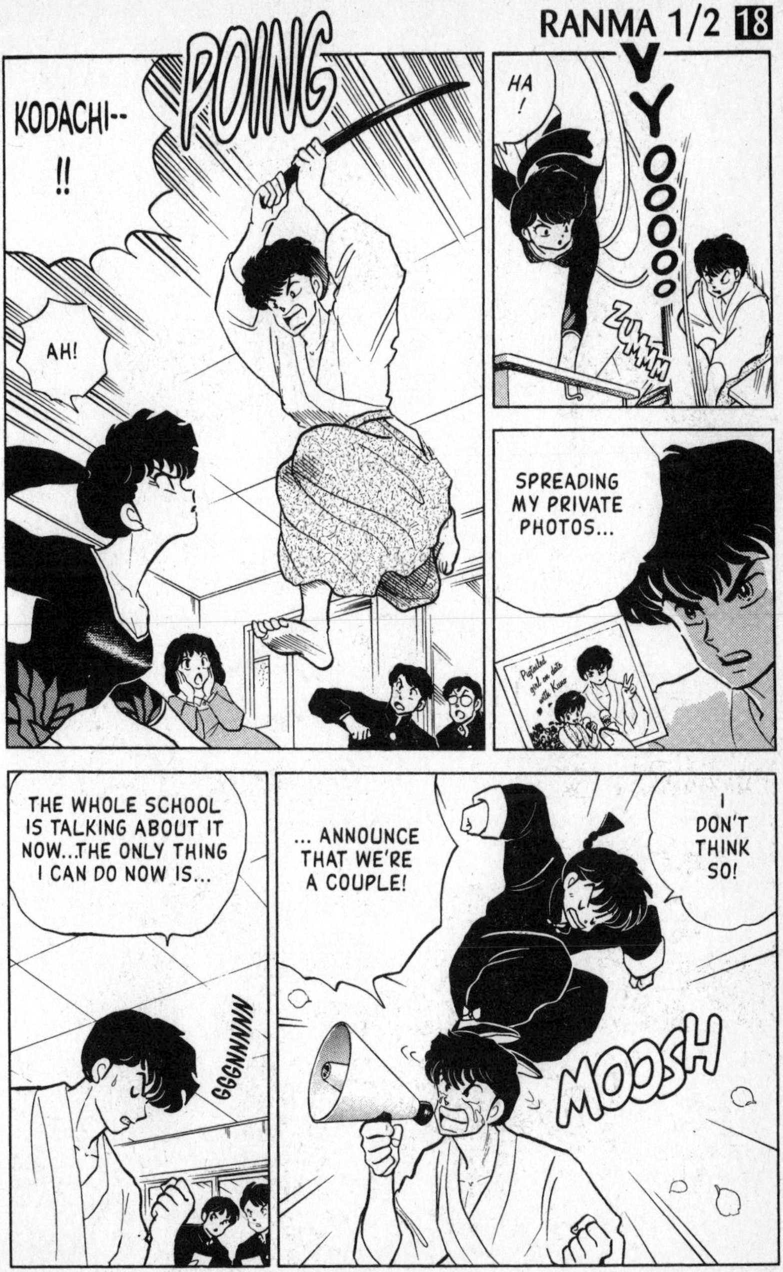
KODACHI-- !!
POING
AH!
HA!
VYOOOOOO
ZUMMM
SPREADING MY PRIVATE PHOTOS...
Pigtailed girl on date with Kuno
THE WHOLE SCHOOL IS TALKING ABOUT IT NOW...THE ONLY THING I CAN DO NOW IS...
GGGNNNNN
... ANNOUNCE THAT WE'RE A COUPLE!
I DON'T THINK SO!
MOOSH

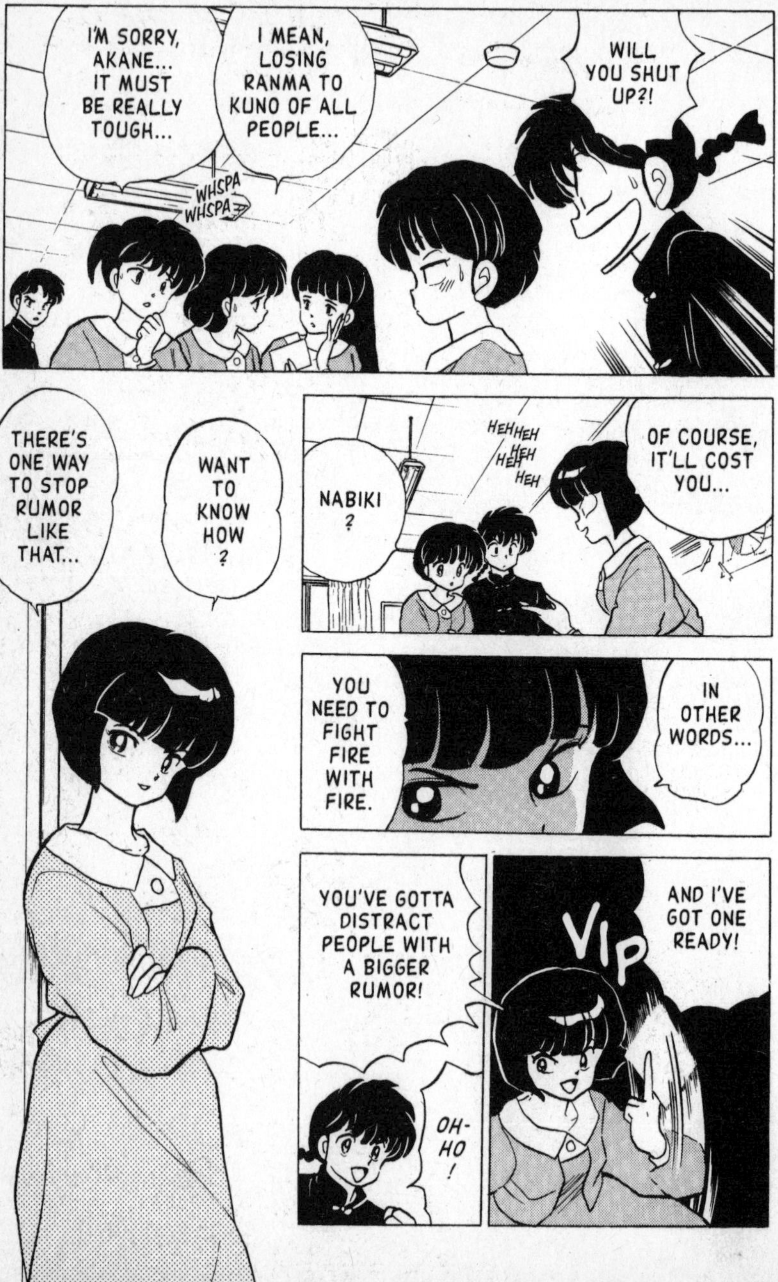
I'M SORRY, AKANE... IT MUST BE REALLY TOUGH...
I MEAN, LOSING RANMA TO KUNO OF ALL PEOPLE...
WHSPA WHSPA
WILL YOU SHUT UP?!
THERE'S ONE WAY TO STOP RUMOR LIKE THAT...
WANT TO KNOW HOW?
NABIKI?
HEHHEH HEH HEH HEH
OF COURSE, IT'LL COST YOU...
YOU NEED TO FIGHT FIRE WITH FIRE.
IN OTHER WORDS...
YOU'VE GOTTA DISTRACT PEOPLE WITH A BIGGER RUMOR!
OH-HO!
VIP
AND I'VE GOT ONE READY!

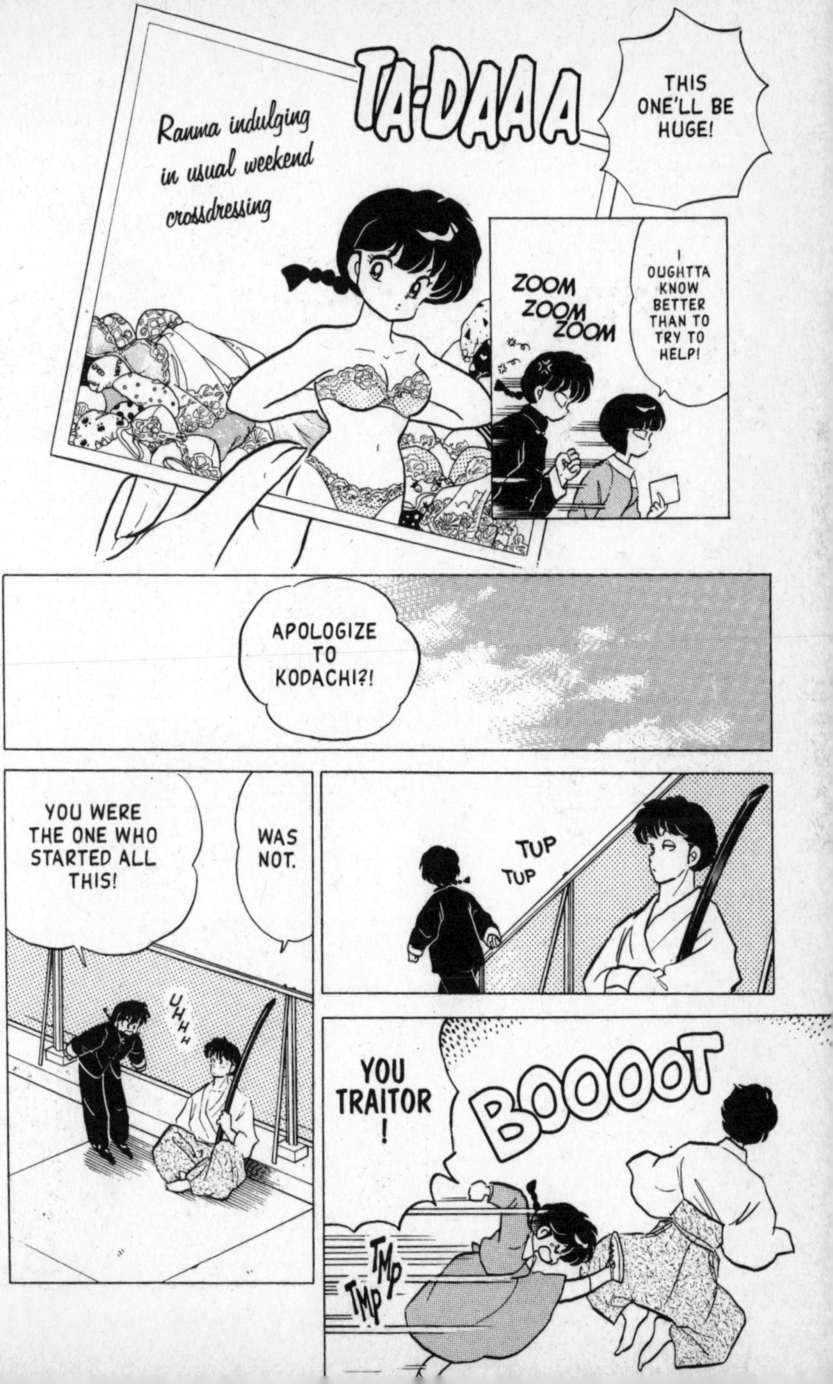
Ranma indulging in usual weekend crossdressing
TA-DAAA
THIS ONE'LL BE HUGE!
ZOOM ZOOM ZOOM
I OUGHTTA KNOW BETTER THAN TO TRY TO HELP!
APOLOGIZE TO KODACHI?!
YOU WERE THE ONE WHO STARTED ALL THIS!
WAS NOT.
UHHH
TUP TUP
YOU TRAITOR!
BOOOOT
TMP TMP

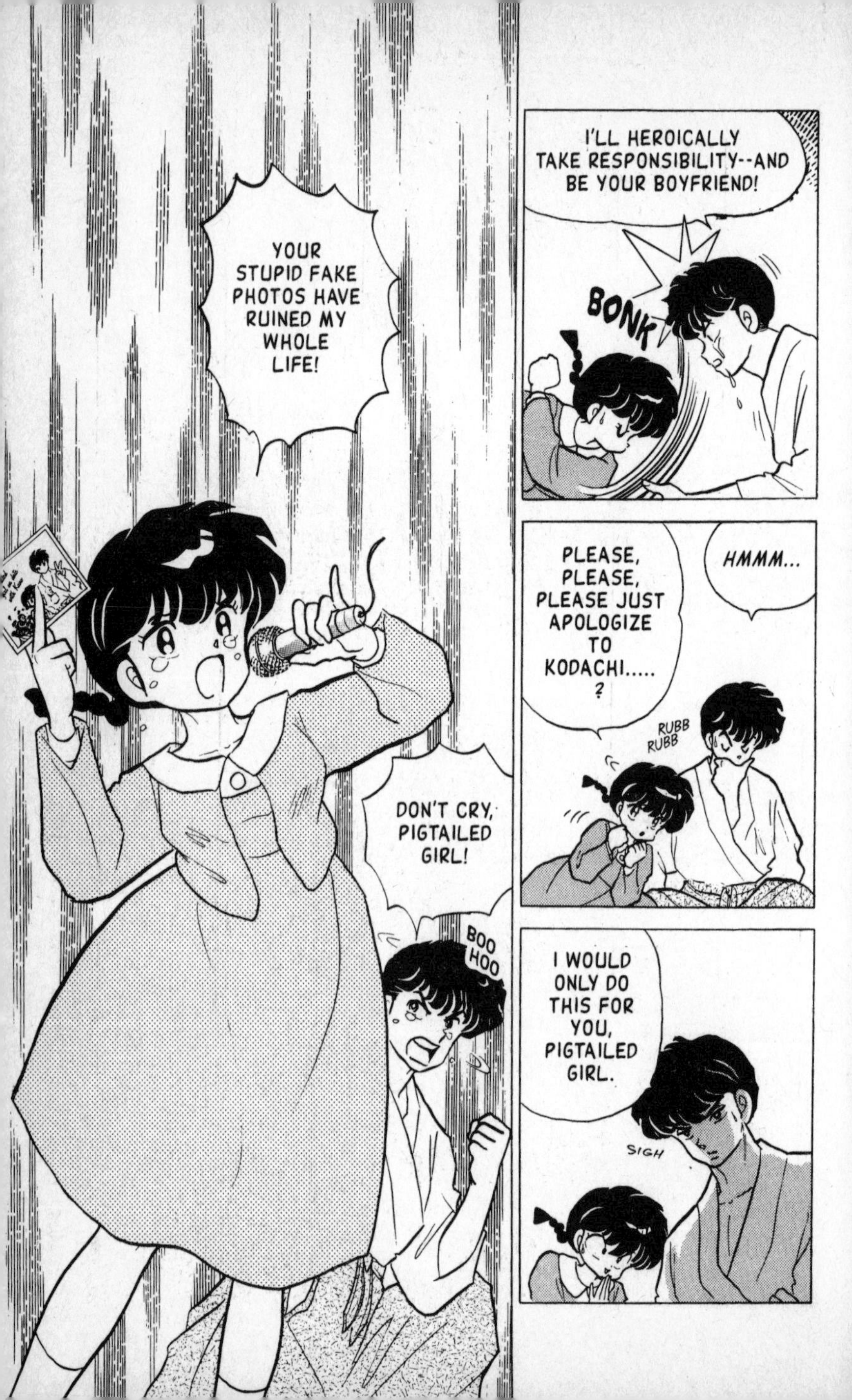
YOUR STUPID FAKE PHOTOS HAVE RUINED MY WHOLE LIFE!
DON'T CRY, PIGTAILED GIRL!
BOO HOO
I'LL HEROICALLY TAKE RESPONSIBILITY--AND BE YOUR BOYFRIEND!
BONK
PLEASE, PLEASE, PLEASE JUST APOLOGIZE TO KODACHI.....?
HMMM...
RUBB RUBB
I WOULD ONLY DO THIS FOR YOU, PIGTAILED GIRL.
SIGH

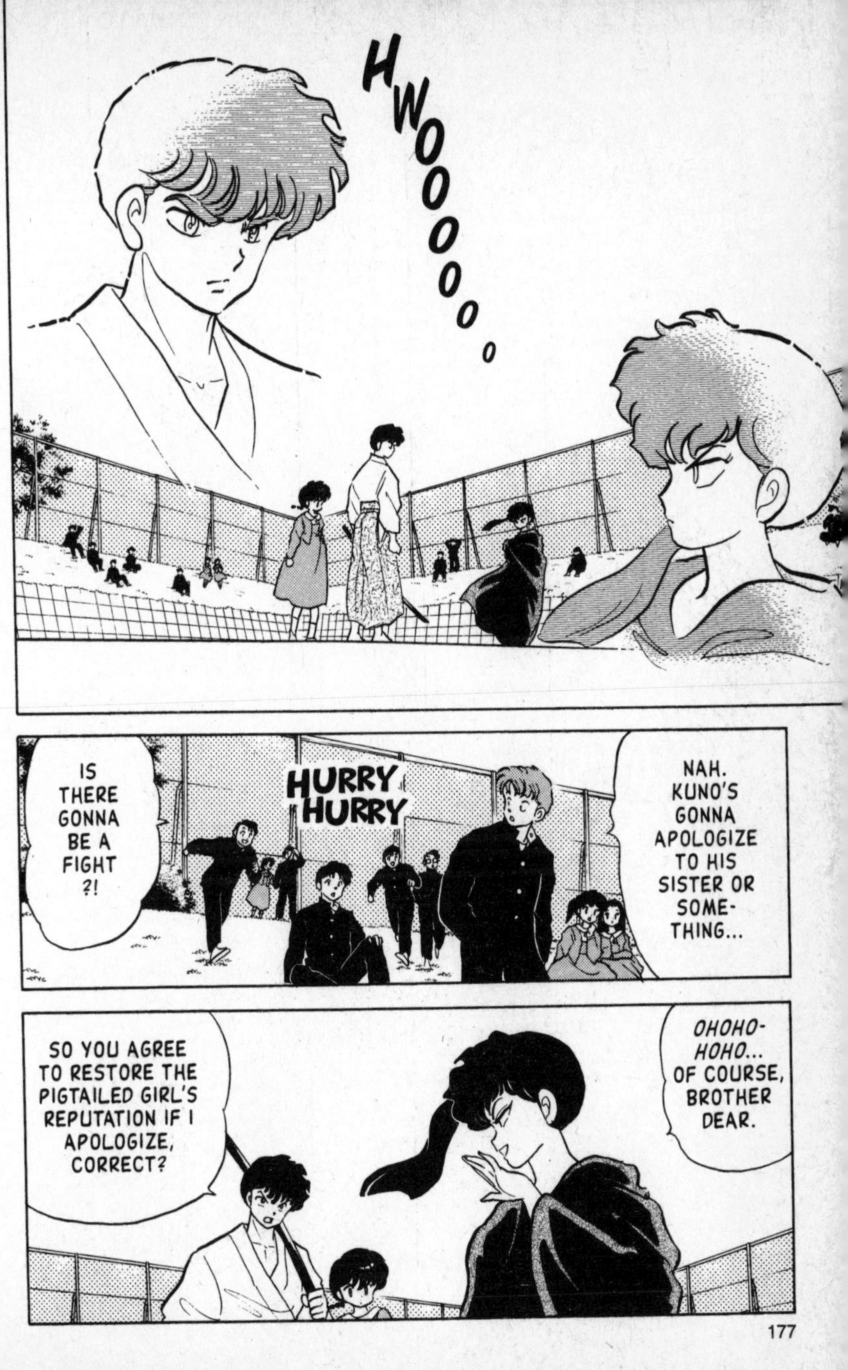
HWOOOOOOo
NAH. KUNO'S GONNA APOLOGIZE TO HIS SISTER OR SOME-THING...
HURRY HURRY
IS THERE GONNA BE A FIGHT ?!
OHOHO-HOHO... OF COURSE, BROTHER DEAR.
SO YOU AGREE TO RESTORE THE PIGTAILED GIRL'S REPUTATION IF I APOLOGIZE, CORRECT?

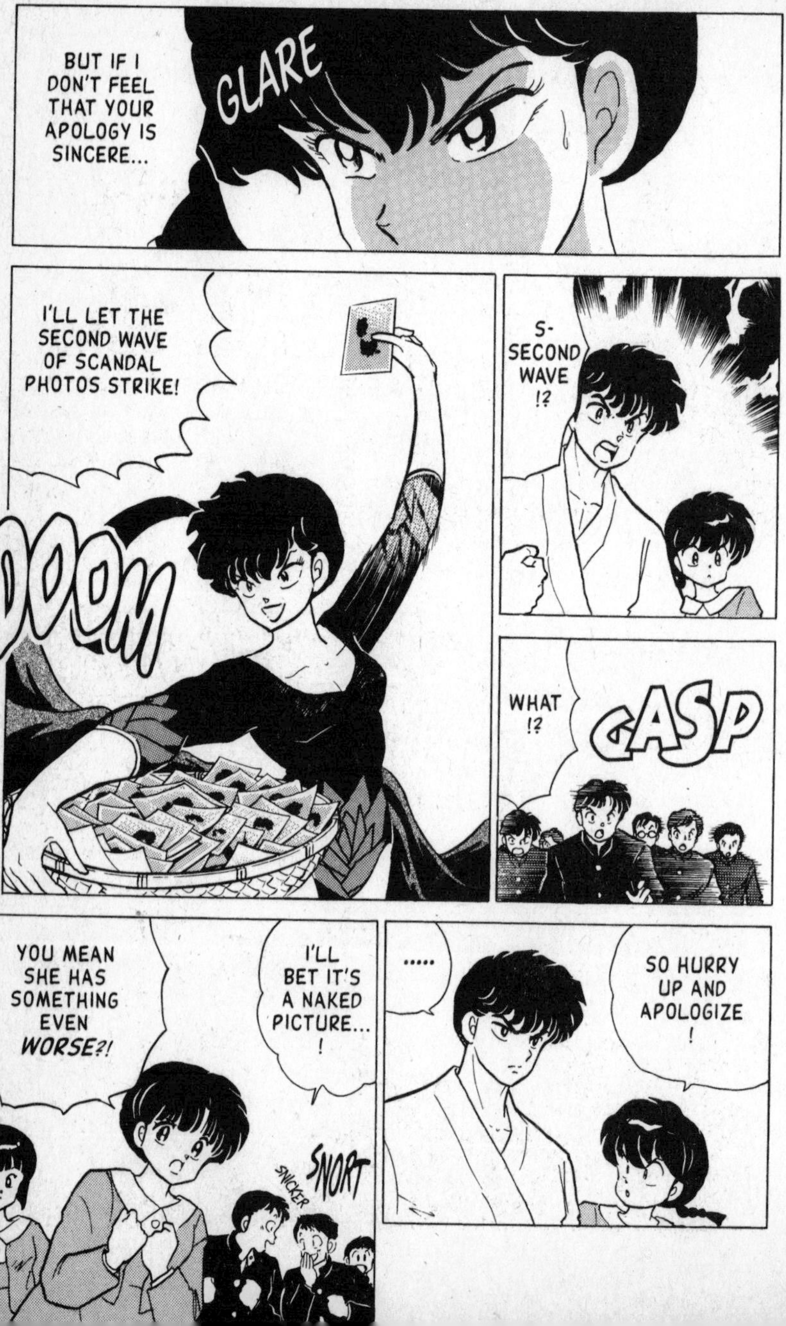

BUT IF I DON'T FEEL THAT YOUR APOLOGY IS SINCERE...
GLARE
I'LL LET THE SECOND WAVE OF SCANDAL PHOTOS STRIKE!
DOOM
S- SECOND WAVE !?
WHAT !?
GASP
YOU MEAN SHE HAS SOMETHING EVEN *WORSE*?!
I'LL BET IT'S A NAKED PICTURE... !
SNICKER
SNORT
......
SO HURRY UP AND APOLOGIZE !

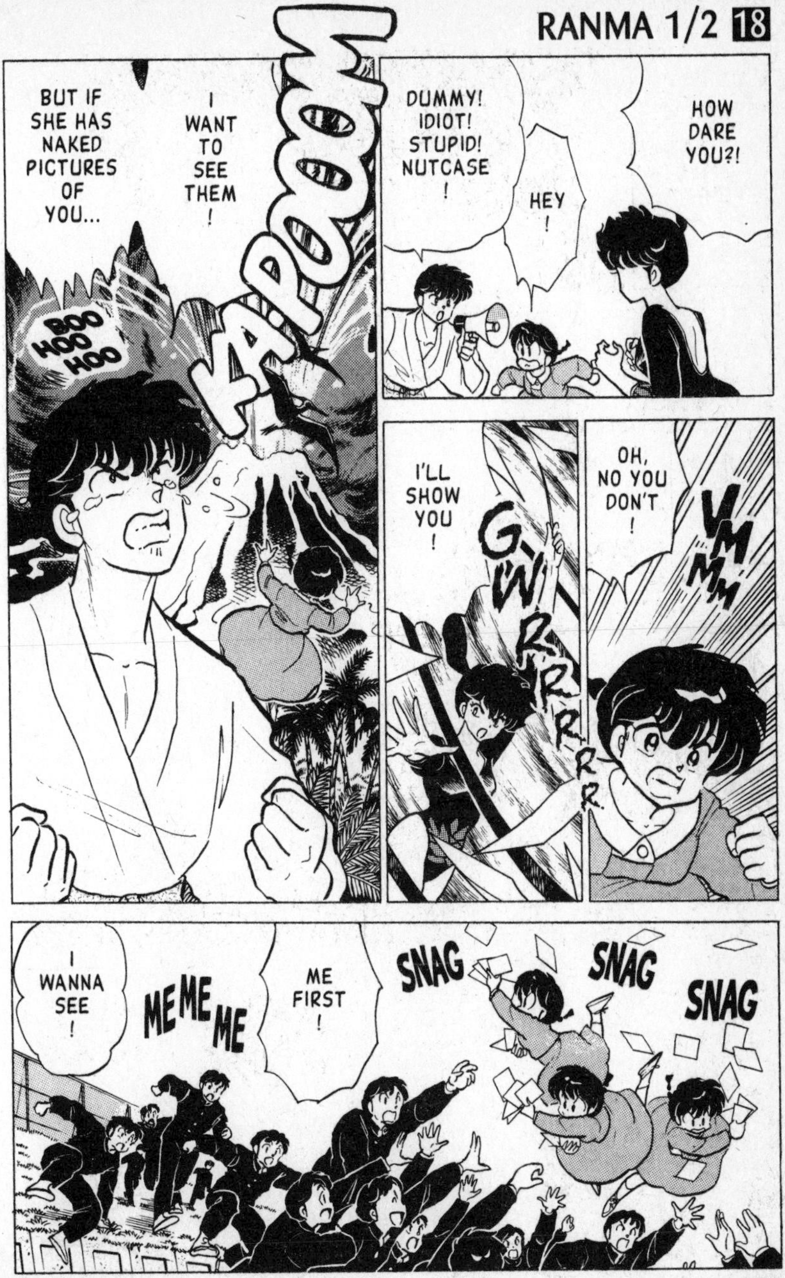
BUT IF SHE HAS NAKED PICTURES OF YOU...
I WANT TO SEE THEM!
KA-BOOM
BOO HOO HOO
DUMMY! IDIOT! STUPID! NUTCASE!
HEY!
HOW DARE YOU?!
I'LL SHOW YOU!
GWRRRRRR
OH, NO YOU DON'T!
VMMMM
I WANNA SEE!
ME ME ME
ME FIRST!
SNAG
SNAG
SNAG

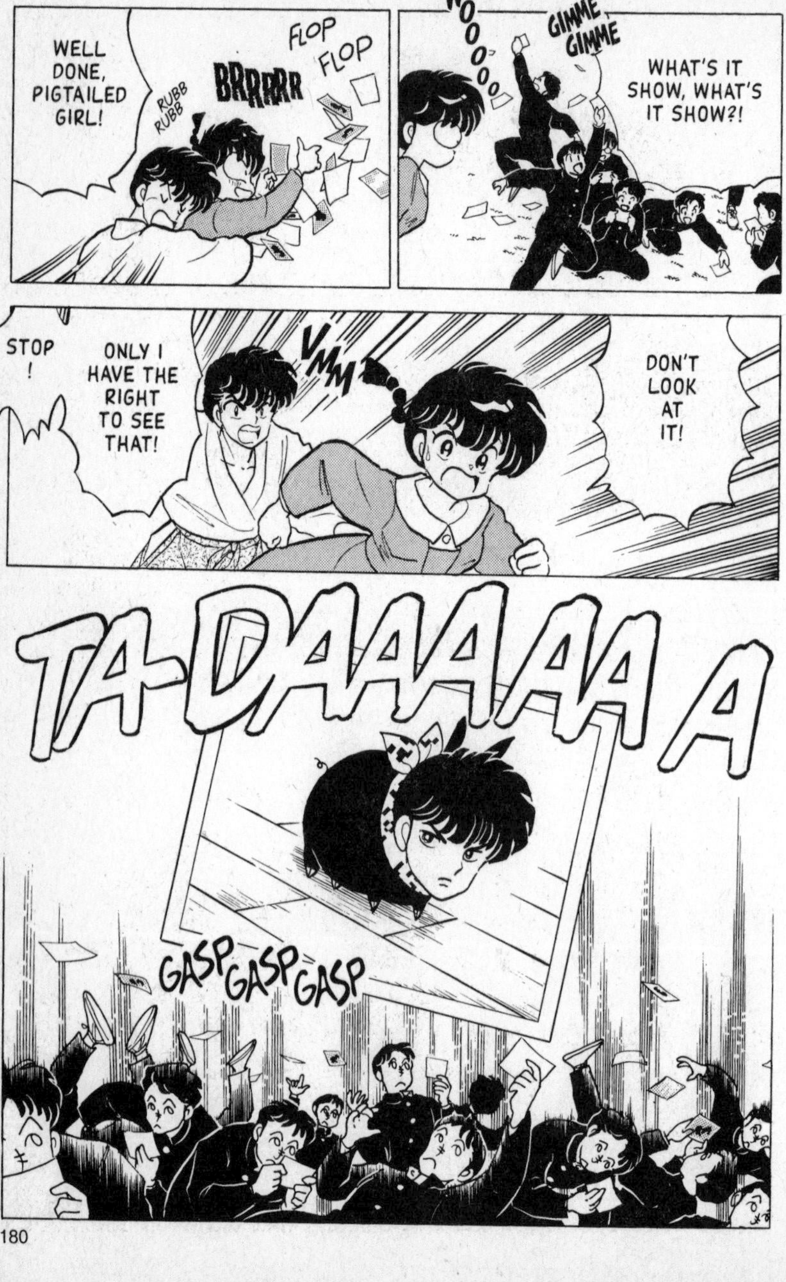
WELL DONE, PIGTAILED GIRL!
RUBB RUBB
BRRRRRR
FLOP FLOP
HWOOOOOO
GIMME GIMME
WHAT'S IT SHOW, WHAT'S IT SHOW?!
STOP!
ONLY I HAVE THE RIGHT TO SEE THAT!
VMM
DON'T LOOK AT IT!
TA-DAAAAA A
GASP GASP GASP

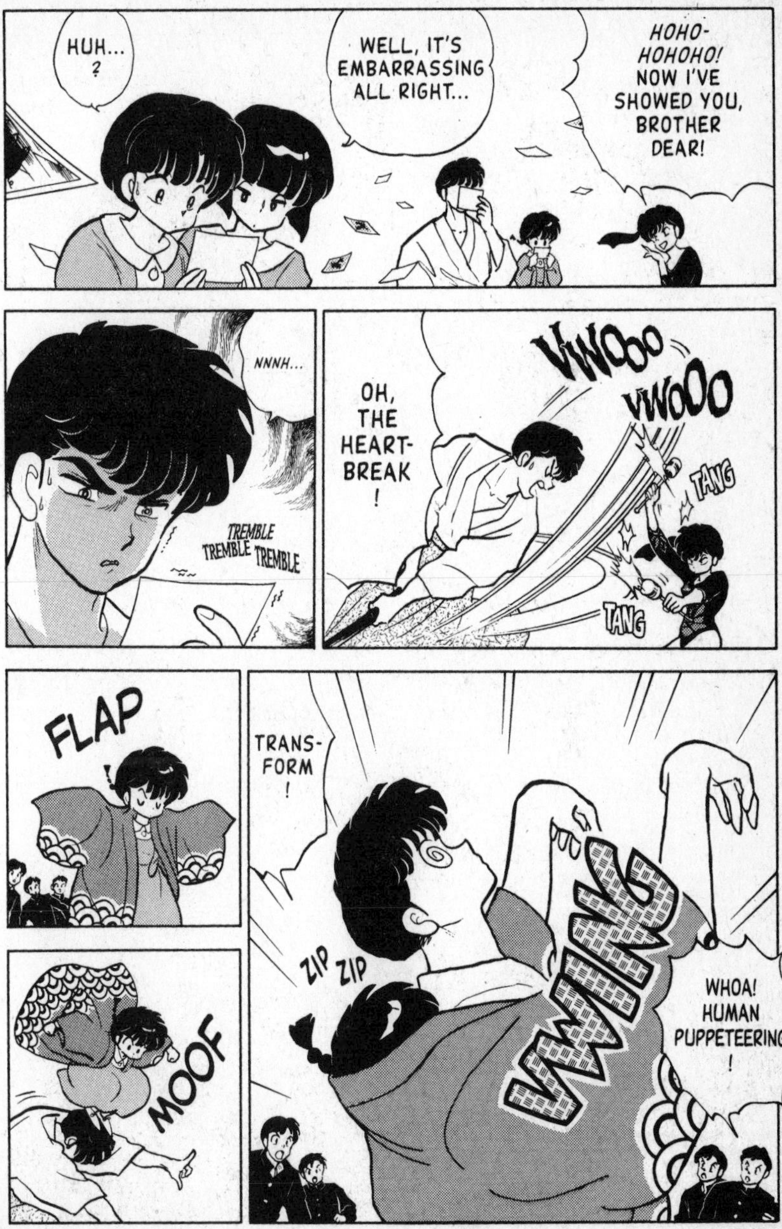
HUH... ?
WELL, IT'S EMBARRASSING ALL RIGHT...
HOHO-HOHOHO! NOW I'VE SHOWED YOU, BROTHER DEAR!
NNNH...
TREMBLE TREMBLE TREMBLE
OH, THE HEART-BREAK!
VWOOO
VWOOO
TANG
TANG
FLAP
MOOF
TRANS-FORM!
WWING
ZIP ZIP
WHOA! HUMAN PUPPETEERING!

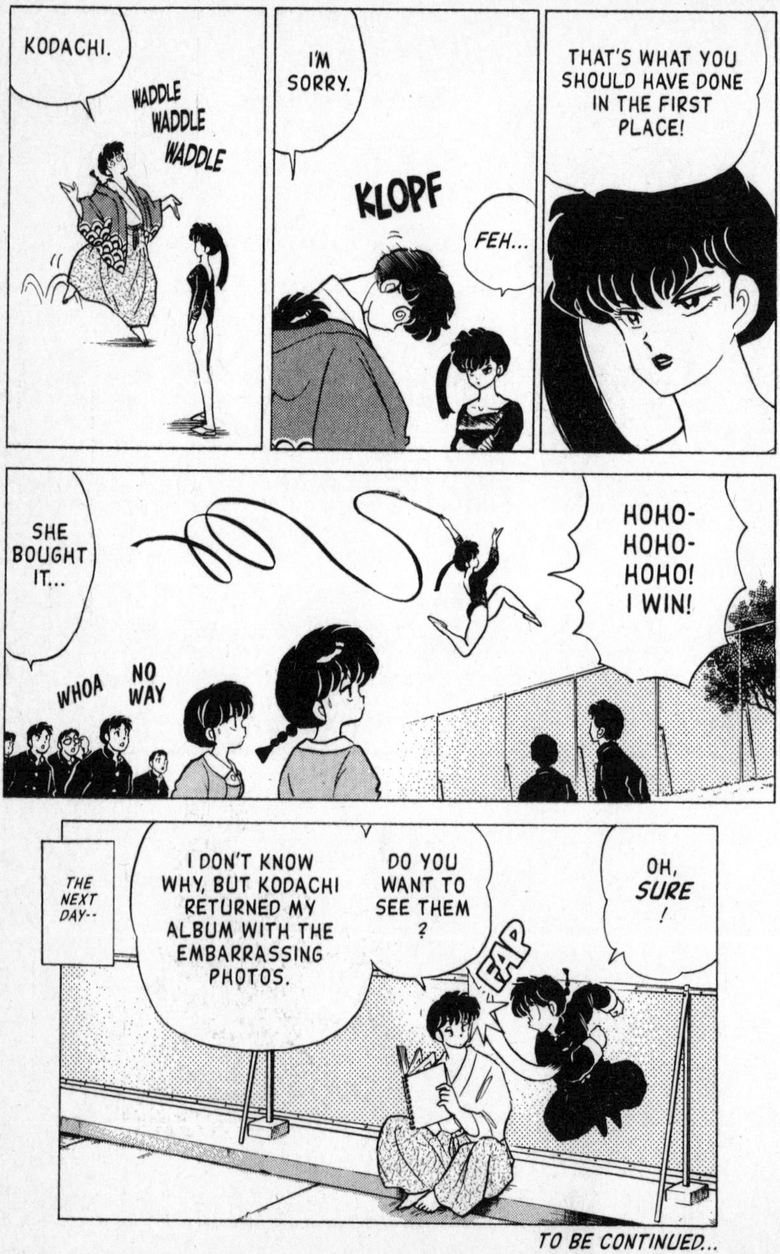
KODACHI.
WADDLE WADDLE WADDLE
I'M SORRY.
KLOPF
FEH...
THAT'S WHAT YOU SHOULD HAVE DONE IN THE FIRST PLACE!
SHE BOUGHT IT...
HOHO-HOHO-HOHO! I WIN!
WHOA
NO WAY
THE NEXT DAY--
I DON'T KNOW WHY, BUT KODACHI RETURNED MY ALBUM WITH THE EMBARRASSING PHOTOS.
DO YOU WANT TO SEE THEM ?
FAP
OH, SURE !

TO BE CONTINUED...

About Rumiko Takahashi

Born in 1957 in Niigata, Japan, Rumiko Takahashi attended women's college in Tokyo, where she began studying comics with Kazuo Koike, author of CRYING FREEMAN. She later became an assistant to horror-manga artist Kazuo Umezu (OROCHI). In 1978, she won a prize in Shogakukan's annual "New Comic Artist Contest," and in that same year her boy-meets-alien comedy series URUSEI YATSURA began appearing in the weekly manga magazine SHÔNEN SUNDAY. This phenomenally successful series ran for nine years and sold over 22 million copies. Takahashi's later RANMA 1/2 series enjoyed even greater popularity.

Takahashi is considered by many to be one of the world's most popular manga artists. With the publication of Volume 34 of her RANMA 1/2 series in Japan, Takahashi's total sales passed one hundred million copies of her compiled works.

Takahashi's serial titles include URUSEI YATSURA, RANMA 1/2, ONE-POUND GOSPEL, MAISON IKKOKU and INUYASHA. Additionally, Takahashi has drawn many short stories which have been published in America under the title "Rumic Theater," and several installments of a saga known as her "Mermaid" series. Most of Takahashi's major stories have also been animated and are widely available in translation worldwide. INUYASHA is her most recent serial story, first published in SHÔNEN SUNDAY in 1996.

EDITOR'S RECOMMENDATIONS

If you enjoyed this volume of Ranma 1/2, then here is some more manga you might be interested in:

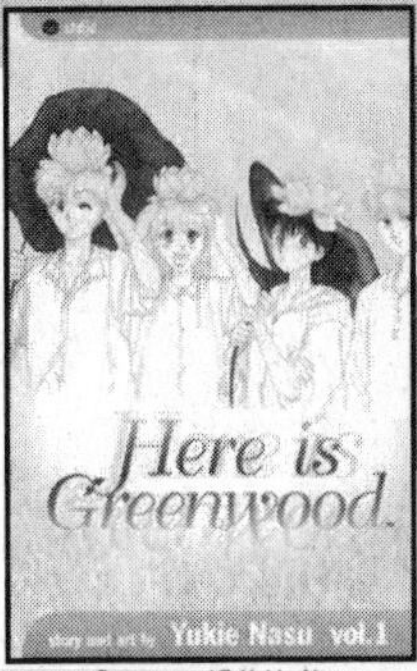
Here is Greenwood.
story and art by Yukie Nasu vol.1

Koko wa Greenwood© Yukie Nasu 1986/HAKUSENSHA, Inc.

HERE IS GREENWOOD

Perhaps written for a slightly older audience than most of Rumiko Takahashi's work, Yukie Nasu's *Here is Greenwood* is exactly like *Ranma 1/2*, except for the martial arts (none), the wacky hijinks (almost none), and the occasional depiction of the adult relationships among its students. Okay, aside from the fact that they both have male high school students in them, they have nothing in common. But they're both cool!

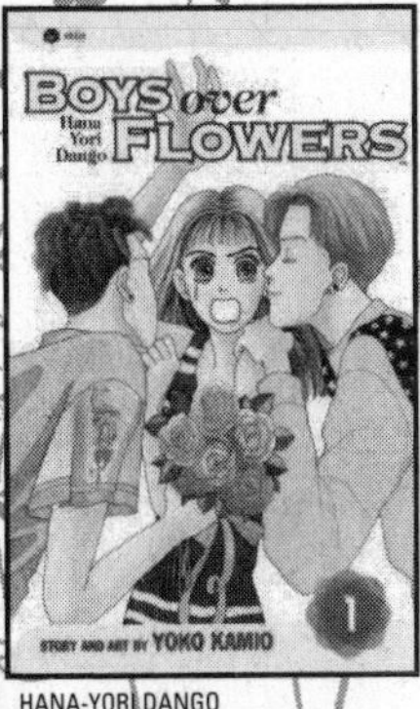
BOYS over FLOWERS
Hana Yori Dango
STORY AND ART BY YOKO KAMIO
1

HANA-YORI DANGO
© 1992 by YOKO KAMIO/SHUEISHA Inc.

BOYS OVER FLOWERS (HANA YORI DANGO)

Another tale of high-school life in Japan, *Boys Over Flowers* (or "HanaDan" to most of its fans) is not without its serious side, but overall tends to fall into the "rabu-kome" or "love-comedy" genre.

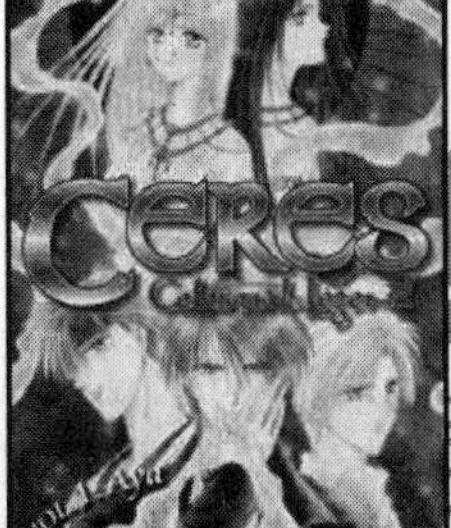
Ceres
YU WATASE
Vol. 1

CERES: CELESTIAL LEGEND
© 1997 Yuu Watase/Shogakukan, Inc.

CERES CELESTIAL LEGEND

Aya Mikage is a trendy Tokyo teen with not much else on her mind but fashion, karaoke, and boys. But a terrible family secret involving an ancient family "curse" is about to make things a lot more difficult.

A Comedy That Redefines a Hot and Cold Relationship!

Due to an unfortunate accident, when martial artist Ranma gets splashed with cold water, he becomes a buxom young girl! Hot water reverses the effect, but when blamed for offenses both real and imagined, and pursued by lovesick suitors of both genders, what's a half-boy, half-girl to do?

From Rumiko Takahashi, creator of *Inuyasha* and *Maison Ikkoku*—complete your collection today!

Ranma ½

A full TV season in each DVD box set

Only $119.98 each!

THE DIGITAL DOJO

action

www.viz.com
store.viz.com

©2003 Rumiko Takahashi/Shogakukan • Kitty Film • Fuji TV

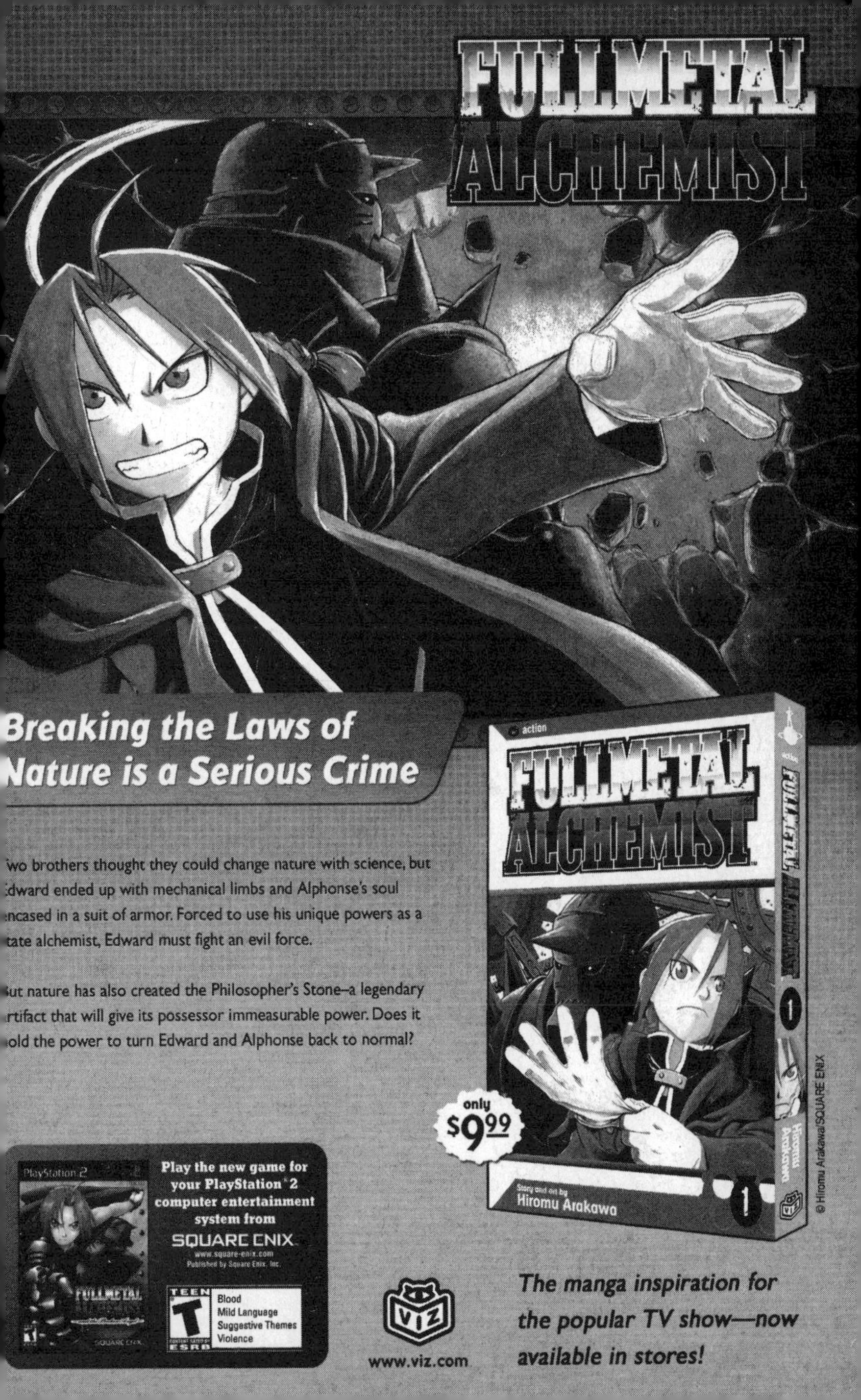
FULLMETAL ALCHEMIST
Breaking the Laws of Nature is a Serious Crime
wo brothers thought they could change nature with science, but dward ended up with mechanical limbs and Alphonse's soul ncased in a suit of armor. Forced to use his unique powers as a tate alchemist, Edward must fight an evil force.
ut nature has also created the Philosopher's Stone–a legendary rtifact that will give its possessor immeasurable power. Does it old the power to turn Edward and Alphonse back to normal?
action
FULLMETAL ALCHEMIST
1
Story and art by
Hiromu Arakawa
only
$9.99
© Hiromu Arakawa/SQUARE ENIX
PlayStation 2
FULLMETAL
Play the new game for your PlayStation® 2 computer entertainment system from
SQUARE ENIX.
www.square-enix.com
Published by Square Enix, Inc.
TEEN
T
Blood
Mild Language
Suggestive Themes
Violence
ESRB
VIZ
www.viz.com
The manga inspiration for the popular TV show—now available in stores!

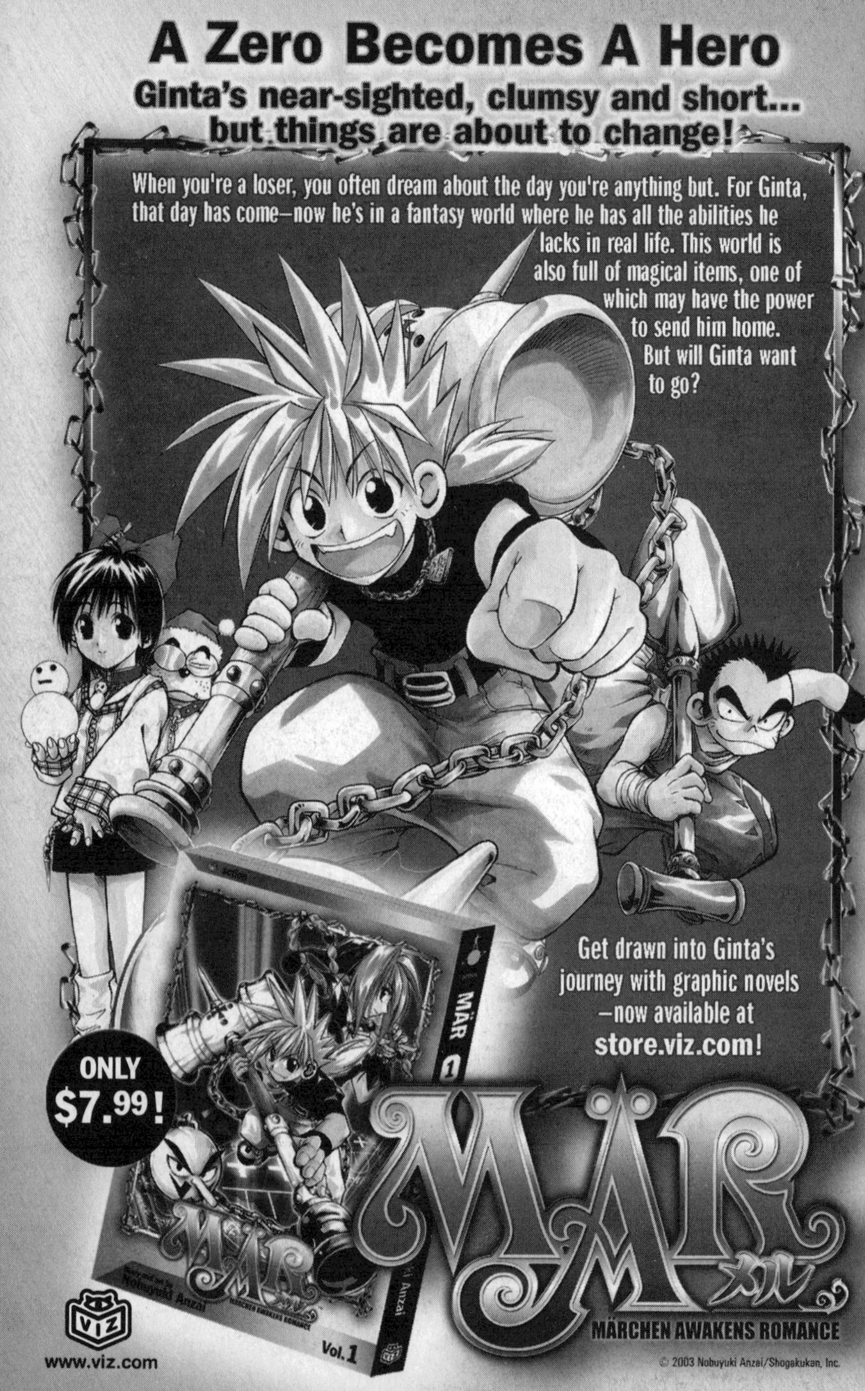
A Zero Becomes A Hero
Ginta's near-sighted, clumsy and short...
...but things are about to change!
When you're a loser, you often dream about the day you're anything but. For Ginta, that day has come—now he's in a fantasy world where he has all the abilities he lacks in real life. This world is also full of magical items, one of which may have the power to send him home. But will Ginta want to go?
Get drawn into Ginta's journey with graphic novels —now available at store.viz.com!
ONLY $7.99!
MÄR
MÄRCHEN AWAKENS ROMANCE
Vol. 1
www.viz.com
© 2003 Nobuyuki Anzai/Shogakukan, Inc.

STUDENTS BY DAY, DEMON-FIGHTERS BY NIGHT!

K E K K A I S H I
【けっかいし】

Teenagers Yoshimori and Tokine are "kekkaishi"—demon-fighters that battle bad beings side-by-side almost every night. They also quarrel with each other, but their biggest fight is the one between their families. Can Yoshimori and Tokine fight together long enough to end their families' ancient rivalry and save the world?

Join this modern-day Romeo and Juliet adventure—graphic novels now available at store.viz.com!

ONLY $9.99!

© 2004 Yellow Tanabe/Shogakukan, Inc.

www.viz.com

All New ACTION Graphic Novels!

action

The latest volumes now available at store.viz.com:

Fullmetal Alchemist, Vol. 1
Kekkaishi, Vol. 1
MÄR, Vol. 1
Battle Angel Alita, Vol. 9 (2nd ed)
Case Closed, Vol. 5
Cheeky Angel, Vol. 6
Excel Saga, Vol. 12
No Need for Tenchi!, Vol. 3 (2nd ed)
Ranma 1/2, Vol. 17 (2nd ed) *
Ranma 1/2, Vol. 18 (2nd ed) *
Ranma 1/2, Vol. 30 *

All books starting at **$7.99!**

* Also available on DVD from VIZ

www.viz.com

FULLMETAL ALCHEMIST © Hiromu Arakawa/SQUARE ENIX KEKKAISHI © 2004 Yellow Tanabe/Shogakukan, Inc.
MÄR © 2003 Nobuyuki Anzai/Shogakukan, Inc. GUNNM © 1991 by YUKITO KISHIRO/SHUEISHA Inc.
CASE CLOSED © 1994 Gosho Aoyama/Shogakukan, Inc. CHEEKY ANGEL © 1999 Hiroyuki Nishimori/Shogakukan, Inc.
EXCEL SAGA © 1997 Rikdo Koshi/SHONENGAHOSHA NO NEED FOR TENCHI! © HITOSHI OKUDA 1995 © AIC/VAP • NTV
RANMA 1/2 ©1988 Rumiko Takahashi/Shogakukan, Inc.

COMPLETE OUR SURVEY AND LET US KNOW WHAT YOU THINK!

☐ Please do NOT send me information about VIZ products, news and events, special offers, or other information.

☐ Please do NOT send me information from VIZ's trusted business partners.

Name: _____

Address: _____

City: _____ **State:** _____ **Zip:** _____

E-mail: _____

☐ Male ☐ Female **Date of Birth** (mm/dd/yyyy): ___/___/_____ (Under 13? Parental consent required)

What race/ethnicity do you consider yourself? (please check one)

☐ Asian/Pacific Islander ☐ Black/African American ☐ Hispanic/Latino

☐ Native American/Alaskan Native ☐ White/Caucasian ☐ Other: _____

What VIZ product did you purchase? (check all that apply and indicate title purchased)

☐ DVD/VHS _____

☐ Graphic Novel _____

☐ Magazines _____

☐ Merchandise _____

Reason for purchase: (check all that apply)

☐ Special offer ☐ Favorite title ☐ Gift

☐ Recommendation ☐ Other _____

Where did you make your purchase? (please check one)

☐ Comic store ☐ Bookstore ☐ Mass/Grocery Store

☐ Newsstand ☐ Video/Video Game Store ☐ Other: _____

☐ Online (site: _____)

What other VIZ properties have you purchased/own? _____

_____

How many anime and/or manga titles have you purchased in the last year? How many were VIZ titles? (please check one from each column)

ANIME
- ☐ None
- ☐ 1-4
- ☐ 5-10
- ☐ 11+

MANGA
- ☐ None
- ☐ 1-4
- ☐ 5-10
- ☐ 11+

VIZ
- ☐ None
- ☐ 1-4
- ☐ 5-10
- ☐ 11+

I find the pricing of VIZ products to be: (please check one)

☐ Cheap   ☐ Reasonable   ☐ Expensive

What genre of manga and anime would you like to see from VIZ? (please check two)

- ☐ Adventure
- ☐ Horror
- ☐ Comic Strip
- ☐ Romance
- ☐ Science Fiction
- ☐ Fantasy
- ☐ Fighting
- ☐ Sports

What do you think of VIZ's new look?

☐ Love It   ☐ It's OK   ☐ Hate It   ☐ Didn't Notice   ☐ No Opinion

Which do you prefer? (please check one)

- ☐ Reading right-to-left
- ☐ Reading left-to-right

Which do you prefer? (please check one)

- ☐ Sound effects in English
- ☐ Sound effects in Japanese with English captions
- ☐ Sound effects in Japanese only with a glossary at the back

THANK YOU! Please send the completed form to:

NJW Research
42 Catharine St.
Poughkeepsie, NY 12601

All information provided will be used for internal purposes only. We promise not to sell or otherwise divulge your information.

NO PURCHASE NECESSARY. Requests not in compliance with all terms of this form will not be acknowledged or returned. All submissions are subject to verification and become the property of VIZ, LLC. Fraudulent submission, including use of multiple addresses or P.O. boxes to obtain additional VIZ information or offers may result in prosecution. VIZ reserves the right to withdraw or modify any terms of this form. Void where prohibited, taxed, or restricted by law. VIZ will not be liable for lost, misdirected, mutilated, illegible, incomplete or postage-due mail. © 2003 VIZ, LLC. All Rights Reserved. VIZ, LLC, property titles, characters, names and plots therein under license to VIZ, LLC. All Rights Reserved.